Mystifying the Monarch

Mystifying the Monarch

Studies on Discourse, Power, and History

edited by

Jeroen Deploige

and

Gita Deneckere

Amsterdam University Press

Cover design: Kok Korpershoek, Amsterdam
Layout: PROgrafici, Goes

Illustration front cover: Jacob Jordaens, *Le roi boit. Repas de famille le jour de la Fête des Rois* [The King Drinks, Family Meal on the Feast of Epiphany] (c. 1638-1640). Paris, Musée du Louvre, (© Photo: RMN – © Jean-Gilles Berizzi).
Painting, depicting a popular ritual of inversion, acquired in Holland in 1787 by the last French king Louis XVI (1754-1793). On 20 June 1792, during an attack by a Parisian mob, Louis XVI was forced to play the role of the mock king in a 'king drinks' rite. In 1793, the year of Louis XVI's decapitation, the Jordaens's painting became part of the collection of the Musée du Louvre.

ISBN-13   978 90 5356 767 8
ISBN-10   90 5356 767 4
NUR   680/698

© Amsterdam University Press, 2006

Contents

Acknowledgements

This book constitutes one of the main results of a research project entitled 'The Sovereign as Father Figure. Towards Practical Linguistic and Text Analytical Methods for Historians', executed between 2001 and 2004 at Ghent University, the Catholic University of Leuven and the Free University of Brussels. We would like to thank our academic partners Jan Blommaert, Jo Tollebeek, Patricia Van den Eeckhout, and Tom Verschaffel for their commitment to this project and the many intellectual stimuli we enjoyed from them. Special gratitude goes to John Barrell, Marc Boone, Luc Duerloo, Jaap van Ginneken, and Ruth Wodak for their contributions to the success of a pleasant, small conference organized in November 2003 as a preparatory step to this volume and hosted by the Royal Academy of Dutch Language and Literature in Ghent. We also feel honoured that Willem Frijhoff, Dominick LaCapra, Joep Leerssen, Gabrielle Spiegel, and Gareth Stedman Jones were willing to take part in the Scientific Committee to this enterprise. The realization of our project and of this volume took extensive advantage of the practical assistance of Claudine Colyn, Margot De Smaele, Greet Donckers, and Linde Vandevelde; of translations offered by Jill Corner, Ingrid Piron, and Donald Pistolesi; and of the meticulous editorial assistance of Juleen Audrey Eichinger. For financial support we could rely comfortably on grants from the Research Foundation – Flanders and from the Faculty of Humanities of Ghent University. Last but not least, we extend our deepest gratitude to the authors who were willing to contribute to this volume and share with us their unparalleled expertise.

Jeroen Deploige and Gita Deneckere
June 2006

Introduction

The Monarchy: A Crossroads of Trajectories

Jeroen Deploige and Gita Deneckere

After the invasion of the humanities and the social sciences by the 'linguistic turn' in the 1980s, a book in which the three concepts of discourse, power, and history are combined can no longer cause surprise. Particularly the work of Michel Foucault has placed its stamp incontrovertibly on this triangle. And it still does so, even after the heyday of the linguistic turn. As Gabrielle Spiegel pointed out recently, Foucault's use of the term *discourse* and his elaboration of the notion of knowledge/power also fostered new currents of historical work in which especially questions of 'practices' come to the fore.[1] If it is true that the major discussions and dissatisfactions engendered by the linguistic turn remain basically at a theoretical level, concrete historical work benefits from Foucauldian theories that emphasize the ways in which discourse is tied to institutions and social practices. Even historians who are reluctant to assume the non-referentiality of language and discourse may well endorse the de-essentializing agenda of the linguistic turn and the abandonment of the positivist idea that discourse is a form of expression. The linguistic turn is in a sense giving way to a 'historical turn' that remains informed by discourse theory but draws the attention away from questions of representation and back to sites of social practice, conceptualized as the effect of discursive formations that themselves undergo constant processes of change. Spiegel sees the new perspectives on the dialectical interplay between discourse and practice as a rediscovery and even rehabilitation of 'the social' that had been weakened and obliterated by poststructuralism.[2]

Insofar as Foucault himself ventured into concrete historical research, one cannot deny that his results were received with considerable criticism, particularly by traditional historians. Those criticisms not only relate to the many historical inaccuracies and doubtful interpretations in Foucault's empirical research, but are also inspired often by a dislike of his denigration of the ideals of the Enlightenment.[3] Yet from a rather unexpected angle, the many-sided French historian Michel de Certeau has made some fascinating annotations on Foucault's 'genealogical' research into the relationship between discursive strategies and the 'microphysics of power', as described for example in *Surveiller et punir*, Foucault's study of nineteenth-century disciplinary procedures in prisons, schools, and hospitals.[4] From Certeau's comments two fundamental, mutually coherent critical observations can be deduced. Foucault's regressive historical approach benefits and isolates only those arguments and practices which appear to have led directly to the nineteenth-century end product he was studying. Hence a strictly linear image has been created of the relationship between power and discourse, in which the Enlightenment gradually appears to corrupt itself. Moreover, this has also led to a tendency to ignore the many practices and voices which have *not* resulted in a reasoned systematization of modernity, but which often have organized space and language and exercised their power less visibly and audibly.[5]

In this collection of essays, the relationship between discourse, power, and history is, perhaps somewhat surprisingly, confronted with one of the oldest and most traditional subjects of historiography: the monarchy. Monarchy, besides being one of the most important institutions in the *longue durée,* can be considered as a challenging pretext for the examination, in very concrete ways, of how historians may deal with language and discourse not only in the critical approach to their sources but particularly with respect to issues of power and authority, of ideology and mystification. There is a remarkable link to be observed between the institution of monarchy – which, of course, has not remained untouched by the finger of time but nonetheless has endured – and the symbolic, discursive order in which it is framed. In spite of the fundamental processes of modernization, secularization, and bureaucratization of power, the affective, archaic, and almost timeless relationship between sovereigns and their 'subjects' still prevails today.

Taking into account Certeau's criticism on the traditional Foucauldian approach, this volume also strives to offer an alternative to the strictly linear thinking which characterizes a great deal of current research into the relationship between discourse and power in a historical perspective. We reject a linear narrative that starts from medieval mystification and leads to the modern demystification of monarchy. Mystification and demystification of power are, after all, two sides of the same coin. In *Talking of the Royal Family,* Michael Billig examined the fascination which monarchy still exerts these days. The sacral character of kingship meanwhile has become outdated completely, and there no longer is any question of uncritical deference for the court. Yet many a modern subject, against his or her better judgement, remains attached to royal mythology. The illusions, which for centuries were staged by the royal entourage, were shattered as illusions, but nonetheless many people still, in spite of this demystification, wish to keep the illusion in place: let the emperor keep his clothes, crown, and jewels; his mystical significance. So we are confronted at the same time with demystification and a consciously persistent demand for mystification. Billig states that the very appearance of being an anachronism – an up-to-date anachronism – marks monarchy as a phenomenon attuned to a postmodern structure of feeling. The postmodernist consciousness is said to recognize images as mere images, whilst accepting the image as reality. Nevertheless, Billig warns us not to exaggerate the novelty of today's monarchical phenomena and says that care should be taken when applying the label of 'postmodernism' to the actual ways in which monarchy is staged and perceived.[6] The historical and diachronic approach of this volume is indeed an invitation to draw parallels among premodern, modern and postmodern times, precisely where the symbolic structure of power and authority is concerned.

Throughout this book, four research trajectories emerge, treating the paradoxical entanglement of mystification and demystification of the monarchy: the sacralization and banalization of the monarchy, its staging and its limitations. Throughout history, the monarchy has been sacralized profoundly by the theories of different generations of political and religious thinkers. The theory of 'the king's two bodies' that we know so well from the work of Ernst Kantorowicz has, in the form of today's constitutional monarchy, even outlived the Ancient Regime.[7] Sacralization, however, has also helped the monarchy to find its way into everyday life. The appropriation and banalization of the monarch are manifest not only in the distribution of all kinds of vulgarized opinions and royal paraphernalia. It is also expressed in procedures of deliberate denigration and profanation of the hallowed kingship.[8] Research into the staging of the monarchy therefore can focus not only on the royal discourse in which monarchs and their courts 'fabricate' the king but also on what was symbolized from below in a rich political imagination, which can be traced in all kinds of texts, plastic arts, objects or (carnivalesque) rituals.[9] Sacralization and staging in this way created environments of hegemonic monarchic ideals which, however, also demarcate essential limitations. Mystification of the monarchy calls to life critical and subversive opinions and practices, tolerates them to a certain extent, but at the same time encourages the screening out of threatening discourse, which, for example, became defined as lese majesty, treason or conspiracy.[10]

So while this volume does not presuppose a linear narrative of mystification and demystification over the centuries, we opt for a diachronic approach, because of the interesting parallels among premodern, modern and postmodern discourse on the monarchy. The determinants of the historical evolution in royal discourse appear to be located not so much in the inherent dynamic of mystification and demystification, as in the changing conditions which determine the circulation of word, image and object. Here the role and evolution of communication and media come under the spotlight, as well as the problem of the audibility of the public sphere, that does not, however, condemn historians to an exclusive focus on the centripetal 'monologic' discourse of the monarchy itself, as will appear from various contributions.[11]

The book is structured by large chronological sections which are linked closely to developments in the potential to create, distribute, and appropriate discourses. The first part deals with the Middle Ages, when there was still no printing press to offer an efficient written communication forum to the general public. Consequently, monarchic discourse then surfaced virtually only as a monologic account in a manuscript culture dominated by religious and, later, also secular elites. Meticulous case studies will, however, put into perspective the reality of this discursive one-sidedness. In the second part on the early modern period, the role of the printing press can no longer be ignored, and the staging of the monarchy becomes gradually determined by the everyday world, by essay writing, pamphlets, performances, reversal rituals, novels, and so on. In the last part finally, the monarchy, confronted with its constitutional limitations and the growing ubiquity of the mass media, is presented in its search of a new *modus operandi*.

In the first chapter, Alain Boureau deals with what is doubtlessly the most fundamental mystification process in the medieval history of monarchy, that is, the growing sacralization of the royal power perceived in Europe from the High Middle Ages onwards. The first question Boureau raises is to what extent this sacralization can be regarded as Christian. He argues that conceptual history and cultural anthropology teach us that the Christian sacralization of the monarchy in fact forms a local interpretation of a universal tendency, in which collective entities are constructed on the basis of the image of their supreme head. Such mystification structures usually result in a common vocabulary in which physical metaphors are associated with supernatural attributes – a 'lexicon' which in medieval Europe was provided mainly by the Christian religion, due to the monopoly position of ecclesiastics in intellectual matters. In addition, these structures display a common 'syntax' in which sacralization becomes concentrated around a number of recurring rites and ceremonies, such as coronations, entries, funerals and so forth, to which the Christian religion offered an integrating principle. They finally lead to a common complex 'discourse' of political transcendence that, certainly in the West, gradually introduces implicit ideas about the State. In this discursive construction, monarchy invented perpetuity for itself outside of, but mirroring, Christian theology. However, despite this successful history of sacralization, the sanctity of kings became less self-evident an ideal as the control of the Church remained unrivalled in the domain of canonization. The Gregorian Reform even brought about a growing separation of the secular and the religious realms, and the Investiture Contest prohibited the success of the never truly realized ideal of a Christian Empire. But when Boureau enters more deeply into the chronological course of the evolution of the idea of sovereignty in the Christian world, attached less to individuals than to the institutional form of government, he is able to point out that the traditional opposition between Church and secular power in fact became neutralized by a shared political theology. While the position of the monarch originally was legitimized by his status as a kind of vicar of Christ, one sees how monarchic power gradually became subjected to a 'pact', requiring the agreement of the subjects, which ultimately led to sacral ideas of 'majesty' and 'sovereignty', stemming closely from the thirteenth-century development of pontifical absolutism. Hence the sacredness of the monarchy never disappeared; it only became increasingly secularized and refined via obvious processes of appropriation.

Boureau concentrates on the analysis of the medieval sacralization of monarchy as a factor in conceptual history. Its demystification, which is mainly a matter of social practices, is behind the scenes in his treatment. Although the high medieval source material does not as yet offer so many possibilities, Jeroen Deploige analyses in a peculiar case study the strong tie between sacralization and the demystification inseparably associated with it. His account begins with a dramatic demystification: the brutal murder of Charles the Good, Count of Flanders, in 1127, which plunged the county into a power vacuum and civil war. Yet the murder quickly resulted in a number of texts in which the unfortunate count was portrayed as a holy martyr. Deploige investigates how such texts took advantage of the existing conventions of the hagiographic genre in the Low Countries in order to attempt an exceptional sanctification of a secular sovereign, despite the growing separation between the secular and the religious realms. At the same time, these texts mirrored, and even contributed to, the important evolution in the sacralization of monarchy at the beginning of the twelfth century, in which we can witness the transition, pointed at by Boureau, from a vicarial model of royal power to a monarchic power which gradually became more conditional. However, this evolution was not evident at all. That is shown particularly by the highly original character of the journalistically organized account by Galbert of Bruges, a text which not only escaped from the strict generic customs of its time but may even be called – in the words of Mikhail Bakhtin – unusually 'dialogic'. Galbert airs ideologies, points of view, perceptions and transcripts of the confusing reality he had experienced, which can be found in hardly any other text of the period. Precisely from this multiplicity of voices, it can be deduced that the sacralization of secular power, which appears to have experienced a smooth development because of the monologic one-sidedness of most of the medieval source material, in reality also became confronted with a great deal of social opposition, mockery and constraint.

That medieval monarchy was particularly aware of the power of the word and the importance of its staging in its pursuit of sacralization and mystification is shown in a very special way in the chapter by Elodie Lecuppre-Desjardin. Here the concrete association with the ideal of the royal *nefandum*, of the sacrosanct silence in which majesty had to cloak itself so as to protect the mysteries of the late medieval State, is put under the microscope. Their silence meant that sovereigns, as those divinely chosen – like Moses, for example – became transformed into icons. By comparative research into the speech habits of Duke Charles the Bold of Burgundy (1467-1477), of King Edward IV of England (1461-1483), and King Louis XI of France (1461-1483), Lecuppre-Desjardin analyses how that ideal was put into practice in several late medieval courts and how it was based on various ideals of authority. Hiding the king as a speaking subject might well underline his sacral presence and the transcendence of his power, yet government still had to be organized and communicated, certainly in the late medieval period, which was pervaded so strongly by humanist ideals of eloquence. The theoretical discussions about this and the descriptions of the royal speech habits bear excellent witness to the quest for an equilibrium between the sacredness of the royal mystery and the risks of banalization run by the requirements of practical government.

Gilles Lecuppre's contribution, however, shows how in spite of the apparent monologism of royal discourse, other voices also emerged from below. Lecuppre deals with the phenomenon of royal impostures in late medieval Western Europe, of wandering hermits, who after crusades and other distant wars gave themselves out to be kings who were believed to have died or disappeared. Although we hardly ever know the discourse of such false pretenders in its original form, usually only from the reactions of the authorities, it is clear that they must have expressed a radical protest against true sovereigns who were deemed to be unlawful or inefficient. Late medieval political deception usually is seen in light of a popular belief in a 'hidden king' who will some day return and restore a long-awaited Golden Age. Lecuppre shows, however, how these impostures were actually based on very technical and realistic concepts of power. The frequently surfacing, eccentric false pretenders did not in the least incorporate a vague and widespread royal archetype. Their demands, manifestos and actions contained a soundly argued defence against the growing monarchic claims of their time. Through their perversion of the official public discourse of royal power, the usually completely implausible royal impostors again contributed, paradoxically enough, to the further sophistication and sacralization of the official royal power.

The chapter by Lecuppre thus convincingly argues that late medieval imposture did not simply constitute a mere parody of kingship but was a well-considered criticism of nascent early modern monarchy. Yet from the sixteenth century onwards, other possibilities emerged to question the growing of royal absolutism. The rise of the printing press, the increasing facilities for the circulation of ideas, and the humanistic culture also created a climate in which intellectual debates could become intensified considerably. The chapter by Jürgen Pieters and Alexander Roose enters more deeply into this kind of intellectual debate, more particularly in sixteenth-century France by such well-known essayists as Montaigne, and tries to situate them in the distinction made by

Michel Foucault between sovereign and governmental forms of royal authority. According to Foucault, the difference between these two economies of power marks precisely the transition from medieval to early modern power regimes. Central to the chapter of Pieters and Roose is a political treatise which constituted a public text known and read by several intellectuals but which, due to its radical character, circulated only in manuscript form for approximately twenty years before finally being published in 1576. Indeed, the early treatise *Discours de la servitude volontaire* of Étienne de La Boétie, a collaborator of Michel de l'Hospital, Chancellor of France, offered a very sharp analysis of the mechanisms of power. It even constituted an attack on the very foundations of the regal system of its time, expressing nothing less than a plea for a form of government that was based on the example of the classical republic. Against the historical background of the development of a truly absolutist theory of monarchy and the growing religious unrest in France, La Boétie questioned why people serve their leaders, hence willingly cooperating in their own subjection. The answer was to be found, according to La Boétie, in the force of habit of the people, as well as in the force of power brought about by the royal *mise en scène* and ceremony. La Boétie's analysis came close to that of Machiavelli in *Il principe*, a work which can be considered as the prototype of the political theory of sovereignty. The growing logic of governmentality hinged upon the subjects' interiorized awareness that it is good to be dominated, but it also stimulated the continual search for better modes of government. Therefore, one could consider La Boétie's critique of the force of habit also as a perfect example of this new political logic.

With the chapter by Kevin Sharpe, we move beyond the history of political thought up to the cultural history of political representation. In his chapter on royal expositions and representations, the consequences of the rise of a print culture and the public sphere are made fully clear. On the basis of the examples of King Henry VIII (1509-1547) and Queen Elizabeth I (1558-1603) of England, Sharpe takes a close look at the Tudors' need for an increasing sacralization of the monarchy. He exposes the processes by which the royal discourse and representation of the monarchy became mystified in the course of the sixteenth century. Sharpe shows revealingly that the process of sacralization was at the same time one of banalization and demystification, since the ability to publicize power and bring regality to the forefront of the cultural imagery also ensured that the monarch became a subject of discourse and an object of the public realm. While Elizabeth I was still very successful in reconciling the mystical with the popular, she left a legacy in which the monarchy had become a public object, an ordinary subject for discussion and gossip, a discontinued mystery. Sharpe argues that the monarchy in a period of development of trade and consumption itself became a product that was not only discussed but also owned by the subjects – who, after all, were starting to develop not only as consumers but also as citizens. For rulers after Elizabeth, the representation of their kingship had become almost impossible without taking into account the important cultural shifts in the perception of mystery and regality. The seventeenth-century civil war, revolution and Commonwealth encouraged these changes further, although, for example, King Charles II (1660-1685) had difficulty in accepting these changes for years. But, as Sharpe emphasizes, in the gradual shift to an uncoupling of the sacred and the political, the narrative of demystification is not straightforward. This relationship between the sacred and the political transcends history; it is peculiar to the complex social psychology which continually shows the need for mystification of authority.

A very explicit form of appropriation of the royal discourse by the common people is encountered in the well-known reversal rituals, which go back to antiquity and the Middle Ages but are exceptionally well documented only from early modern times onwards. In his chapter, Marc Jacobs traces the history of a repertoire of customs, stories and images involving imaginary or fake rulers, like the Three Kings, 'bean kings', and other 'rulers for a day'. Throughout the centuries in pre-revolutionary Europe, these representations have helped to imagine, discuss, perform and even construct the figure of a king and his court and to reflect on notions like 'absolute authority', theatricality and discontinuity in relation to royalty. Genuine royal courts dealt with these practices very ambiguously. On the one hand, there was the constant worry to keep any mockery within bounds. On the other hand, however, it appears that genuine rulers started to take part within and outside their palaces in the competitions to choose the king for a day. Through this new appropriation, they participated resolutely in the ritual banalization of regality. This dramatized display of their 'being ordinary' could at the same time encourage the mystification of their genuine kingship, something of which the late nineteenth- and twentieth-century monarchs would at a later date become very aware. But as Jacobs shows in the last case of his survey, in late eighteenth-century France, Louis XVI could postpone only temporarily his dramatic fate by taking up his caricatural role in the 'king drinks' rite on 20 June 1792.

While the staging of the monarchy still could be controlled and censored to a large extent during the Renaissance and later by the royal administrations, this became more difficult with the individualization of reading, which was brought about by the growing distribution of literature in a time when enlightened voices increasingly argued for freedom of press and of opinion. In her contribution, Lisa Jane Graham puts the emphasis on the discursive mechanisms which constitute and undermine political authority. She shows how fiction, more specifically the genre of the novel, demystified royal authority in eighteenth-century France. The novel established connections between private matters of the heart and public affairs of state. By elaborating a subjective language of interiority, novelists subverted the monarchy's staging of its own image and challenged the principles of secrecy and spectacle that guided the cultural politics of the crown. Where royal ceremonies reinforced the distance between sovereign and subject, the novel drew the two closer together. The novel eroded the fear and reverence that had traditionally surrounded the French king and did this by using literary techniques of parody, scrutiny and criticism articulated through the construction of character. The triumph of literary character constituted an 'uncrowning' that threatened royal authority. The decision to cast the king as a character in a novel established an analogy between kingship and fiction. Once the king acquired fictional character, he lost control of his political character. The novel demystified the king and encouraged demands for accountability that proved incompatible with theories of divine right and absolutism. Graham's analysis focuses on form, the early French novel, to demonstrate its impact on content, the demystification of kingship. The author draws together theories of the novel with historical interest in print, communication, representation and consumption. Following Michel de Certeau, she claims that textual appropriation offers a site both for the production of meaning and resistance.

The French Revolution marks the transition of monarchy as a divine investiture to a monarchy legitimized by the nation. This process, which had started long before 1789, was associated with a loss of the magical, with a desacralization of the monarchy and a separation between the king and the divine. The nineteenth-century constitutional monarchies arose not by the grace of God but by the grace of popular consent. In successive rounds of democratization, 'the people' were increasingly involved in politics, while the crown had to relinquish real power in constitutional systems. At the same time, however, the image of the royal family continued to play a very important role in several mass democracies into the twenty-first century. Kings and queens and their family stories became popular objects, easy to identify with. The 'magical touch of royalty' can be regarded as a charismatic aura somewhere between grandeur and everyday reality. Where monarchs had to move among their people, they should not overdo it; the element of mystery had to be preserved, and the king had to stay on his pedestal. The growing exposure through the developing mass media thus contributed to the establishment of popular monarchy and also to its banalization and trivialization. The media played, and still play, a remarkable double role both in creating the myth of the monarchy and in demythologizing it.

Although obviously a privileged channel, the consolidation of the press during the nineteenth century was not the only medium which brought the monarchy closer to the people. From Maria Grever's contribution it becomes clear that the extraordinary mixture of magic attraction, sublimity and 'ordinariness' of kings and queens could be demonstrated during World Exhibitions. Being part of a broader visual culture, these grand spectacles offered an unprecedented opportunity to promote a populist monarchy and to sustain a royal culture industry on a mass scale, while thousands of visitors had a chance to gaze at 'real' kings and queens. From the mid-nineteenth century onwards, World Exhibitions celebrated progress and needed the support of governments and royal houses financially, but also ceremonially: magic and glamour were ensured by the presence of royals. Grever, too, deals with the symbolic power of the monarchy as the embodiment of the nation in the nineteenth century. She compares the emerging popular monarchy at the World Exhibitions of 1851 and 1867: how monarchs exposed themselves and represented their nation with modern means and (re-)invented discourses, and how the masses consumed and (re-)appropriated this royal spectacle. Again we see the staging of domesticity and familiarity in combination with royal grandeur. Moreover, in the staging of Napoleon III (1852-1870), the historic reference to the time of the Roman empire was very emphatically present, with the object of reconfirming patriarchal structures. Monarchs were shown as *paterfamilias*, their wives as loving mothers. In the press, copious commentary was devoted to their dress, jewels, family relations, and dynastic genealogy. The mix of unapproachability and nearness was an essential component in the imaging and appropriation of the royal family.

In his influential analysis of the constitutional monarchy published in 1867, Walter Bagehot distinguished between the 'dignified' and the 'efficient', parts of politics, in which the royal show element was seen as a kind of dissimulation of the 'efficient' parts. The contributions by Jaap van Osta and Henk te Velde each examine this phenomenon from a different point of view. Jaap van Osta follows Bagehot when he looks at the popularization of the British and Dutch monarchies in terms of a shift from a 'political' to a 'ceremonial' monarchy. As symbol and promoter of national unity and consensus, the monarchy strove to forge a greater identification with the population, which required deliberate exposure in the public sphere. Particularly the private life of rulers had to be made public. Royal celebrations around births, marriages, funerals and other life milestones grew in the late nineteenth and early twentieth century into national ceremonies, such as the Jubilees in Great Britain or the Queen's Birthday in the Netherlands. The popularization of the press went hand in hand with the popularization of the monarchy. A flourishing souvenir culture pointed to a new wave of commercialization, although from Sharpe's contribution it appears that the monarchy as a 'product' or consumer article can hardly be called a modern innovation. Also, the fear that commercialization and banalization would undermine the mystery of the monarchy was and is a phenomenon which transcends time. And while we must refer national differences in staging the monarchy back to differences in the socio-political context of the countries being examined, according to Van Osta the personality and theatrical abilities of the monarchs should not be overlooked.

In his contribution to this volume, Henk te Velde starts with the changes the British historian David Cannadine identified in royal rituals during the years 1870-1880. However, Te Velde criticizes Bagehot's distinction between the symbolic and theatrical sphere and the sphere where real politics were practiced, and argues that the theatrical side of the parliamentary establishment also should be examined. For instance, the political duel between the British politicians Gladstone and Disraeli in the 1870s indicates the personalization and popularization of politics in general. Not only the monarchy erected a narrative of identification with the nation. Politicians also developed into political stars, and their speeches were widely published and distributed; people used relics of Gladstone's felled trees as 'small pieces of authority'. So no mass democracy without theatre, certainly not from the late nineteenth century onwards, when the 'masses' became politically emancipated. Te Velde attributes the differences between British parliamentary culture and the Dutch, in which the theatrical element was less present, to the extent of centralization of the state. The great tribunes of the people in the Netherlands came from outside the parliamentary system, where the development of a phenomenon such as *Koninginnedag* (the Queen's Birthday) in the late nineteenth century similarly can be linked to the evolution of mass politics. If we want to understand nineteenth-century politics and monarchy, it is clear that both the popular interest in the monarchy – which was more than a naïve belief in fairy tales – and the cultural side of the efficient parts of the constitution, especially the House of Commons, should be taken seriously.

Gita Deneckere focuses on the annual speech from the throne in Belgian history: a ritual in which monarch and parliament were symbolically linked and intertwined. Although there was never an official end to the ritual, no speeches from the throne have been held in Belgium since 1918. In its heyday, the speech from the throne had both a political and cultural element, bearing 'efficient' as well as 'dignified' aspects of royal power. The purpose of the speech was essentially symbolic, in the sense that the pact between the monarch and the nation was renewed and ratified every year. The speech from the throne also had a 'substantive' aspect: it conveyed a political message when the king on that occasion announced the government's policy programme. The king who acts as the mouthpiece of national politics is consistent with the ministerial responsibility and the adage that 'the King can do no wrong'. Therefore, the king also can *say* no wrong – the ministers are responsible for what he says and must cover the immune king. The mere fact that the king speaks bestows an exceptional splendour on the government's address: the role that the speech from the throne plays is a ceremonial one, whereas the government is responsible for the political message. Although the ceremonial aspect of the speech from the throne hardly changed between 1831 and 1918, it appears that its political text evolved in terms of the changing socio-political context and the king's position in it. Seeing that the struggle between the parties made the realization of a national consensus increasingly less self-evident – except in time of war or threat of war – the speech from the throne became more and more politicized, and the king's words could no longer surpass or remove the divide in a neutral manner. The fact that the speech from the throne became a source of conflict and could have political repercussions that were at odds with its function to promote unity explains why the ritual ceased to exist in Belgium, unlike the situation in the Netherlands and Great Britain.

Furthermore, at the end of the nineteenth century, Belgian socialists managed to subvert the speech from the throne in a rather spectacular way. The disruption of the strongly symbolically sensitive circumstance of the speech from the throne was aimed at bringing their demand for universal suffrage to the very pith of public attention. It is an indication of the fact that the 'theatre of the state', with the royal family in the principal role, does not work unilaterally from above. If it is true that the royal theatre contains a kind of magical spell to enchant people and to provide the political regime with a firm popular base, nevertheless this *mise-en-scène* went a long way to meet feelings from below. As in the earlier chapters of this book, we must not only pay attention to the ways in which authority was staged but also try to decipher the discourse of ordinary people that goes beyond the official rhetoric. Maarten Van Ginderachter takes up the challenge and peruses letters from Belgian citizens to the royal family, written in the period 1880-1940. The most common reason for writing to the king was to ask the royal family for money or help in kind with a so-called *letter of request* or *demande de secours*. This renewed interest in sources from 'ordinary people' is part of a recent reaction against one of the central assumptions of the field of discourse studies, viz., that analysing the production of a certain discourse amounts to studying its consumption in society. Using James C. Scott's concept of the 'public transcript', Van Ginderachter's essay asks to what extent the 'official' royal imagery resounded at the base of society. The letters of request constitute the public transcript of royalism as produced by the subordinate. Through their letters, ordinary people appealed to royal philanthropy, a practice which stemmed from the Ancient Regime and demonstrates how paternalism functioned as a basis for authority and how this official paternalist discourse was appropriated from below. Although by consequence it does not involve the unfiltered, authentic voices of the lower (uneducated) classes, it is precisely the dialogism which makes the letters interesting. It is striking how the image of the king as father of the nation appears in Belgium only after World War I, which should be linked to the personal characteristics of the unpopular King Leopold II (1865-1909). Appeals to the kindness and generosity of the royal family also appeared only after the war in the discourse of the letter writers. A shift occurred from a loyal, devoted and submissive attitude to a more affective and loving one, in which, for example, the maternal aspect of

Queen Elizabeth was prominently featured. Once more, the success of the modern monarchy seems to depend on the interplay between 'ordinariness' and 'extraordinariness' of the royals.

Today, the royal family saga still seems to be a firm base for the popularity of the monarchy as a postmodern phenomenon. That the many recent scandals at various European courts have cast just a limited stain on the royal escutcheon indicates that royal public relations continue to be remarkably successful in making people forget the facts and making myths match what people want to believe. Hence the main finding of this collection of essays may be that anything but a straightforward historical tale can be told of advancing demystification of the monarchy. For the present-day monarchy, it seems that even while the absolute logic of the rationalization of power should lead to its abolition, the continuity and enduring popularity of the monarchy actually indicate that this logic bumps up against a barrier, behind which the irrational nucleus of authority and power can be suspected. The problem of continuity and discontinuity in the four research trajectories of sacralization and banalization, of staging and the limitation of discourse about and of the monarch, thus boils down to the historization of the inherent ambiguity of the discursive relationship between monarchs and their subjects.

Monarchy's Medieval Monologism?

How Christian Was the Sacralization of Monarchy in Western Europe (Twelfth-Fifteenth Centuries)?

Alain Boureau

In the old French romance *Merlin*, composed in about 1220, a long passage is devoted to the question of King Uther Pendragon's heir. All the barons are convinced that no land or city can survive without a leader. However, the legitimacy of the new king, Arthur, seems to them very doubtful. And yet, according to the romance, this choice is the will of God, who through his prophet Merlin caused the young Arthur to be begotten and reared to manhood. Arthur's eventual success after a long, hard struggle requires miracles and immediate divine intervention.[1] This episode demonstrates that the office of kingship, thought necessary to mankind, is very difficult to establish, even when God makes his will quite clear. In the romance, supernatural support triumphs but must be recognized and acknowledged. The supernatural nature of kingship is not a given; it must be established.

A Shared Sacrality

Does Christianity play a significant part in the process of sacralization we see at work in *Merlin*? It would seem not, judging by the general atmosphere of the romance, in which God may represent any benevolent supernatural power. The process of choosing follows paths that are far from virtuous, since it involves adultery, forcible sexual union and trickery. Even its function seems uncertain. In short, Christianity appears to be only a vehicle for myths that convey the *caractère surnaturel* – the 'supernatural nature' – of kings.

It is not by chance that I refer to the subtitle of the French original of Marc Bloch's *Les rois thaumaturges* (1924).[2] The terms of this title demonstrate the non-specific aspect of sacred monarchy. The word *thaumaturge*, or wonderworker, is not just a scholarly doublet that expresses the power to work miracles. Its implicit theology stands aloof from the Christian religion, in which only God can make miracles, since it is a 'supernatural nature' and not a grace that is bestowed on the kings of France and England. And yet Bloch pays little attention to the 'Celtic' or 'Germanic' roots of medieval myths of royalty. The event that decisively changed the direction of the medievalist's academic career was the Great War. We must not underestimate the trauma suffered by a brilliant intellectual, dedicated to the idea of pure reason, on being plunged without warning into the irrational world of the trenches, where the ultimate goal of defending one's country was expressed in old-fashioned notions of honour and devotion to the leader that alone could explain why self-sacrifice was noble.

This tremendous shock led Bloch to study the historical roots of the phenomenon. The research he undertook to write *Les rois thaumaturges* enabled him to combine his concern for scholarly accuracy with a new slant postulating the universality of the leadership cult. The principle of monarchy was so universal and so timeless that to many it seemed to be a transcendental element of human life, as indeed the common usage of the adjective *royal* as a synonym for *excellent* or *paramount* in so many languages indicates. It appears therefore that Bloch relied on the anthropology of James George Frazer's *Golden Bough*, whereas intellectually he might have been expected to lean towards Émile Durkheim or Marcel Mauss.[3] This little mystery has always puzzled commentators of his work. Although Frazer's book represented an out-of-date anthropology, it interested Bloch as being a sort of encyclopaedic dictionary of beliefs corresponding to the universality of devotion to monarchy.

What he was looking for was a universal *lexicon* of the cult of monarchy, predating any *syntax* or *discourse*, that could be connected to a particular culture. This lexicon comprised a small number of irreducible elements, frequently using the metaphorical aspect of language like the miraculous royal touch, the aura or the fable of the necessary relationship between a body and its members. In this case, Christianity provided a possible framework, but other religions could also provide one.

Although the two intellectual traditions have little in common, since the 1950s the ongoing study of sacred monarchy has been found in the projects and publications of scholars whom I have called 'neo-ceremonialists', especially in the United States, the first of whom was Ralph Giesey, a direct follower of Ernst Kantorowicz. Giesey and his own disciples constructed syntaxes of sacralization, claiming that these universal lexical elements formed part of a continual process, passing through the ritual stage proper to a culture.[4] They were actually concerned less with the sacralization of the monarchy than with the ritual basis of a transcendence. In this respect they were following an American tradition which, probably influenced by the experience of building a nation whose political principles predated any written constitution, sought in the political life of the Middle Ages the traces of a proto-democratic and/or proto-state doctrine destined to flourish on both sides of the Atlantic in the eighteenth century. In this sense, Giesey's work was perhaps less broadly influenced by his collaboration with Kantorowicz than by the work of the medievalist Joseph Streyer, which dominated American medievalism for years and was applied to the Renaissance period by William F. Church's publication of *Constitutional Thought in Sixteenth-Century France*.[5]

The neo-ceremonialists, notably Sarah Hanley, even more than Giesey himself, eventually were influenced by a cultural anthropology which asserted that the authenticity and origin of sacred monarchy were to be found in its rites.[6] It was therefore necessary to consider the royal ceremonies as 'text', following the injunctions of Clifford Geertz, who by dealing with cultural practices and objects in this manner gave them an apparent autonomy.[7] And despite the multiple meanings that might be suggested by the notion of 'text', cultural anthropology tends to limit cultural processes to symbolic behaviours of unequivocal meaning, doubtless because the real author of the 'text' is not the historical protagonist but the author-decipherer. Here again, the Christian religion offered little more than an integrating principle, as necessary as any other to the particular working out of a syntax based on the constant elements of sacred vocabulary.

This organized grammar took on a more specific, more 'Western' aspect in Ernst Kantorowicz's version. For him, political transcendence constituted a true discourse in Western Europe, which gave birth to an idea of statehood that has scarcely any cultural equivalent. To fully grasp this trend, it is necessary to start from the central principle underlying the concept of *The King's Two Bodies*: '*dignitas non moritur*' [dignity does not die].[8] This formula undeniably contains an element of the metaphorical, with a literal term (*dignity, function*) and a figurative term (represented by the verb *to die*). Bearing in mind that the metaphorical process basically turns on the predicate, what we have here is a well-worn metaphor: in the fourteenth century Lucas of Penna glossed 'does not die' as 'lasts forever' [*quod semper est*]. The statement seems commonplace, extending to the secular institution a principle established in the domain of religion: the Church, the Apostolic See, does not die. Hence, institutional history indicates a displacement, a shift. Kantorowicz's brilliant idea was to reveal a new metaphor by placing the emphasis on the subject and not on the predicate. If dignity does not die, that is because it is compared to a living being, a person. The predicate *non moritur* thus creates a paradigm of living, immortal subjects that combines institutions (dead metaphors), divine subjects (theological predications) and mythological beings (allegories) or fictional ones (living metaphors): Empire, Mystical Body, Angel, Christ, Treasury, King, Phoenix.

Through the discursive contributions of some jurists and artists, Western man succeeded in constructing the imaginary yet effective space of an institution in which each person could exist both collectively and individually. The generalized establishment of the State and the idea of the public good made people forget the novelty of this process, which gave a structure to populations hitherto at the mercy of the disintegration of feudalism and of divided and contradictory loyalties. However, Kantorowicz was careful to not provide a direct political transcription of his discoveries; he simply observed how royalty invented a legitimate perpetuity for itself outside of, but mirroring, theology.

The sacralization of royalty was demonstrated widely, but as working to the benefit of the State and at the expense of Christianity, which offered only a store of metaphors. From Bloch to Kantorowicz and his successors, the Christian sacredness of the monarchy continued to be of minor and secondary importance.

A Christian Sanctity of Royal Power?

We seem at last to touch on the modes of a Christian sacredness when we come to the subject of the sanctity of kings. Sanctity, though not peculiar to Christianity, is seen here in particularly rich and developed forms. Nonetheless, there were degrees of sanctity, and it could easily be adapted to be simply a declaration of excellence. The pivotal figure of St Louis exemplified the possibility of a convergence of Christian sacrality and royal sanctity.[9] But this was an isolated instance, and royalty scarcely benefited from this convergence.

There is hardly any substantial trace of a living, hereditary sacrality associated with ancient German royalty. This limitation of the possibility of monarchical sanctity was reinforced on the Church's part by the separation of the secular and the religious realm brought about by the Gregorian Reform in the eleventh century, at the same time as the Holy See took charge of canonization procedures. The sainthood of the laity in general, despite the greater attention paid to ordinary Christian values, was still limited and was held in far less esteem. At best, it reflected virtues fully developed within the domain of the Church.

The medieval Church continued to hold up a biblical mirror to kings' faces in which, however, the image of the good monarch is often obscure. A famous description of the royalty to come is found in the Book of Samuel, where the people of Israel demand a king in place of the government of the Judges: their abuses and oppression are clearly forecast.[10] The sins and crimes of the wise and learned kings of the Old Testament, David and Solomon, are continually referred to; wisdom is conferred on them by God at specific moments, as though miraculously and not as a *habitus* or a gift. In about 1270, Gerard of Abbeville, one of many commentators, glosses the prophetic dream of Solomon as follows:

> Solomon, in this dream, does not merit the gift of wisdom, although in this instance he is granted the gift
> [*licet ibi obtinuerit*], because he has not been granted the gift of wisdom through the merit of contemplation but through the grace of revelation.[11]

Passively and functionally experienced inspiration is contrasted with the slow, active process of contemplation, the churchly, even clerical, source of Christian wisdom.

The absolute authority of the pope, as it slowly developed from Innocent III (1198-1216) to Boniface VIII (1294-1303), was based largely on the notion of a permanent institution of the law through papal decree. The idea of the *beata stirps* – of lineal sanctity, strongly maintained by the royal houses of France, Anjou and Hungary – was not sufficient to outweigh the ecclesiastical monopoly on sanctity and canonization.[12]

As a rule, the position of the prince in the Church was defined by *ministeriality*: the king was, at best, a secondary minister of religion. It was in this sense that the papacy tolerated the royal miracle-healing established in England and France in the twelfth century. The flow of grace could be channelled through the king's person on the day of his coronation rites, under specific circumstances controlled by the Church. But this intermittent, infrequent ministeriality was still of minor importance compared to that of the priest, who had daily charge of this flow of grace. The temporary status of deacon that the liturgy of the coronation rites conferred on the new king, sometimes cited as a proof of the sacrality of Christian kings, actually demonstrates its strict limits.[13]

Another possible way to Christian sacralization was autonomous and so obviated the mediation of the Church, understood as an institutional entity. A potential Christian sacrality surrounded the monarch as emperor. Indeed, the Empire as a totality – as a universality of the faithful, in its eschatological dimension – still represented a horizon of expectation for medieval Christians. We can discern parallels here with Gilbert Dagron's indispensable analysis of the Byzantine situation: the sacrality inherent in the Byzantine emperor came from the status of priest-king which he had inherited from the Old Testament through the figures of Melchizedek and David.[14] A careful analysis of the rites of coronation and the solemn procession in Byzantium shows clearly that this sacerdotal function did not derive from the Church. The Byzantine Church maintained the same tight control over the sovereign's religious domain as did the Western Church and granted only limited areas of participation in the holy mysteries. The office of the priest-king or priest-emperor had no ecclesiastical character.

In Byzantine Christianity we can discern the ongoing unobtrusive but authoritative Christian presence of the biblical image of the priest-kings, Melchizedek and David, beyond and within their absorption in Christ. This should encourage occidentalists to look about for possible parallels. Meanwhile, let us look at one that shows both affinities between East and West and the emergence of something specifically Western. Angelus Clarenus (Pietro da Fossombrone), at the end of a long and tumultuous life as a Franciscan rebel, wrote a commentary in about 1321-1323 on the Rule of St Francis in which he refers twice to the figure of the priest-king in a particular context. Commenting on the precept that allowed the brothers, in case of necessity, to eat whatever food was available, Angelus adds, 'as the Lord said speaking of David, who ate the offerings of bread which only priests were allowed to eat'.[15] Later he recalls the visit of a German brother, a master of theology, who came to ask St Francis's permission to move away from the brothers who would not follow the Rule to the letter (that is, from most of the Order). It seems that Angelus Clarenus was projecting into the life of Francis the much later dispute (after 1270) between the partisans of the strictest poverty and the majority of the Order. Francis replied that the request had already been granted by Christ and by himself. Then he blessed the brother, putting his right hand on his head saying, 'Thou art a priest forever according to the order of Melchizedek' (Psalm 109.4).[16] It should be remembered that Francis was never consecrated a priest but remained a sub-deacon. Angelus Clarenus's reconstruction depicts the faithful adhering to the rule as a priest-king, an emperor in his faith, apart from the Church or against it. The rebellion of the Spiritual Franciscans must be seen, of course, in an eschatological framework. It is not without interest that this text was written a few years after William of Ockham (1285-1349) took his case to Emperor Louis IV of Bavaria (1314-1347), and it sheds some light on this episode.

Pope Gelasius's (492-496) division of the two sources of government for Christians – of which Pierre Toubert has recently published a blistering analysis[17] – left no space for an aspiration to a third power, that of inspiration. The difference in the Eastern Church is probably due to the fact that the emperor – the soon-to-be nostalgic image of a past, possible and future Christian universality, with threatened borders – could take on this third function of power which in the West was left open to prophets, to dissidents or, in a more secular version, to the new institution of learning, the university.[18] This eschatological Old Testament reservation, outside the Church's power and accepting of absolutism, could still be found some centuries later. It is undoubtedly the diffuse nature of this Christian sacrality unrelated to the Church that is missing from studies of the political history of sovereignty.

But the Church's hostility to the idea of empire persisted. It is apparent in many well-known confrontations such as the Investiture Contest, the fierce battle between Frederick II of Hohenstaufen (1215-1250) and the papacy, and the prosecution of Louis IV of Bavaria. The Christian empire scarcely existed in reality, although it aroused violent debate.

The medieval Church overwhelmed all other power through its ubiquitarian reality,[19] which took the place of empire through the flexibility of its polyhierarchic system.[20] This powerful entity reduced the prestige of the secular authorities to a local, partial authority. The scope of its domination gave it a monopoly on discourse and argument for centuries, because it held the scriptural mould of demonstrations.

Sovereignty and Political Theology

In fact, despite all discursive superficiality, the Christian sacrality of monarchs gained ground in unexpected ways, being attached less to individuals than to the institutional form of government. In that institutional form, the traditional opposition between the Church and secular society was neutralized or, rather, became part of the same whole. In the long run, one can distinguish three types and three ages in the accomplishment of a considerable theoretical change in the doctrine of sovereignty through a clear expression of Christian and communal sacralities. This accomplishment led to 'absolute' power that provided itself, in the fourteenth and at times even in the thirteenth century, with powerful doctrinal instruments: sovereignty, majesty and the notion of the State.

In the first place, power in general, understood as lieutenancy, was constituted on 'vicarial' lines. The vicarial system is quite easily explained in the realm of ecclesiastical power. The pope is called the Vicar of Christ, thus the Vicar of God. St Peter or the apostles held on earth the place of the Word at the Incarnation, having been expressly delegated by God. It matters little that the nature of vicarial authority was subject to endless challenges, which were only briefly interrupted by the triumph of the papacy early in the second millennium. Until the thirteenth century, the occasional instance of vicarial legitimacy was questioned, but not the principle of it, which also played a part in the gradual sacralization of the whole body of authorities, hierarchized according to how close they were to the original source of truth: the Gospels, then in descending order the Epistles, the canons of the Councils and the patristic writings, ranked in an order of truth defined by tradition.

According to an ancient pattern of ecclesial doctrine, there exist in this world only two kinds of universal power, *regnum* and *sacerdotium,* both directly or indirectly ordained for the purpose of salvation. Secular power, *regnum,* followed the same pattern of lieutenancy, based on the royalty of Christ.[21] Kings only could aspire to the prosperity that justified their power by submitting to ecclesial control. There again, all disputes, until the Investiture Contest in the eleventh century, were concerned only with the source of the delegation: was it God himself, the papacy or the Church? The vicarial construct of double power, which crystallized legitimacy in a single origin, developed for a millennium with great flexibility: depending on where the place of lieutenancy was established, the secular power had a greater or lesser degree of independence.

But it was less the challenge of the Empire than the logic of the ecclesial doctrine that endangered the system of vicarial legitimacy by increasing it and combining it with functional legitimacy. This challenge to the sole vicarial legitimacy originating with St Peter came from various quarters: the bishops claimed a legitimacy of their own, based both on continuous transmission since the Apostles and on the importance of the pastoral office, especially in the major crises and particularly between 1280 and 1290, which pitted the secular clergy against the begging orders protected by the papacy. The priesthood, whose representatives, in the same circumstances, identified themselves with the tradition of the seventy disciples, gradually took on a greater concentration of sacrality and absorbed the ideas of *auctoritas, magisterium* and *ministerium*.

The system of double power was threatened, however, by the claims of a third power, the structural presence of which was laid down by the early Church in charismatic and prophetic functions, which had of course been incorporated into the 'priestly-episcopal' function since the third century.[22] But the revival of prophetic and mystical inspiration from the twelfth century on, followed by the development of university learning, led to this third source of power being legitimized as *studium*, and finally rendered the legitimacy of any exercise of power conditional and open to question.[23]

The traditional vicarial model seems to have become slowly worn out by the start of the second millennium. The separation of the religious and secular spheres aimed at by the Gregorian Reform in the late eleventh century specialized the royal or imperial function by claiming that it was subject to the moral control of the Church.[24] Manegold of Lautenbach, a German regular canon and a friend of Gregory VII (1073-1085), used the word *pact* to designate the source of legitimacy of secular and imperial power, but this was a matter of demonstrating the *conditional,* rather than contractual, nature of this power, even if the theology and the practice of the pact played an important role in the High Middle Ages.[25]

Manegold described this conditionality in rather blunt terms, saying that if a lord did not hesitate to dismiss, without compensation or consideration, a swineherd who did his job badly, how much greater reason was there to get rid of monarchs whose job was to watch over the salvation of their people and yet left them to wallow in sin.[26] This kind of treatment of kings is found two centuries later during another conflict, between Boniface VIII and the French King Philip the Fair (1285-1314), over an investiture: according to the Pope's accusers, in 1303 he had threatened to depose the monarch 'like a farm boy' [*sicut unum garsionem*].[27]

The third age in the erection of a cohesive theory of power was based on the notion of sovereignty, stemming closely from the theology of the Trinity.[28] In medieval political thought, the idea of sovereignty has long seemed secondary: historians of political thought have tended to believe that nothing was established firmly in this domain before Jean Bodin (1530-1596) or before the definite existence of a State or, more precisely, of a distinction between government and State. Alternately, they reduced the idea of sovereignty to the absence of any superior source of power or control at the level of political entities. In this sense, Innocent III and Philip Augustus (1180-1223) were joint forces in defining sovereignty in the kingdom of France. It is true that medieval language lacked the vocabulary to describe the emergence of a concept more specifically rooted in the exercise of a potentially absolute power, above and beyond the hierarchical degrees of the Church, the city or the kingdom. The word *superioritas* describes it less well than *maiestas*.[29] But since Walter Ullmann,[30] historians of pontifical power have taught us to identify forms of political legitimacy based on the unnamed but precise idea of sovereignty, fully developed since the pontificate of Innocent IV (1243-1254) on the Church's part and, since the early fourteenth century, on the part of the secular powers. Where Michael Wilks speaks of 'sovereignty' in his famous book on the publicists and Augustinus Triumphus (1243-1328),[31] Jacques Krynen prefers to use the notion of 'absolutism'.[32] In the past few years, many studies have been written about the instruments of this 'sovereignty': examples include the recent books on the distinction between absolute power and ordained power by Lawrence Moonan and by William Courtenay.[33]

The bitter debate about the Immaculate Conception of Mary[34] in the early fourteenth century comes under the heading of 'political theology', to use an expression coined in 1922 by the German jurist Carl Schmitt in the context of a critique of parliamentary government. Schmitt showed how the State could not be based on the rule of law; prior to the machinery of government, sovereignty, defined as pure decision, must be recognized: 'The sovereign is the one who makes the decisions in an exceptional situation.' The notion of political theology reveals that this structure of sovereignty secularized religious domination: the exceptional situation was the equivalent of the miracle. In quoting the French jurist Frédéric Atger, Schmitt makes the analogy more precise: 'The prince develops all the inherent virtualities of the State by a sort of continual creation. The prince is the Cartesian God transposed into the political sphere.'[35] This idea, long suspect as a result of Schmitt's commitment to the Nazi cause, has since become commonplace, a way of describing a simple aspect of theology applied to a political subject. However, its narrow sense, unburdened of the original polemical context, is useful to us. The expression describes a transitivity of the theological process, which still was not detached from other fields of thought.

The debate over the Immaculate Conception of Mary dealt with the divine power in that it broke free of the most universal and most necessary law (the conception of mankind in a state of sin). In the case of this debate we do not even need to speak of transposition: law and privilege are analysed in such universal terms that the shift from theological to political, from divine to princely, does not require any recourse to analogy. The mission in quest of salvation and the continual creation defined all great power.

The articulation of sovereignty which takes into account both the Creation and the march of time (that series of changes) reaches the point where sovereignty can be called an institution, going back to a key term in the doctrine of

Innocent IV. Pontifical absolutism, as it slowly grew from Innocent III to Boniface VIII, was mainly based on this idea of a permanent institution of law through papal edict. The essential contribution of the debate over Mary was to go back to the doctrine from the viewpoint of the common or privileged subjects of sovereignty. The rival powers could not reach an agreement, but the clash of their extreme claims did create a core of theory common to two opposite positions. The ways to Christian sacralization were very obscure.

Political Assassination and Sanctification. Transforming Discursive Customs after the Murder of the Flemish Count Charles the Good (1127)

Jeroen Deploige

> The office of the first hour was completed and also the response of the third hour, when Paternoster is said, and when the count, according to custom, was praying, reading aloud obligingly; then at last, after so many plans and oaths and pacts among themselves, those wretched traitors, already murderers at heart, slew the count, who was struck down with swords and run through again and again, while he was praying devoutly and giving alms, humbly kneeling before the Divine Majesty. And so God gave the palm of the martyrs to the count, the course of whose good life was washed clean in the rivulets of his blood and brought to an end in good works. In the final moment of his life and at the onset of death, he had most nobly lifted his countenance and his royal hands to heaven, as well as he could amid so many blows and thrusts of the swordsmen; and so he surrendered his spirit to the Lord of all and offered himself as a morning sacrifice to God.[1]

It is in the famous diary of Galbert of Bruges that we can read this colourful and dramatic account of how the childless Charles, Count of Flanders, ended his life on 2 March 1127, during Lent, in the Bruges church of St Donatian. The description is pregnant with symbolic meaning, of which three particular aspects touch at the core of this chapter. By referring so explicitly to the 'good life' of the count who, while praying and giving alms, received the 'palm of the martyrs', this fragment most overtly deploys a discourse recognizable as religious and, more specifically, as hagiographic. At the same time, by pointing not guilelessly at the count's 'royal hands' that were lifted to heaven during his martyrdom, it also conveys in a rather implicit way some early twelfth-century political and ideological discussions on the nature and the regal aspirations of the count's power in Flanders. Finally, despite the highly Christological portrait that is depicted here, we cannot isolate this description from a very disturbing historical context. While Charles may indeed be compared to a 'morning sacrifice' murdered by 'wretched traitors', we have to situate Galbert of Bruges's stirring report in the very ambivalent reality of a clearly orchestrated and brutal demystification of political power, followed by a nearly immediate reaction of sacralization. As a matter of fact, the discursive originality of Galbert's text is, as we will see, not only revealing but also closely connected to a much divided. historical context, to an age experiencing profound social and political change.

Charles, born c. 1082/86, was the son of King Canute IV of Denmark (1080-1086) and of Adela, daughter of the Flemish Count Robert I the Frisian (1071-1093). After the murder of her husband in Odense in 1086, Adela returned to Flanders with her little son, where she married Duke Roger of Apulia. The young Charles was thus educated at the court of his uncle Count Robert II (1093-1111) and Robert's son Count Baldwin VII (1111-1119). In 1119, Charles 'of Denmark' received the county from his childless dying cousin Baldwin. Charles's reign was said to have been a vigorous one, especially with regard to internal politics. He succeeded in limiting the needless use of violence in the county and in bringing internal peace. That was not only appreciated by the rural population, who were often victims of the feudal brutality of local lords and looting knights, but certainly also by the growing urban groups, who stood to benefit greatly from safe roads and markets for their commerce. During the severe famine of 1124-1125, Charles implemented measures that stimulated the planting of fast-growing crops and countered usury, both strong efforts to protect the poor and the weak.

However, while optimizing his administration and the management of his demesnes, he was confronted by a very delicate problem. In 1091, nearly thirty years before Charles came into power, the direction of the county's demesnes and fiscal collections had already come into the hands of a certain Bertulf, provost of the count's canonical chapter of St Donatian and, in that position, chancellor of the county administration. Bertulf belonged to the clan of the Erembalds, a family of un-free men who had taken advantage of the possibilities of social mobility and who had worked their way up as ministers of successive counts until they finally managed to dominate all kinds of important secular and ecclesiastical functions in the county. Charles hoped to break their power and return the Erembalds to serfdom, using as a pretext a lawsuit against one of their many violations of the peace in the county.[2] The Erembalds were very well aware of the count's threat. At the instigation of Bertulf, they conspired against Charles, carefully planning the murder that ended his life. But after the murder of Charles, the Erembald clan quickly lost control of the situation. Moreover, they had overestimated the support they might receive from the Bruges townsmen and from the population of Flanders. Some of the murderers and traitors, among them the provost Bertulf, succeeded in escaping from Bruges, but they were later captured and executed. Others held out under siege for a month and a half but finally were captured as well.

Because Charles had no children of his own and had never named a successor, central authority broke down into a chaos of lawlessness and looting. News of the murder spread very fast all over northwestern Europe and quickly reached Charles's suzerain, the King of France, Louis VI (1108-1137). At first, the King managed to make excellent political capital out of the situation.[3] Despite the existence of several candidates, he succeeded in having a new count elected within just a few weeks. Moreover, he was able to impose a strategically very interesting new count: his Norman brother-in-law William Clito, grandson of William the Conqueror (d. 1087) and Matilda of Flanders. William Clito at that time lived very much in discord with his uncle Henry I of England (1100-1135), with whom Louis was embroiled in a rivalry of power.[4] The young and ambitious William Clito initially seemed to the Flemish nobility and urban elites to be a very acceptable new count, who could take over Charles's role as righteous peacemaker. It looked as if the unproblematic election of William Clito and the final punishment of the traitors had resolved the political impasse in Flanders rather quickly. However, in 1128 a civil war broke out. The new Count William became more and more compromised as he refused to respect the privileges that he had accorded to the Flemish towns, and his discord with Henry I threatened the good economic relations between England and Flanders. Among the several challengers of William, one pretender was moving to the forefront: Thierry of Alsace, another blood relative of the murdered Charles. Supported by a coalition of townsmen and some nobility, he would end up at the end of July 1128 as William's successor after the latter's sudden death on the battlefield.

Since Henri Pirenne's edition in 1891 of Galbert's work,[5] the events in Bruges and Flanders in the years 1127-1128 have fascinated generations of historians, who have analysed the political circumstances,[6] juridical aspects,[7] solidarities,[8] mentalities,[9] rituals,[10] and historiographical issues[11] surrounding this turning point in early twelfth-century Flemish history. It is not my purpose in this chapter to enter into a discussion with that research tradition. Rather I would like to analyse here the problem of Charles's quick sanctification and its narrativization, against the background of the medieval sacralization of monarchy, through the lens of a discourse analysis, drawing chiefly upon the genre theory of the Russian language theoretician Mikhail Bakhtin.

Genre and Context: Bakhtin's Theoretical Framework

Mikhail Bakhtin's genre theory is not a traditional literary one, based on the formal or semantic characteristics of literary texts. His theory starts from the simple fact that linguistic communication is always realized in the form of individual, concrete utterances by the participants in varying fields of human activity.[12] These utterances are characterized by a number of rhetorical features, which insure that they can never reflect the reality of that social field perfectly. But although Bakhtin stresses the importance of content, style and composition – typical criteria for traditional literary typologies – he does not consider those elements to characterize a so-called 'speech genre' or 'discourse genre'. For Bakhtin, discourse genres result from an interplay between specific communication contexts in which the utterances are produced, and intertextual and intersubjective discursive conventions and repertoires to which the utterances appeal. Bakhtin's understanding of genre is thus situated on the level of socially negotiated discursive customs. His approach is also very historical: he argues that every genre is always subject to evolution because the context for communication is always different and influenced by new historical circumstances. The repertoires of discourse genres always become more differentiated and more complex. They change not only as a result of new contexts of communication but also through dialogue with the existing genre conventions. Discourse genres are for Bakhtin 'the drive belts from the history of society to the history of language'.[13]

The flow chart adopted here (Figure 1) summarizes the most important aspects of the Bakhtinian genre theory.[14] Conceived in the 1950s, this theory can easily be consolidated by more recent insights deriving from sociology and literary studies. The notion of relatively independent social fields, with their own structures and internal logics, for example, has been implemented thoroughly by the sociologist Pierre Bourdieu.[15] The idea that genres are always subject to a continuous historical process of creation and modification of what can be called a 'horizon of expectations' has become central to the reception aesthetics of Hans-Robert Jauss. As Jauss put it, new texts evoke for their readers (or listeners) 'a horizon of expectations and rules which are familiar thanks to earlier texts, and which immediately undergo more variations, rectifications and modifications, or which are simply reproduced'.[16] Further, one can find in Michel de Certeau's analysis of the 'practices of everyday life' a very inspiring conceptualization of how people, according to specific contexts and positions of power, can appropriate cultural goods and repertoires. Certeau differentiates, for example, between the strategic modelling of cultural goods, among which we can count discourse genres, by those social agents that hold true positions of power and the more tactical appropriation and silent transformation of these goods by the less powerful.[17]

There exists, of course, a countless number of discourse genres, and Bakhtin even differentiates between primary genres, used in daily speech, and secondary or more complex genres that are most often written.[18] A fine example of such a complex discourse genre, which was very popular in the Middle Ages

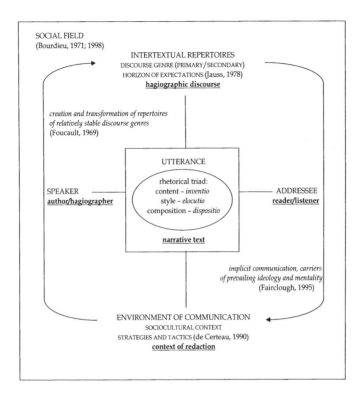

Fig. 1. The Place of Hagiography in the Bakhtinian Genre Theory

and for which there certainly existed a well-developed horizon of expectations, is the 'hagiographic discourse'.[19] It is precisely the way in which this hagiographic discourse was employed in the immediate aftermath of the unexpected murder of Count Charles, in order to narrativize and surmount discursively the disturbing reality in Flanders in 1127, that I will analyse in the following paragraphs.

On the basis of this specific case study, I would like to draw special attention to the interrelatedness of contexts and discourse genres. On the one hand, we will be confronted with an illustration of how new contexts always slightly modify, transform or sophisticate existing repertoires of discourse genres – something already revealed, for example, in Michel Foucault's theories on the production of discourses.[20] On the other hand, discourse genres are always at the same time vehicles of implicit communication. Because they rely upon a unity of form and content, they are excellent carriers of existing ideologies and mentalities. In recent years, the unmasking of this implicit ideological communication has become the focal point of the new linguistic discipline of critical discourse analysis.[21]

Sanctification through Genre Transformation

The assassination of Charles may have been well prepared by a conspiracy of several leading persons in the county's administration and in Bruges's military and judicial apparatus, who recently had climbed their way up in the feudal society and who had gained a lot of influence thanks to their position of power, not in the least among the average citizens who did not have such strong feelings for the traditional nobility.[22] Nevertheless, the murder was very unexpected and immediately caused a shock wave of dread throughout the county. This can be derived from a number of narratives – chronicles, annals reports, etc. – that echo the mourning and describe the public chaos after Charles's death.[23] Almost immediately after the murder, a first series of elegies and epitaphs was published, in which Charles was extolled as the most ideal ruler the county could ever have desired.[24] One of the oldest epitaphs, probably dating from April 1127, described him as the father of the orphans, protector of widows, saviour of the fatherland, protector of the churches and, finally, as a pacifier.[25]

Two extremely interesting texts, however, written in the immediate aftermath of the assassination, went even further in their narrativization of the events and without reticence ascribed to Charles 'the Good' the airs of a saint and a martyr. The first text to appeal overtly in its description of Charles's brutal death to a hagiographical horizon of expectations was the *Vita Karoli*, written in the summer of 1127 by the regular canon Walter at the order of the Thérouanne Bishop John of Warneton.[26] Walter had started his ecclesiastical career at the abbey of the Augustinian canons of St Martin in Ypres and had been appointed in 1116 by Bishop John as archdeacon of the Flemish part of the diocese of Thérouanne.[27] Walter's *Vita* constituted an average example of a well-crafted and nicely structured traditional hagiography. In the first part of his text (ch. 1-14), he describes Charles's origins and exemplary rule. He subsequently throws light, as if in a negative mirror, on the origins and the outrages of the Erembald clan (ch. 15-25). Central to the text are three chapters in which Charles's martyrdom is described in a very biblically styled way. Then follows the account of the events leading to the burial of the count (ch. 29-33). Finally, the last and largest part of the hagiography deals with the persecution of the murderers (ch. 34-54). The text only contains some three explicit descriptions of miracles, but the stories of the fall of the conspirators do function in a certain way as a kind of divinely fated and hence miraculous punishment stories.

The second and today even more famous narrativization of the events is written down in the above-cited text *De multro, traditione, et occisione gloriosi Karoli comitis Flandriae*, written by a clericus in the count's fiscal administration, Galbert of Bruges.[28] For two months after the murder, Galbert kept a kind of journal – now lost – of the confusing events he was witnessing. In the summer and fall of 1127, he reworked his daily notes, added some extra chapters and prefaced his text by a prologue and a biographical account praising Charles's roots, youth and exemplary reign. In this revised version, especially in its first 23 chapters, Galbert clearly wanted to model his account according to the specific hagiographic discourse typical of a passion story. This hagiographic discourse gets concretized by the praise of Charles's origins and good works, by the description of his violent death in terms of an unmistakable martyrdom, by the account of the failed attempt of the acquisitive monks of the Ghent abbey of St Peter's to get hold of the body of the count in order to add it to the collection of relics of their abbey (which had become from the tenth century onwards the necropolis of several Flemish counts) and by the description of a miraculous healing of a cripple that would have occurred during this tumult. As Jeff Rider has argued, there are good reasons to assume that shortly before his revision, Galbert took note of Walter of Thérouanne's hagiographical work.[29] We can even extend this hypothesis and presume that he may have felt himself strengthened and inspired by the work of the authoritative archdeacon to style his own text too in a hagiographical way and to present Charles straight out as a real martyr. After the outbreak of the civil war in Flanders in 1128, Galbert resumed his work to record the new developments on a regular basis. As we will still see below, his text finally escaped from the traditional hagiographical customs to become a journalistically organized history.

The fact that Walter of Thérouanne and Galbert of Bruges made use of a hagiographic discourse in order to sanctify their hero Charles can be considered a fine example of the process of appropriating and transforming a powerful existing discourse genre, in this case in the very specific context of a dramatic political parricide. Indeed, if we take a closer look at the existing hagiographic genre conventions in the Low Countries in the early twelfth century, then we cannot say that Charles's panegyrists have chosen a discursive convenience. Charles was a contemporary personality, he was considered to be a martyr and he was a layperson. None of these characteristics was self-evident for hagiographically described heroes at that moment.

The hagiographic tradition in the Southern Low Countries was of course an old one, with roots in the Early Middle Ages. An examination of all the known hagiographic texts written since the 920s – that is, in the two centuries preceding the events of 1127 – reveals that the number of contemporary persons described in these two centuries was still very limited.[30] In the approximately 220 texts composed during these two centuries, we meet only nine saints who were hagiographically described within a half century after their death. Except for Charles, only two of those nine were honoured within five years after their death: the enigmatic Armenian tramp Macarius, who had arrived in Ghent in 1010 as a 'pseudo-bishop' of Antioch and had died shortly after; and the reformist abbot Thierry of St Hubert, whose life ended in 1086.[31]

The honour of martyrdom was, in the early twelfth century, still nearly exclusively reserved for those religious heroes who had died for their faith in confrontation with pagans. In Christianized Europe, such a death had become very hard to aspire to. But the spirit of the crusades may have stirred up the ideal of martyrdom again. In northern and eastern Europe, where Christianization had not yet been completely accomplished, it was still possible to get killed by pagans, or at least by 'foes of the faith'. However, up to the 1120s, a murder committed by fellow Christians was but very rarely considered as a cause of martyrdom and that would remain the case in the next centuries. In the hagiographical tradition of the Southern Low Countries before 1127, we meet only one case of such a martyr: Godeliph of Gistel, a Flemish married woman who was allegedly killed around 1070 at the instigation of her brutal husband and who was portrayed in 1084 in a hagiographical text as a martyr of marital fidelity, exactly in the period in which the Christian sacrament of marriage was in full development.[32]

That same Godeliph, with her social profile otherwise so different from that of the Flemish count, was also the sole layperson in the Low Countries to gain the status of a saint in the two centuries preceding the murder of Charles. In this span of time, it was nearly exclusively important ecclesiastical prelates who inspired hagiographers. Among the nine contemporary persons who had preceded Charles as heroes inspiring hagiographical efforts, we find, for example, next to Godeliph, five reformist bishops and three powerful abbots.

In the religious and literary field of the 1120s, it was hence an absolutely innovative undertaking to describe a count such as Charles, notwithstanding his positive image of Christian prince and victim of an assassination, in a sanctifying discourse. Neither Walter nor Galbert were members of a traditional centre of hagiographical activity. Both were coming from a recently emerged urban background: Walter as secular canon originating from Ypres and living in Thérouanne; Galbert as clericus in the count's administration in Bruges. That the murder of Charles was perceived and narrativized in a completely different way in the traditional, monastic circles of literate activity appears clearly in the *Translatio sancti Jonati*, which was composed in 1127, shortly after the murder, in the old Benedictine abbey of Marchiennes in the extreme south of the county.[33]

The monks of Marchiennes always had lived on very good terms with Count Charles, who had succeeded in limiting the feudal violence even in the southern confines of his county and who thus had protected the estates of the abbey against possible violations and usurpations by the local aristocracy.[34] Gualbert of Marchiennes, the author of the *Translatio sancti Jonati*, was also the presumed poet behind the anonymous elegy *Huc ades, Calliope* in honour of the murdered Charles.[35] But despite the fact that the *Translatio* enters at length and very explicitly into the assassination of Charles and into his former role of

protector of the abbey, the count is nowhere in this text depicted as a true martyr or described in a hagiographical way. On the contrary, this text is devoted to
a true traditional saint, the seventh-century abbot Jonatus, whose relics had
been literally mobilized in the aftermath of the murder by the Marchiennes
monks in order to protect one of their villages against possible violations by
local lords, after the authority of the count had disappeared temporarily. Even
though Jonatus never did receive widespread veneration after the temporary
translation of his relics, the cast in this text remains unmistakable: the count
had been a good secular protector, while St Jonatus was considered as a religious patron who could be helpful to compel divine protection after the breakdown of the secular authority.

Of course, there were examples of well-known older hagiographic texts
describing early medieval martyred kings, especially in the Anglo-Saxon tradition of before the eleventh century.[36] The seventh-century King Oswald of
Northumbria, for example, who was reported to have been killed during a
campaign against the pagan King Penda of Mercia, was still venerated in
Flanders in the late eleventh century.[37] But in the Christian heartland of
Europe, it turns out that even contemporary monarchs of royal or imperial status were but very rarely commemorated in a hagiographical discourse during
the High Middle Ages. The Ottonian Emperor Henry II (1002-1024) and the
pre-Norman English King Edward the Confessor (1042-1066) were the last
known examples, both still preceding the Gregorian Reform with its redefini-
tion of the relationship between *sacerdotium* and *imperium*.[38] As Alain Boureau
already noted in the previous chapter, royalty scarcely benefited from the convergence between Christian sacrality and royal sanctity from the High Middle
Ages onwards.

However, as Gábor Klaniczay has well established, the influence of the
Ottonian attempts to develop a notion of hereditary sanctity and of a *beata
stirps* has had, from the second half of the eleventh century onwards, a very
important reception in the peripheries of Western Christendom, for example
in Hungary with the canonization of several kings and princesses of the
Arpad dynasty. The old Anglo-Saxon tradition with its several martyred kings
was revived especially in the Scandinavian confines of Europe.[39] The fate of one
of those kings was even very well known to both Walter of Thérouanne and
Galbert of Bruges. Around 1100, no one less than Charles's own father, King
Canute of Denmark, killed in 1086 in St Alban's church of Odense by rebelling
nobles under the command of his brother Olaf, was gaining much fame as a
Scandinavian 'protomartyr' in the recently Christianized northern European
periphery.[40] Although it seems unlikely that there were already circulating
manuscripts of the *Passio Canuti* in the Low Countries in the early twelfth century, Charles's biographers did not remain untouched by the parallels between
Canute and his son.[41]

Later in the twelfth and thirteenth centuries, we find increasingly more examples of contemporary lay saints, but the phenomenon of martyrs killed by fellow Christians remained rather rare and exclusively reserved to important prelates who were assassinated in the context of the ecclesiastical and papal movement of reform.[42] The best known example of this new kind of martyr was of course the reformist Archbishop Thomas Becket, killed in 1170 in Canterbury Cathedral because of his conflict with King Henry II (1154-1189) and officially canonized by Pope Alexander III as early as 1173. The martyrdom of Thomas immediately gained international resonance, not only in terms of veneration and spread of his cult but also as a source of hagiographical inspiration. For example, when the just-ordained Liège Bishop Albert of Louvain was killed in 1192 by German envoys because the German emperor supported another candidate for the bishop's seat, Albert immediately was compared, in a hagiographical narrative, to Thomas Becket.[43] But as we can learn from a poem, probably written at the end of the twelfth century in the Beauvaisis in northern France, certainly outside of Flanders, the murder of Thomas must also have evoked reminiscences of the old fate of Charles the Good. Indeed, among a collection of preserved hymns and elegies dedicated to the martyrdom of Thomas, we find a poem entitled *Non lingua fari*, in which an allusion is made to the early twelfth-century Flemish count.[44]

The hagiography of Charles, which was rather unusual in its own region and time, hence constituted an important transition point in the history of the genre and of the practice of sanctification. On the one hand, it fitted in with the early medieval tradition of martyred kings, which was temporarily remerging in the periphery of Christianity; on the other hand, it was paving the way to a new kind of martyr, which, however, would become reserved to only a few important clerics active in the movement of ecclesiastical reform.

Narrativization and the Implicit Advocacy of Royal Ideologies

By strategically choosing a narrative which corresponds to a hagiographical horizon of expectations, Charles's panegyrists inscribed their narrativizations of the events they had witnessed in the specific ideological framework that hagiography, as a discourse genre, silently imposes. Their sanctifications of the murdered count are strengthened by the ample use of biblical citations that stress the divine character of the secular lord. Neither writer neglects the historical details that may help to stress the sacral character of the assassination: that Charles was murdered during Lent, in a Church, while praying and after having given alms to the poor. The most important implication of interpreting the martyrdom of Charles through a hagiographical lens can be discovered in the fact that both Walter of Thérouanne and Galbert of Bruges described the terrible and disturbing crime in terms of a well-designed and meaningful divine plan. In Walter's *Vita Karoli*, that providential plan is revealed by a very eschatological interpretation and presentation of the event. As David Van Meter has analysed acutely, Walter succeeds in exalting the historical Charles with his surprising defeat and death up to the level of an agent of God's peace, by portraying him as true Christological hero in search of self-sacrifice after an exemplary public life as protector of the poor, of peace and of justice. In his death, Van Meter summarizes, 'Charles realized his full potentiality as a Christian ruler, and the sudden loosing of divine justice upon an entire generation of evil men'.[45] In his *De Multro*, Galbert added yet another providential logic to this image of the sacrificed count personifying the Eucharist. With reference to Exodus 20.5 or Deuteronomy 5.9 – 'Since God is wont in the severity of his punishment to correct the iniquities of the fathers unto the third and fourth generation'[46] – he considered the murder of Charles and the subsequent execution of Bertulf as logical divine punishments of two earlier crimes in late eleventh-century history.[47] Indeed, on the one hand, Charles's own ancestor Robert the Frisian had received his count's office in 1071 in an illegal way at the dispense of the sons of his older brother. Provost Bertulf and his clan members, on the other hand, owed their influential positions to the fact that their ancestor Erembald only had become castellan of Bruges after having murdered his master Boldran.[48]

However, using a discourse genre does more than to imply the adoption of a pre-existing general model to interpret and to explain certain aspects of a specific culture or social reality. As we have seen above, it also enables speakers or writers to communicate implicitly, and hence more tactically, ideological choices or preferences which are not necessarily characteristic to the discourse genre itself. Genres are in other words excellent vehicles for the (re-)affirmation and advocacy of values and ideologies. This can be noticed very well in Walter's and Galbert's narratives, too. While both authors use a traditional discursive form, they do not hesitate to inject their accounts with rather innovative political theories. Central to their texts, for example, is the idea that Charles should be considered as the ideal, natural monarch, who became a martyr of justice. Walter even literally asks, 'which other reason could there have been for his martyrdom except justice?'[49] This stress on the monarch as a personification of justice may have been very recognizable and was based upon old ideals which we can find already in the early medieval 'mirrors of kings'. Very innovative, however, is the fact that this justice of the monarch becomes linked, by both Walter and Galbert, to very contemporaneous political concepts and aspirations.

When Charles is presented as a fair pacifier, we should situate this image in the context of the Peace and Truce of God movements, which originally had emerged at the very end of the tenth and the first half of the eleventh centuries as ecclesiastical initiatives to limit feudal violence and private warfare, yet had been adopted rather quickly by a few important secular princes, who could invest themselves in this way with some sort of messianic aura and judicial power within the borders of their own 'theocratic' principality.[50] Already from the early eleventh century onwards, the Flemish counts Baldwin IV (988-1035) and V (1035-1067) prominently manifested themselves as champions of the Peace of God.[51] This policy was also considered an important instrument to underline the independency of the count's authority vis-à-vis the weaker French royal suzerain, especially from the beginning of the twelfth century onwards, when the traditional ecclesiastical Truce of God evolved to the more secularized 'public peace' (*Landfriede*) under the immediate authority of the secular prince.[52] The increasing power of the rather independent county to the detriment of the French king was also mirrored in the emergence of a new 'patriotic' terminology. From the 1060-1070s onwards, the county of Flanders occasionally became characterized as the *monarchia Flandrenis*, as a principality governed by an authority legitimated by God, stemming from old Carolingian royal roots.[53] In 1110-1011, in his *De laude Flandrie*, the canon Peter Pictor sang the praises of Flanders being the *domina patriarum* or the 'mistress among the fatherlands', and some ten years later, his colleague Lambert of Saint-Omer adopted a *Genealogia regum Francorum comitumque Flandriae* in his famous encyclopaedia *Liber floridus* in which he typified Flanders as a true *regnum* or realm.[54]

Also, the narratives of Walter of Thérouanne and Galbert of Bruges teem with expressions like *patria Flandriarum* or *regnum Flandriae*.[55] Even the dictum *pro patria mori*, which Ernst Kantorowicz still thought had gained momentum only in the thirteenth century, can already be retrieved in Galbert's text, when he supposes that the besiegers of the church of St Donatian, who were trying to capture some of the conspirators who were still hiding in the church, were rather bent on the treasure of the count than considering 'how noble it would be to die for father and fatherland'.[56] Of course the count too is presented as the *pater patriae*, the *patriae defensor*, the *comes patriae*.[57] The relationship between the traditional ideal of justice and the more recent concept of the fatherland is actually expressed very literally by Galbert when he states that 'God [...] carried off to the place of the saints the one who had been killed in the cause of justice in the fatherland'.[58] Completely in line with this stress on the Flemish *monarchia* or *patria*, Walter and Galbert also take the opportunity to underline that Charles was of royal origin on his father's side. Galbert goes the furthest in his attempt to elevate Charles up to the level of real kings. He is eager to mention that the count had refused the German emperor's crown (1123) as well as the crown of the Kingdom of Jerusalem (1125).[59] He stresses in his prologue that Charles's power and honour surpassed that of many other kings.[60] In the citation at the opening of this chapter we have seen already how Galbert describes Charles's 'royal hands', lifted in the air at the moment of his martyrdom. He finally also sighs that Charles was 'more worthy to be a king than the count of wretched traitors'.[61]

It is not surprising, therefore, that in their sanctifications Count Charles's biographers also sought to portray their hero according to the current ideologies of their time concerning the sacralization of kingship. However, we may notice some differing nuances between Walter of Thérouanne and Galbert of Bruges. By using a very explicit and well-balanced hagiographic structure, Walter left no doubt that his hero was to be considered a saint. As I indicated above, it is mainly by sketching a very Christological portrait of Charles that Walter seems to have appropriated the contemporaneous discourse of sacralization of the monarch. Unconsciously, he still echoes the anti-Gregorian tractates of the so-called Norman Anonymous, written around 1100 and developing the concept of the king as a natural lord endowed with spiritual qualities by the grace of God.[62] In the way his deeds and death are described by Walter, Charles effectively bears both the characteristics of an ontological 'image of Christ' and of a functional 'vicar of Christ'.[63] Even his murderers fit into this image in a very eschatological way, as they are compared at length with the Jews, who killed Jesus outside the city gate with their tongues although not with their hands, because they failed to recognize their Lord.[64]

A comparison of Walter's discourse of sanctification to Galbert's narrativization of the events in 1127 mirrors in some way the twelfth-century shift, described by Ernst Kantorowicz, from a liturgical kingship, in which the king is seen as a vicar of Christ, towards a law-centred kingship, in which the king is considered as the father and son of justice, as the lord and the minister of the law.[65] Indeed, in Galbert's work we retrieve the traditional image of the Catholic prince and legitimate father figure – a *dominus, pater, advocatus* – who had won his spurs as a protector of peace and justice.[66] Moreover, Galbert, who seems to have been very experienced in legal matters, not only depicted Charles as a Christ-like sacrament but also described in detail the requirements that were set by his contemporaries for a new count. In these descriptions we are confronted with the growing conditional bases of secular power. A good lord's justice had to be in service of the common good, of the *bonum commune* of society. This becomes clear for the first time when Galbert cites a letter received by the citizens of Bruges on 20 March 1127 from Thierry of Alsace, who presented himself as the best possible candidate to the office of the count:

> If, out of respect for right and kinship, you send back a favourable reply to me, I shall hasten to become your count, and I shall be just, peaceful, tractable, and concerned for the common good and welfare.[67]

One week later, the chief citizens of Bruges and the leading men of the castellany replicated this idea and swore on the relics of their saints that their new count had to be one 'who will be willing and able to serve the common interests of the land'.[68] At the same time, however, Galbert ventilates subtleties deriving from the political theology of his time, which continue to stress the sacrality of kingship. When he describes, for example, how on 6 April 1127 King Louis VI and the new Count William Clito had to reconfirm the prerogatives of the Bruges chapter of St Donatian, Galbert stresses the fact that the king was obliged to respect these, not only as a person but also because of the dignity (*dignitas*) of his kingship.[69] Royal Dignity – which had to be maintained for the sake of the whole realm – was going to become a very pivotal concept in the development of the idea of royal transcendence.[70]

However, from that same agreement between the king and the canons of St Donatian we can also conclude that the person occupying the office of the count was considered as the king's substitute only during the absence of the latter. Although he seems to have been persuaded by the sacred character of kingship, Galbert's narrative – just like Walter's – only aimed at sanctifying Charles as a person and not really at sacralizing the office of the count. This prudence, which contrasts with the many attempts to glorify the Flemish *patria* or *monarchia*, may be understood in the context of the growing influence of the Gregorian Reform and its separation of the secular and the religious realm.[71] However, the dream of a *regnum Flandriae*, at the level of a true kingdom, did not completely evaporate in the subsequent decades. Ludo Milis, for example, has clearly shown how the counts Thierry (1128-1168) and his son Philip of Alsace (1168-1191) continued to highlight their kingly virtues, by the specific royal symbolism on their seals, in order to assert themselves with regard to their French suzerain.[72] And even though Walter and Galbert did not try to develop a discourse sacralizing the office of the count, they managed to elevate the political parricide on Charles up to the level of a true regicide thanks to their explicit stress on Charles's royal origins.

Social and Discursive Fault Lines and the Multiplication of Voices

It is striking that in the course of history, several political murders took place in or around sanctuaries. Since antiquity, churches and other religious buildings had constituted public spaces where violence should be banned, where asylum could be found and where a potential, unarmed victim should normally find himself protected by the sacred setting. Some browsing through the sixth-century *Historiae* of Gregory of Tours reveals that from the Early Middle Ages onwards, violation of church asylum constituted a highly efficient transgression in private warfare.[73] Sacred services in sanctuaries, moreover, are usually organized following a strict timetable, which allows careful planning of a murder. Even in our own times, this has led to several political assassinations in or close to temples. We can think for example of Archbishop Oscar Arnulfo Romero from El Salvador, one of the leaders in the movement of liberation theology, who was killed on 24 March 1980 while celebrating a mass in a hospital of one of San Salvador's outskirts, officially by members of a right-wing death squad. Or we can consider the charismatic founder of the Palestinian Hamas movement, Sheik Ahmad Yasin, who was assassinated on 22 March 2004 by Israeli rockets as he left a mosque in Gaza.

While political murders in sanctuaries are often inspired by practical motives rather than by an aspiration to ritual transgression, it is noticeable that the double demystification they bring about – murder and desecration – induces a very strong tension in the narrativization and catharsis of these shocking events, as well as in the immediate praise, through all kinds of texts and discourses, of the victim. It is, in other words, the 'poetics' rather than the 'politics' of transgression that try to ritualize the events.[74] This purgation of emotions is also frequently achieved in a very innovative way. Important historical fault lines thus often become intimately intertwined with discursive fault lines. We have seen above how Walter of Thérouanne successfully appropriated a traditional genre in a very unusual situation by couching the extraordinary events in Bruges in a hagiographical plot. Sometimes, however, a discursive fault is brought about by a nearly complete abandonment of the current generic customs. The narrative emplotment of a social historical fault line can lead, in other words, to completely new forms of expression. This had already happened once some fifteen years earlier, in 1112, on the occasion of an important communal revolt in the northern French city of Laon, where, among others, the bishop of the town had been assassinated during an escalating conflict with the urban population. We are best informed on this turbulent revolt, which can be situated in the same social atmosphere as the events in Flanders in 1127-1128, by a highly original narrativization entitled *Monodiae*, by the Benedictine abbot Guibert of Nogent.[75] In order to come to a good understanding and explanation of the events in Laon, Guibert not only described the revolt itself in detail; in his analysis of the failed ecclesiastical leadership of his time, he also included his own personal life history, preceding his account with the oldest known autobiography of the Middle Ages, written after the example of St Augustine's late-antique *Confessiones*.[76]

In the immediate aftermath of the events in Bruges in 1127-1128, it is of course Galbert who transformed and even provoked most strongly the existing genre conventions of his time.[77] There exists however some discussion on the character of his work. The traditional point of view considers Galbert's journal as an incredibly lively eyewitness report of an average intellectual, attached to his count, to his *patria* and to his city, who, under extraordinary circumstances, accidentally invented a completely new literary genre.[78] In one passage in his *De multro*, Galbert also strengthens this perception:

> And it should be noted that in the midst of such a great tumult and the burning of so many houses [...] and in the midst of so much danger by night and conflict by day, even though I, Galbert, had no suitable place for writing, I noted down on tablets a summary of events until finally, in a longed-for moment of peace during the night or day, I could set in order the present description according to the sequence of events. And in this way, though in great straits, I transcribed for the faithful what you see and read.[79]

Recently however, Jeff Rider argued that Galbert was not at all such a naïve chronicler, but that he was, on the contrary, a gifted author with a very personal historiographical skill, who succeeded in imposing linguistic order upon chaotic reality in an absolutely sophisticated way.[80] Although the traditional view of Galbert's work may be a bit naïve and too positivistic, the more recent stress on his literary qualities does not provide ground for underestimating the social complexity of the environment in which Galbert had to arrange his thoughts.[81]

This chapter is not the place to develop a detailed analysis of Galbert's literary skills and cultural background, as Rider's work remains unrivalled in that respect. However, it is important to stress here that Galbert did not invent a completely new discourse genre. Rather his text should be considered as a very creative and unusual blend of several well-known repertoires of his time. I have already shown how Galbert managed to appropriate several features of the hagiographic discourse: in his description of Charles's exemplary biography and passion, in the few miracles he has recounted, and in his accounts of what happened with Charles's relics. In other chapters of his *De multro*, we also find passages that closely resemble religious *exempla*, the official language of charters, privileges, legal texts and judicial investigations, the liveliness of oral reports. It is even possible to consider his day-by-day descriptions as a very refined and unusually inspired adaptation of the traditional annalistic historiography, in which historiographers and chroniclers noted down, year by year, the most remarkable events of their time.[82]

Very important, however, for the interrelatedness between discourse, power, and history is the fact that precisely this blending of repertoires enabled Galbert to write a highly unusual multi-voiced account, to write a narrative strongly characterized by what Mikhail Bakhtin has called 'dialogization', not only between related texts but even within one single narrative.[83] In the history of literature, according to Bakhtin, such dialogism only truly emerges in the modern novel. As Lisa Jane Graham nicely illustrates in this volume, the development of that genre has played a very emancipative role in history because it was able to mobilize many conflicting ideologies, undermine traditional authority and ventilate social criticism through the construction of different literary characters. The majority of medieval literature, however, especially at the beginning of the twelfth century when the clergy still possessed a strong monopoly on writing, was still very undialogized or monologic: authors such as Walter of Thérouanne voiced in their text only one authoritative and hegemonic discourse.[84] Galbert, in contrast, expresses in his one work *De multro* many points of view, corresponding to the different political echelons and social solidarities of his time. He even enables us to listen to subversive voices that normally were never expressed in clerical texts. In the first and reworked part of his *De multro*, describing the events of 1127, Galbert frequently uses for this purpose several rhetorical means such as direct speech, the inclusion of silent gossip about the Erembalds as well as about the count, and even a rare interior monologue attributed to provost Bertulf, the brain behind the conspiracy.[85]

A very special kind of multiplication of voices was realized in *De multro*, however, when Galbert resumed his work in the course in 1128 in order to describe the civil war which had broken out in Flanders. Above, we have seen how in the first part of his narrative, which we only know in its revised version, Galbert succeeded so well in discerning a divine plan behind the terrible events. But when, in the summer of 1128, Thierry of Alsace finally managed to become the new count to the detriment of the perished Count William Clito, Galbert got very confused. In contrast to William, Thierry belonged, after all, to the lineal descendants of Count Robert the Frisian, who had come to power in 1071 in such an unjust way:

> It may well be asked why, therefore, when God wished
> to restore the peace of the fatherland through the death
> of one of the two, He preferred that Count William
> should die, whose claim to rule the land was more just,
> and why on the contrary Count Thierry did not die
> who seemed unjustly put in his place; or by what justice
> God granted the countship to the one who forcibly
> seized the office?[86]

As Jan Dhondt has analysed so penetratingly, we are able to notice here how bit by bit Galbert starts doubting the providential logic he had discerned so far in the succession of events.[87] While he continued to consider William Clito, who had been recognized as Flanders's new count by the noble elite of the peers of the county, as the rightful successor to Charles the Good for a very long time, it turned out, all at once, that he had to look for a new explanation due to the final victory of Thierry, whom he had always seen as an illegitimate pretender. This Thierry moreover had been supported by a certain Lambert of Aardenburg, one of the rare surviving participants to the betrayal who, to Galbert's consternation, had been able to clear himself of any guilt, thanks to his success in enduring a trial by fire.

At the end of his records of 1128, Galbert nevertheless still tries to make his peace with the election of Thierry. It is clear, however, that he has been obliged to adjust his own points of view, to question his own former convictions and to speak with a new voice in his own story. Due to the outcome of civil war, Galbert did not really succeed in realizing a true providential emplotment in his narrative.[88] Until the middle of July, he still held the opinion that 'the citizens were [...] acting unjustly in that while their lord was still alive they had put another lord in his place, and neither was the one justly cast down nor the other justly set up'.[89] Only after the unexpected killing of William Clito on the battlefield some weeks later did he try to understand and to interpret, in his somewhat isolated concluding paragraphs, the success of Thierry, by characterizing William, in the same way as so many nobles and citizens had done before, as a tyrant and as another punishment by God. Hence on this specific point, Galbert's narrative does not really manage to surpass the narrative structure of an average chronicle, in which, as Hayden White has shown, a true plot can hardly be induced. While writing, a chronicler does not know the outcome of the events, and yet he is not able to prepare the logic of that outcome through the events recounted earlier.[90] This is probably also the reason for the abrupt ending of Galbert's work and for the fact that he did not revise the second part of his diary in the same way he had revised his narrative of the events of 1127.[91]

At the same time, however, it is precisely this mental unsteadiness which allowed Galbert's description of the troubles of 1128 to achieve a level of multivocality which was never expressed before in the medieval literary tradition. It is mainly in this part of his work that he expresses expositions that did not square at all with the typical clerical transcript of reality usually aired in high medieval texts: for example, Galbert is not afraid to ridicule the bidding up of excommunications by the churchmen of his time and the superstitions of some local priests whom he literally considers as 'idiots'.[92] Most important for the issue of the 'sacralization of the monarch' is that, in the second part of his narrative, Galbert has given a voice to social groups who were not concerned at all with that sacralization, or at the very least, who did not consider it as a safeguard against princely arbitrariness. Indeed, Galbert's text contains the rendition of several public speeches and documents which allow the modern reader to get a rare glimpse of the way in which, very early on, ideas about 'constitutionalism' between prince and population were publicly negotiated. There exists some discussion about whether Galbert reproduced these speeches literally or crafted them to a certain extent, but what is sure is that they do contain subversive ideas and points of view which Galbert did not always share himself, as he seemed rather attached to the more traditional monarchical ideas.[93] Hence the fact that he did integrate them in his narrative is already very unique and significant of the dialogization in his text.

In the harangue of Ivan of Aalst, one of the peers of Flanders who would soon become a supporter of Thierry of Alsace, directed to William Clito in the crowded marketplace in Ghent in February 1128, we can notice how, as Raoul Van Caenegem put it, 'the contractual and "ascending" theory of power bursts clearly and even brutally into the open'.[94] Ivan emphasized how the ruler had to respect his promises made to the people and how the people had the right to dismiss a lawless and faithless prince. Comparable ideas were also aired on 10 April 1128 by the citizens of Bruges, when they formulated a message to the French King Louis VI in order to complain about William Clito's policy. They described William as someone who was 'contrary to reason, contrary to the law of God and men' and even went so far as to deny the king his suzerain's right to interfere in the election of a new count.[95] As Van Caenegem has suggested, these positions seem to be clearly inspired by anti-imperial theories which had been developed in the last quarter of the eleventh century in the context of the Investiture Contest, for example in the *Liber ad Gebehardum* of 1085 by the Alsace monk Manegold of Lautenbach.[96] Could it have been thanks to some councillors of Thierry of Alsace that certain ideas from this treatise have finally spread their influence even right into some Flemish urban marketplaces?

The multi-vocality in Galbert's narrative must certainly have been recognizable for his contemporaries, as many of them had been among the witnesses of, or even among the participants in, the tumult of 1127 and the ensuing war and public debates of 1128.[97] However, his work escaped too much from the existing literary horizon of expectations and did not fit in the discursive customs that were still completely dominated by a powerful elite of clerics and their noble protectors.[98] For the newly installed regime of Count Thierry and his successors, the *De multro* was not favourable enough; for the ecclesiastical elites it was probably too critical; for the citizens of Bruges and other Flemish towns, who might have been Galbert's most obvious audience, it remained too intellectual.[99] Hence, Galbert's discursive tactics were doomed to fail. Just like Guibert of Nogent's *Monodiae*, written after the Laon revolt of 1112, Galbert's *De multro* was hardly read or copied in the Middle Ages, and its formal originality has never been imitated since. This fate marks also the big difference between Galbert's work and Walter of Thérouanne's *Vita Karoli*. Walter's explicit hagiographic textualization was much less ambitious: faithful to its generic features, it was aimed mainly at the promotion of Charles's local canonization and cult.[100] Although Charles has never been canonized – only in 1884 was he officially beatified for regional veneration – Walter's attempt was rather successful. His text was read widely during the Middle Ages, and even today it is possible to discern the existence of at least nineteen copies of his text.[101] But it is of course thanks to the unique multi-vocality of Galbert's *De multro* that we have such a lively insight into the fact that the sacralization of power – be it the king's or the count's – which otherwise appears as a smooth development because of the 'monologic' one-sidedness of the majority of our medieval source materials, must also have been confronted in reality already early in the twelfth century by protest and public debates and by negotiation and practical restrictions, especially in the context of growing social differentiation and urbanization in the county of Flanders.[102]

'Et le prince respondit de par sa bouche.' Monarchal Speech Habits in Late Medieval Europe

Elodie Lecuppre-Desjardin

> 'When I use a word,' Humpty Dumpty said in rather a
> scornful tone, 'it means just what I choose it to mean –
> neither more nor less.' 'The question is,' said Alice,
> 'whether you can make words mean different things.'
> 'The question is,' said Humpty Dumpty, 'which is to be
> master – that's all.'[1]

Although Alice's adventures offered a wonderful subject for lovers of surrealism or students of Sigmund Freud's theories, we must not forget that these stories were written as a children's book in which children expressed their frustration at always being brought under the yoke of adults' authority. This conversation extracted from the meeting between Alice and Humpty Dumpty perfectly reflects one of Lewis Carroll's favourite leitmotifs, which suggested the relationships between words and power. In his work, by turns, words are authorized, forbidden, broken off, given, and so on, according to an incredible hierarchy headed by queens and kings. The characters of Carroll's story know perfectly well that the absolute control of speech is synonymous with power, because as Quentin Skinner said, after John Austin, 'to utter any serious utterance is both to say something and to do something'.[2] Carroll's work is thus not just a rhetorical means designed to introduce my subject but a mine of interrogations able to guide my own thought about connections between power and speech, especially speech acts.

Ernst Kantorowicz underlined on several occasions that majesty was always surrounded by silence, a sacred silence which protected the State's mysteries and which lay at the heart of the *nefandum* category recently studied by Jacques Chiffoleau.[3] Because they were the Lord's Elects, monarchs had to adopt an imitative behaviour which converted them into icons.[4] If we want to convince ourselves of that principle inherent in the very essence of the authority of monarchs, we can find its foundations in the Bible. The book of *Exodus* shows us Moses complaining about his inability to be a ringleader. The Lord, having listened to his moans, answers him that his brother Aaron would be his mouth:

You shall speak to him and put the words in his mouth.
I will be with your mouth, and with his mouth, and will
teach you what you shall do. He will be your spokesman
to the people: and it will happen that he will be to you a
mouth and you will be to him as God.[5]

In a way, Moses by his silence would become a God for his people. Thus, princes, thanks to their reserve, increased their prestige and could be considered as Embodied Order.

The function of speech – or, to be more precise, the function of the absence of speech – in the elaboration of the princely majesty is quite clear. Nonetheless, the juxtaposition of this principle of silence with practical experiences has not drawn the attention of many historians. Except for Jacques Le Goff and his study about St Louis, only rare scholars have decided to observe princely speech habits in European courts.[6] Yet, it is worth undertaking the task of reconciling ideals with the practical necessities of government, especially at a time deeply marked by humanist thought and its praise of eloquence. For this reason, I will observe in this chapter the behaviour of three princes at the end of the Middle Ages. In examining not only the habits but also the texts which depicted Charles the Bold, Duke of Burgundy (1467-1477), Edward IV, King of England (1461-1470 and 1471-1483), and Louis XI, King of France (1461-1483), I hope to shed light on the political habits of utterance according to geographical space and, above all, according to the different ideas of authority that their status showed.

Speech Habits: Between Spontaneity and Protocol

My first point will rely on a lively report developed by the chronicler Philippe de Commynes in his *Memoirs*. In 1464, on the eve of the War of the Public Weal, a group of great French feudal lords gathered, led by Charles the Bold, Count of Charolais, against King Louis XI. The Earl of Eu and the Chancellor of France, Pierre de Morvillier, were sent by Louis XI to Philip the Good, Duke of Burgundy, to complain about an alliance that Philip's son Charles had formed with Francis, the Duke of Brittany. During the reception of the embassy in Lille, as Philippe de Commynes related it, the French chancellor publicly charged Charles the Bold with treason, and Charles, flying into a rage, tried to utter something in his defence. But the French chancellor, without losing his quiet arrogance, did not hesitate to hush him, claiming that he was here to speak not to him but to the Duke of Burgundy.[7] Then began a sort of lively ballet, where words were included in the game of the most elaborate choreography. Charles, deeply hurt by this rebuff, turned to his father and asked him for authorization to reply to the French chancellor. But the Duke of Burgundy answered that it was the duty of a father to protect his child and that he was going to talk to the French ambassador himself.[8] Charles apparently believed that he had to deliver his own version of these events, and he took advantage of the night to develop a well-turned speech. When, the following day, the same characters gathered for another public audience, Charles entered the room, dropped onto one knee in front of his father and began to explain his position, as if he were alone with him. Philip the Good concluded the scene by requesting the favour of the king. But Philippe de Commynes could not close this episode without mentioning that had Philip the Good not been present, Charles would have spoken more rudely.[9]

Of course, in this narrative written by a political observer, the emphasis fell on the events, in other words, the beginning of the War of the Public Weal, but Philippe de Commynes, traditionally indifferent to the rituals of ceremony, did not hesitate to describe a diplomatic protocol pregnant with meaning.[10] As far as we are concerned, this episode highlights two parameters on which the link between power and speech partly rested, viz., the humanity of the prince and the weight of the ceremonial system. The whole scene is actually depicted as if the characters had been installed in a stage setting with a part to play in the ordinary performance of a diplomatic meeting. Philippe de Commynes insisted on this contrast between the personality of his characters and the attitude required by their status, especially for Charles. Of course, princes' speech depended on their own prolixity. In contrast to his father, who was a silent man, Charles, according to the Flemish jurist Philip Wielant, was very fond of uttering harangues and proclamations and, moreover, had been born with a most violent nature, passionate to the point of insulting his servants and counselors:

> Le duc Philippe parloit peu, et s'il disoit quelque note, il
> estoit bien assis, et au contraire le duc Charles se délec-
> toit de faire longues harangues. De la bouche du duc
> Philippe ne partoit jamais parolle villaine ny injurieuse;
> sy faisoit-il bien souvent le duc Charles, quant en soi
> courouchant il apelloit ses gens traictres et dagues de
> ploncq.[11]

The information given about speech habits by chroniclers of this period is rather scarce and typically was intended to express an ideal portrait of an ideal prince, a point to which I shall return. Nevertheless, some indications allow us to isolate the attitude of some rulers, proving that *benevolentia* was connected not only with an individual's status but also with his personality. Philip Augustus was 'in sermone subtilis', according to Rigord of Saint-Denis; Louis IX, according to Joinville, never hesitated to answer 'de par sa bouche'; and Charles V was a very eloquent man according to Christine de Pisan. But Bernard Saisset, Bishop of Pamiers and enemy of the king, is reported to have declared about Philip the Fair: 'the king is like an owl, the most beautiful of birds, but worth nothing. He is the most handsome of men but he stares fixedly in silence. [...] He is neither man nor beast, he is a statue.'[12] So it is difficult for us, from this observation of the psychological parameters, to develop a model which might express an unbroken evolution toward an increasingly important role or, indeed, a less significant one for speech in the implementation of monarchy.

At the same time, the study of protocol is more interesting for underlining the code system used by speech. First, in the meeting before Duke Philip the Good, we notice that despite the agitation of Charles the Bold and his great capability to utter discourses, the hierarchy is perfectly preserved. The Duke of Burgundy is the only one authorized to allow speeches in a public audience. Moreover, when Charles, Count of Charolais, decided to plead in his own defence, his speech was delivered as if he and his father were alone in a private space, pretending to ignore the presence of the other officers. Thus, the ceremonial system of fixed rules and accepted behaviour in force at the court of Burgundy was not transgressed. The message of the French king was sent to the Duke of Burgundy, and it was the Duke of Burgundy who answered it. We must admit that the court of Burgundy was a real stickler for the rules. Chronicles abound in examples that set its rules of protocol apart from those of French or English courts.[13] While Charles the Bold made it a point of honour to dispense justice publicly, although by avoiding direct contact with his people, thanks to an incredible display of splendour, Louis XI was admired for his simplicity with everyone. Edward IV, furthermore, was depicted by an Italian ambassador as a very 'easy access' man, and by Henry VII's court historian Polydore Vergil as a king who 'by reason wherof, and of humanytie which was bred in him aboundantly, wold use himself more famylyarly among private persons than the donor of his maiestie requyryd [...]'.[14]

Nevertheless, we must be cautious and take into account the different venues in which princely speech made itself heard. The official character of certain events automatically adjusted the degree of formality of the discourse. It seems obvious that if Louis XI could joke and make puns in private company, his position as king forbade him any misbehaviour. And if he chatted without restraint with Italian merchants in Bruges in 1457, he could act in such a way because he was not yet the King of France, just the Dauphin in exile.[15] In the context of the General Estates that he convened in 1468, the use of a spokesman like Jean Juvénal des Ursins, who asked three questions to the assembly in the name of the king, seemed better suited to the situation.[16] The use of a spokesman is proof, according to Pierre Bourdieu, that the authority of language lies not inside the words uttered but in the status of the men who pronounce them. In a slightly provocative sentence, he declared that the 'spokesman is an impostor equipped with the skeptron'.[17] In Homeric literature, the man who decided to speak in front of an audience was equipped with a stick which symbolized his new function. Thus, the weakness of his power is linked not with his eloquence but with the symbolic resources accumulated by the group for which he stood. Of course, Jean Juvénal des Ursins or the Chancellor Hugonet commanded the respect of the audiences because they respectively spoke for the King of France and for the Duke of Burgundy. But alongside these considerations, which orbit around questions of social status, the use of a spokesman increased the distance between the ruler and his audience and thus strengthened his majesty. From this perspective, the introduction of professional speakers is thought-provoking. It raises questions first about the image of the prince and his protection, and second about techniques of government and ideas of power at the close of the Middle Ages.

The Eloquence of the Prince: An Ideal of Wisdom

Let us now turn to the advice professed by Philippe de Commynes. Because of his professional experience as an ambassador throughout Europe and as courtly counsellor, Commynes developed an opinion about the public appearances of monarchs. According to him, it is possible to show the prince in public only if he has the necessary qualities. The prince must be wise, honest and fair, and if he is not, then it is best to show him as rarely as possible. And when we must see him, he should be correctly dressed and well informed about what he has to say. Like a puppet in the hands of political professionals, the prince was put under close watch, and his words as well as his clothes were considered to be a mirror of his dignity. Indeed, chroniclers often brought together, in their portrait of princes, appearance and eloquence. For example, Commynes's contemporary Thomas Basin depicted Louis XI in these words: 'As simple in his finery as in his speech.'[18] So the vigilance expended on princely speech could also be explained by the principle adopted in all pedagogical treatises. According to them, eloquence is the reflection not only of education but also of wisdom.

In his *De regimine Principum,* which was a sort of practical textbook about the art of ruling, Giles of Rome (c. 1247-1316) explained that, thanks to a good education, the prince could build an ideal image of his dignity based on wisdom and virtue, and could thus appeal to his people to imitate his model. By a sort of logical deduction, then, speech was associated with self-control, which was the *temperentia* praised by all political theoreticians of that time.[19] This model, which castigated those who were too outspoken, was deeply fixed in people's minds. And courtiers tried to adopt the same model of behaviour. The *Enseignements paternels,* written in the middle of the fifteenth century by

Ghillebert de Lannoy, Knight of the Golden Fleece, for his son, proved the wide circulation of this ideal of moderation worthwhile for everyone whatever the level of nobility.[20] His abundant advice about silence is summed up in the beginning of his text:

> La première, comment c'est belle chose et proffitable à
> ung noble homme, soit prince, duc, ou conte ou autre
> en mendre degré de noblesse, avoir silence en la bouche.
> Et entens par silence mesure et attemprance à son parler.
> Et pour quoy fu dit le proverbe: Se ung fol se taist, il est
> réputé pour sage, si non que chascun doit avoir la bride
> en la bouche pour la sçavoir tirer, en soy taisant quant
> mestier est, et laschier pour parler quant nécessité le
> requiert?[21]

According to Ghillebert, the first piece of advice is that it is good and beneficial for a noble man – i.e., prince, duke, earl, or men of less noble lineage – to have silence in his mouth. And silence means moderation and temperance in his speech. As the saying goes, a madman who says nothing is supposed to be a wise man. Among the different arguments that Ghillebert suggested is the biological one, which claimed that if the tongue is kept naturally prisoner in three jails (lips, teeth and palate), there must be a good reason – of course, planned by God.[22] The rest of the arguments are more traditional, emphasizing the risks that the chatterer runs if he begins to gossip, to make some frivolous utterances or just to say stupid things, especially in the court. The *fama* of the nobleman is at stake.[23] In other words, pedagogical treatises were unanimous in condemning excessive speech.

Silence is golden. Conversely, misplaced speeches became a means to blame princes for their lack of dignity. Thomas Basin, who would have done anything to ruin the reputation of Louis XI, laid stress on the verbosity of the prince. This is only one among a plethora of apt quotations:

> Il avait une telle fringale de paroles qu'il permettait à
> peine à ceux qui se trouvaient près de lui de parler à leur
> tour. Aussi un personnage très important disait de lui
> parfois ce qui était la vérité même: 'Dès le matin depuis
> son réveil, il ne fermait pas la bouche et sa langue ne
> cessait pas d'être en action jusqu'à ce que, la nuit
> revenant et la tête sur l'oreiller, le sommeil l'obligeait à
> s'arrêter.[24]

In Basin's words, Louis XI is very talkative, but without dignity or seriousness in his eloquence. He was so prolix that his loquacity led to boredom. According to the chronicler, he very often interrupted the person he was talking to... and if he began to answer he could not manage to stop himself. Basin emphasized that the king could not keep silent even though the wise Solomon had said that chattering is on the road to sin; and scarcely a day passed that the king did not utter some malicious gossip just because he had an uncontrollable weakness for liking to talk, and so on.[25] Admittedly, Louis XI himself easily confessed that his tongue had cost him a lot since his birth.[26] But the accusations developed by Basin belonged to the archetype of the bad sovereign. And both the modern legend of Edward IV as an immature prince and the bad reputation of Charles the Bold as a choleric prince were partly based on that kind of argument.

The image of princely dignity – the sacralization of the monarchy – was heavily influenced by this principle of moderation applied to the whole life of the prince and, by extension, to his habits of speaking. The episode of Charles the Bold's failed Joyeuse Entrée into Ghent, on 28 June 1467, proved that he who sows the wind reaps the whirlwind. Charles, who let out a stream of abuse at rioters, simply managed to stir up their rage. And by insulting them, he broke the iconic dimension of his dignity and encouraged people to scorn it.[27] Conversely, a well-balanced discourse could, in the same extremely tense circumstances, save a prince in acute danger. When he landed in Yorkshire on 14 March 1471, Edward IV had few men with him, and before the city of York he was faced by the city-dwellers in arms. But Polydore Vergil says that Edward used speeches in order to avoid armed conflict:

> But he gave curtless speaches to every of tholder men
> and rewlers by name, cawling them worshippfull and
> grave magistrates, and he made theme many fayre
> promyses, and besouwght them to suffer him to be safe
> in his owne towne.[28]

Of course, the urgency of the situation made the king act quickly, but the dispatch of messengers or heralds would have been a good approach. At that time and in that country, the eloquence of men seemed to have become a sign of wisdom.

We have to be careful here. The rehabilitation of the *vir bonus dicendi peritus* was not the prerogative of Renaissance humanism alone. Of course, all the *Orationes in laudem oratoriae facultatis* uttered in the Quatroccento Italian universities made eloquence famous. But the praise of eloquence considered as a harmonious union between wisdom and style was just the expansion of the rule of government that had been pursued in the Italian cities since the thirteenth century and had been present in some medieval texts and in political advice throughout the rest of Europe.[29] In her study on the union of wisdom and eloquence before the Renaissance, Cary J. Nederman has demonstrated that sometime before 1266, before Brunetto Latini wrote *Li Livres dou trésor*, in which the first quality of a ruler is eloquence, the speaker's art associated with the love of wisdom inevitably led to the well-being of the state.[30] This is evident in the commentary on Cicero's *De inventione rhetorica,* written around 1130 by Thierry of Chartres. Some centuries later, eloquence reappeared in some political treatises, such as those of Christine de Pisan, but also in speeches and some paternal advice, always considered as an ideal of virtue

Progressively, eloquence left the category of virtue and majesty which symbolized princely dignity, to be assigned to the qualities characterizing, above all, the efficiency of governments.

Speaking for Ruling

In Italian cities, those who acted in a political capacity had to master the art of rhetoric. According to Marc Fumaroli, in the European world after the Roman Empire, the earthly city needed a ruling discipline of speech. Rhetoric generates civil order, it was taught, as does Roman law, with which it has numerous affinities.[31] Such ideas, promoted by numerous Italian intellectuals such as Guido Fava, Brunetto Latini, Bartolomeo della Fonte, Lorenzo Valla or Marsilio Ficino, could not have been confined to Italy. Of course, we must admit that as regards England, the settlement of Italian intellectuals began only after the end of the War of the Roses, under the protection of Henry VII (1485-1509).[32] With regard to the Burgundian court, Arjo Vanderjagt and Richard Walsh claim that, despite the intensification of the commercial and political relationships with Italy under Charles the Bold, Italian courtiers were not humanists.[33] And in France, the friendship of Louis XI with individual Italians does not justify talking about the influence of humanists. Nevertheless, the absence of Italian intellectuals in those courts was not enough to deny the influence of humanism. Other signs indicated a renewal of interest in the art of rhetoric or its practice in these courts.

In the English kingdom, Edward IV needed no instructional treatises to express himself by his own mouth. If he seems to have listened to the lessons of the tutor sent by his father, he was not very fond of intellectual matters.[34] His speeches were pragmatic, above all, even if the House of York was not insensitive to its image. On several occasions, the rolls of Parliament praised his speeches. Some examples: in his first parliament, in November 1461, he made a speech from his throne, thanking the commons for their true hearts and tender considerations. In June 1467, he spoke again to the commons with the aim of putting their minds at rest about taxes.[35] But Parliament was not the only platform for his expression. We have heard him in front of the gates of York in 1470, and in 1471, we find him in the Star Chamber, when the mayor and the corporation of Nottingham complained about rioters being maintained by Henry, Lord Grey. The sovereign 'by his own mouth asked and questionned' Lord Grey about his connection with the accused, and then 'gave the same Lord Grey in strait commandment and injunction' that he should not support or favour any persons within the town of Nottingham.[36] And so on. But this habit of open speech was not so common elsewhere.

Let me consider the *Rosier des Guerres,* an instructional book ascribed for a long time to Louis XI himself but written, in reality, by Pierre Choisnet.[37] In this political testament dictated by Louis XI to his doctor and astrologer around 1482, chapter 3, dealing with justice, grants an important part to *eloquentia*. The chapter opens with these remarkable sentences, which openly proves the influence of Cicero:

> Toutefois si comme l'or surmonte toute maniere de metal, aussi est la science de bien parler plus noble que nul art du monde: dont Tulle dit que la plus haulte science de peuple gouverner, si est rhetoricque, qui est science de bien parler car si parolle ne feust cité, ne seroit ne nul establissement de justice, ne de humaine compaignée.[38]

This book, which has been insufficiently studied, marks a turning point in the conception of the exercise of power. The French kingdom was not alone in welcoming the ideal of an eloquent sovereign whose verbal capacity is a basic requirement for the well-being of the common good. All in all, this classical ideal was in the mind of figures who were responsible for the education of young princes like Louis XI or Charles the Bold. It is not my purpose here to develop the influence of those concerned, but let me mention the work of Cardinal Jean Jouffroy (1412-1473), who was a student of Lorenzo Valla in Pavia between 1431 and 1433 and then courtier of Philip the Good.[39] His enormous library, replete with ancient classical and Christian authors, his career from Italian humanist circles to the court of Burgundy, must have changed his political behaviour. And the speeches of both Charles the Bold and his chancellor Hugonet, which were full of quotations from Lactantius, Augustine and Cicero, plead in favour of that evolution.[40] Nonetheless, if Charles the Bold was able to utter discourses, he always sent his chancellors as spokesmen first, even if he refuted his counsellors immediately afterwards, as in Saint-Omer on 15 July 1470 in front of the French ambassadors, or during the meetings of the General Estates as in Bruges on 12 January 1473.[41] *Eloquentia* seemed to be under the control of ceremonial rituals which were guarantors of princely majesty.

Conclusion

Speech seems to have been seen alternately as an iconic ideal of the monarch's dignity and a necessity for a more effective implementation of power. Only the quest for *sapientia* seemed to be able to reconcile morality and politics, that is to say, princely virtue and the well-being of the Common Good. Thus, speech's place can be considered a sign of the nature of power in the hands of the different sovereigns observed.

Discussion of the importance of *eloquentia* in English literature at the time of Edward IV is rather scarce. For example, Sir John Fortescue, one of the king's teachers, did not say one word about speech in his *Governance of England*. Edward, like other kings of England, had a pragmatic approach toward government. Even if he was surrounded by chancellors and counsellors, in a parliamentary monarchy the king had many occasions to engage in discourse. The dialogue between prince and subjects was inherent in the exercise of the king's power since the *Magna Carta* (1215), and it was sustained by an institutional mechanism on different levels. That the king had recourse to speech is so obvious that it seems that there would have been no reason to develop any theory about it. In the Low Countries, Charles the Bold had to face a similar political atmosphere, especially in Flanders, where – following an evolution started at the time of the murder of Count Charles the Good in 1127 – decisions were taken by the great councils in every important town.[42] It seems that in the effort to protect his ambition for supremacy and compensate for his lack of kingship, Charles preserved all the symbols of majesty, among them the use of spokesman and the respect for silence, even if he was very eloquent. Finally, in France, monarchy had no need to resort to any expedients for commanding respect. There they faced the problem of the efficiency of government, and this is certainly the reason why Philippe de Commynes explained that it is better to leave the state's business in the care of professionals, even discourses, harangues and diplomatic conversations. In other words, speech reflected a policy option of government at the crossroads of sacralization and banalization.

Ideal Kingship against Oppressive Monarchy. Discourses and Practices of Royal Imposture at the Close of the Middle Ages

Gilles Lecuppre

On Ascension Day, 24 May 1487, in the aftermath of the War of the Roses, the Dublin cathedral of Christchurch became the unusual setting of a magnificent royal ceremony, imbued with local colour. Gerald Fitzgerald, Earl of Kildare and Governor of Ireland, supervised the proceedings and acted in a sense as a 'kingmaker'. Around him were gathered the upper crust among Anglo-Irish lords and prelates, including the Archbishop of Dublin and four of his suffragans. 'German' armoured captains, that is to say Flemish mercenaries, completed the concerted dramatization and reminded everyone that, thanks to the elite of modern armies, victory would soon follow on the very ground of England. The nearby kingdom was even represented by two eminent peers: Viscount Francis Lovell, Richard III's former counsellor, and, above all, John de la Pole, Earl of Lincoln, the same nephew of King Richard who had long been regarded as his heir presumptive. After a stylized but rather dignified church service, all of them gave their approval to the coronation of a ten-year-old boy as Edward VI, 'King of England and France'. One detail should be stressed a little more than the English historian Michael Bennett did in his study of the event and its sequel: on the head of the new sovereign was put, as a crown, a small circle taken from a statue of the Holy Virgin located in the neighbouring parish of 'St Mary de la Dam'.[1] In a kingdom where supreme authority was challenged so frequently and during times when coups d'état were succeeding one another at such a speed, the supernatural support of Christ's Mother was very welcome. After the traditional acclamation offered to the young Edward, in remembrance of the old election procedure of any new leader, the crowd outside the cathedral, so anxious to see the monarch, made itself heard. The tallest among the nobles, Lord Darcy of Platen, as another St Christopher, raised the child onto his shoulders so that the good people could rejoice. The whole ceremony ended with a big banquet.[2]

There remained only one minor trouble. The Lord's anointed was not Edward, Earl of Warwick, the son of the late Duke of Clarence and thus the last surviving Plantagenet, but an ordinary boy from Oxford whose father may have been an organ maker. His name was Lambert Simnel, whereas the real

Edward was kept in the London Tower. What the Dubliners witnessed was merely another manifestation in the medieval tradition of political imposture. However, the scenes which took place on that ceremonial day were pregnant with meaning. The taste for performance, the resolute harmony among various levels of political society, and even the celestial protection granted to the odd monarch were part of a sound criticism of the way in which the modern state was about to threaten the ideal of the royal father figure.

Political imposture proved an almost ordinary means of opposition at the close of the Middle Ages. It mainly was witnessed in Flanders, Germany and England, even though other territories were perfectly aware of the fraudulent practice and exploited it now and then.[3] Pseudo-hermits or pseudo-pilgrims who pretended to have come back after a long time of penance thus tried to seize the crown by impersonating a dead or vanished king. They were soon followed in their attempt by younger would-be princes such as Lambert Simnel. While some particularities of Western medieval civilization – the importance of anchorites, crusades, and distant wars or, more commonly, faulty memory – enabled such hoaxes, they principally rested on the objectives of scheming parties. At the core of the phenomenon, aristocratic plots expressed a radical protest against the supposed illegitimacy or inefficiency of the true sovereign, who therefore had to take up a difficult challenge. Other sources of discontent usually obscured the trickery. The feigned leader often acted as a spokesperson for victims of the growing 'modern state', or as a puppet in the hands of foreign powers. Although usually not much affected by messianic or prophetic charisma, impostors often embodied the ideal of a traditional paternalistic kingship, as opposed to the reality of an increasingly oppressive monarchy.

I intend to show that, in this regard, the original project, which consisted in displaying a purified princely figure, was quickly lost in the necessary invective against the ruling monarch and that this very invective inevitably revealed in the background a small clique of opponents of the regime with less pure intentions. The discursive construction of royal imposture usually followed three steps. (1) A successful *captatio benevolentiae* generally constituted the bravura passage of new self-declared kings. According to the exordia of their public performances, these alleged missing persons suddenly reappeared to lay claim to the throne; with their incredible stories, they had to fill in the gap which separated a public death or exile from a renewed extraordinary mandate. (2) Then, the most brilliant or better supported among them behaved as kings. They gave a concrete expression to the kingship they were embodying or living. (3) At last, they harshly criticized the existing power structures, by denouncing both the turpitudes of individual monarchs and the abuses and growing demands of contemporary monarchy.

Focusing on the discourse of royal impostors presents us with the problem of scarce and biased sources. Legitimate and victorious power, not to say legitimate *because* victorious, naturally destroyed, distorted, and disciplined every hostile argument in order to incorporate it into its own orthodox interpretation of events. Since it was so evidently connected to subversion, the public utterances of pretenders rarely survived in their initial form. We are thus condemned to lend our ears to adulterated pleas in favour of defeated, captured and frightened impostors – rebel leaders who were always gagged too soon and who lacked their former lustre. We are also forced to consult later moralizing and submissive chroniclers to try and reconstruct erased pieces of writing, which expressed alternative views on kingship. Nevertheless, we also dispose of a handful of letters, treaties, tracts and even an autobiography left by those men who would be king – sources which obviously also merit our attention. However, when studying medieval imposture, we are obliged to understand the concept of 'discourse' in a wide-ranging sense, including not only the impostors' own writings or reported speeches but also what can be inferred from their practices and from the arguments and behaviour of those who supported or manipulated them.

Impostors Entering the Scene. Stories of Suffering and Redemption

Usurpation of identity required a carefully thought-out scenario, since it had to account for a long absence and explain the dramatic changes that occurred in the princely personality. At this stage, adventurers understood perfectly well they needed to bring an additional charisma to the part they were playing, so as to arouse in their subjects a feeling of veneration, admiration, or compassion. For their stories and their own propaganda, they borrowed recognizable storylines from narratives which were more or less commonly shared at their time. The evolution in the selection of those narrative patterns is noteworthy. Impostors used to keep up with fashion, by following in turn popular hagiographic themes, marvellous Eastern impressions, highlights of the Bible or beautiful vernacular tales.

Throughout the last four centuries of the Middle Ages, a dozen counterfeit aristocrats or monarchs chose the disguise of wandering clerks or pilgrims while assuming a too-transparent incognito. In addition, their present state enabled them to give explanations for their disappearance. Until then, they were thought to have died on the battlefield or in far-off countries. However, so they pretended, they had relinquished worldly possessions to meditate on their faults and to do penance for their private or public sins. In Flanders, the most famous case occurred in 1224, near Valenciennes, when Count Baldwin IX of Flanders, also Count of Hainault and first Latin Emperor of Constantinople, seemed to be back for good as a dignified beggar, after escaping the jails of

Ioannitsa, King of the Vlachs and Bulgarians. After long roaming in Eastern countries, he had withdrawn to the forest of Glançon. No matter that the true Baldwin had been executed in 1205 – a bushy beard and a favourable context helped his understudy to conceal his identity and to catch his dupes' attention.[4]

Sometimes, indeed exactly as other saintly hermits had done before, medieval impostors added mortification to their daily sufferings.[5] That was, in the 1360s, the key to the doctrine of the Thuringian Konrad Schmid. He led a sect of millenarian flagellants and later compelled his supporters to call him 'Emperor Frederick', in remembrance of the German Emperor Frederick II, who had died in 1250 and now was said to have been resurrected. Whether sincere or not, those penitents usually lost their anonymity thanks to a reputation which stemmed from their *vita aspera*. Their rough conditions of living were regarded systematically by their followers as unquestionable signs of perfection and sanctity, whereas their opponents denounced them as temporary shams.[6] Whether it was just another trick or simply prudence, most impostors seemed reluctant to assume their new identity at first. Bertrand de Rays, a minstrel who passed himself off as a hermit, vigorously denied it when the local gentry tried to get him to admit that he had been a companion of the above-mentioned Baldwin of Flanders and Hainault and, ultimately, the Emperor-Count himself. According to the thirteenth-century *Chronique rimée* of Philippe Mousket, Bertrand feigned to laugh at them and compared them to Britons, who were said to wait for King Arthur's impossible return:

> Tant qu'a lui sont el bos venu
> Cil de Valencienes apriès;
> Et moult estoit cascuns engriès
> Qu'il desist k'il estoit lor sire.
> Mais il ne noioit bien et sire,
> Et dissoit que Breton estoient
> Ki Artu encore atendoient.[7]

The most rewarding identities for humbugs to assume were those of prominent personalities who looked able to guide their people towards salvation. Baldwin of Flanders had gained an imposing stature by putting on the Byzantine imperial crown, and he even looked very like the last Roman emperor, an apocalyptic hero who would bring peace and fertility after times of trouble.[8] Frederick II, the German emperor, was an amazing character who had won the crown of Jerusalem and fought against papal power.[9] He was bound to come back after his death. And so he did, no fewer than seven times, through reckless aged doubles.[10] One of them, named Tile Kolup, was burnt at the stake in 1285. According to the *Annales Blandinienses*, he was at once replaced by another social misfit:

> After he [Tile Kolup] was burnt, another one appeared
> and said that he had risen after three days from the
> burned body and ashes of the said burned one. Wander-
> ing through several villages and cities, he was finally cap-
> tured in the Ghent graveyard of St Bavo by the bailiff of
> Ghent and handed over in iron chains; but subsequently
> freed from the arrest of the bailiff, he was finally hung
> on the gallows near Utrecht.[11]

As time went by, the future sovereign who would free everyone from all clerical exactions became the holy model in popular opinion. Another impersonation of the famous Staufer Frederick II, the above-mentioned Konrad Schmid, leader of the crypto-flagellants, was therefore doubly saintly.

All those ghostly princes pretended that they had left their worldly existence for a long while after meeting with a serious defeat. Their new public life was accordingly a second chance to correct former military routs and personal political failures. Because there is mercy for everything, their alter egos intended to do better, to smooth out past blunders and to offer to their people a purified and ideal monarch. In the Holy Roman Empire, at the end of the 1330s, a rootless pseudo-Edward II, the enigmatic William le Galeys, succeeded in charming the people by propitiatory prophecies, whereas his model had proved unable to do so for lack of patience and humility. The pilgrim had no partisans and seemed to act out of sheer sympathy for King Edward, his model, which was not the case of the several fake Baldwins (of Ardres and of Flanders) and Fredericks.[12] But what could be preferable to mere perfection as a political programme? Having saved their own souls, saintly kings ingenuously promised salvation to their flock.

Later impostors, in the fourteenth and fifteenth centuries, were recruited no longer from apparently religious old people but from men in their forties or even beautiful teenagers, whose fresh faces were meant to reveal natural distinc-tion and to inspire pity in those considering their misfortunes. Conspirators manifestly found inspiration in folk tales speaking of substituted babies or chil-dren spared by their tormentors. It was a sign of the times: feigned princes now tugged at the heartstrings of their contemporaries and relied on the fabulous to heighten their fabricated kingship. In the first half of the fourteenth century, this new stratagem gave birth to an alternative Edward II of England or to a pseudo-John the Posthumous of France, founding their puzzling claims on such pathetic appeals.[13] During the English Wars of the Roses (1450-1485), as the royal Lancastrian branch was grappling with the no less royal Yorkist one, the physical extinction of all pretenders of the latter party led to the sudden necessity of inventing new ones. In the 1480s and 1490s, three false heirs of the Yorkist cause successively stressed the hard times they and their share of slaughtered parents and brothers had gone through, in order to denounce more easily the unfair usurpation of their rival Henry VII and to benefit from the miraculous aura of survivors.[14] Thus, Perkin Warbeck, who styled himself Duke Richard of York, Edward IV's second son, was explicitly compared, in a letter his benevolent 'Aunt' Margaret sent to Pope Alexander VI, with the biblical Joas who, according to *Kings II* and *Chronicles II*, was providentially protected from the wrath of Athalia and, after being brought up in the utmost secrecy, raised to the Israeli throne.[15]

Impostors Taking the Floor. Two Imaginary Paths to Kingship

Either holy anchorites or victims saved from sacrifice, pretenders, as soon as they introduced themselves, resolutely placed kingship in a distant sacred sphere. This was, after all, a means to underline their own difference and their adversaries' lack of legitimacy. But how did they articulate their views on princely status? We consult two documents that vividly illustrate two impostors' thoughts and feelings on their claim to kingship. These sources are all the more exceptional as they both came from the impostors themselves or, at least, from their companions or shadow-cabinet. The first was written in Italian between the 1360s and the 1420s, after the patent collapse of the delusions of grandeur which motivated the hero, Giannino Baglioni, alias John the Posthumous, the last Capetian King of France.[16] The second was conceived, in 1496, as a pugnacious text on the eve of the invasion of England by the Scottish King, James IV, who was ready to help Perkin Warbeck, the would-be Richard IV, to regain his dubious rights.[17] On the one hand, we get a fascinating insight into a tremendous, tenacious, but isolated desire for power, and on the other hand we see a polemical manifesto in the tradition of the great Yorkist criticism.

After a very stirring life, Giannino Baglioni spent his last years in Provençal or Neapolitan prisons, where he wrote down his genealogy and adventures. These texts were transmitted to his descendants and compiled in an authorized autobiography. Giannino's family still totally agreed with what their famous ancestor pretended about his real and royal origins. He argued indeed that, to prevent his assassination when he had been a newborn infant, clever barons swapped him for his wet nurse's child. That child had lived for only five days and was known therefore as King John the Posthumous (November 1316). Giannino himself was brought to Siena, where he found out the whole matter some forty years later. From then on, he canvassed European courts incessantly for their support – in Hungary, Naples and Avignon – and sent countless letters, often being manipulated by unscrupulous people of all sorts. He finally led a group of mercenaries who attacked the Papal States and was arrested by the Seneschal of Provence. I will summarize here his memoirs, for such a hypertrophic ego would need several chapters to be fully dissected. Giannino was ready indeed to believe any kind of assertion that confirmed him in his opinion, but basically portrayed himself as a peaceful and universal sovereign in the continuity of the excellent Capetian lineage. Were he to gain power to rule, he claimed, war would cease, Jews would come back to France, and Muslim states would be subjugated. But beyond those naïve clichés, Giannino complacently described the phases of his martyrdom. In Marseilles, he was nearly lynched, cooked in boiling water or burnt at the stake. Songs and poems were composed to make fun of him, calling him 'Joan, Queen of France' and a prostitute. He was even accused of forgery and sodomy, he was beaten up, and he suffered food poisoning:

> Poi esso ancora lo' nfamo che esso aveva fatto fare moneta falsa in Vignone, et mostro al populo di Marsilia cierte monete false, et disse, che l'aveva trovate adosso a detto G. quando fu preso doppo la praticha, che fecie quando si collo dala finestra; et tanto lo' nfamo di sua boccha, e per sua famiglia, et con letare, che faceva venire da Vignone, et ancho ordinato con cierti Galeotti et giente di piccolo affare, e male disposti, a' quali dava alcuna volta mangiare, e bere; di che al tutto delliberato fu per la maggior parte de' marsaliesi che'l dotto G. fusse morto vitoparosamente di fuocho, et bollito, et trasconato e posto aleffe et fatto di lui tutti li stracii, et vitoperi, che mai fusse fatti a veruno mal uomo, et fecie fare sonetti et canzoni molte ladie, e villane di lui, et cantare in su la sua [blank], e farle cantare per la terra, e facievalo chiamare la Reyna di Francia Giovanna, et quasi come fusse una meretrice, e tutti li strazii, e vituperii, e parole vilane, faceva fare, e dire al detto G. e feciele dare il veleno tre volte, e facievali dare mangiare cose stanthie, e puzolenti.[18]

These lines lead one inexorably to draw a conscious parallel with the pathetic figure of Christ Mocked. The whole passage might well be inspired by Giannino's memories of the Sienese collegiate church San Gimignano, decorated with frescoes recounting the Christ's Childhood and Passion.[19] Giannino praised scorned kingship, as only humiliation could ennoble his otherwise disastrous career. He even succumbed to the temptation of martyrdom.[20] Along the lines of imaginary monarchy, Giannino thus also walked a path of purity.

Thoroughly different is Perkin Warbeck's pompous proclamation, which aimed at more political, that is to say more practical, results and was part of a collective and rather considered plan.[21] His entourage mastered tried and tested rhetorical formulas and arguments, and new ones were invented for the occasion.[22] Pseudo-Richard consequently criticized the ruling King Henry VII's low birth, actions and ministers and concluded that the kingdom needed to be saved from evil counsel. Henry was accused of attacking the true nobility. He indeed had executed William Stanley, his own chamberlain, and many others, who were exhaustively cited.[23] Henry wrongfully had imprisoned the Earl of Warwick and deprived him of his estates in order to enfeeble his power, which meant that the earl could not aid his cousin 'Richard IV'. Royal blood had been polluted: Warwick's sister and other royal ladies had been married to Henry's kinsmen and friends of 'simple and low degree'.[24] The low-born were now favoured as councillors, and a number were named as the 'principal finders, occasioners and counsellors of the misrule and mischief now reigning in England'. In addition to this usual Yorkist language, there also followed a list of complaints more specifically directed to Henry Tudor. He abused and broke sanctuary laws. He was a traitor who murdered and robbed people. He was an extortioner with a cruel policy of taxation. The self-declared Duke of York and true King of England promised to set right all these crimes. To this end, he asked for the help of the whole kingdom and promised that any who until then had been his enemy would be pardoned, should they support him. A general reform would be advanced by the impartial administration of 'the good Laws and Customs heretofore made by our noble progenitors Kings of England [...] according to the effect and true meaning they were first made ordained'. Warbeck humorously alluded to Henry's potential flight and offered a reward of £1000 for his capture. Although this 'clarion call' did not have any effect, it was still very comparable to the various declarations made a decade earlier during the War of the Roses. Theoretically speaking, Warbeck certainly still held monarchical ideas which had proved themselves for a long time. However, his manifesto also displayed various types of remonstrance against an execrated government, whose overthrow would put an end to his own and his fellow conspirators' winter of discontent.

Kingship against Monarchy. The Negative Print of the Ideal Sovereign

A careful analysis of the main arguments elaborated in the aristocratic circles supporting royal impostors clearly reveals that imposture meant much more than a personal contest for the crown. Their discourse of discontent even offers us at the same time the antithesis of what was expected of true kingship and of ideal sovereigns, a 'negative print' of a prince's mirror.

Launching a full-scale attack on their adversaries' lineage deficiencies certainly was the first move, and it was fair enough, since dynastic order had spread all over Europe. Everyone felt that blood-legitimacy had gained acceptance through use and that such criticism was to the point. The kings, counts and knights who backed an alleged Woldemar of Brandenburg in the mid-fourteenth century reminded their enemies of the superiority of the old native Askanian family over the younger, foreign, Bavarian Wittelsbach branch.[25] The competing Margrave, Louis V the Brandenburger, had after all been chosen by his own father, the Emperor Louis IV of Bavaria, to succeed to the title. His origins, methods and southern advisers were soon resented by local nobility and towns that preferred to discover 'their' old prince in the clothes of a hermit. Likewise, Giannino Baglioni, from 1356 onwards, blamed the Valois for the misfortunes that befell France.[26] Having lost his mentor (the Roman senator Cola di Rienzo, who had convinced him that he was John the Posthumous and that Philip VI and John II had been wrongfully elected and crowned), the poor lunatic waited for a miracle at home. Giannino's royal secret was revealed precisely when the news of a French disaster on the battlefield of Poitiers reached Siena: his supporters detected a sign of divine ire in that important battle during the Hundred Years' War. Giannino's confessor, Fra Bartalomeo, pointed at the advanced decay of the neighbouring kingdom: Calais had already fallen into English hands (1347), and now, John II had become the captive of Edward III of England. It was clear that Giannino should reign, since 'John I' naturally prevailed over John II. One and a half century later, Perkin Warbeck castigated Henry VII's grandfather, Owen Tudor, for being ignoble.[27] By birth, Henry was an absolute outsider, especially when compared to the 'direct lineage' the pseudo-Duke of York boasted about. The Tudor rival even had illegally conquered England as a refugee devoted to French interests.

Any impostor pointed the finger at his rival's tyranny: his power was groundless and, what is worse, unfair. Taxation, war, bad relationships with the nobility, personal indignity, natural calamities, food shortages and epidemics nourished the main reproaches to bad princes. The individual and functional dimensions of kingship often were very intertwined in these perceptions. In the beginning of the fourteenth century, the real Edward II of England was mocked by a false Edward II for his uncouth manners. According to the impostor, John of Powderham, a nurse or a midwife had swapped him, the true heir to Edward I, for the son of the queen's groom or carriage-driver. Several sources, for example the *Chronicle of Lanercost*, report that John of Powderham's story was inspired by Edward II's well-known rustic tastes:

> When this was reported the whole community became
> excited and greatly wondered, certain foolish persons

yielding adherence to this fellow [John], all the more
readily because the said lord Edward resembled the elder
lord Edward in none of his virtues. For it was commonly reported that he [Edward II] had devoted himself
privately from his youth to the arts of rowing and driv-
ing chariots, digging pits and roofing houses; also that
he wrought as a craftsman with his boon companions by
night, and at other mechanical arts, besides other vanities and frivolities wherein it doth not become a king's
son to busy himself.[28]

The above-mentioned Ludwig of Brandenburg was reviled for his libidinous
inclinations, and Henry VII for his greed.[29] Food shortages, famines, or plague
were imputed to contemporary unsuccessful princes.[30] Thus, two chroniclers
noticed the proximity of bad harvests and political troubles surrounding the
second accession of 'good' Count Baldwin in Flanders in 1224-1226. Joan, the
unable princess, was chastised by God's wrath, whereas the generous hero
could parade as a saviour.[31]

Condemnations of surtaxes, questionable foreign affairs or class-specific injustice were more important, because they seemed to apply to the new monarchic
state as a whole. Tile Kolup, the new Frederick II of around 1285, was given a
warm welcome by a league of West-German overtaxed towns: Neuss, Wetlzar
and even Frankfurt, the city where imperial election usually took place.[32]
Henry VII's fiscal policy gave Perkin Warbeck a heaven-sent opportunity to stir
up Cornish crowds against another Scottish conflict, one for which Warbeck,
amusingly, was partly responsible![33] The counterfeit 'Richard IV' landed in Corn-
wall two months after the battle of Blackheath near London (17 June 1497),
where an army of Cornish and Devonian peasants had been defeated by royal
troops. Eight thousand rioters joined Warbeck's meagre forces of, initially, only
some 300 men. Angry about the war taxation, the peasants dashed along with
Warbeck's men towards Exeter with a vengeance. International tensions and warfare also fuelled the plotters' arguments. The group around pseudo-Baldwin was
hostile to Countess Joan's Francophilia and wished to form an alliance with England, whose King Henry III sent a letter to welcome the old crusader back home
and to suggest a renewal of ancient treaties.[34] At the beginning of the fifteenth
century, a double of Richard II had gathered at the Scottish court all kinds of
opponents to Henry IV, who naturally then made contact with Welsh rebels.[35]
Warbeck's advisers successively sought French, Irish, Flemish, and Scottish help.[36]
Early in his career, in 1493, he wrote to Isabella, Queen of Castile, to inform her
about his misfortunes, and he mentioned in passing that he had received envoys
from Maximilian, King of the Romans, James IV, King of Scotland, John, King
of Denmark, and other princes. European diplomacy was at stake.[37]

More significantly, radical protests focused on the king's attitude toward some aristocratic factions, who considered themselves as deprived of their privileges. They felt themselves removed from the political scene or fallen into disgrace one way or another. In this respect, Warbeck's 1496 harangue spoke for itself. This feigned monarch's government was populated with nobles who had come down in the world, by former officials who had been dismissed, or even by apparently obedient servants who were ready to betray their legitimate master, for they felt it frustrating to be rewarded below their merits. In the middle of the thirteenth century, Philip of Catania, once a member of the imperial chancellery in Sicily who now resented his ousting by King Manfred, became another false Frederick II's partner in crime.[38] A good century and a half later, William Serle, chamberlain to King Richard II and also known as the murderer of the king's uncle, Thomas of Gloucester, stole Richard's signet. He used it to seal letters which purported to come from the Plantagenet and which facilitated the creation of another pseudo-Richard by the Scottish court.[39] At the end of the fifteenth century, William Stanley, chamberlain of Henry VII, was scheming with Perkin Warbeck's party for the deposition of his former benefactor. Not only because of loyalty to Yorkism but also out of personal frustration, he sent money to the rebels.[40] Philip of Catania, William Serle, William Stanley – all of them were expecting a general redistribution of dignities, titles, lands and charters. And that is, of course, why they prompted their favourite actor, so as to keep monarchy under their supervision. Impostors' discourse therefore may be considered as a last-ditch stand of, among others, those who were nostalgic for a vanishing feudal era.

Conclusion

Medieval imposture initially pretended to raise royal status to sanctity and heroism. In its strife for martyrdom or martial success, those fake sovereigns' quest apparently purified their spirit even though they often were the naïve puppet of a cabal. Yet choosing the mere image of a previous king enabled a direct attack on the actual leader. By re-defining kingship, aristocratic plotters aimed to restore their fullest prerogatives. Their paroxysmal assertion of kingship had to lead to a true moderation of the actual monarchy. However, their conspiracies and false kings were always unmasked eventually.[41]

Medieval imposture was not a mere parody of kingship, performed by unlucky thespians. It only superficially hurt or degraded the kingly figure and was mainly an expression of a nostalgic, reactionary stance. Moreover, impostors spread a discourse of bruised pride: many a magnate could forgive the monarchy for its internal evolution, on condition that the sovereign continued to grant equal amounts of love to his main servants. Political imposture was very significant, whether or not the undertaking was crowned with success. Each instance of imposture ventilated ideas about what kingship really needed, and about what conspiring fringe groups perceived as adulterations. From the sum of plots can be inferred the features of the average ideal king, which was a most traditional one. A native, he inherited royal blood from a long line of ancestors; he had a special relationship with God, thanks to the hard times he had endured, which enabled him to bring back peace and prosperity or to heal serious rifts after decades of trouble. Hence, imposture negatively mirrored the 'public transcript' of the nascent early modern monarchy, which was experienced as an obvious vector of usurpation, war and taxation. The discourse of demystifying the reigning sovereign in a certain way even reinforced the sacred character of true kingship.

Medieval subversion, which rested on rather technical and realistic conceptions of power, stands in sharp contrast with what happened next, since, in early modern Europe, political imposture was generally connected to the popular belief in a 'hidden king' who would return to restore a long-awaited Golden Age.[42] From that time onward, as the emerging public sphere led the royal archetype to become more widespread and political society considerably broader, we begin to see the true process of banalization of kingship, leading to numerous pseudo-tsarevitches and the so-called Louis XVII. However, as far as the Middle Ages are concerned, clever plotters created a king after their own hearts and their own advantages, if necessary even with a little help from the Holy Virgin. Was not her coronet as worthy as any miraculous oil?

Monarchy and the Emergence of the
Public Sphere

The Art of Saying 'No'. Premonitions of Foucault's 'Governmentality' in Étienne de La Boétie's *Discours de la servitude volontaire*

Jürgen Pieters and Alexander Roose

In 1562, the French King Charles IX (1560-1574), then aged twelve, was introduced at a meeting of his court in Rouen to three 'cannibals'. The anecdote is documented in Montaigne's beautiful essay of that name (I, 31).[1] The strange creatures, members of the Brazilian Tupinamba tribe so famously described by the sixteenth-century French traveller Jean de Léry and, later, by Claude Lévi-Strauss,[2] had been imported from the New World that Charles's grandfather, Francis I (1515-1547), had once hoped to lay claim to.[3] The cannibals were in a way staged in Charles's court and subsequently put up for inspection. They were gazed and marvelled at, as if they were monsters at some fancy fair or other, only to be scrutinized like the exotic paraphernalia that were collected in books by contemporary naturalists. Their presence served not merely to alleviate the curiosity of the French, though. The 'cannibals' also functioned as background characters or, worse still, props in a fascinating power play whose leading role was assumed by a twelve-year-old boy, soon to be declared *majeur*.[4] The strange creatures added to the power of the French monarch, as both witnesses to and products of a series of hard and difficult overseas adventures that could only have been dreamed of a few generations before. Under the reign of this youthful monarch, it would seem the French navy not only promised to finally sail beyond the pillars of Hercules, but also would begin to bear the fruits of an empire in which people from different cultures and creeds willingly joined ranks as subjects of one superior being, the king whom they all would gladly serve.

As the conversation between Charles IX and his three new subjects came to an end, the cannibals were given the opportunity by one of those present to divulge their thoughts on their new leader, the French king. The *impromptu* offer is more surprising than it may seem, since it entails the possibility of a subversion, albeit momentary, of the traditional hierarchies involved in the spec(tac)ular display of regal power. For a moment, the monster is given the possibility 'to marvel back' as it were, and to say what it cannot but avoid thinking: that the spectacle in which it participates is a peculiar and curious one that provokes more questions than it can answer, questions moreover that touch upon the foundations of the societal organization of which the spectacle itself is a clear product. What obviously struck the three cannibals more than anything else was the fact that a number of strong bearded men willingly obeyed a mere child. Why on earth did they not choose one of their own to command the others, they wondered. Furthermore, it also seemed strange to them that some people clearly revelled in wealth and luxury while others were almost starving to death. Montaigne, who was present at this little spectacle and who also talked for a while with the leader of the cannibals, considered the three men wise enough to hold them dear. But then again, he added, with a twist of the superior irony that runs through his *Essais*, they do not dress the way we do – 'ils ne portent point de hauts-de-chausses' (I, 31, 214).

Montaigne's cannibals express their bewilderment in front of a society that no longer seems to oppose men of power to those who lack power. The fact that strong and truly powerful men allow themselves to be dominated by a child, who in their eyes is by definition without any real power, is already an indication of this. In what follows, the bewilderment of the cannibals will be read as a sign of the advent of the new 'governmental' conception of power that Michel Foucault locates in the course of the sixteenth century and that is centrally concerned with a set of ever-returning questions that Foucault sees cropping up in several social fields: 'Comment se gouverner, comment être gouverné, comment gouverner les autres, par qui doit-on accepter d'être gouverné, comment faire pour être le meilleur gouverneur possible.'[5]

In the logic of 'governmentality', Foucault argues, power is no longer taken as the automatic outcome of physical strength and force; its origins are much more diffuse and harder to trace down. Consequently, the division of political and social systems can no longer be analysed in terms of a distinction between those who are 'in' power and those who are not, but in terms of much less clear-cut distinctions between those who govern and those who are governed. This change, as we will see, has a number of important conceptual consequences with respect to the possibility of resistance against power and the definition of both tyrants and princes.

Montaigne and Étienne de La Boétie

Montaigne returns to the problem of government and conduct repeatedly in his work.[6] The question of how to govern oneself both underlies and nourishes the enterprise and the writing of the *Essais*.[7] The famous essay on the instruction of children, for instance, one of the highlights of the humanist pedagogy, is a reflection on the art of conducting and governing children. Originally, the problem of the government of the State was to occupy a central position in the first edition of the *Essais*, since it is the single most important question treated by Étienne de La Boétie in his *Discours de la servitude volontaire*, the text that Montaigne intended to include in his *Essais*. Also, Montaigne wonders at several points in his texts whether it suffices to know how to govern oneself in order to govern others.[8] In the full course at the Collège de France in which he develops his analysis of the concept of governmentality, Foucault does mention Montaigne, without however referring to the *Discours sur la servitude volontaire*. He also stresses the renewed interest for the philosophy of the Stoics – La Boétie was, like Justus Lipsius and to a certain extent even Montaigne, a neo-Stoic – which obviously is a central factor in the return of the general preoccupation with questions of how to govern oneself. It is hardly coincidental that Montaigne was highly appreciative of the political treatises of the neo-Stoic Lipsius.[9] Here, moral philosophy and political philosophy begin to join hands: those who govern politically need to be able to show to the people how to overcome their personal miseries, just like they themselves do when they are faced with personal adversity and disorder.

Montaigne's reading of the cannibals' momentary 'deconstruction' of the masquerade of regal power comes close to a shorthand analysis of the famous treatise written by his friend Étienne de La Boétie, the *Discours de la servitude volontaire*. Montaigne had hoped to include his friend's text in his own collection of essays, but he ultimately decided not to, because La Boétie's text was being used by a number of Protestants in their struggle against a group of Catholic extremists in the king's surroundings. Some truths, Montaigne felt, are better left unsaid. He decided, therefore, to centre his own essays around La Boétie's poems rather than the prophetic text his friend had written in his prime.

In a way, the *Discours* had laid the foundations of the friendship that Montaigne and La Boétie both shared and cherished (I, 28). Long before their first encounter, Montaigne had read La Boétie's sharp analysis of the mechanisms of power, and he had understood well enough why nobody dared to publish the manuscript that circulated among intellectuals. The *Discours* was to some extent a public text, but one that better remained unpublished,[10] Montaigne realized, because the ideas that its author propagated in it were at least as dangerous as the seemingly naïve critique of the cannibals on the phenomenon of the *enfant roi*. Like the three Tupinamba, La Boétie attacked the very foundations of the regal system, but he did so on a more systematic basis, holding nothing less than a plea for a form of government that was based on the example of the classical republic. In print, moreover, the subversive power of this text would be far less momentary than the passing remark of some or other Brazilian Indian.

The few reflections that we have of Montaigne on La Boétie's *Discours* underscore the text's potential threat, even though the author of the *Essais* seems to have done everything in his power to take away this impression.

Describing the text as a mere rhetorical exercise written by a youthful author, Montaigne suggests that we take the *Discours* as a sin of La Boétie's youth.[11] While he does admit that the author of the *Discours* would have preferred to have been born in the most famous republic of his time – 'que s'il eut eu à choisir, il eut mieux aimé estre nay à Venise qu'à Sarlat: et avec raison' (I, 28, 195) – he simply adds: well, who would not? Still, Montaigne stresses that there is no one he knows of who detested violence and revolutions as much as La Boétie. If only for that reason, he would have done anything in his power to safeguard the peace in his country. Montaigne's careful extenuation of La Boétie's rhetorical exercise is as correct as it is ambiguous. It is true that the author of the *Discours* played an active and pacifist part in the troublesome times in which he lived, as a collaborator of the Chancellor of France, Michel de l'Hospital. After the States-General of Orléans, the Chancellor had asked the young and loyal jurist La Boétie to defend his policy of religious toleration before his colleagues of the Bordeaux parliament.[12] What Montaigne fails to stress, though, is the fact that the war in question was a religious one, not a political struggle in which the fight was one between republicans and royalists.

The Mind of a Poet

La Boétie loved poetry. He wrote poems himself, both in Latin and French, and he also adorned his *Discours* with a number of literary quotations. He opens his text with a line from Homer, the book of books as far as Renaissance enthusiasts of Antique philosophy were concerned. For the reader inspired by the treasure troves of the booming humanism, it offered a perfect *incipit*:

> 'D'avoir plusieurs seigneurs aucun bien je n'y vois
> Qu'un sans plus soit le maître, et qu'un seul soit le Roi.'
> Ce disait Ulysse en Homère parlant en public. S'il n'eût
> rien plus dit, sinon 'D'avoir plusieurs seigneurs aucun
> bien je n'y vois', c'était autant bien dit que rien plus;
> mais au lieu que pour le raisonner il fallait dire que la
> domination de plusieurs ne pouvait être bonne, puisque
> la puissance d'un seul, dès lors qu'il prend ce titre de
> maître, est dure et déraisonnable, il est allé ajouter tout
> au rebours:
> 'Qu'un sans plus soit le maître, et qu'un seul soit le
> Roi.'[13]

La Boétie opens his text by inverting the old saying that one can serve only one master. To serve many masters is worse than serving one, he argues, if only because it is horrible to serve one in the first place. We should be careful, La Boétie adds, not to give too much weight to Ulysses's words, since his argument was determined primarily by the circumstances in which it was given. He voiced his idea in order to appease a group of rebellious officers, not in order to make a general truth claim about the workings of power. Still, the reference does function by way of a *caveat*. What will be at stake in his own text, La Boétie goes on to say, is exactly that: the fundamentals of power. Rather than stage a debate about the ideal form of government,[14] this text aims to bring centre stage the quintessential question to which every form of societal organization needs to have an answer:

> Comme il se peut faire que tant d'hommes, tant de
> bourgs, tant de villes, tant de nations endurent quelque-
> fois un tyran seul, qui n'a puissance que celle qu'ils don-
> nent; qui n'a pouvoir de leur nuire, sinon tant qu'ils ont
> vouloir de l'endurer; qui ne saurait leur faire mal aucun,
> sinon lorqu'ils aiment mieux souffrir que lui contredire
> (*SV*, 26).[15]

The question, in other words, is the one asked by Montaigne's cannibals after they had encountered the young French king: how come 'so many grown men, bearded, strong and armed, who were around the king [it is likely that they were talking about the Swiss of his guard] should submit to obey a child, and that one of them was not chosen to command instead' (I, 31, 216).[16] It would be quite understandable, La Boétie suggests, if people put their fates in the hands of a virtuous person who at one or other critical point in their lives helped them in a substantial way. But this is not how things are wont to go: people do not simply obey their leaders; they serve them, willingly submitting themselves to enslavement. To La Boétie, this is a crucial difference, one that comes close to the insights of Antonio Gramsci and Louis Althusser into the workings of hegemonic systems, whose success is largely based on the fact that those subjected to them willingly co-operate in their own subjection.[17] To La Boétie, however, the mechanism of 'servitude volontaire' is not simply a matter of ideological consensus and unenforced negotiations between those who govern and those who are governed. Human beings, he asserts, allow themselves to be not simply governed ('gouvernés') but also tyrannized ('mais tyrannisés') (*SV*, 27). Patiently and passively they undergo the most cruel sufferings, committed not by a foreign army or by a group of barbarians against whom they are expected to defend their belongings but by one man, a little man, moreover, 'un hom-meau, et le plus lâche et femelin de la nation; non pas accoutumé à la poudre des batailles, mais encore à grand peine au sable des tournois' (*SV*, 27).[18] How on earth is this possible, La Boétie exclaims? Cowardice is too narrow a ground to explain this bizarre phenomenon. It would be a matter of cowardice if four men allowed themselves to be intimidated by one lord. But what is it that urges a million people and thousands of cities to allow themselves to be subjected by one single man, a tyrant at that? They arm the hand that strikes against them, they feed the monster that now and again throws something at them to eat. They stuff the attics of their houses only to have them pillaged by him; they raise their children so that he could send them off to war or so that he could use them as servants of his whims, the hangmen of his revenge (*SV*, 30). Even animals would not allow this to happen, La Boétie wryly concludes.

The Once and Future King

The quotation from Homer's *Odyssee* with which La Boétie opens his text can be read as an echo from a political treatise with which he may have been familiar and which continued to cast its shadow over the political and juridical controversy surrounding the French monarchy in the second half of the sixteenth century: Claude de Seyssel's *Le Grant Monarchie de France* (1518). One of de Seyssel's key maxims, as John W. Allen puts it in his survey of the book, is the idea that 'men find it more easy and natural to obey a single chief than to submit to control by a group of any sort'.[19] According to Allen, the idea serves as an apt synthesis of its author's pragmatic defence of the monarchy. Even though de Seyssel is in principle far more in favour of an aristocratic form of government, in which a group of noble and trustworthy men have been elected collectively to perform the manifold duties of a king, he fears that in practice this form of government is destined to lead to corruption and internal strife.[20]

De Seyssel's pragmatic defence of the monarch's power, while clearly influenced by a thorough reading of Machiavelli's *Il Principe*, is also grounded in his personal political experience. As an adviser of and minister to Louis XII (1498-1515), he knew that the stability of the monarchy depended to a large extent on an effective system of checks and regulations that involved a careful balancing between the central power of the divinely ordained king and a set of local customs that derived mainly from a feudally organized society. In the first half of the sixteenth century, though, during the reign of Francis I, the equilibrium that was essential to the system de Seyssel held so dear came under an increasing strain, as several groups of jurists began to develop arguments for a truly absolutist theory of monarchy which, if not in practice then at least in theory, could justify the unlimited juridical sovereignty of the king, in both political and religious matters. Returning to the fundamentals of Roman law, the French king's jurists aimed to set up a political apparatus that could make a decisive break with the largely feudal organization of both State and Church under Francis's predecessors.

Even though the practical organization of the monarchy under Francis I did not fully adhere to the theoretical ideals of absolutism, the first half of the sixteenth century was marked by a growing tendency towards the centralization of state power. The reigns of Francis's successors – Henry II (1547-1559) and his sons, Francis II (1559-1560), Charles IX and Henry III (1574-1589) – are characterized by the same *étatistic* drive, but the growing religious unrest in the third quarter of the sixteenth century seems to have hampered the gradual development of a distinctively absolutist regal practice that set in under the reign of Francis I, as many Protestant factions joined more local and regional attempts to delimit the political powers of a centralized government. As Michel Foucault puts it in his survey of the period in his 1978 course at the Collège de France, the sixteenth century is structurally characterized by the conjunction of these two intersecting historical developments: 'concentration étatique' on the one hand and 'dispersion et dissidence religieuse' on the other.[21]

The year in which Charles IX was introduced to the Tupinamba cannibals with which we began this text is often seen as marking the formal beginning of the religiously inspired civil wars that broke up France until well in the 1590s. From the very beginning, the strife between Protestants and Catholics resulted in the publication of numerous pamphlets and speeches surrounding the problem of the monarchy. A number of these were collected in the so-called *Mémoires de l'Estat de France sous Charles IX*, published in 1576 by Simon Goulart. La Boétie's text was one of these. Written at least two decades earlier, the text seems to contain no direct references to the political circumstances out of which we now assume it grew, but it would seem that its defence of republican forms of government functioned as an explosive new given in a religiously inspired struggle over the monarchy.

In the early years of Charles IX's reign, the policy with respect to religious diversity and dissent was rather tolerant, more tolerant at least than that of Charles's predecessors, Henry II and Francis II. The latter's short reign was heavily determined by the severe Catholicism of the Guise family, whose impact declines considerably after the death of Francis II. The new regal policy is from then on determined and decided by Charles's mother, the Catholic queen Catherine de' Medici, wife to Henry II, who served as the official regent to Charles while he was still a minor. As a token of her new, more tolerant policy, Catherine appointed a new Chancellor in 1560: Michel de l'Hospital, whom we mentioned earlier and in whose service La Boétie worked. 'In the years 1560-1561 the government of France,' John W. Allen writes, 'directed by Catherine de' Medici, was endeavouring to avert civil war by the establishment of a partial and localized toleration of heretical or "reformed" worship. L'Hospital, as Chancellor, expounded and defended the new policy in a series of remarkable public speeches.'[22] The new Chancellor's policy of toleration goes hand in hand with a new view on the role of the king that seems to mark a new stage in the genealogy of regal absolutism. Even though there are considerable theoretical discrepancies between, for instance, de Seyssel's view of kingship and that of de l'Hospital, they share a considerable degree of pragmatism. Like de Seyssel, de l'Hospital is aware of the dangers involved in pure absolutism. What the monarchy needs is a system of checks and balances that can counter the potential dangers of sheer regal arbitrariness. But what the monarchy also needs, de l'Hospital argues, is for the king to behave like a shepherd to his subjects, all of them. In Allen's words: 'The ideal which de l'Hospital was setting before France was that of a national government without legal limitation to its powers: a government not independent of religion, for the King holds authority from God, still less indifferent to religious opinion, but seeing in the maintenance of peace, order and justice its essential function and owning a duty to secure as far as possible the welfare of all its subjects, irrespective of creed.'[23]

'Even the Oxen under the Weight of the Yoke Complain'

According to Montaigne, the point of germination of La Boétie's text may well have been Plutarch's dictum that 'the inhabitants of Asia served one single man because they could not pronounce one single syllable, which is 'No' (I, 26, 156).[24] Indeed, La Boétie is convinced that it suffices to say 'No' only once in order to bring down tyrants:

> Soyez résolus de ne servir plus, et vous voilà libres. Je ne veux pas que vous le poussiez ou l'ébranliez, mais seulement ne le soutenez plus, et vous le verrez, comme un grand colosse à qui on a dérobé sa base, de son poids même fondre en bas et se rompre (SV, 30).[25]

How then is it possible, he goes on to wonder, that so many people forgot how and when to say this single word? After all, freedom is a natural right, shared by man and animal alike. An elephant that can no longer escape imprisonment buries his teeth in a tree in order to break them, because he knows that those who hunt him down are only in it for the ivory. He prefers to live toothless rather than undergo even the shortest period of imprisonment. A fish caught in the fisherman's nets will do its utmost to escape, La Boétie remarks, but man seems to willingly subject himself to the dictates of one single person. How on earth is this possible? La Boétie's answer is as straightforward as his recurrent question: it is the force of habit. Much in the way that Aristotle teaches us that we arrive at virtue by being repeatedly virtuous,[26] one can also get used to vice, La Boétie believes. Inserting yet another reference to Homer, he wonders: if a certain group of people were to live in the dark for six months, would those who are born during this period not grow accustomed to a life of darkness, strangers to the desire for light, which, after all, they have never known (*SV*, 38)?

The force of human alienation is so decisive that for many the desire for freedom seems unnatural, La Boétie concludes. Still, in true neo-Stoic vein[27] he points out that if we were truly to live according to nature – 'si nous vivions avec les droits que la nature nous a donnés et avec les enseignements qu'elle nous apprend' (*SV*, 31)[28] – then we would surely listen to our forefathers, submit ourselves to reason and would never be anyone's slave. After all, every human being participates to some extent in the order of reason. While one could argue about the origin of reason, there is no denying that nature, God's servant and Man's governess, created us out of the same mould. Mother Nature gave us the earth as our abode, she gave us the same house and produced us on the basis of the same pattern. And since we all share the same fate and are all equal, it cannot be reasonably argued that it was nature's purpose to condemn some persons to slavery. According to the (neo-)Stoics, things must be considered in the broader perspective of Universal Nature or Universal Reason.[29] For them, in fact, Nature equals Reason – 'la nature, étant toute raisonnable' (*SV*, 32).[30] Moreover, the innate reflex that causes humans to defend their freedom indicates that freedom is a natural right. As we have seen, animals only give up their freedom after a long and hard fight, and even domestic animals, La Boétie argues, suffer from imprisonment:

> Même les bœufs sous le poids du joug geignent
> Et les oiseaux dans la cage se plaignent (*SV*, 33).[31]

Why, then, has man lost his memory of a former, originally free life and with it the urge to reclaim that original freedom? 'Quel malencontre,' he exclaims, 'a pu tant dénaturer l'homme?'(*SV*, 33). Again, La Boétie's answer is quite straightforward: the force of habit, he remains convinced, plays a large role in all of this. Once more he uses a classical example to make his point: Mithridates eventually got used to poison by drinking small portions of it daily. The seeds of goodness and freedom that nature planted in us are subject to change, depending on the climate, the soil in which they are nurtured and the gardener's efforts. The logic is sustained by yet another example from antiquity: the Spartan leader Lycurgus, La Boétie writes, made this perfectly clear by means of the following experiment. Two dogs from the same nest were separated from birth, one being raised in a kitchen while the other became part of a hunting troop. Several years later Lycurgus took the dogs to the marketplace and confronted them with a bowl of soup and a hare. The tame dog immediately made for the bowl of soup, while the other ravaged the hare.

Kings can similarly determine and train their subjects. Whatever man feeds himself on seems natural, as do the things that he commonly does. Only freedom and reason, neither of which can be tainted by habit, are original qualities, La Boétie remains convinced. Kings have a number of means available to take away the freedom of their subjects: violent means, obviously, but also more subtle ones. Again La Boétie refers to an example from ancient history to make his point: When the people of Sardis, the capital of Lydia, tried to rise against him, Cyrus, the Emperor of Persia,[32] faced a dilemma. He did not want to destroy the beautiful city of Sardis, but neither could he afford to station a large part of his troops there, in order to maintain peace. He therefore introduced bordellos, taverns and playhouses in the city and decreed by law that the Sardinians had to make use of them. Subsequently, La Boétie writes, the king's arms could be laid to rest – 'il ne fallut tirer un coup d'épée' (SV, 42).

The example is instructive to La Boétie in more than one respect. Because the inhabitants of Lydia developed a great number of plays, he takes it that the Latin word for it is derived from them: ludi, after all is close to lydi (SV, 42). The reference is more than a passing one, since it serves La Boétie to point out that many tyrants make use of their subjects' 'natural' propensity toward the 'ludic'. Theatres, plays, comedies and other performances, gladiators, strange animals – all of these serve as bait meant to lure people into voluntary servitude; they are the price paid for freedom and the tyrant's mightiest weapon. In great enthusiasm people cry out loud 'Vive le roi!', La Boétie writes, as the king returns something that he had originally stolen from them. Power is a matter of presentation and ceremony, La Boétie concludes. Roman tyrants always assumed the title of tribune of the people. The kings of the Assyrians and the Medes always delayed their public appearance, so that their people would more firmly believe in their divine superiority. The subjected nations feared the king whom they had never even seen. La Boétie also points to the example of the Egyptian kings who presented themselves to their subjects with a cat on their head. What would seem ridiculous to most free men was greeted by the Egyptians with reverence and wonder.

The theatre, La Boétie concludes on the basis of these examples, is a double instrument of power. People who go to the theatre are looking for distraction and will not easily rise against the tyrant. Moreover, the mise en scène of royal power turns out to be a major factor in upholding the political status quo. The king's public appearances are political performances that serve to confirm and strengthen the power they are meant to praise. Likewise, La Boétie continues, the miracles that kings are said to perform also heighten their prestige and power. The finger of Pyrrhus once healed a sick spleen, he reminds us; it is hard to imagine that he was not alluding to the miraculous powers of the French kings, 'les rois thaumaturges' as Marc Bloch called them.[33] Ever since Robert the Pious (996-1031), French kings were said to heal those afflicted with scrophulosis by touching them and saying: 'le roi te touche, le roi te guérit'. In 1569, Charles IX touched over two thousand sick people. It goes without saying that this extraordinary phenomenon was used by defenders of absolutism to stress the divine origins of royal authority.[34]

The Force of Power

A number of tyrants, La Boétie observes, some of whom were themselves surprised at the fact that so many people were willing to undergo the evil done unto them by one single man, made use of religion to strengthen their power. 'Ils voulaient fort se mettre la religion devant pour garde-corps, et, s'il était possible, emprunter quelque échantillon de la divinité pour le maintien de leur méchante vie' (SV, 45).[35] But this abuse will be punished by the gods, La Boétie feels, just like Salmoneus was punished by Jupiter because he claimed he could perfectly imitate the god's thunder and lightning. With this classical example from the Aeneid, La Boétie seems to realize the dangerous actuality of his treatise. How is it possible to talk about kings and their abuse of power in general without simultaneously criticizing the kings of France? 'Les nôtres semèrent en France je ne sais quoi de tel, des crapauds, des fleurs de lys, l'ampoule et l'oriflamme' (SV, 45).[36] Legend had it that the coat of arms of Clovis, the King of the Franks (481-511), was illustrated with toads.[37] The lily is an even clearer topical reference. The enumeration in itself may be taken as a signal of scepticism, an allusion possibly to Cornelius Agrippa's book on the mistakes of his times, which listed all the animals that several armies selected in order to adorn their standards: the Romans opted for an eagle, the Phrygians for a piglet, the Goths for a bear, the Alanians for a cat, the first French for a lion, the Saxons for a horse.[38] The reader expects the passage to lead to the conclusion that 'our kings' are different. And so it does, to a certain extent, were it not for La Boétie's ambivalent phrasing of it: 'si semble-il qu'ils ont été non pas faits commes les autres par la nature, mais choisis par le Dieu tout-puissant, avant que naître, pour le gouvernement et conservation de ce royaume' (SV, 45-46).[39] It 'seems'[40] as if our kings are supernatural. The outcome of this passage is rather bizarre: nature equals reason, but here there appears to be something that is above reason, a *deus ex machina* that somehow does not seem to fit in La Boétie's stoical world-picture.

What, then, La Boétie wonders, is the central mystery of power, 'le ressort et le secret de la domination' (SV, 47)?[41] We are wrong to conclude, La Boétie writes, that its secret lies with the army. The guards that are holding the fort are only there to scare off a number of poor peasants; they are not the ones who keep a tyrant on the throne. According to La Boétie, the king owes his power to the few immediately surrounding him, a limited group of councillors and companions, to whom he listens as they give him advice and who are accessories to his wrongdoings. In turn, this small group of councillors has power over a larger group of some five hundred to whom they give privileges and favours: they govern the lands and they rule with force, so much so that they can only maintain their position because their degree, their subservience, and their ties with the immediate circle around the king protect them.

La Boétie makes use of the metaphor of the organic and natural structure of the political body to give meaning to the phenomenon of power. If in a human body decay or putrefaction sets in, all the bacteria assemble in that spot. So it goes with tyranny: as soon as a tyrant shows up, rabble and thieves assemble around him, who in a republic would be relatively harmless. The tyrant controls his subjects and, in order to do so, relies on others.

> Voilà ses archers, voilà ses gardes, voilà ses hallebardiers;
> non pas qu'eux-mêmes ne souffrent quelquefois de lui;
> mais ces perdus et abandonnés de Dieu et des hommes
> sont contents d'endurer du mal pour en faire, non pas à
> celui qui leur en fait, mais à ceux qui endurent comme
> eux, et qui n'en peuvent mais (SV, 48).[42]

La Boétie makes clear that the king's power does not revolve around the power of his soldiers, the dexterity of his archers, or the cruelty of his infantry. His power is sustained, rather, by the few nobles who are part of the council that surrounds him and to whom he has granted a number of special liberties and riches. Those in turn are surrounded by a number of people to whom they, in turn, give a number of privileges. The mechanism of humiliation is accepted by those who can humiliate others; one allows oneself to be bereft of freedom on condition that one can take away freedom from others. The pyramid of power thus becomes broader and broader, it includes more and more people, to the point at which those who profit from the system outnumber those who yearn for their lost freedom. The system is so strong and so permanent that it destroys, unnoticed, our natural and original drive for freedom. And those who remember this freedom will consider it unnatural.[43] The hierarchical system, founded upon the systematic withdrawal of freedom and the upholding of inequality, is experienced as natural. Our natural drive for freedom is either forgotten or taken as unnatural; subjection as normal. La Boétie's contemporary, Guillaume de La Perrière, in contrast, argues in his *Miroir politique* that the hierarchical structure is natural. The bees, La Perrière writes, 'les mouches à miel', have only one king, who determines all their doings:

> Au surplus nous voions que nature: que dis ie, nature?
> ains le conditeur de la nature, a exprimé ce Royal &

> unique gouvernement, tant aux choses animees, que non
> animees, à celle qu'il donnast à entendre aux humains,
> que unique gouvernement est meilleur que tout autre.
> Les mouches à miel conduictes & poussees par leur
> instinct naturel, ont un seul Roy, sous l'authorité duquel
> elles combatent, disposent leurs negoces, travaillent &
> vivent socialement, recognoissans un Roy pour leur seul
> chef & gouverneur, comme est loisible de veoir en Varo,
> Virgile, Columelle, Palladius, Constantin Cesar, &
> autres autheurs, qui ont escrit de l'agriculture.[44]

The hierarchic organization, and the inequality of rights that follows from it, is also part of the organic natural order that God created. Inequality in nature legitimates the pyramidal power structure. This is the very point that Baldassare Castiglione makes in his *Book of the Courtier* (1529), when he has Octavian exclaim: 'Marke ye whether Deere, Cranes, and many other foules, when they take their flight doe not alwaies set a Prince before, whom they follow and obey. And Bees (as it were) with discourse of reason, and with such reverence honour their King, as the most obedientest people in the world can do.'[45] La Boétie inverts this: freedom and equal rights are the foundations of natural order. But in La Perrière's system, the analogy of the bee also serves to show that the king's power is not founded on the possibility of the exertion of violence:

> Aussi tout gouverneur doit avoir patience, à l'exemple
> du Roy des mouches à miel, qui n'a point d'esguillon, en
> quoy nature a voulu montrer mystiquement, que les
> Rois & gouverneurs de Republique doivent envers leurs
> subjects user de beaucoup plus de clemence que de
> severite, & et d'equité que de rigueur.[46]

Like the bee, the king needs to be patient and wise in order to take care of his subjects. That is what Nature shows us in a 'mystical' way. It is not so much that La Boétie's text rejects any mystical foundation of power; rather, he shows that power is founded on a mystical vacuum.[47] Moreover, La Boétie's text is not marked (or marred) by the prescriptive rhetorics of *Le Miroir Politique*.[48] *Le discours de la servitude volontaire* is not a king's manual; it offers an analysis of the power structures that continue to characterize the monarchy well into the Renaissance. Its purpose is not to stress what kings should do but to show what kings really do in order to stay kings.

Foucault and Governmentality

Despite their differences, the texts by La Perrière and La Boétie make clear the extent to which the historical moment from which they derive marks a true turning point in the history of the concept of power. On account of this change, the sixteenth and seventeenth centuries bear witness to a striking number of discursive attempts to prepare future kings for the exercise and maintenance of this new type of power. Hence the profusion of writings on the nature of monarchical power and the true plethora of *Institutions politiques* that, contrary to similar texts from a previous age, are no longer limited to the definition and delimitation of a number of moral principles that the good prince needs to uphold. In his 1978 course at the Collège de France, Michel Foucault referred to this development as the advent of a politics of 'gouvernementalité'.[49]

The specificity of the sixteenth-century logic of governmentality resides in its marked difference from what Foucault labels a Machiavellian logic of 'sovereignty', in which the position of the ruler with respect to his subjects and to the geographical area in which they are contained is defined according to three principles: singularity, exteriority and transcendence. What is crucial in the Machiavellian concept of power is the idea that the prince or king is, in fact, not really part of his principality. He is exterior and superior to it, and it is his sole purpose to retain both his power and the principality in which it is invested. His concern lies not so much with the physical space which his subjects occupy, nor with the subjects themselves, but with the bond of power which relates him to his principality.[50] His main concern is to uphold this power and to guarantee as much as possible the status quo which allowed him to rule in the first place.

In his course, Foucault pointed out the central position that Machiavelli continued to occupy in the debates on the nature of political power that came out of the sixteenth and seventeenth centuries.[51] While La Perrière distances himself from Machiavelli's analysis by stressing the natural legitimacy of monarchic power and the banishment of violence that results from it, La Boétie's analysis comes close to that of the Florentine in that he points out the very mechanisms of power, like Machiavelli in *Il Principe*. Unlike Machiavelli, however, La Boétie stresses above all that the king in no way needs to resort to violence in order to secure his authority since his subjects have integrated the power structure to such an extent that they stop questioning it and would never try to overthrow it with violence.

In governmental texts, this sovereign logic is either substituted for or complemented by a new stress on the 'interior' position of the prince or king: the one who rules is located within the field of power which the logic of governmentality installs. This new logic also involves a different finality of government: it is less self-focused, even though of course it also aims for a certain status quo of power. But its goal is ultimately directed elsewhere: not upon itself but upon what several sixteenth-century texts define as the common good, 'le bien commun'. In his contradistinction between the governmental and sovereign logics of power and authority, Foucault quotes extensively from the text that we just mentioned, Guillaume La Perrière's *Le Miroir Politique, contenant diverses manières de gouverner* (1555), where the ideal of government is defined as 'droite disposition des choses, desquelles l'on prend charge pour les conduire jusqu'à fin convenable'.[52] Here, as elsewhere in La Perrière's text, the goal in question is that of 'le bien commun'. The concept is not new. It is even central to the definition St Thomas proposed of the king as 'celui qui gouverne le peuple d'une seule cité et d'une seule province, et cela en vue du bien commun'.[53] In this definition there is no distinction whatsoever between the one who governs his people and the one who exercises his powers of sovereignty. In the exercise of his functions, the king behaves like a shepherd and, ultimately, like a God.

The central word in the quotation from La Perrière is *conduire*, the idea of conduct, which, even though La Perrière seems to limit it to goods, can also be applied to the king's subjects. As Foucault sees it, between 1580 and 1660, the sovereign ruler assumes a new task that no longer can be defined within the framework of traditional sovereignty. 'Le souverain qui règne,' Foucault writes, 'le souverain qui exerce sa souveraineté se voit, à partir de ce moment-là, chargé, confié, assigné à de nouvelles tâches, et ses nouvelles tâches, c'est celles précisément de la conduction des âmes.' The latter phrase may suggest a certain amount of recourse to the traditional pastoral model, which can be found in certain medieval treatises on politics. Foucault makes clear, however, that like the logic of sovereignty, that of pastoralism undergoes a number of decisive changes in the period on account of the imminent disintegration of the presence of the divine in the world. The role of the king is no longer limited to that of one who aims 'à prolonger sur terre une souveraineté divine qui se répercuterait en quelque sorte dans le continuum de la nature'.[54] Hence, the Prince can no longer rely on the traditional pastoral model nor on the model of the *paterfamilias* – as could Caesar, to borrow the example of La Boétie.[55] It no longer suffices to occupy himself with his political affairs like a shepherd takes care of his flock.

The example of Michel de l'Hospital, with his stress on a king who is shepherd of all of France's sheep, irrespective of creed and breed, turns out to be instructive. Making use of a metaphor borrowed from the traditional pastoral paradigm, de l'Hospital advocates a new *raison d'état* in which it is stressed that from now on the king has to govern, to conduct and control his subjects rather than rule over them. This art of government, which is neither pastoral nor sovereign, rests upon a type of rationality that owes its success to the State's ability to decipher the minds and penetrate the souls of those governed. To a certain extent, La Boétie seems to have foreseen this change in his conception of a power that would like, in the manner of Momus, to slightly modify man as he was forged by Vulcan: 'Mome, le dieu moqueur, ne se moqua pas trop quand il trouva cela à redire en l'homme que Vulcain avait fait, dequoi il ne lui avait mis une petite fenêtre au cœur, afin que par là on pût voir ses pensées' (SV, 39).[56]

Foucault couples the religious idea of the pastoral government of the souls of the faithful to the political transformations that occurred in France in the course of the sixteenth century.[57] His purpose in doing so, he stresses, is not to suggest that there is a simple transfer of 'pastoral logic' from the religious sphere to the political one. The process is more complex than that, involving not only an intensification of all sorts of pastoral practices of spiritual welfare and control but also an extension of these practices to new domains of everyday life.[58] As a result, the questions dominating the logic of governmentality are linked with the problems of conduct, the conduct of self and of others: 'Comment se conduire? Comment se conduire soi-même? Comment conduire ses enfants? Comment conduire sa famille?'[59]

Foucault's genealogy of governmentality must be analysed more thoroughly to reveal its full potential for the historiography of sixteenth-century culture. Of interest here is the fact that his sketch of the period makes clear that the logic of governmentality also entailed a new conception of the role of the king. La Boétie's analysis does start from the persona of king who governs in the way Machiavelli's examples seem to do.[60] The text by La Boétie is the site where old debates – on the nature of tyranny, on the best model of government (republic, monarchy, aristocracy) – are reinvested[61] in order to produce an answer to new questions. To a large extent, La Boétie's text belongs to the paradigm of sovereignty. In most of the examples that La Boétie addresses, the king is exterior to his kingdom; he literally stands above his subjects. Also, his position is potentially very fragile. La Boétie stresses this fragility throughout, if only in his sustained suggestion that the king *can* be overthrown as the result of a simple, collective 'No!' The king, then, will do anything to strengthen his position and maintain the power that is invested in it. His policy is directed not toward the organization of a virtuous society, the success of which is defined in either moral or economical terms (or, indeed, in both), but exclusively toward the maintenance of his power. In this sense, La Boétie's text participates in the Machiavellian analysis of power against which Guillaume de La Perrière reacted.

At the same time, there are also elements in the *Discours* that suggest at least a family resemblance to the governmental logic that Foucault tries to lay bare. La Boétie longs for a political system in which the Prince operates as a governor and not as a tyrant. He is astonished to see so many people 'non pas obéir, mais servir; non pas être gouvernés, mais tyrannisés' (SV, 27).[62] The debate on the nature of tyranny and the comparison between the advantages of the republic over the monarchy (and vice versa) are reinvested in an attempt to fashion the principles of a form of government that offers to those who are governed a model that preserves their liberty, even to the point where they themselves turn out willingly to defend this liberty to the very end: 'Entre gens libres c'est à l'envi à qui mieux mieux, chacun pour le bien commun, chacun pour soi' (*SV*, 40).[63] La Boétie understands very well, therefore, that there is a thin line between a tyrant and a good governor: tyrants also invoke 'le bien public et soulagement commun' (*SV*, 43) – 'public welfare and common good' – in order to legitimize their political measures. Free men are willing to serve and to take arms, to serve in an army in order to protect their freedom. Foucault[64] shows how military service, in the governmental society of the nineteenth century, turns into a moral duty, an ethical choice of a excellent citizen. In these societies, desertion is not an escape out of the horror of war; it becomes a very unusual way of expressing a political resistance to the power of a government trying to organize the conduct of its citizens. Foucault's analysis of governmentality comes close to a mode of ideology that is supported by the active participation of the subject in his/her subjection. Whereas the politics of sovereignty are founded, to a large extent, on the king's possibility to dominate and subject by means of violence and fear, the politics of governmentality hinge upon the subject's awareness that it is good (maybe even necessary) to be dominated, that one becomes a better and more prosperous subject if one submits oneself to the power and the providence of the shepherd king. As such, Foucault's notion of governmentality reminds one of Gramsci's description of the politics of hegemony which, as we have shown, is strikingly similar to La Boétie's key notion of 'servitude volontaire'. While he hints occasionally at the theoretical possibility of a collective refusal of the king's or the prince's power, La Boétie stresses throughout that this possibility will never materialize, precisely because of this phenomenon of voluntary submission.

> Comme des plus braves courtauds qui au commencement mordent le frein et puis s'en jouent, et, là où naguère ruaient contre la selle, ils se parent maintenant dans le harnois, et tout fiers se gorgiasent sous la barde (*SV*, 38).[65]

The parallel with the Gramscian analysis may even be taken further. Only an intellectual elite[66] is now and then reminded of the existence of an original freedom that has since been lost, La Boétie seems to suggest occasionally. In contrast to 'le gros populace' (*SV*, 39), the slaves who are proud of the chains that bind them, these intellectuals maintain this memory of freedom: they are not obsessed with their present condition. In this sense too, La Boétie's text seems to anticipate Gramsci's analysis. Processes of cultural hegemony are involved in the support of central power. That is why tyrants are so keen to control and contain the doings of an intellectual elite; that is why they support networks of communication that foreclose the possibility for scholars and students of the humanities to communicate.[67] The collective refusal will never materialize, this much La Boétie knows. A massive 'no' has become impossible. The focus on the question of modes of conduct in the sixteenth and seventeenth centuries also results in the awareness, Foucault suggests, that there are always alternative and better forms of conduct. The question of how to be governed incites the question 'how *not* to be governed', as Foucault puts it, and it is clear that the formula is relevant to La Boétie's critique of contemporary forms of government and conduct.[68] Foucault links up this important development with a number of historical phenomena in the sixteenth and seventeenth centuries, of which he singles out three: (1) the development of an early form of biblical hermeneutics (a large-scale query into the historical existence of the Word of God), (2) the rise of new scientific theories and conceptions, and (3) the debates surrounding the use and actualization of Roman law. (The latter is the discursive field with which La Boétie was most familiar, one could argue.)

Foucault's point in 'Qu'est-ce que la critique?' should not be misunderstood. The drift of it is that the governmental production of the search for alternative modes of conduct and government (of modes of explicit counter-conduct even) is not detrimental to this new logic of governmentality but rather intrinsic to it. One could even say that it is the very reason of its success, in the sense that the search for other, better modes of government becomes part of this new political ratio that is centred around and centrally focused upon the idea of improvement and productivity. The ultimate goal of the system is not so much (or rather: not merely) to uphold and secure power (as was the case in the ideology of sovereignty) as to instil in the minds of the subjects the idea that what the system is doing is good and a cause for advancement. In a certain sense, the logic of governmentality is anathema to a politics that thrives upon habit and the consistent enforcement of the status quo. The ideals of governmentality are accumulation, improvement, production and change, ideals that are inherent to reason and lie dormant in nature. As such, the logic of governmentality needs people to say 'yes' for a good reason and to refuse to say 'no' for the same good reason, not simply because they have forgotten to.

Seen in this light, La Boétie's critique of the force of habit is a perfect example of this new political logic. One could even argue that his defence of the ideal republic (an idea which at first seems strange to the governmental defence of the monarchy as advocated by La Perrière and his likes) ultimately serves the cause of governmentality. La Boétie's critique of the traditional sovereign entails a plea for good citizenship, for a form of government that allows citizens to prosper and to continue to prosper, and that involves them responsibly in their own prosperity. The pastoral conception of monarchy of the sort defended by de l'Hospital and La Perrière is not what La Boétie has in mind for the achievement of this goal. His ideal is that of the republic of Venice, as we saw earlier:[69]

> Qui verrait les Vénitiens, une poignée de gens vivant si librement que le plus méchant d'entre eux ne voudrait pas être le roi de tous, ainsi nés et nourris qu'ils ne reconnaissent point d'autre ambition, sinon à qui mieux avisera et plus soigneusement prendra garde à entretenir la liberté; ainsi appris et faits dès le berceau, qu'ils ne prendraient point tout le reste des félicités de la terre pour perdre la moindre point de leur franchise (*SV*, 35-36).[70]

For the Venetians, liberty involves the structural impossibility of one person ruling all the others. A political model such as the monarchy, La Boétie is convinced, excludes the possibility of a politics of compromise. La Boétie responds to a new question – this new form of power that excludes the possibility of classical forms of resistance: the art of saying 'no' – with ancient remedies. His text indicates, despite his flawed conclusions and the central aporia in which it results, that the nature of power has definitely changed.

Sacralization and Demystification. The Publicization of Monarchy in Early Modern England

Kevin Sharpe

Representation and Regality

The defining terms of our volume have, until recently at least, seldom appeared in the same sentence, even the same book. Indeed 'discourse' and 'monarchy' have for the most part been separated by disciplines and by the separate, often antagonistic, approaches of critics and historians. For more than two decades, critics and theorists have drawn attention to the relationships among languages and signs and power and authority from a variety of perspectives. Working from entirely different positions and faculties, scholars as different as Michel Foucault and Clifford Geertz have powerfully argued that authority, even power, is and was not constituted simply by institutions and armies but, rather, depends upon words, images, rituals – representations.[1] Representations, they have posited, not only displayed power but also endeavoured to construct and sustain it. To govern was to publicize.

These perspectives were most forcefully brought to bear on our approach to the history of early modern England not, at least initially, by historians but by those literary critics called 'new historicists'. Combining neo-Marxist and Foucauldian approaches with Geertz's brand of symbolic anthropology, new historicists insisted that in early modernity power was culture – representations and texts; and, correspondingly, that power could be most incisively interrogated through the texts of early modern culture: verse and drama as much as pamphlet or sermon.[2]

Such an approach helpfully redirected scholars to early modernity's own preoccupation with texts and with discourse. Central to Renaissance humanism (a set of values as well as an educational programme) was a belief in, a concern with, the power of words. The early modern students' extensive and rigorous training in rhetoric assumed a connection between social status and the capacity to argue and persuade, between rhetoric and authority. And it was a connection fully comprehended and strengthened by monarchs who patronized the new learning, employed the best humanist scholars as royal servants, and who felt the need to master languages and the art of rhetoric themselves. As more than a few observers began to comment, in early modern England, agility with arguments (*topoi*) became as important as skill in arms, and rhetorical flair emerged as the principal courtly art.[3]

Where historians were concerned, a particular group – in origin more a duo – were finding a somewhat different path to the study of history and language. From the 1960s, with different emphases but in similar ways, Quentin Skinner and John Pocock refigured approaches to the history of political thought by arguing for an address to language and to paradigmatic linguistic shifts as the markers – and makers – of larger changes in political ideas and polities.[4] As I have argued elsewhere, though the methodology of what came to be termed the 'linguistic turn' had implications for all historical writings, Skinner and Pocock concentrated on canonical texts of political theory: on Machiavelli, Hobbes and Locke, not on royal speech, statute or proclamation. In reality they became in some ways a subdiscipline, and their work, though venerated, was long viewed as exotic, at the margins rather than the centre of history.[5]

Certainly political historians, who still claimed (indeed claim) the centre paid little attention to language – even royal language. No historian of early modern English monarchy has analysed royal speeches, letters or proclamations as rhetorical texts or as representations of regality. None has studied other genres of royal writing, such as prayers, translations, paraphrases or poems.[6] The works of Elizabeth I (1558-1603) and James I (1603-1625) have been edited by literary scholars and still sit unexamined by historians of society and state.[7] This lack appears all the more striking in our own twenty-first century moment. For example, when President George W. Bush makes a speech, the media report not simply – often not primarily – what is said, but also report on the arts and strategies of self-presentation: grammar and syntax, the deployment of personal or inclusive pronouns, the use of affect, the evocation of memory – or anxiety; and they go beyond reporting on tone, gesture, and body language to delve yet further into psychology. By contrast, when historians cite the words or addresses of early modern monarchs who inhabited a culture obsessed with the arts of persuasion, they limit discussion to the content of what is spoken or written. And all too often historians of politics pass over the principal object and subject of royal words – the audience. Rhetoric, the art of persuasion, was premised on dialogue: on the presence of others who needed to be persuaded, probably because they held different views. In addition to injunctions to subjects, royal (and other official) speeches, proclamations, and statutes were acts of persuasion directed to auditors and readers who, whatever their predisposition to obedience, needed to be won over to particular courses. Moreover, royal rhetoric had to adjust to and perform differently in sometimes radically shifting circumstances. Who would doubt, even if historians have not quite written about it in these terms, that Henry VIII (1509-1547) had to construct a new language of regality after the break from Rome, or that Charles II (1660-1685) and Queen Anne (1702-1714) had to alter modes of royal self-presentation after the revolutionary events of 1649 and 1688?[8]

The shifts in the linguistic and symbolic paradigms of their representation, the adaptations and deployments of traditional languages and tropes, is an as yet unwritten study of early modern government. My purpose here is more modest. It is to identify, by means of three cases, some shifting historical circumstances and the relationship of those circumstances to royal self-presentation in early modern England. By circumstances I mean not only events – Reformation, regicide or revolution – but changes in the media of representation, in the audiences for and receptions of royal address, in the culture of commerce and consumption in which royal texts and artefacts circulated, in fine in the modes of publicizing authority itself.

I argue that the break from Rome compelled a renewed emphasis on and a programme of sacralizing royal authority.[9] And I want to suggest that the process and media of publicizing sacred kingship served, seemingly paradoxically, to demystify it – by casting the mysteries of rule into a public domain. Further, I shall dare to suggest the reverse also: that the demystification of power stimulated at key moments a desire for sacred authority. Rather than a Whig or modernizing narrative of rationalization (though I believe there remains a measure of truth in that), I shall suggest a complex and shifting psychology of power, which we may yet recognize, but which has a very specific early modern history that needs to be brought up and analysed.

The centrality of the word in early modern culture was not only an aspect of the new humanism; it also owed much to what were to be the religious upheavals of the age. Perhaps every faith has been constructed on the words of some foundational prophet or text. In the case of Christianity, the Bible is explicit: as St John's gospel chapter 1, verse 1 reads: 'in the beginning was the Word'. The Word was God, and his son Jesus was the Word made flesh. Moreover the Bible connected the authority of words directly with secular political power, in the words of Ecclesiastes 8.4: 'where the word of a king is there is power'. Both as a prince and as Christ's representative on earth, the monarch's authority rested on Scripture and the injunctions of Scripture: on the Word and on his own words which a Christian prince took from his faith. In preliterate society, the royal word quite literally determined courses of action, legal judgements, grants of estate, fortunes, and lives. Even in a preliterate society that moved from memory to written record and then, in early modernity, to print, the royal word – spoken as well as 'writ' – was still foundational and determining.[10] It was Elizabeth's supposed naming her successor on her deathbed that finally secured James VI of Scotland the throne of England.

The early modern period witnessed, if anything, a new preoccupation with the Word. As, first within the Catholic church, men began to ask questions about or challenge the practices or teachings of the church, debate turned to the meaning of Scripture. Some scholars sought the solution to threatened schism in biblical philology, the search for the lost language of Adam that would restore to fallen man direct access to God's locution, and in a perfect text of Scripture on which all could agree.[11] But, as we know, the Reformation exploded from different readings of Scripture into different texts of the Bible and into a myriad of vernacular Scriptures and exegeses which appeared to replicate the biblical story of Babel. For all that it underlined the vital authority of the word, the Reformation rendered Scripture, God's Word, unstable and multiple, the text of many nations, communities, denominations, and, ultimately, readers.[12] Given the foundation of royal authority on the Word, these developments could not but have profound consequences for Christian princes. Indeed, the Reformation made it all the more important for the ruler to determine the meaning of Scripture, so as to preserve unity and authority, but in the end made it impossible for him to do so. Attempts by successive English monarchs to establish an official text of Scripture and, beyond, to determine who could read it and how it was interpreted proved futile. In translation, the Word was Everyman's, and the logical outcome was that royal words, in some measure, became Everyman's too.

In England these developments coincided crucially with the first age of print. The vernacular Bibles, unlike say the earlier Wycliffe Bible, were published and broadly disseminated: they were open to all who were literate and beyond to those who heard Scripture read; and in turn they advanced literacy and debate. As I have argued elsewhere, print presented princes with both a medium and a problem.[13] Print enabled the publicization of regality – the printing not only of statutes and proclamations but also of royal processions and pamphlets, prayers and poems. Officially approved texts were published with printed royal licence or privilege.[14] Yet while it provided new opportunities to authority, print gave rise to new difficulties which compromised it. The printed word may have been delivered by authority, but it was consumed in communities of readers or alone by men and women who, increasingly in a divided nation, interpreted it differently. And print was a medium of communication open to critics as well as supporters of authority. In Germany, cheap print and woodcuts pilloried the authority of the clergy and church; in England, Henry VIII found his attack on Luther answered in excoriating terms and circulated back to his subjects.[15] With publication, he discovered, came contest. It is this dilemma – the need to publicize authority and the risks in doing so – that is my subject in this essay, and it is one I wish to address by brief remarks on three English monarchs over a period of revolutions, from Reformation to Restoration.

Tudor Representations

Henry VIII was the first English king of print: a monarch who, throughout his reign, published in an attempt to enhance his authority and to make it sacred.

As early as 1521 Henry obtained the title Defender of the Faith as a result of publishing a defence of the seven sacraments against Luther's assault on church orthodoxy.[16] When he failed to secure a divorce from Rome, Henry, no longer wishing to represent himself as the lieutenant of the papacy, sought directly to figure himself as God's own agent and exegete, in his patronage of an English Bible. On the engraved title page of the Bible, Henry sits enthroned beneath the godhead, scrolls from his mouth mingling with those of the Lord himself. The king presents with both hands 'Verbum Dei' to bishops and nobles seated left and right beneath his throne, who pass the book to preachers and magistrates and on down to civilians, even men in prison, who cry out 'God save the king'.[17] Henry VIII also wrote and published specifically and polemically to advance his case. His *A Glass of the Truth* of 1532 staged a dialogue between a lawyer and a divine who, through discussion, come to concur about the 'plain truth' and rights of the king's suit for a divorce and to wonder how any might find it 'disputable'.[18] A decade later, with the realm sharply divided over doctrine, he wrote again in an attempt to impose a royal orthodoxy which he discerned as essential to the maintenance of royal authority. In *A Necessary Doctrine* (1543) Henry, mingling his own with Scriptural injunctions, sought to define the faith and underline the necessity of obedience to a ruler whom God had appointed as his spokesman.[19] Henry published, that is, in order to define and control; and in proclamations and statutes banning apprentices and women from access to the English Bible, he sought to determine readership and interpretation.[20]

Such control was not only beyond him, however: in publishing, Henry unwittingly contributed to the very debates and differences he wrote to suppress. We have noted Luther's immediate rejoinder, which worsted Henry in an encounter published throughout Europe. Moreover, Henry's work survived to provide weapons for critics of his later, less orthodox, courses, enabling the royal words to be turned against the king. As for *A Glass of the Truth,* not only did the dialogue form enable and encourage reader debate, but the king's justification of his divorce also led him to divulge explicit details concerning Queen Katherine's virginity at the time of their marriage.[21] In opening his troubled conscience and justifying himself in public, Henry published what had been *arcana imperii* and himself. There can be no doubt that such publicization fuelled public curiosity and debate: about the king's interior life, his privacy, and his sexual body. Royal publication allowed subjects to read Henry's texts against each other and encouraged them to widely publicize 'the king's great matter'. Tavern talk and rumour pilloried Anne Boleyn as a seductress and whore, and print lent authority to rumour, re-distributing it alongside royal text into what we will categorize as an emerging public sphere.[22] Royal proclamations against rumour and statutes making words treason evidence official panic at a loss of control in an England in which, whatever the proscriptions or penalties, it proved impossible to police all who did 'print or write or else speak, sing or declare' of state matters.[23] Indeed, whatever his distaste for it, Henry himself had recognized public debate, not least in ventriloquizing it in *A Glass of the Truth*. The divorce, the break from Rome, and the doctrinal disputes that ensued necessitated Henry's writing, arguing, and presenting himself as sacred. But such acts of representation publicized and, by plunging royal words into the arena of public debate, began to demystify his authority. As we shall see, both the necessity to publish and its demystifying consequences only increased as the century progressed.

For Henry's daughter from his marriage to Anne Boleyn, the difficult dilemma we are discussing was exacerbated by her sex. Not least from Mary Tudor's (1553-1558) loss of control of her representation and Elizabeth's own contribution, while princess, to that failure, Queen Elizabeth fully appreciated the importance to her rule of her image and her words. However, in addition to being (in the eyes of Roman Catholics) illegitimate and a heretic, as a woman Elizabeth was proscribed from the public sphere and from publicizing herself, that is, from speaking and writing. Though rule depended upon acts of speaking and writing, female publication and loquacity were associated with whoredom. Moreover, after the radical Protestant evangelism of Edward VI's brief reign (1547-1553), followed by the Catholic reaction under Mary, the public realm was more than ever divided, and the need to assert royal authority was both greater and more problematic than ever. The conventional historical orthodoxy is that Elizabeth brilliantly overcame those difficulties and strengthened the crown. Whatever her particular political failings, she proved brilliant in the arts of representation, in her image and words. Elizabeth I, as scholars since Roy Strong have argued, successfully sacralized her authority, presenting herself as Gloriana, the Deborah, the Judith, and most of all the mystical Virgin – an icon impenetrable to rational scrutiny and debate.[24]

Such a portrait, significantly, is taken more from visual than verbal representations of the queen. Though a few famous speeches have often been quoted, Elizabeth's works, her letters, prayers, poems, and translations have only just begun to be edited and have yet to be seriously examined.[25] Nonetheless, in all the various genres in which she wrote, Elizabeth's writings complicate the usual picture of her representation and disclose the complex ambiguity of mystery and publicity which is my subject. Let us take, for example, Elizabeth's prayers. Several volumes of these were published throughout her reign and, whether she authored them or not, were issued or received as hers. Some were published with an engraved frontispiece of the queen in her closet, without any of the trappings of majesty, kneeling in prayer before a Bible and before her God.[26] As with the title of one collection, *Precationes Privatae,* the scene is one of privacy: we have a sense of eavesdropping on a queen alone in her private devotions, oblivious to our gaze.[27] And yet, of course, the private is here published and printed. The prayers publicize Elizabeth as devout, as a queen fully aware of her duties to God, even in language that soothes anxieties concerning gender, as God's 'handmaid'.[28] I want to suggest that, as with other texts of the queen, notably her poems and translations, here Elizabeth pursues a strategy for negotiating a royal dilemma and one exacerbated by her sex. That is, *she publicizes the private, while endeavouring to keep public matters private,* under her personal control. This may add an unexplored dimension to the observation often made about her use of a language of love. For love was in early modernity (and still is) both an intimate and a social discourse. Amorous language enabled Elizabeth to make public comment whilst retaining a sense of intimacy, just as her representation as the virgin queen rendered mysterious a queen who deployed with kings, courtiers, and commoners the informal and familiar word or gesture. It is in this neglected respect, I suggest, that Elizabeth most skilfully turned the disadvantage of her sex into a resource. For though – and she often used the masculine noun – a prince, as a woman Elizabeth was not 'public'; and though as a woman she was 'desired', as queen she was unavailable, at least to her subjects. By skilfully negotiating this privacy and publicity, through the use of genre as well as language, Elizabeth endeavoured, as she knew she must, to be both mystical and familiar, sacred and popular – the dream combination for rulers even to this day.

Did she succeed? To that key question the answer must be less clear than conventional historiography has given: yes and no. For though Elizabeth undoubtedly succeeded in being regarded both as sacred icon and good queen Bess, for all her desire to do so, she could not control how she was debated and presented. Recently, important work on Elizabeth has identified the extent of alternative images of the queen and the number of writers and speakers who 'dissed' her in ways quite destructive of mystery.[29] At various points before and throughout her reign, there were rumours that Elizabeth was pregnant: by Seymour or Leicester, by Hatton or the Earl of Essex. Stories circulated in and out of print of her offspring or, contrarily, of her genital abnormalities which rendered her infertile; or of her lesbianism which made her monstrous.[30] As Hannah Betts has shown, especially in the last decade of her rule, Elizabeth was the subject of an explicitly pornographic literature which exposed in words and blazons the ultimate mystery of female rule, 'those secrets [that] must not be surveyed with eyes' – the vagina – to public imagination and comment.[31]

Such counter representations of the queen were ironically stimulated by her own acts of representation, still more by the erotic language and forms of her self-presentation.[32] Through printed and published images and words, Elizabeth fostered public desire; but in doing so she rendered herself a public object as much as a mysterious icon. As I shall observe later, Elizabeth's reign witnessed a huge increase in publications, panegyrics, and portraits of majesty and saw a vogue for medals and mementoes of the queen. Elizabeth was not only

desired but also was consumed by a broad public and, in some measure, pene-
trated and owned by them in the process. Both in her lifetime and for centuries
after her death, Elizabeth was (perhaps still is) made to stand for many things
she would not have supported – radical religious reform the most obvious
among them.[33] Though she sought to limit its meaning and political performance, Elizabeth became in two senses the people's princess: a queen constituted
by and for a variety of people, as well as a loving ruler over them.

Moreover, in the process of publicizing herself, Queen Elizabeth helped to
foster developments and changes in the culture of representation and publicization that were to prove vital, in some cases fatal, to the exercise of royal government. By the end of her reign, the queen advanced and had to respond to
new conditions: an increase in print and public discussion; the emergence of a
metropolitan and consumer society stimulated not least by the royal court;
most of all the increasing centrality of monarchy in the public imagination and
a broad fascination with figures of authority and power and its representation.
Though they are large subjects which cannot be adequately treated here, we
must touch upon each of them insofar as they affected the publicizing and the
dilemmas in the publishing of regality.

Publicity and Politics

If Henry was the first English ruler to inhabit a world of print, the medium
rapidly took off, stimulating a wider readership that in turn accelerated print
production. The figures tell the story: where in the 1530s, on average about
eighty books were published annually, by the end of the century annual publications exceeded 250.[34] The expansion of print was accompanied by a clear perception that it carried with it a loss of royal control. As early as Edward VI's
reign, the government complained of 'divers printers and booksellers' who
published and sold 'whatsoever any light fantastical head liketh to invent'.[35]
Attempts to ban books only added to their frisson and commercial success. In
particular, pamphlets dealing with matters of state were, as a proclamation of
May 1551 put it, 'spread and cast abroad in streets at such privy corners where
they might best publish their malice'.[36] As we know, from mid-century on, the
increase in published output increased exponentially. But what has been less
remarked is the relationship of this to the monarchy and its own publicizations
of regality. As a perusal of a chronological catalogue of STC books – books
printed in England or in English before 1641 – discloses, over the second half of
the sixteenth century there was a marked increase in the number of books
about monarchs and courts, even books with terms like 'majesty' in the title.
The growth in print was stimulated by a wider public interest in regality and in
turn furthered that interest, making it all the more necessary for the queen and

government to use the medium and attempt to regulate it. For to not use print was to surrender it to others: as Joad Raymond has demonstrated, from about 1580, a 'business of news' emerged in England with pamphlets independent of earlier official directions and financed by a market.[37] Though pamphleteers were often loyal, the Martin Marprelate tracts, attacking the church hierarchy in a popular genre and plain prose, underlined the need for official responses and defences and so furthered even more the discussion of politics in print, as did momentous events abroad and at home, notably the Armada.[38] Whatever their mutual discomfort at times, print and authority were becoming inextricably interrelated and increasingly dependent upon each other. Through print, Elizabeth's speeches to parliament became addresses to the nation, just as the stories of her actions, progresses, and suitors provided good copy for the commerce of print.[39]

These developments and relationships gave rise to the emergence of a public sphere. The phrase was first coined by the German sociologist Jürgen Habermas to describe a condition that he regarded as a herald of modernity at the beginning of the eighteenth century. In Habermas's formulation, first published in 1962 but only translated into English in 1989, a bourgeois public sphere emerged at the dawn of the Enlightenment to replace the representational state and to provide a rational critique of sovereign authority.[40] For all the stimulus it has provided, there are many historical objections to Habermas's model, but over the last decade or so historians have rather been competing to push it further back into early modernity.[41] Accordingly, David Zaret has argued for the Civil War as the dawn of a public sphere in England; Joad Raymond sees its emergence with the birth of news pamphlets and news in the first decades of the Stuart age; and Peter Lake argues for an Elizabethan public sphere formed in and by confessional disputes and foreign threats combining in moments of crisis, such as the Anjou match or Armada.[42] While I would want to argue that Henry's divorce and the obsession with rumour was the moment a public sphere was formed, the important point is that by Elizabeth's reign, it not only existed but also was *seen* to exist and was itself the subject of discussion and representation. An account of a pageant staged for Elizabeth on her visit to the Earl of Leicester at Kenilworth in 1575 contains a scene which has elicited surprisingly little comment. During the entertainment, a Captain Cox is presented, carrying with him copies of Virgil and Spenser's works, Colin Clout (perhaps Skelton's poem) tales of Robin Hood, almanacs, and popular ballads – a remarkable bricolage of elite Latin and English writers with the texts of low culture, in the hands of a mere soldier.[43] Four years later, the pamphlet *News From The North* features, in conference with Simon Certain, one Piers Ploughman who enters an inn with a pile of books to discuss whether magistracy was ordained by God![44] In such cases, print is imagined and staged as the stimulus to, in this instance, radical political debate, even among those below the literate elites and whose names – Cox and Ploughman – may stand for Everyman. Such instances lead us to ponder whether the complaints of figures such as Dr. Richard Young were more than mere rhetorical paranoia. 'Who is there,' Young lamented in a sermon of 1575, 'be he of never so vile and base condition, what artificer, servant, prentice, but hath a commonwealth in his head and nothing in his mouth but the government of commonwealth and church'.[45] While he bears powerful witness to it, Young clearly disapproved of a public sphere which was rendering *arcana imperii* the stuff of tavern talk.[46] But not all commentators were as negative. A 1576 English edition of Francesco Patrizi's *A Moral Methode of Ciuile Policie* proclaims the view that 'it goeth not well in that commonweal [...] where citizens [...] dare not speak freely'.[47] Perhaps the notion of counsel lent itself to broader interpretation in the new world of print and publicity.[48] But whatever the views of the queen or her government, address to a public sphere and participation in public conversation were necessary. And with royal participation came both an impetus to yet further publicization and even some legitimization of it.

Print was part of a larger commerce that was itself in many ways related to developments in the culture and representation of authority. The wider cultural and ideological reach of commerce and consumption have been valuably explored for eighteenth-century England.[49] By contrast, little attention has been paid to the early modern period, the age of the birth of capitalism and a metropolitan culture of consumption and commodification, beyond a somewhat narrow concern with trade and economics. Commerce and commodification, however, were important to the early modern publicization and reception of authority in a number of ways. First, and a subject to which I shall briefly return, theatre was the first commercialized leisure industry, and it not only connected the crown and court, through the various Queen's companies or Lord Chamberlain's men, but also ubiquitously staged regality, as many of the most popular plays were those about kings and courts.[50] A fascination with power had other commercial expressions. From quite early in Elizabeth's reign we sense a desire to possess some personal memento or image of the queen. A draft proclamation of 1563 indeed acknowledges the 'desire' of 'all sorts of subjects both noble and mean' to acquire some portrait of Elizabeth and announces plans for a licensed image to satisfy it. From about 1572, perhaps to mark Elizabeth's triumph over smallpox as well as the rising of the Northern earls, a series of medals representing Elizabeth was issued;[51] from the 1580s the production of portrait miniatures became, in Roy Strong's words, almost a factory production;[52] and after 1588 even such lowly objects as playing cards figured Elizabeth and her victory.[53] The interest in regality was not confined to Elizabeth. From her reign, books of engraved images of all the monarchs of England were published as commercial enterprises.[54] But it was Elizabeth herself who made the monarchy part of the material culture of consumption.

Fig. 1. Souvenir Plate in Honour of Queen Elizabeth (1600)

Copies of the queen's speeches and accounts of her progresses poured from the presses along with verse panegyrics on her reign.[55] Souvenir plates like the one in the Museum of London (see Figure 1) and other artefacts evidently found willing purchasers who desired to 'own' something of the Queen. If Henry VIII was the first prince of print, it was Elizabeth who was the first monarch of the marketplace – the object of consumption and capitalist desire.

The performance of royal representation in a public sphere and the immersion of regality into a commercial society were to effect vital changes in the relationships between sovereigns and subjects, and in the perception and discussion of those relationships. Because in England there was no standing army or paid bureaucracy to enforce royal wishes, the monarch had always needed to 'secure compliance', in Penry Williams's phrase, through patronage and negotiation; aristocratic involvement in royal government was enshrined in the obligation of counsel.[56] Ultimately, authority depended on the compliance of the people which, for all the repetition of injunctions to obedience and deference, also needed to be secured, at times by withdrawal of unpopular measures (like the Amicable Grant) or by sops to the people's wishes.[57] Over the sixteenth century, however, the course of events and royal policy, notably the popular and nationalistic rhetoric deployed to support the break from Rome, involved the commonalty more than ever in the affairs of state. The Tudor ideology of the 'commonweal' may have been an official programme to cement unity at a time of threatened division, but it served to advance ideas of a polity in which the people were participants as well as subjects. Like the language of love, increasingly deployed by rulers over the sixteenth century, the discourse of the commonweal implied an element of reciprocity in the relationships of ruler and ruled. Neither the relationship of these developments to an emerging public sphere of print and rumour, nor the contribution of these languages to changes in political thinking, to the imaginings of politics, towards the end of the century has been adequately considered. But it may well be that they were the stimulus to that imagining of what Patrick Collinson and others have called a 'monarchical republic' in Elizabeth's reign.[58]

By the last decade of the Queen's rule there was certainly a lively debate about, even interrogation of, the business of politics and the exercise of power. As Malcolm Smuts and others have argued, we discern a broad interest in Roman histories, especially Livy and Tacitus, and in the accounts of (good and bad) princes, republics, and favourites that they recounted.[59] Though he was not published in translation until later, the figure lurking behind discussions of power and politics was, of course, Niccolo Machiavelli, who was widely known in Italian editions and, among the students at Oxford, Cambridge, and the Inns of Court, through bootleg manuscript translations.[60] Machiavelli infamously stripped authority of its foundation in Christian religion and ethics to expose the naked force and guile behind the exercise of rule. His works cast a shadow over early modern Europe and were the subject of near-universal condemnation. But Machiavelli's challenge to traditional thinking and his language had equally a nearly universal impact.[61] Even Elizabeth I echoed the Florentine when she wrote to William Lambarde 'now the wit of the fox is everywhere on foot'.[62]

Perhaps the most radical of all Machiavelli's moves in *The Prince* was his exposure of the exercise of rule as an artifice, as a business involving performance, misrepresentation as well as representation, and at times dissimulation.[63] In England the representation and performance of monarchy in a public sphere drew attention not only to the monarchy, as we have seen, but also to its performances – and perhaps to power as a series of performances. Scholars have frequently quoted but not, I think, sufficiently pondered the novel and increasing use of metaphors of the stage to describe rule in late sixteenth- and early seventeenth-century England. In Elizabeth's words to her Parliament in November 1586: 'Princes, you know, stand upon stages, so that their actions are viewed and beheld of all men.'[64] Most obviously her metaphor, often repeated, was prompted by the newly erected theatres being built around London from the 1570s in response to market demand. But, as I have suggested, theatre itself was related to, and drew much of its material from, an interest in princes and power. The growth of the theatres, I would suggest, was one expression of the impact of the Tudor monarchs on the cultural imaginary. But the theatre became a Machiavellian space in which authority – that is, monarchy – was not only represented and performed but also scrutinized as representation and performance. Was Henry V a virtuous prince or a dissimulator who by artful rhetoric and disguise manipulated his subjects? Was his success dependent on craftiness and guile, as much as on faith and bravery? Theatre staged kings as human and fallible and represented their doubleness – their interior as well as public life, their sexual desires, jealousies, and passions as well as public acts.[65] If the events and representations of Henry's reign had opened such subjects, theatre returned its own radical staging of them into a public sphere of political debate and imagining. Plays not only represented, they also helped to refashion politics, in both broad and specific ways. As Elizabeth famously observed, 'I am Richard II. Know ye not that'.[66]

Representation and Revolution

Elizabeth has been praised for her skilful efforts to negotiate the necessity to publicize her rule and the need to retain some element of mystery: to be both sacred and popular. Whatever our evaluation of her success, it is clear that the circumstances of that negotiation changed over the half-century of her reign, and that she was by no means the least of the agents of change. Admiration for the queen's success at the business of representation, in the eyes of many contemporaries as well as historians, was undoubtedly strengthened by what appeared to be the conspicuous failures in these arts of at least her first two Stuart successors. It may be, however, that here, as in other respects, Elizabeth's legacy was far from unproblematic. During the last years of her reign the figuring of the queen as an iconic mask suggests some attempt to retreat from the glare of public scrutiny, as well as to deny the devastating political consequences of her mortality.[67] And, as I have suggested, though she skilfully turned the limitations of her sex in many ways to her advantage, in so doing she gendered the art of royal representation, the portrayal of private and public bodies, in ways that male successors could not emulate. But most of all, her bringing herself and the monarchy to the centre of public attention bequeathed a condition, a challenge, and a role to a successor which required the most skilful of performers on the public stage.

The traditional narrative is that Elizabeth's Stuart successors not only failed in these arts but failed spectacularly. Interestingly, they failed very differently – or in completely contrasting ways. James VI and I, we have learned, from a Scotland where the sacralization of regality had not reached English heights, demystified and debased monarchical authority by his vulgar behaviour, debauched court and disregard for his representation and image.[68] Charles I (1625-1649), by contrast, preoccupied with his representation, emphasized the sanctity of his kingship and through careful attention to ritual mystified the royal body but, silent and remote, appeared detached from his people.[69] Each characterization is too simplistic. James I wrote Scriptural paraphrases and exegeses not least to underpin his divine rule; Charles I's court had some reach into popular culture, and the king certainly cared about the love of the people.[70] But it is the different emphases in their representation that remain striking. These may be explained straightforwardly in terms of character and personal style. But in both cases – one thinks of James's writing a verse libel to answer his detractors, or an occasional common touch by Charles – there appears to have been an element of strategy, that is, a consciousness of the art of representation and of its difficulties.

It may be that, as well as their quite individual failings, the tensions between the king's two bodies – the public and private, the need to sacralize and yet demystify royal authority – could no longer be contained, as early seventeenth-century newspapers, city comedies, satires, squibs, and libels stripped away the veils of mystery. Certainly during moments such as the Overbury affair, the exposure of the court, of courtiers and, by implication at least, of the king to public examination and verbal vilification reached new heights.[71] As political discontents and divisions mounted from the 1620s, contemporaries began to note the changed tenor of public debate. Later there was widespread talk of the 'paper bullets' that had preceded, and enabled, the outbreak of violence in civil war.[72] One might argue that the Civil War, still more the regicide, was made possible only by a long process of demystification which had rendered monarchy a human condition and the monarch a man, to be arraigned and judged for his crimes. But again I would suggest that, though inviting, such an argument is too simple. For in some ways it was the mystification of sovereignty that led to violent revolution, to political iconoclasm. And as events were swiftly to manifest, subjects as well as rulers faced the complexities of the sacralization and demystification of authority.

For all the broad circulation of squibs and libels critical of the court or crown, we should not forget the popular desire for keepsakes of Elizabeth, some venerated as near-sacred icons. Nor should we fail to note that some of the disappointment with James I stemmed from his failure to sustain the mystery of monarchical rituals and kingship. Charles I, then, may not have been entirely wrong in thinking that the mystification of rule might also be popular. Certainly, as he faced conflict, defeat, imprisonment, and then death, he endeavoured to garner the support of the people for sacred kingship. And his appeal, perhaps too late for his personal victory, was successfully to repaint kingship in sacred hues. It has often been observed that the *Eikon Basilike,* supposedly Charles I's own account of his life and last days, was published on the day of regicide. What has not been noted is that the day of the execution of a divine king also saw the publication of the text of the most powerful sacralization of monarchy, a work that was immediately a popular bestseller and that went into thirty-six editions in the year of publication.[73] The famous Marshal frontispiece, depicting the king as a Christ figure, gave rise to miniatures, medals, and objects figuring Charles as sacred martyr which circulated into popular culture, as well as among the king's immediate followers.[74] Like Elizabeth, Charles became a popular icon, a subject of veneration and commemoration, albeit in different ways. I have argued elsewhere that the short-lived English republic may have been undermined by the powerful image and memory of sacred kingship.[75] But it was undermined as much by its own lack of the mystical and the sacred. Though defended in part as the work of divine providence, the republic was presented and justified in a new rationalist, utilitarian language which seems never to have gained widespread, certainly not popular, support. Indeed, the most articulate spokesman for *de facto* government, Thomas Hobbes, was condemned as much in parliamentarian as royalist circles and became, not unlike Machiavelli to whom he owed a debt too rarely acknowledged, a demonized figure for decades after the publication of *Leviathan* in 1651.[76] The respective fortunes of the *Eikon Basilike* and *Leviathan* not only nicely capture the continuing engagement with both the sacralization and demystification of authority at a critical moment, they also warn us not to subscribe to a Whig narrative of the rationalization of power as the cause and consequence of revolution.

If the Civil War did not have its origins in a simple desacralization of authority, neither was its legacy one of rationalization and demystification, even after eleven years without monarchy. If anything, the experience of civil war and republic, and as much the determination not to see them repeated, suggested a need and sharpened a desire for the mysteries of regality. On the other hand, the lessons of civil war and regicide could not safely be forgotten, chief among them that mystery and divinity had not secured a crown. The ambiguity about sacralization and demystification that was an early modern condition therefore, not surprisingly, resurfaced at the Restoration, albeit in somewhat different ways. 'Let a prince,' advised the author of *England's Beauty* in 1661, perhaps with Charles I's failings in mind, 'show himself affable to the people, but let him not suffer himself to be contemned', held in contempt, despised, and pilloried.[77] 'Matters of policy, the arts of government,' a sermon of Edmund Callamy still asserted in 1680, 'are things too sacred to be profaned by unhallowed hands.'[78] Yet as another preacher had by this time come to acknowledge, men were 'arguing pro and con, making it a moot case whether monarchy be the government that God approves or whether the nation (was) as happy under a republic'.[79] Far from being silenced by its revolutionary explosion during the 1640s, the noise of print and public debate in Restoration England spilled out into coffee houses and clubs as well as congregations and street corners.[80] Whatever mystery subjects desired in their new king, it was a mystery that had to be enacted on a public stage and in a public sphere, by a man who was 'affable', as well as a monarch who was sacred. If that did not present difficulties enough, one senses that, for all the invocation of the past, some had come to see that the arts of representation were just that – arts, a fiction as well as a performance, still more that the claim to mystery itself may be no more than 'poetical and rhetorical flourishes'.[81] At the Restoration, that is, English men, and now more than ever women, sought a ruler who could reconcile seemingly irreconcilable needs and who could sustain and render believable what at some level they sensed were fictions of state, not truths of faith.

No monarch was better suited to that impossible brief, no ruler of early modern England more successful in negotiating ambiguity, than Charles II. The king's own experiences had been of sacred authority and the indignities of flight and exile; his upbringing had been orthodox Anglican and his companions in exile Catholic, but his tutor had been Hobbes. He had heard from his father the importance of convictions and principles, yet had lived for twenty years a life of compromise and manoeuvre. He had been schooled in sincerity but had necessarily learned disguise. And successive circumstances had led him to perform as pious son, martial leader, rightful heir, king in exile, man of the people, diplomat and merciful sovereign. Perhaps such experiences naturally endowed him with the qualities he needed. But Charles certainly intuited, with greater acuteness than most, the doubleness of his position. And he negotiated the ambiguity brilliantly. No king touched more than Charles to cure the king's evil.[82] At the same time, none was more openly available to his subjects, walking unattended in St James's Park.[83] Charles joined his people on the streets of London to assist with quenching the Great Fire;[84] and infamously he paraded his mistresses and publicized his sex life in a manner that suggests strategy.[85] Charles II was not only both mystical and familiar but also, as I have argued elsewhere, made his very ordinariness a means of elevating his kingship, of attracting public affection and support.[86] For sure, Charles was sharply criticized in satires, but by the end of the reign, while a public monument commemorated his role in fighting the Fire, his monarchy was lauded in sacred strains not heard for decades. Unquestionably, it was the crisis of the Popish Plot and the renewed threat of civil war that led many again to emphasize the sacred.[87] But Charles had made it possible for the sacred to be popular – and indeed for the 'affable' to be mystified.

His personal acumen is nowhere better demonstrated than in the fate of his successor and brother, James II (1685-1688). James saw Charles's triumph, but it is not clear that he understood the ambiguities at its core. He emulated the script of – he embodied – sacred kingship without pursuing popularity (and he had enjoyed that as Duke of York); and he lost his throne. But even the 1688 Revolution did not simply mark a modernizing stage on the road to a rational attitude to power.[88] Revealingly, the last of the Stuarts, Queen Anne, appears to have drawn on the examples of her most successful kin in an attempt to nego-tiate the ambiguities of the sacred and demystified. Like Charles II, she fre-quently touched – she was the last monarch to do so – for the king's evil; and she adopted Elizabeth I's motto, along with other representational tropes, as her own.[89] But she presented herself, too, as the mother, and on canvas she appears almost as a bourgeois housewife, with no hint of the mystical or iconic.[90]

If Anne's sex was again a resource, so unquestionably were her dynasty and her nationality. The Hanoverians, who enjoyed no such advantages, attained neither sacred status nor popularity. Significantly, they were the first rulers to be represented in that site of demystified power, the (sometimes scatological) cartoon. Eighteenth-century England is often presented, and indeed often fig-ured itself, as an age of reason. But even at the end of my sketch, I would not want to suggest the ambiguity of sacralization and demystification resolved. The narrative is rather one of a dialogue and tension between the sacred and demystified, both related to the necessary process of publicizing and publishing authority. It is, as some have observed, a narrative that continues because it expresses a still deeper psychological doubleness – a desire for and loathing of authority that is founded on the love and fear of that analogue of the sovereign, the father.[91] And recent experience in England has familiarized us with the ten-sions within the modern royal family, between notions of mysterious majesty and popular accessibility, not to mention given us a princess whose ordinari-ness served to render her sacred. For all that they may endure, however, the ten-sions and ambiguities in authority of sacralization and demystification need to be historicized and have, in early modernity, their specific, key moments. That the moments of greatest difficulty in resolving this ambiguity were moments of political crisis and revolution, and that the rulers who most successfully nego-tiated the ambiguity died peacefully in their beds, only underlines the impor-tance for the master narrative of a subject yet to be explored.

King for a Day. Games of Inversion, Representation, and Appropriation in Ancient Regime Europe

Marc Jacobs

> Just as one cannot understand daylight, white, and happiness without the contrast of night, black and sorrow, so too the boundaries of rule were defined by the existence of its opposite.[1]

New computer and video games enable us to become mayor of Sim City, to be a ruler in the Age of Empires, to be Caesar or Louis XIV for a few hours. By just entering the computer shop we already hope to experience that the 'customer is king'. Children celebrating their birthday are crowned in the classroom or in a McDonald's outlet. In kingdoms like the United Kingdom, Belgium, or Spain there are hundreds of reigning queens today: beauty queens for instance. In France or the Low Countries, there were, in any given year of the early modern period, many hundreds of temporary kings for a day, for a week or for a year. Mock kings were elected in corporations, in villages and in neighbourhoods, in winter, spring, summer or fall. Ordinary people who won the popinjay shooting competition in the local archers' guild became king for a year. However, this could also happen to persons of royal blood, as the famous example of the Infanta Isabella in Brussels in 1615 illustrates perfectly. In the cradle, the daughter of the Spanish King Philip II (1556-1598) seemed to be destined to become a queen. But the only acting queen's title she could achieve in history as *lieu de mémoire* was that of an archery competition, an event that was cultivated so intensely that in Belgium, four centuries later, the notion of archer's queen is still associated with Isabella. This leads us right into the heart of this chapter. Common people could dress up or act as a king, a queen or a court member. Even more interesting, however, is what happens when even real kings and rulers become king for a day, or when a fake court subjects a real court.

'King for a Day', 'the King drinks' or the 'Bean King' are different names of the game I focus upon in this contribution. It took place in households on 6 January or Twelfth Night, also known as the Feast of the Three Kings. Since the early modern period, in some regions, groups of star singers have dressed up as kings to roam in the streets, evoking the magi visiting Christ. Alongside these customs and other performances, stories and images of such 'Winter

Kings' circulated for centuries. The number of twelve nights refers to a threshold phase in the festive year cycle, marked by the winter solstice, Christmas and, in many regions, the beginning of a New Year: a time packed with rites of passage. Next to mock popes, bishops – as echoed in Santa Claus – and Winter Kings, all sorts of 'rulers for a day' took up their temporary festive reign in this liminal period. The concept of liminality, developed by Arnold van Gennep and Victor Turner, refers to a betwixt-and-between phase in rites of passage. Van Gennep analytically divided rites associated with passing from one collective or individual state or status to another into three stages: (1) separation; (2) a liminal phase involving seclusion from everyday life and rules; and (3) reaggregation. In the liminal phase, special rules of conduct and order apply, for example under the authority of a mock ruler.[2] Building on Van Gennep's work, Turner has generated interesting theories for the study of ritual processes, for example by observing that among participants living outside the norms and fixed categories of the social system, a feeling of solidarity and unity emerges, *communitas*, and that this also has a structure, although its purpose is antistructural.[3] Turner emphasized the role of deep communication in liminal contexts, both to individuals and to society at large. Rites of passage fulfil a crucial task: inculcating a society's rules and values in those who are to become its full-fledged members or in those who renew or upgrade their commitment.

In cultural history since the 1970s, it has become widely accepted that rites and images about the 'world turned upside down' actually reinforce the normal social structures and hierarchy, both on a cognitive level and by performing a safety-valve function.[4] The point to be made in this contribution is that many 'king for a day' rites, stories and images also worked that way in Ancient Regime Europe. The proliferation of these representations in the early modern period reflects, and is even related to, the evolution of notions of authority within households of all sorts, including the metaphorical national households of new, centralizing monarchies. It was significant for the concept of royalty that paper or other crowns and other regal paraphernalia were abundantly available outside real courts, in private homes and inns. The huge quantities of circulating printed king's letters or paintings representing 'the king drinks' scene reveal that we are dealing with a powerful format. By extension, the question arises of whether the representation of the Three Kings adorning the almost naked and vulnerable Child King also helped to construct and comment upon royal status and entitlements in the last two millennia. I furthermore wish to explore the special significance of these phenomena when they took place in a real court or when a real, reigning monarch was involved – in situations with an embedded Russian dolls-effect. The 'king for a day' format could be used to reinforce but also to attack royalty. Which historical examples are available? The proof of the pudding may be discerned in the French Revolutionary period, when an Ancient Regime in Europe with roots in early medieval and Roman empires was turned upside down and an old system dismantled. Did the 'king drinks' format also work in that huge festival of liminalities, and at what price?

Emperor Nero as Saturnalia King

In the *Annales* of Tacitus (c. 55- c. 117), the narrative about the last days of the life of Britannicus begins with a strange scene:

> On the holiday of the Saturnalia a group of his age-
> mates was playing, among other games, at being king by
> dice-roll, and this lot had fallen to Nero. And so he
> assigned to others various tasks that would not embar-
> rass them, but Britannicus he bade rise and advance to
> the center to sing a song – expecting that mockery of
> the boy would follow, since he was unaccustomed to
> sober parties, let alone drunken ones. But Britannicus
> with equanimity began a song in which he alluded to his
> own exclusion from his home and fatherland and
> throne. The result was a rather too obvious pity, for
> night and revelry had done away with dissimulation.
> And Nero understood the ill will against him and inten-
> sified his hatred.[5]

The audience seems to have made a fatal mistake by forgetting the presence of the real emperor and, hence, the necessity to continue playing the double role. This led straight to the death of Britannicus, Nero's stepbrother and son of the previous emperor Claudius in the year 55. Commentator Suetonius suggested that Nero was jealous not only of Britannicus's birthright and growing influence but also and in particular of his singing voice. The version of Tacitus throws another light on the matter. The scene of the murder, instant death by poison during dinner, has the same characteristics: everyone was expected to keep up appearances at all times. The imprudent courtiers fled, giving away that something was really wrong, and hence taking serious personal risks. Nero explained that Britannicus had had a seizure and then observed the reactions of the others present.

Shadi Bartsch used these extreme cases of keeping up appearances to discuss 'theatricality' in her book *Actors in the Audience*. The reversal of the normal one-way direction of the spectators' gaze depends on them knowing that they are themselves watched. The unequal distribution of power requires all those present or even playing alone to constantly monitor their behaviour – or else.

The model applied to the life of Nero shows a very complex construction. Where do the exchanges characterized by theatricality stop? The extreme power of Nero amounts to the ability to impose his own fictions upon the world. Tacitus portrays a man whose power is characterized by his ability to decide what truth in the public realm will be: the audience is compelled to follow a script over which the ruler has total control. But it works in both directions. By introducing the notions of public and private transcripts, James Scott emphasized that we get the wrong impression if we visualize actors perpetually wearing fake smiles and moving with the reluctance of a chain gang. There is always some margin for appropriating the performance. Deference and flattery can be artfully manipulated to achieve other objectives: crucial elements to understand how and why royal courts function.[6]

Thinking through an upside-down king's game played in a place fraught with theatricality is revealing. Everyone knows it is just a game, where the royal status and several roles to be played in his neighbourhood are only temporary and context-related. Everyone involved is supposed to loosen up and play along, but even in this liminal situation, the usual power relations are still very much present. It illustrates the importance of dealing with highly ambiguous situations, with multiplicities of meaning, and with the implicit ability to mobilize formats from other contexts.[7] The most extreme situation we may think of is a scene from the last days of Louis XVI (1754-1793). It will conclude our journey through an Ancient Regime, starting in the Middle Ages and ending in the French Revolution.

From Saturnalia to Twelfth Night

In ancient Rome, the religious rites of 17 December, the feast of Saturn, continued in profane festivities for two to seven days: the Saturnalia. Shops and institutions were closed. Public gambling was allowed. Masters served their servants at mealtimes. As the story about Nero illustrated, lots or dice were thrown in age groups, to choose one member as a king of the feast.[8] The Kalendae devoted to Janus – 1 January being the start of the Roman Year from 153 B.C. onwards – were marked by even more merry-making. In between, there was also the winter solstice, fixed at 25 December in the calendar of Julius Caesar.

The new Christian feast of the Nativity, celebrated on 25 December in the second half of the fourth century (first certain record in 354), replaced the Birthday of the Sun, the object of worship in a cult sponsored by the Roman Empire between 274 and 323. Fixing and celebrating a birthday of Christ worked like a magnet, extinguishing the Roman feasts just mentioned but reshuffling important elements, rites and metaphors to other feasts that popped up in its orbit. A whole string of holy days and invented traditions clustered between 24 December and 6 January in the late Roman Empire and the Early Middle Ages. The Eastern churches celebrated Epiphany, the baptism of Christ by John the Baptist, on 6 January from the second century onwards. In the medieval Western Christian world, the adoration of Christ by the magi gradually eclipsed other stories and elements connected to 6 January, while also – in the long run – appropriating elements of the old Saturnalia feast. Matthew 2.1-12, 16 mentions an unspecified number of wise men coming from the East with myrrh, frankincense and gold to worship the Child. By the sixth century, these characters frequently were combined with the figures of kings, predicted in Psalms 72.10-11 as people coming to honour the Messiah, a link first suggested by Tertullian (160-220). This feast overwhelmed the original notion of Epiphany. In 567 the council of Tours declared the twelve days between the Nativity and the Epiphany as one festive cycle. By the eighth century, the Christian appropriation of twelve days of celebration following the winter solstice was in place, including 1 January, declared to be the feast of Christ's Circumcision.[9] Recent studies by Ronald Hutton and Richard Trexler provide ample information on this fascinating early medieval fixation, construction

Fig. 1. Mosaic of the Adoration of the Magi *(561), Sant'Apollinare Nuovo, Ravenna, Italy. This representation was commissioned by the Byzantine monarch Justinian (d. 565). The upper bodies of the magi were repainted centuries later, which explains the presence of the names above the figures. Notice the Phrygian bonnets.*

and invention of these Twelve Days as a system, of the Twelfth Day in particular, and of the story of the Three Kings (see Figure 1).[10]

A few months before the canonization of Charlemagne (800-814) in 1165, the gift by Frederick Barbarossa of relics of the 'Three Kings', translated from Milan, to the archbishop of Cologne soon became a major attraction. Gradually, in the following centuries, a visit to the Cologne shrine became part of the rite of passage of the new German kings in the Middle Ages.[11] This illustrates how important the invented stories, traditions and images of the Three Kings 'of Cologne' had become for religious and political legitimacy and representation of German and other kings. The format of the Three Kings or the theatrical overlay of the magi was also used for international encounters and joint performances by European royals in the fourteenth and fifteenth centuries. The strongest example is probably the meeting in Paris on 4 and 5 January 1378 between Charles V of France, the Holy Roman Emperor Charles IV and the latter's son Wenceslaus, King of the Romans, who acted out the magi drama. Richard Trexler concluded: 'The royals of Europe, and their bourgeois emulators, had cast themselves as magi – or as one particular magus. They seemed to derive their authority by reenacting the biblical event that featured those they emulated.'[12]

Already by the twelfth century, religious communities had invented their own upside-down tradition. The 'feast of fools' was seen as an exercise in humility of the higher clergy, as they temporarily handed leadership in religious ceremonies around New Year to the lower clergy. Since the thirteenth century, the feast was familiar in cloisters and chapters in France until its gradual repression in the fifteenth century and its abolition in the sixteenth. From France it spread into the Low Countries and the British Isles. A similar feast was that of the 'boy bishop'. It grew out of a custom in German areas where the junior clergy and assistants of cathedrals were allowed to hold mock processions on the holy days of Christmas. In several regions in the twelfth century, the custom intertwined with the cult of St Nicholas and the election of a cathedral choirboy to impersonate the bishop on his feast on 6 December or on 28 December, the feast of the Holy Innocents, one of the aforementioned Twelve Days in the orbit of Christmas that has appropriated Saturnalia features.[13] Sandra Billington suggested that:

> The Christian justification for midwinter customs of
> inversion was Christ's humble birth, which was cele-
> brated as the ultimate and Pauline example of the lowest
> in society as 'kyng of chrystmas' [...] Christ features
> throughout medieval drama as the apparent mock, fool
> king, whose greater kingdom, not of this world, is
> misunderstood by men conscious only of their worldly

power, and it would seem from the crown of thorns that this was how he was treated in his own time. The seasonal dethronement of kings at Christmas was a reminder to those in power of their relation to Christ and of the limitations of their human authority.[14]

At the end of the thirteenth century, with an early notice on the year 1282 in a Tournai chronicle of Gilles li Muisis (1272-1353), the first traces are found of an interesting feast that echoed Saturnalia descriptions of abundant eating, drinking and the appointment of a king for a day or an evening.[15] For the sumptuous banquets that marked Twelfth Night, a special cake was baked that might contain dried fruit, flour, honey, or spice but also always contained a pea or a bean.[16] Whoever found the pea or bean became King or Queen of the Pea or Bean for the evening. The sixteenth and seventeenth centuries are considered the high days of this custom, although the custom is still known in several European regions in the twenty-first century. Since the Late Middle Ages, the number of human beings acting and being treated as a king for a winter's day or evening, temporarily sky-rocketed every year on January 6.

As I have pointed out above, this was only the tip of the iceberg of the use of royal titles and paraphernalia outside the context of 'real' dynastic successions, courts and official state ceremonies. A significant portion of the total mock king population was connected to the Winter season. Famous in medieval and early modern fantasy were the stories, songs and plays of the battle between Winter and Summer, often personified as kings. This gave inspiration to represent or re-enact their adventures on stage, in feasts or even in collective actions. Sandra Billington recently published an impressive catalogue of Winter Kings and Queens on the British Isles in the early modern period.[17] In the fifteenth and sixteenth centuries, youth groups or neighbourhoods on the European continent also enacted mock winter monarchies or constructed their worlds in ice or snow, like the realm of 'le Roy de Clacquedent' in 1434 in Artois, or the 'roy de glace, duc de gellee, comte de neige', mentioned in a late fifteenth-century text in the same region.[18]

Kings' Chits and Printing

The transition from the Middle Ages to the early modern period is characterized by the implementation of techniques of exercising power at a long distance. Strong examples are the seafaring and military technologies related to the great discoveries and the printing press. Richard Trexler has demonstrated brilliantly the connection between the discoveries and the story about the magi. Prester or Priest John was said to be a descendant of the three kings and

Fig. 2. The Adoration of the Magi, *by Vasco Fernandes (?) (c. 1504). This painting was commissioned at the occasion of Cabral's discovery of Brazil in 1500: one of the magi represents a Native American.*

the ruler of a homeland rich enough to yield the presents brought by the magi. His localization in Ethiopia is one reason for the breakthrough of the black magus from the 1440s onward. The quest for the magi in the late fifteenth and sixteenth centuries was a matter not only of exploring sacred geography but also of economics – a search for homelands with great wealth in spices and precious metals. In diplomatic missions to the pope, Portuguese diplomats (for example in 1485 and 1514) referred to Psalm 7.2 ('The kings of the Arabians and of Saba shall bring gifts, and all princes shall adore thee and all nations shall serve thee') to legitimate their expeditions. Both on his first (1492) and second (1495) trip, Columbus referred to the magi, as for example the mistaking of Cuba for Sheba/Saba illustrates. The inclusion of a Native American with feathers as a magus in a 1504 painting of the adoration, commissioned at the occasion of Cabral's discovery of Brazil in 1500, speaks volumes (Figure 2).[19]

The introduction of mass-produced kings' letters or chits was an important development that introduced the king's game to many families and groups in early modern society. The kings' letters [*billets des rois, koningsbrieven...*] were woodcuts, occasionally copper engravings, that were subdivided into compartments of images and connected to an appropriate poem. The compartments and the accompanying texts were cut into strips that served both as lots and as small scripts for the kings' play to be enacted on Twelfth Night. The person who drew the lot or script of 'king' played the king's role, and so on, yielding a whole court. There were variants with sixteen figures and variants with thirty-two figures, including female courts around queens. In the Holy Roman Empire, the first traces of an election of a king and a court by drawing these *lootjes* were found in 1550.[20] Marnix of Saint-Aldegonde projected it to heaven in *Den Byencorf der h. Roomsche Kercke* (1574) and even pushed the argument so far to suggest that St Mary had become 'queen of heaven' by getting the bean from a cake:

> Jae hy heeft eenen yegelick zijn Ampt ende Office
> voorgeschreven ghelijck men op de drye Conincx-avont
> eenen yegelycken zyn ambt en office met briefkens
> uutdeylt: onse L. Vrouwe heeft de Boone uut de Koeck
> ghecreghen, ende is de Coninghinne der Hemelen.[21]

It is striking to notice that the first mention in Dutch of the use of a king's letter in combination with the bean custom constitutes a vicious attack on the legitimacy of the notion of royal divinity and divine royalty.

Fig. 3. Characters on a Kings' Letter, *by a collaborator of Maerten van Cleve (1527-1581). This painting, dated in 1575, shows eighteen characters on a kings' letter, with their titles.*

A painting by a collaborator of Maerten van Cleve (1527-1581), dated to 1575, shows eighteen characters on a king's letter, along with titles (Figure 3). Interesting is the fact that there is an alternation of men and women, and that women are given roles such as councillor, secretary, surgeon and fool. There were several possible figurations of that one-day court, as we can deduce from the royal monopoly for three years granted on 7 October 1596 to Laureys van Secillien to print and sell 'all kinds of kings' letters' [*alle soorten van Conincxbrieven*].[22] A king's letter published in 1635 by Abraham van den Bosse (1602-1676) counts twenty-four characters. It includes a kind of small manual on how to use a king's letter and includes role descriptions such as:

Le Roy.
A ce coup je suis dans la gloire
L'on me sert comme un Roy.
Bachus me fait maintenant croire.
Que je suis Prince quand je boy.

[...]

L'escuier tranchant.
Tout les bons morceaux que je trouve.
Je les presente honnestement.
A ce Monarque de la febve.
Qu'pert son Royaume en dormant.[23]

In fact, these examples also refer to another repertoire, not necessarily connected to Epiphany. In an early sixteenth-century letter, the Spanish humanist Luis Vivès (1492-1540) told the story of a drunken sleeping man who was selected to be subjected to the role of 'king for a day', with real court members playing along when the man awakened and got through the day. In many similar variants in the sixteenth and seventeenth centuries, the court in question was presented as that of the Duke of Burgundy, Philip the Good (1419-1467), in fifteenth-century Bruges or Brussels. The Duke allegedly set up the event to teach the court members about vanities. It was later transformed into an instructive play for young potentials of elite groups in seventeenth- and eighteenth-century colleges.[24]

The Winter King and Queen

One of the trigger events of the Thirty Years War (1618-1648) became associated with the notion of 'Winter King', in particular in court circles and educated elites in the seventeenth and eighteenth centuries. In the early 1620s, it was even the talk of the town, in the streets, shops and inns throughout Europe. The story of the Count Palatine Frederick V (1619-1620), after his marriage in 1613 to the English Princess Elizabeth, is famous.[25] He was the Elector Palatine and leader of the Protestant Union. After the death of the esoteric Emperor Rudolph II (1612) and just before the death of Emperor Matthias (1619), the fanatical Catholic and Habsburg Archduke Ferdinand became King of Bohemia in 1617, quickly ending the policy of religious toleration in that region. On 26 August 1619, the Bohemians, claiming that the crown of Bohemia was elective and not hereditary, asked Frederick to become their king. Frederick accepted, counting on the support of the Union and, although in vain, of his father-in-law, the English King James I (1603-1625). Frederick ascended the throne on 4 November 1619. Ferdinand II (1619-1637), by now Emperor, sent the army of the Catholic League under the command of Tilly and Bucquoy. The famous Battle of the White Mountain (Wittenberg) on 8 November 1620 resulted in the defeat of the Bohemian troops. King Frederick had to go on the run with his wife Queen Elizabeth and their children and ended up in The Hague; his crown did not witness a second winter. Frederick V was henceforth known by his nickname, 'the Winter King', also a reference to the mock kings of Christmas, Epiphany or Carnival.

Frederick V was an obvious target to connect the idea of temporary king to a real royal person, and hence a problem for collective image building of royalty. A tsunami of caricatures, pamphlets and booklets followed the symbolic 1620 earthquake in Bohemia and Wittenberg.[26] In Antwerp the pamphlets *Postillon pour chercher le Roy déchassé de Prague* and *Postillioen uutghesonden om te soecken den verjaegden Coninck van Praghe, 1621* were published by Abraham Verhoeven two months after the Wittenberg battle.[27] The Dutch version was part of the famous series *Nieuwe Tijdinghen*, since 1617 the first regular 'newspaper' in the Spanish Netherlands, published by Abraham Verhoeven (c. 1575-1652), an information broker well connected to the Brussels courts and information networks.[28] The newspaper issue was reproduced, copied and appropriated in several manuscript collections in the Spanish Netherlands and the Dutch Republic. *Postill(i)o(e)n* is the story of a post rider trying to locate Frederick after his flight from Prague. One episode refers to an inquiry in Frederick's base town Heidelberg, where the rider asked the Calvinist ministers and notables if they were hiding Frederick in order to make him king for a day [*koning lappeken*] on Twelfth Night.[29] In a newspaper issue of Verhoeven's dated January 1621 (no. 8), a special poem entitled *Coninck-feest van den Palatin* (Kings' Feast of the Palatine) was published, next to a translation in French, *Joyeux Billets et rhimes pour créer le roy*. Frederick was presented as *Coninck Lappeken van corte rijcken*, literally 'the fake king of short empire'. Count Heinrich Matthias of Thurn, head of the Bohemian Protestant nobility and a key figure in the Defenestration of Prague in 1619, acted as the chamberlain. The Protestant Union was presented as the bad councillor; James I as the steward [*hofmeester*] who noticed that things were going wrong. Count Ernst von Mansfelt was the 'voorsnijder'. He was sent by the Duke of Savoye with troops to help the Bohemians. He cut the pieces so big that the king almost choked.[30] And so on... In short, a sharp political analysis of the European chessboard at the moment of the fall of the Winter King was presented in several popular formats and games about the temporary festive king.[31]

In the so-called *Roffelpot*-polemics of 1621, rhymed texts in Dutch and French were exchanged between Catholics and Calvinists. These texts toyed with the references to *Koning-lap* [King Fake] and the membership of carnival guilds when discussing the impact of the story of the King of Bohemia on public opinion. The connection between carnival, the 'king for a day' and alcohol was very powerful.[32] In a brilliant and controversial book, Frances Yates explained the crucial importance of the court of Frederick V and its subsequent downfall for what she provocatively called the *Rosicrucian Enlightenment*. She claimed that this chemistry between magic, alchemy and the Cabala experienced an Indian Summer under the Winter King and that this was a significant phase on the road to the so-called Scientific Revolution in the seventeenth century. Yates discussed one of the 'king for a day' images by pointing out that the image of the Habsburg Eagle triumphing over the prostrate figure of Frederick, who lost the crown of Bohemia while supporters put feathers, symbolizing Palatinate towns, into the Eagle's wings, was in fact a reference to passages in the Rosicrucian manifestos.[33] In any case, these images were multivocal, appropriated in several networks and had an important effect. They were part of a very broad propaganda campaign against the Winter King but were the very opposite of a win-win-operation – especially for elective royalty and even for the emperor.

Over and over again, use of the format or images of temporary kings or the Epiphany in order to make a statement on international dynastic politics proved to be a very strong weapon. Important changes took place in the first half of the sixteenth century that saw the disappearance of royals from paintings in which they were pictured as magi adoring Jesus, at a moment when mass production gained momentum. For example, Maximilian (1493-1519) appears in many adorations, Charles V (1530-1556) in some, and their successors Philip II and Emperor Ferdinand are absent in such paintings. Trexler suggested that this was connected to the fact that the printing press revolutionized the forms of legitimacy and also criticism.[34]

The format of the kings' letters proved useful, for instance to comment on relations between the Turkish and the Austrian empires, in particular in the early eighteenth century.[35] An interesting early modern example is an engraving by the Dutch artist Romeyn de Hooghe (1645-1708). In 1689 he published a print with the title *L'Epiphane du Nouveau Antichrist*, which represented James II (1685-1688), Louis XIV (1643-1715), William III (1689-1702), the pope and other leaders (Figure 4). The format that had been used three centuries earlier to legitimate royal interactions was turned into a powerful weapon against royal figurations. A more recent powerful example is an image of the 'three kings from the East' by the Dutch cartoonist Louis Raemaekers (1869-1956), published for the first time in 1914 (Figure 5). Contemporary commentators recognized them as Emperor Wilhelm II, Emperor Franz Joseph, and the Turkish sultan, bringing weapons and war as a present to Mary and a frightened child, symbolizing humanity. The publication resulted in a series of complaints by the German government at the highest level. A price was set on Raemaekers's head by the Germans. This even resulted in a court case against Raemaekers in the Netherlands for bringing the safety and neutrality of the state in danger. It is telling that among many caricatures and images against aggressors from the German and Austrian empires, precisely this image touched the right cord.[36]

Fig. 4. L'Epiphane du Nouveau Antichrist, *by Romeyn de Hooghe (1645-1708). In 1689 the Dutch artist de Hooghe published this engraving in which James II (1685-1688), Louis XIV (1643-1715), William III (1689-1702), the Pope and other leaders are represented.*

Fig. 5. The Three Kings from the East, *by Louis Raemaekers (1869-1956). In 1914, the Dutch cartoonist Raemaekers depicted Emperor Wilhelm II, Emperor Franz Joseph, and the Turkish sultan, bringing weapons and war as a present to Mary and her frightened child Jesus.*

Feasting and Begging

Anke Van Wagenberg-ter Hoeven has published a catalogue of eighty-seven sixteenth- and seventeenth-century images, in particular paintings and engravings, about Twelfth Night in the art of the Northern and Southern Netherlands.[37] Two aspects of the festive repertoire were portrayed: on the one hand the celebration at home, the so-called Twelfth Night; on the other hand the celebration in the streets, the Star singers. The majority of representations in the Low Countries deal with the feast indoors. The king or *dominus festi* was often presented drinking or, better, holding a glass in his hand, cheered on by grown-ups and children around a table with food and drink. The theme of star singers of Twelfth Night is depicted from about 1630 way into the nineteenth century. However, Wagenberg-ter Hoeven discovered an interesting shift: towards the end of the seventeenth century the number of depictions of the domestic feast diminished, and the number of depictions of the Star singers increased. This reflects a general evolution in early modern Europe of Epiphany celebrations and other festivities between Christmas and New Year, moving from the idea of rich men who gave endlessly for a day or an evening to a practice of begging kings. The analogy with the growing need of rulers to take up credit and to increase taxations in the context of the process of state formation, in particular for financing war, is very striking: the 'fiscal prince' emerged. In a comparative research of folklore studies, Trexler showed that the custom of groups of begging magi in the Christmas period emerged in Europe between 1460 to 1570. The number of references to kings as public beggars singing beneath a spinning star dates increased after 1550. Young people introduced themselves singing as 'three kings coming from afar' and begged for food or other presents; a folkloristic practice which stood the time until today in many a country.[38]

The domestic and public customs required all kind of royal paraphernalia in paper or other materials that normally do not show up in, for instance, probate inventories of private persons. Both the bean-in-the-cake and the king's letters were used not only in homes but also in corporations, like for example archers' guilds.[39] It was not uncommon for the game to get out of hand or spill over outside the house or the inn, to a temporary empire of misrule. Two examples should suffice. On 7 January 1499, the *Jeunesse* of Racquinghem near Aire-sur-la-Lys designated a *roi de fortune*. Every adolescent had to obey under sanction of being thrown in the river. The refusal of some subjects to obey and assemble in a cabaret nearby resulted in a mock battle that turned into a real fight and bloodshed.[40] In Brussels in 1719, the butchers' guild proceeded like other guilds to elect a king. On 30 and 31 January they marched through the city, accompanied by a music band. The elected king Anthoen de Coster wore a crown on his head. They shouted not only the traditional 'Den coninck die drinckt' but also references to the political situation, like 'Vivat Philippus', 'Vivat den Hertog van Maine', 'Vivat Beyeren' and even 'Den keyser is maer eenen hontsfot', or the Dutch equivalent of 'The emperor is nothing but an hound dog', later echoed in a famous song by Elvis Presley, the King of Rock 'n' Roll. Five members of the butchers' guild, including the 'king', were arrested. The next day four others who demanded their release were also arrested. Eventually four of them were sentenced to banishment for ten years, despite political pressure. Of course this had to be seen in the context of a series of protests by the guilds in 1718-1719, eventually resulting in the death punishment of the Brussels master of the tilers' guild, François Anneessens (1660-1719), and five others.[41]

The possibility of things going wrong, and the consumption of huge quantities of alcohol and food, did not go unnoticed by the authorities. Several decrees and prohibitions were issued by church, municipal and other authorities during the early modern period. This was the case not only for the Counter-Reformation. Already on the eve of Epiphany 1531, Martin Luther heavily rejected the customs and even the story of the three kings and proposed to focus on the baptism of Jesus. In the history of the Reformation, the martyr of the law professor Jean de Caturce in Toulouse in January 1532 is a *cause célèbre*. He made the mistake of using the feast of Epiphany to ventilate his ideas inspired by his reading of Scripture and tried to replace the cry 'Le Roy boit' with 'Christ règne dans nos cœurs'. After a trial in the *Parlement de Toulouse*, Caturce was burned on the Place St Étienne on 23 June 1532. However, the impact of these men, or for example John Calvin, remained limited in the history of the 'king-for-a-day' customs.[42]

The official attention was also due to the fact that mock kings provided an excellent way to mock real kings and other rulers. The king's feast even offered the enlightened philosophers in France an excellent occasion for reflection. In the early 1770s, Denis Diderot became Bean King three times. In his poems about these experiences, he reflected on the difficulties to 'do the right thing' when in possession of absolute power. Authors like Voltaire (1694-1778) also used the format or allusions to it.[43] Recently, Paul Downes described the 1776 American wave of crowning, humiliating, parading, burying or burning effigies of the king of England:

> It was not just that the colonials killed their king 'in metaphorical terms'; it was also the king's privileged relationship to the order of the metaphor, the profane substitution, that the revolutionaries were attempting to rid themselves.[44]

Next to the custom, the very format of the kings' letters could be used for political statements, as for example in the Southern Netherlands in 1792 to comment on the French Revolution and on political struggles in the big cities.[45]

King for a Day in Real Courts

What happened in the Ancient Regime when the two worlds met? I do not refer to practices of using leftovers and second-hand material from real courts in mock king festivities.[46] I ask instead how kings and their court celebrated Twelfth Night. References to Twelfth Night are abundantly available in sources and studies dealing with courtly everyday life, the year cycle and the festive culture in European courts. Especially when someone of the royal family turned out to be elected King of the Twelfth Night, and in particular when incidents occurred, it tends to be recorded in archives, popular publications or biographies. The most famous example is that of the French King Francis I who, in the Epiphany season of 1521, was wounded in a mock battle – with snowballs, eggs, and apples – against the King of the Bean of the household of the Count of St Pol.

The literary variants of the above-mentioned Luis Vivès story of the drunken man are all situated in court surroundings but are not yet documented in non-literary sources such as account books. Other variants are. At the court of Navarre in the second half of the fourteenth century, the king tended to appoint a poor child or a lower courtier's son – like in 1361 his barber's – to be dressed royally and to act as a 'petit roi de la fève' during Epiphany, in exchange for money or grain for the family. Remarkable and tragic are the three requests by court poet Alonso Alvarez de Villasandino to King John II of Castile (1406-1454) to nominate him as 'Rey de la faba' instead of a poor child. In the fifteenth and early sixteenth century, stories circulated about rulers of the Bourbon or d'Este families who went on the streets as 'poor' magi to collect money in order to redistribute it. Trexler emphasized the importance of these changes that also shed new light on the evolution in popular culture in the seventeenth century we discussed in the previous paragraph:

> Already in the fifteenth century, princes were rethinking the nature of the prince as a fiscal and a monetary creature. No longer the purely liberal giver, he was now a collector, and the resulting gift became a proof of the prince's legitimacy as a representative of his people.[47]

The idea that the magi gave the wealth of their nation to Jesus could be reoriented.

Some fifteenth-century sources document that gold, frankincense and myrrh were given by Henry VII (1485-1509) and James IV (1488-1513) in the Chapels Royal of England and Scotland. From the sixteenth century until today, a royal presentation of frankincense, myrrh and gold takes place every year on 6 January. This event survived the English Reformation, in particular because of the added value of expressing a direct relation between monarch and God, without having to resort to a papal intermediary. Every English sovereign presented them personally until the mad King George III (1760-1801) was unable to. Then the gifts were presented by a representative in the name of the monarch on a dish or, since Queen Victoria (1837-1901), in a red bag. This tradition stands today.[48] The English monarchs, in particular since Henry VII, also offered gifts to the boy bishops of several chapels, in particular the Chapel Royal. Henry VIII (1509-1547) banned this in 1541 as an offence to the ecclesiastical dignity of which he was the guardian. They were restored by the Catholic Queen Mary (1553-1558) in London in 1554, but vanished again when she died and the Elizabethan Reformation took momentum.[49]

One of the most systematic searches for mock or 'bean' kings in real court settings was conducted by Hutton for the English and Scottish medieval and early modern courts. There are traces of the 'bean' custom at the English courts of Edward II and Edward III (1327-1377). Account books mention a 'bean king' being rewarded at Christmas in 1315, 1316 and 1335. But the custom seems to have faded in the courts in the following decades before returning strongly between 1450 and 1550. Henry VII of England paid for the services of a Lord of Misrule and an Abbot of Unreason during all Christmases from 1489 onward. James IV of Scotland paid for a King of the Bean and an Abbot of Unreason from the 1490s onward. Lady Margaret Beaufort, Henry VIII's mother, had a budget for a Lord of Misrule in the Christmas season. Henry VIII continued the custom and promoted it in university colleges. Under his son Edward VI (1547-1553), the Lord of Misrule custom peaked. The Duke of Northumberland financed large mock courts and spectacles. A man called George Ferrers occupied the position of royal Lord of Misrule with grand style. He had his own coat of arms, three pages, eight councillors, a clergyman, a philosopher, an astronomer, a poet, a physician, an apothecary, a Master of Requests, a civil lawyer, two gentlemen, a couple of jugglers, acrobats and comic friars. He even entertained an ambassador who spoke nonsense and an interpreter to decode. The spectacle was designed to amuse not only Edward and his court but also the people of London. Part of the programme was an official tour in the city of London and a welcome by the London sheriff's Lord of Misrule and his mock personnel. The official state visits were enacted in all details as for an adult king, including the item that the mock 'royal cofferer' threw money to the crowd. Eventually, it ended in a banquet provided by the Lord Mayor or Lord Treasurer.[50]

When Edward died, 'Bloody' Queen Mary succeeded him. The Duke of Northumberland was executed. No royal Lord of Misrule was ever appointed again in England. From then on, the usual Master of the Revels performed his usual functions all year long. The Lord Mayor and sheriffs of London decided never to appoint a new Lord of Misrule after 1554. At the Scottish court however, a new variant was cultivated: a 'Queen of the Bean'. The most famous episode was registered in 1563 in the presence of the Queen regnant Mary (1542-1567), when the favourite Mary Fleming was chosen as Bean Queen and covered with jewels. In 1564 lady-in-waiting Mary Beton was Queen of the Bean: her silver gown covered with jewels echoed the image of Queen Elizabeth (1558-1603).[51] Mary's son James did not revive the practice: the heyday of the temporary 'bean monarchy' thus was situated in the royal court from mid-fifteenth to the mid-sixteenth century.[52]

In the households of sixteenth-century English nobility and in the university colleges, Christmas mock sovereigns were well established. In a recent publication Hutton underlined that in the early fifteenth century, figures like 'Prester John' or King Balthasar were found to preside over festivities, and at the end of the fifteenth century 'bean kings' replaced them.[53] In the London law schools of the Inns of Court, kings were appointed from the early sixteenth century onwards. At Lincoln's Inn, the 1519-1520 season knew 'a King over Christmas' and a 'King over New Year's Day'. These could be high-ranking officers, but also students or real lords. One of the episodes deserves special mention, as the aforementioned real Winter King is involved:

> In 1635 Charles I himself asked the Middle Temple to appoint a student to provide a Christmas diversion for his nephew, the exiled Prince Palatine, who was on a state visit to England. A young Cornishman, Richard Vyvyan, was duly elected 'Prince d'Amour', and contributed £6,000 of his own money towards the £20,000 which the Inn spent on feasts, dances, and a masque, between Christmas Day and Shrovetide.[54]

According to Hutton the end was near in England:

> What killed the taste for those figures among the English ruling classes was an experience of genuine 'misrule' and political inversion in the form of the Civil Wars and Revolution of the 1640s. When the traditional political and social order was restored in 1660, almost nobody felt much like simulating that experience any more. [...] Misrule metamorphosed into a much more harmless, inexpensive, scaled-down and domesticated form, based apparently upon the reintroduction to England from Europe of the medieval tradition of the 'bean king'.[55]

In many courts on the continent, including the French Court, the custom of appointing kings for a day or a festive week was cultivated actively. On 5 and 6 January 1649 the mother of Louis XIV was elected Queen of Beans after she found the bean in the cake. She was cheered with the words 'La reine boit'. Later that night she snuck out of the court in Paris, in full Fronde.[56] In the Low Countries, Prince William III of Orange loved the feast before he came to the Isles. He was very proud to be elected king on Twelfth Night in 1662 in the house of his grandmother in The Hague. The fact that he would mount the English throne a few years later gave this special significance and ensured a reference in history. The account of the election was published in the *Hollandtze Mercurius* of January 1662: publishing stories about these festive events increased their impact well beyond the household or palace, even in space and time.[57] Everyday life at court, and even recurrent events like the game of the bean king, had effects well beyond the palace walls and the figuration of those present. The household of the Sun King is the paradigmatic example of this evolution.

The Versailles court became the central theatre of French politics and power under Louis XIV. The significance of an account of the domestic kings' feast on Epiphany 1684 that was published in the *Mercure Galant* of June 1684, an early modern 'mass' medium, should not be underestimated. The 1684 Epiphany feast in the *grand appartement* of the king with four tables for the ladies and one for princes was described in detail, including all the names of the 'bean kings' at each table and the diplomatic games they played. Louis XIV ordered the feast to be repeated one week later. This time the Sun King himself had the bean in the king's cake at his table: 'On pouvait dire qu'il était roi par sa naissance, par son mérite et par le sort, qu'on ne pouvait appeler capricieux ce soir-là.' The feast was once again a big success. Several remarks of the reporter in the June issue of the *Mercure Galant* are highly significant. The king and other members of the highest nobility did their best, by using humoristic publications and quotes from Molière (1622-1673), to try to mitigate theatricality, the fact that 'chacun avait de la peine à prendre un air libre devant le roi'. It is remarkable that it took an upside-down feast of royalty to have a very rare kind of warm family feeling at court, as was noted in the *Mercure Galant*.[58]

Louis XVI Drinks

The last French king of the Ancient Regime, Louis XVI, knew the Twelfth Night custom of the Bean King well. In the 1780s, he was personally involved in the acquisition of the famous seventeenth-century painting *Le roi boit* or *Repas de famille le jour de la Fête des Rois* of Jacob Jordaens (1593-1678) (see the cover image of this volume).[59] Today this painting is exhibited in the Louvre. The fact that this masterpiece and indeed the Louvre palace itself are now 'national heritage' and property of the French Republic is directly linked to the French Revolution that started with the Storming of the Bastille in 1789.[60] The king was not removed immediately: in this topsy-turvy context, Louis XVI continued to act as a king for three more years. But on 22 September 1792, the French republic was proclaimed officially and the curtain – and literally his head – finally fell, in a regicide by guillotine on 21 January 1793.

After being forced on 5 October 1789 to move from Versailles to the heart of Paris, the King and his court were based in the Tuileries palace until 10 August 1792, when another episode struck a fatal blow to the royal status. The military problems and defeats of the French revolutionary armies in 1792 led to riots and rebellions. The anger did not focus on the Constituante but once again on the King and the representatives of the Old Regime. The so-called 'Storming of the Tuileries palace' by the Parisian populace on 10 August was the violent end of regular court life and the transition to the last months of Louis in 'prison'. The successful storming of the palace on that day had been preceded by an aborted full-fledged attack of the Tuileries palace twenty days earlier, on 20 June. A big Parisian mob entered the royal palace. The National Guard was helpless. Louis XVI's life was in real danger. This was clearly a crucial moment in the history of the French monarchy: the King versus his riotous subjects. How did Louis XVI manage to buy a few weeks of extra time as a king in a palace? Which symbolic language was left? He was abandoned by his soldiers, his court, his advisers,... and was under direct, physical pressure by the crowd. He had to act, in many senses of this word, in order to save his life. The Cordelier revolutionary Pierre Gaspard Chaumette (1763-1794) described this crucial scene in detail:

> On donna un grand coup de hache à une autre porte. Louis XVI la fit ouvrir lui-même et se mit à brandir son chapeau en l'air en criant de toutes ses forces: 'Vive la nation!' [...] En un clin d'œil la salle fut remplie d'hommes armés de piques, de faux, de bâtons armés de couteaux, de scies, de fusils, de fourches etc. On plaça les tables de la Déclaration des droits de l'homme face à face du roi. Il se déconcerta et chercha à s'agiter pour se remettre. Alors ce ne fut qu'un cri: 'Sanctionnez', disait-on, 'sanctionnez les décrets qui doivent sauver la France, rappelez les ministres patriotes, chassez vos prêtres, choisisses entre Coblentz et Paris.' Le roi tendait la main aux uns et aux autres, agitait toujours son chapeau. Enfin, ayant aperçu un bonnet rouge entre les mains d'un citoyen, il en couvrit sa tête, puis il se mit à boire à même une bouteille 'à la santé des sans-culottes', qui de leur côté criaient 'Le roi boit!'. Il promit tout ce que demandaient les citoyens. Alors ils évacuèrent peu à peu les appartements [...] Enfin à dix heures du soir tout fut évacué et Paris se trouva dans le plus grand calme.[61]

The 'king drinks' rite saved Louis XVI's life on 20 June 1792, but this worked only once. No rites could top the regicide that soon followed. The custom of the king drinks had lost its power: it was no longer a game of inversion.[62] This can be learned from the episode on 17 Nivôse of the Year II (1794) when an overzealous revolutionary committee of the Marie in Paris concluded that it would be necessary for the *conseil-général* to issue a *circulaire* to all revolutionary committees, because 'king's cakes' were being sold for January 6th. Bakers selling the cakes with beans and people taking part in the Bean King's feasts had to be arrested. The *agent national* (the revolutionary version of *substitut du procureur* and political liaison officer of higher authorities) intervened at this point and debunked the problem. He focused on technicalities, that a revolutionary committee could not communicate with other *comités* but should refer to the police when the *sûreté de République* was in danger and to the administration of 'substances' for abuses of wasting flour on cakes instead of bread.[63] At the same time he questioned the priority of this issue when symbolic violence was downplayed by direct, bloody, political violence during the Terror. What could 'king for a day' mean in such circumstances?

Conclusion

In this contribution we examined the history of a repertoire of customs, stories and images involving imaginary or fake rulers such as the Three Kings – for whom there is no hard evidence, notwithstanding their alleged relics in Cologne – 'bean kings' and 'bean queens', and other 'rulers for a day'. Throughout the centuries in pre-revolutionary Europe, these representations have helped to imagine, discuss, perform and even construct the figure of a king and his court and to reflect on notions like 'absolute authority', theatricality and discontinuity in relation to royalty. This worked on a symbolic-cognitive level but also as a ritual safety valve in power-laden situations like abbeys, universities, bourgeois households, and indeed noble and royal courts. The evolution of forms and images in the sixteenth and seventeenth centuries seems to echo some major evolutions of kingship. Suggestions and representations of mock kings could also be used to mock kings, as strong examples like that of the Palatine Winter King in the seventeenth century showed. 'King for a day' was a powerful, funny but potentially dangerous idea or performance in the context of early modern courts of reigning rulers who tried to aspire to continuity and exclusivity. All these events are not merely 'anecdotes' but had multiple functions in a system of symbolic violence – or its negation – around kingship and court life in a world full of theatricality. Napoleon Bonaparte, who was an eyewitness to the events in the Tuileries on 20 June 1792, immediately grasped that a point of no return had been reached by the monarchy when he saw Louis XVI showing himself with the red cap at the windows overlooking the garden filled with a riotous crowd. Time for myths and rites about royalty were over. Napoleon commented that those in power should have used the cannon to sweep off four or five hundred of them and set an example, but that now it was too late. The 'king drinks' custom of Epiphany in winter, publicly performed by a king in order to escape real and present danger in mid-summer 1792, had turned the inversion inside-out: a symbolic nuclear explosion. Royalty would never be the same again.[64]

Fiction, Kingship, and the Politics of Character in Eighteenth-Century France

Lisa Jane Graham

Historians and literary scholars agree that the relationship between politics and literature acquired unprecedented force during the reign of Louis XIV.[1] The literary field that emerged in the late seventeenth century shaped itself through and against royal authority. The Sun King promoted literature as part of an aggressive cultural project to extend and consolidate his rule. By mobilizing authors to craft his image, the king ceded control to writers whose output he then attempted to police. Moreover, literary activity in France inherited traditions of resistance from the sixteenth-century tracts of the Huguenots to the pamphlets that flooded the streets during the Fronde.[2] Thus, the crown had felt the sting of the pen long before it sought to tame it through academies and censorship. The combined pressures of propaganda and censorship created a tense climate for writers in search of patrons, status, and remuneration. While some directed their talents toward the crown, others experimented with new genres such as the novel that enabled self-expression and criticism.

This chapter traces the evolution of royal character between the realms of statecraft and fiction. Political character derived from the Renaissance idea that a ruler should inspire obedience through exemplary behavior and affection rather than force. The prince adhered to a higher moral standard because his conduct embodied the dictates of God and reason. This moral imperative justified the mystery surrounding statecraft that only the sovereign could decipher through his superior reason. The importance of character formation guided the educational treatises written for future kings since the Middle Ages known as mirrors of princes.[3] As these texts reiterated, princely power carried moral responsibilities that were ignored at great cost.

Derived from the Greek, the original meaning of character as an imprinted or engraved mark persisted as the term entered moral and aesthetic discussions in seventeenth-century France. When applied to social taxonomy, characters referred to fixed qualities that distinguished human temperaments. The popularity of the genre, inspired by the rediscovery of Theophrastus's text, *Characters*, reflected its ability to buttress values of hierarchy and stability through its classification of human dispositions and behavior. This inflection accounts for the success of Jean de La Bruyère's best-selling *Les caractères*, a satirical dissection of Louis XIV and the court society he created as a symbol of his power.[4]

La Bruyère's text reinforces the psychological theory of character that grounded personality traits in physiology. The treatise delineates types in order to train individuals to know their place and where they stood in relation to one another. In politics, character entails a consistent public performance that requires education; the different roles derive from their natures. As La Bruyère recognizes, the superficial quality of character that smoothed social interaction entailed a loss of psychological depth and motive. His mockery points to a more complex and individuated notion of character that developed in fiction in the eighteenth century. Early French novelists drew on La Bruyère's emphasis on inner and outer selves to define a genre that aimed to instruct readers while entertaining them.

As royal historiographers recorded the exploits of the Sun King for posterity, an alternative script took shape in the hands of authors experimenting with a fictional technique called the novel.[5] Blending the traditions of epic and romance with current events, novels probed the human heart and developed a language to express the role of the emotions in human behavior. This endeavor fleshed out the individual but also revealed the limits of reason as a guide to character. By elaborating a subjective language of interiority, novelists subverted the crown's hegemony on culture and taste. They also challenged principles of privilege and hierarchy that structured Ancient Regime society and government. Ironically, as character acquired greater sophistication in eighteenth-century literature, it undermined a coherent understanding of the self.[6] This development threatened classical conceptions of royal character and the theories of rule that shaped it.

The two forms of character I have identified could not share the king's body because they were fundamentally at odds with one another. This tension peaked in the middle of the eighteenth century with the vogue for allegorical novels in France.[7] In these novels, authors used the empirical aims of fiction to dispel the mythical claims of monarchy. The novels mark the triumph of literary imperatives over political mandates: the literary requirements of character trumped the sanctity of the king. As the Marquis d'Argens observed:

> Tis difficult to distinguish the different forms, and …
> the internal motives of different characters…. But a
> good author paints them, sets them plainly in sight, and
> exposes them as they really are.[8]

This remark underlines the novel's commitment to full disclosure contrasted with the principles of secrecy and spectacle that guided the cultural politics of the crown. Where royal ceremonies reinforced the distance between sovereign and subject, the novel drew the two closer together.[9] The novel eroded the fear and reverence that traditionally had surrounded the French king through literary techniques of parody, scrutiny, and criticism articulated through the construction of character.

These principles constituted the 'specific danger inherent in the novelistic zone of contact' by enabling the reader to enter the world of fiction and explore it freely.[10] While the two worlds, that of the novel and that of the reader, intersect and overlap, they operate according to different rules and assumptions. The novel would come to question hierarchy and privilege in favor of experience and criticism. The king moves on the same plane as all the characters, and his fate depended on authorial intention, not divine will. For these reasons, the triumph of literary character constituted an 'uncrowning' that threatened royal authority. By revealing the subjective nature of all decisions and the limits of human reason, the novel demystified the king and encouraged demands for accountability that proved incompatible with theories of divine right and absolutism.

This analysis focuses on form, the early French novel, to demonstrate its impact on content, the demystification of kingship. It draws together theories of the novel with historical interest in print, communication, and representation. Although historians sense a connection between the explosion of print and the erosion of royal authority, they separate questions of form and content in their analysis of political criticism.[11] Too much attention has focused on the content of texts, images, and utterances and not enough on modes and mechanisms of communication. To counter this tendency, I have turned to Michel de Certeau, who warns against the ideology of 'consumption-as-a-receptacle'.[12] In his analysis of the act of reading, Certeau insists that textual appropriation offers a site both for the production of meaning and resistance. Although Certeau recognizes that 'to read is to wander through an imposed system', he emphasizes that readers invent as they wander. The reader assumes primordial importance in this model because 'the text becomes a text only in relation to the exteriority of the reader'.[13] By redefining consumption as an interpretative activity, Certeau's model enables a multifaceted approach to the historical text.

This emphasis on reception captures the social life of language as it moves among individuals, groups, and institutions. In his recent research, Robert Darnton turns from questions of production to those of circulation to assess the role of clandestine literature in propelling political change in eighteenth-century France. In order to track criticism, Darnton reconstructs the communication networks through which information circulated, got amplified, policed, and distorted.[14] Extending his analysis to 'mixed media' such as gossip and song, Darnton emphasizes that the spread of the message, how it reached the public and took hold, mattered more than where it originated in sociocultural terms. Rejecting a 'genealogy of ideas' approach, he proposes mapping communication systems in order to highlight the feedback and convergence that transform information into ideology.

In shifting from production to reception, however, Darnton risks leveling the differences between literary forms and between oral and print media. Although transmission shapes the message, form plays an equally, if not more, determining role. While different media may reinforce a message through overlapping content, they do not achieve this goal in a uniform way. These formal paths must be identified before they are combined. I will illustrate this argument through a sample of allegorical novels from the 1740s in which Louis XV appears as a character. Even when the portrait of the king is flattering or anodyne, the techniques of fiction challenge the ontological claims that grounded royal authority. In contrast to official propaganda and royal ceremonies, these novels were not commissioned and controlled by the crown. Louis XV lost control of his character in this decade, and neither he nor his successor managed to reclaim it.

Political Character and Linguistic Authority

In his *Testament Politique*, Richelieu offered an unblinking evaluation of Louis XIII's character as part of his blueprint for reforming French absolutism. Drawing on Renaissance theories of statecraft, Richelieu identifies character as the essential piece of sovereignty and emphasizes that a spotless reputation is the king's most valued resource at home and abroad:

> La réputation est d'autant plus nécessaire aux princes
> que celuy duquel on a bonne opinion fait plus avec son
> seul nom que ceux qui ne sont pas estimés avec des
> armées. Ils sont obligez d'en faire plus d'éstat que de leur
> propre vie et ils doivent plutôt hazarder leur fortune et
> leur grandeur que de souffrir qu'on y fasse aucune
> brèche, estant certain que le premier affoiblissement qui
> arrive à la réputation d'un prince est, pour léger qu'il
> soit, le pas de plus dangereuse conséquence à sa ruine.[15]

Echoing Machiavelli, Richelieu insists that reputation instills obedience more effectively than force and thereby provides a stronger foundation for rule.[16] A strong character reflected the king's capacity to subjugate personal inclinations and passions to the dictates of reason. Richelieu worried about Louis XIII whose sensitive temperament weakened his resolve at crucial moments.[17] According to Richelieu, subjects will love their king if they see that reason guides his decisions. A prince who falls prey to passion courts derision that leads to disobedience.

Richelieu assigns character the weight of law in his definition of sovereignty. The king must set a good example:

> Rien n'est plus utile à un establissement que la bonne
> vie des princes, laquelle est une loy parlante et oblig-
> eante avec plus d'efficacité que toutes celles qu'ils pour-
> roient faire pour contraindre au bien qu'ils veulent pro-
> curer.[18]

The public nature of his charge requires that the king be circumspect in his speech and actions. For Richelieu, language plays a crucial role in maintaining the delicate balance of reason and reputation that is the bedrock of sovereignty. On the one hand, Richelieu implores the king to discipline his use of language:

> Les coups d'espée se guérissent aisément, mais il n'en est
> pas de mesme des blessures de la langue, particulière-
> ment par celles des roys dont l'autorité rend les coups
> presque sans remède s'ils viennent d'eux-mesmes.[19]

On the other hand, he warns that kings must be careful not to offend or alien-ate their subjects:

> La raison requiert qu'ils ferment leurs oreilles aux mes-
> disances et faux raports, et qu'ils chassent et bannissent
> ceux qui en sont autheurs comme peste très dangereuse
> qui empoisonne souvent les cœurs et les oreilles et
> l'esprit de toux ceux qui les approchent.[20]

Richelieu viewed language as a double-edged sword that could reinforce or undermine royal authority, and this assumption guided his cultural policy. On the one hand, he founded the Académie Française in 1634 and charged it with the task of codifying the French language by preparing a dictionary.[21] On the other hand, he applied it to the juridical realm by expanding the definition of *lèse-majesté* and punishing it severely.

As part of his efforts to protect the crown from its enemies, Richelieu elab-orated a theory of treason that added language, written and spoken, to conspir-acy as serious threats to the person of the king. He included the publication and dissemination of defamatory libels in the revised list of crimes punishable as treason.[22] Louis XIV pursued Richelieu's agenda when he created a police force in 1667 and charged it, among other tasks, with tracking opinion and repressing seditious speech and writing. Moreover, the police treated all allu-sions to the king, even imaginary threats, with suspicion since his name was not a public commodity. The Bourbon monarchy and their policing agents recognized the power of language and claimed it as a royal prerogative in order to control the image of the king.

But the crown lost its monopoly on the word in the eighteenth century due to the explosion of printing, the rise of literacy, and the flourishing trade in underground literature. The death of Louis XIV in 1715 ushered in an era of social change and cultural awakening. When previously taboo subjects were questioned, even the king's character became a topic of jest, as Montesquieu indicates in his best-selling novel, the *Lettres Persanes*:

> On dit que l'on ne peut jamais connaître le caractère des
> rois d'Occident jusques à ce qu'ils aient passé par les
> deux grandes épreuves de leur maîtresse et de leur con-
> fesseur. On verra bientôt l'un et l'autre travailler à se
> saisir de l'esprit de celui-ci, et il se livrera pour cela de
> grands combats: car, sous un jeune prince, ces deux
> puissances sont toujours rivales; mais elles se concilient
> et réunissent sous un vieux.[23]

As a young writer dedicated to enlightened ideals, Montesquieu experimented with fictional forms and irony to develop a skeptical view of authority. His success raised concern about the novel's subversive potential and the crown's inability to suppress it.

Like Richelieu, the police officers who tracked public opinion in eighteenth-century Paris perceived connections among print, ridicule, and loss of authority. They understood that the king had lost control of his character, as the following report from May 1740 indicates:

> On parle dans le public d'un petit livret qui coure, fait à
> l'occasion des plaisirs que le Roy prend dans ses petits
> appartements, on prétend que celui qui en est l'auteur
> est des plus hardis parce qu'il dépeint le Roy et ces
> favoris d'une manière peu avantageuse, que son but ne
> peut tendre qu'à rendre Sa Majesté méprisable non
> seulement à ses sujets mais aussi à tous les étrangers,
> entre les mains desquels un tel ouvrage tombera [...] [24]

By the middle of the eighteenth century, the police feared that the world of clandestine publication threatened to erode the king's political authority at home and abroad. To understand this shift, we must examine the formal techniques developed by authors since the late seventeenth century. The narrative strategies of early French novels escalated familiar complaints to a dangerous level by implicating the reader in a critical epistemology that ultimately required judgment.

Narrative Techniques and the Effects of Fiction

Authors of novels immediately found themselves on the defensive about the genre they had created. The novel stood at the center of the debates between the Ancients and the Moderns that raged at the end of the seventeenth century. Critics denounced the novel for debasing taste and corrupting morals.[25] In their efforts to refute these attacks, French novelists confronted the dilemma of reconciling the search for veracity with moral instruction. Crébillon *fils* (1707-1777) captured this tension in the preface to *Les Égarements du cœur et de l'esprit*:

> Le fait, préparé avec art, serait rendu avec naturel. On
> ne prêcherait plus contre les convenances et la raison. Le
> sentiment ne serait point outré; l'homme enfin verrait
> l'homme tel qu'il est, on l'éblouirait moins, mais on l'in-
> struirait davantage.[26]

This empirical outlook distinguished the novel from its closest kin, epics and romances, by grounding characters in recognizable time and space. Moreover, the novel established connections between private matters of the heart and public affairs of state. This last trait reinforced the novel's subversive capacity and the crown's efforts to suppress it.

As Joan DeJean argues, the late seventeenth-century novel took the flat notion of character and fleshed it out by providing a vocabulary for describing states of feeling and being.[27] This language of the emotions not only identified their psychological force but also highlighted the shortcomings of reason as a guide to behavior. Passion determined action for characters in novels as much as, if not more than, rational judgment. This last point proved significant when the character in question was the king of France. The king appeared just as vulnerable to passions as any other character, and this image undermined his claims to superior wisdom. Once exposed, the king's promiscuity remained troubling, despite efforts to contain it within the bounds of fiction.

Fiction required narrative techniques to uncover the emotions and communicate them to readers. Madame de Lafayette (1634-1693) developed the interior monologue as a strategy for getting inside a character's head to capture the conflicting dictates of reason and passion. By collapsing the distance between readers and characters, these monologues facilitated greater emotional connection. For the king, the loss of distance meant a loss of protection, since readers evaluated the king as they would any other character. The interior monologue linked intention to action by putting words in the king's mouth, making it impossible to shield him from blame. The interests of different characters competed for the reader's attention and forced a critical response. Finally, the novel's expository methods favored partial truths that undermined absolutist claims in any domain. The subjective, at times intimate, nature of the reading experience furthered this fragmentation.

The allegorical novels or *romans à clef* that flourished in the early eighteenth century combined elements of the real and the marvelous. They used the device of a key to characters as a screen for the persons and events described. Yet, as the police reports made clear, these allegories were transparent: the reliance on a key reinforced the principle of making applications to actual persons and events. When comparing different copies of the same novel, one observes that some included printed keys while others had handwritten ones. Moreover, eighteenth-century readers left their traces in the text itself, often writing in the names of the various characters between the lines or in the margins. As Darnton suggests, deciphering keys was a literary game for an elite trained to decode a political culture based on secrecy, conspiracy, and allusion.[28] The authors of these satirical stories borrowed narrative techniques developed in the novel and directed them toward their political and social agendas. Although the authors mocked and criticized the king, they rarely questioned the monarchy as the form of government best suited for France.

Despite the docile ideological thrust, the methods of exposition subverted royal authority. The blurring of truth and fiction made it difficult for the reader to distinguish between the two and, hence, to respect the boundaries of obedience. The more readers identified with characters and events, the more confident they felt intervening and passing judgment. Authors justified their scrutinizing of the royal character by claiming the higher purpose of moral instruction. Since much of this literature emanated from the same court in which the fictional intrigues took place, the king was simultaneously a prime target and a designated reader. Authors reminded both the king and his entourage of their flaws and responsibilities. From this perspective, literary character offered a tool for correcting flawed political character but it did so with methods that deconstructed the authority claimed by those same figures.

The Fiction Effect

To illustrate the impact of these literary techniques on perceptions of royal character, I have selected four allegorical novels published between 1745 and 1750: *Tanastès* (1745) by Marie Bonafon; *Les amours de Zéokinizul* (1746) by Crébillon *fils*; *Voyage d'Amatonthe* (1750) by the Chevalier de Rességuier; and, finally, *Les Bijoux indiscrets* (1748) by Denis Diderot. Each is a *roman à clef* and focuses on Louis XV, his mistresses, ministers, and members of the court. Three of the four authors were imprisoned when the police identified their responsibility for the works in question. Their arrest reflects official concern about the proliferation and popularity of these clandestinely published novels. The stories blend references to current affairs with elements borrowed from fairytales, oriental tales, libertine literature, travel narratives and epistolary novels. Except for *Les Bijoux indiscrets*, these novels have fallen into obscurity despite their popularity at the time.[29]

Although Chancellor d'Aguesseau had singled out the novel for repression in his 1737 edict regarding the policing of the book trade, his efforts drove the novel underground rather than deterring authors.[30] Still, the edict reflects the crown's concern about the dangers of fiction as well as its vulnerability to attack. Moreover, the efforts to censor the novel affirmed its status as an experimental and subversive genre. The genre offered members of the reading public a glimpse inside the palace corridors, combining policy and gossip similar to magazines today. In addition, these novels entertained members of the court, including the king, with their wit and malice.

At first glance, these novels rehearse tropes about a weak king who is controlled by his passions and enslaved to women and evil ministers. It is difficult to recover their capacity to provoke offense if we focus on the content alone. Instead, we must follow the police commissioners and listen to their concerns as they surface in the dossiers. The police never dismissed these novels as frivolous or escapist, even when their authors offered these arguments in self-defense. They planted spies in the publishing trade who alerted them to suspicious titles, authors, publishers and booksellers. The police responded with repression, often acquiring copies of the books in question to verify the damage for themselves.[31] Authors sought protection by blaming either their readers for drawing applications or their publishers.[32] Nonetheless, all four authors sensed the popularity of the material and risked publication to profit from the demand.

When the police arrested Marie Bonafon in 1745, she was living at Versailles in the service of the Princesse de Montauban.[33] Bonafon explained that she had been inspired by recent events, including the king's illness at Metz in 1744, to write a story with topical interest to earn some money. She insisted that while she had mocked the king, she had never meant to cause offense. The Chevalier de Rességuier made a similar point after his arrest, when he asserted: 'J'adorais le Roi, j'étois l'admirateur de ses vertus, et cependant j'ai osé porter mes traits satiriques jusqu'à lui.'[34] Both Bonafon and Rességuier wrote as allies, not opponents, but as the police reminded them, the king's character was not available for fictional purposes of either criticism or entertainment. In all four novels, the king was demoted twice, first by the author who created his literary character, and second by the other characters who manipulated him in their own interests. While none of these fictive kings was vicious, they all appeared variously as weak, hedonistic, and untrustworthy.

In *Tanastès*, Bonafon doubles the character of the king to contrast two forms of rule: monarchy and despotism.[35] Bonafon uses this device to criticize Louis XV without attacking him directly, because Louis XV is, in effect, both kings. The bad king, Agamil, is enslaved to his scheming mistress, Ardentine, and cedes all control to her. Bonafon recalls Richelieu's notion of exemplary behavior to chide the selfish Agamil. The reference to a king who abandoned his duty for sexual dalliance struck a chord among French readers concerned about Louis XV's capacity to lead them in a time of war.

Bonafon uses interior monologue to flesh out Agamil's character and to collapse the distance separating the king from the reader. For example, after his marriage to Sterlie, Agamil wrestles with his pledge of conjugal fidelity but refuses to give up his mistress. He justifies his behavior by reminding himself that 'un Roi n'est pas fait pour être victime des loix qu'il impose aux autres'.[36] Previous descriptions of despotism had always distanced the threat in time and place, but Bonafon puts the reference inside the mind of the royal character. This gesture aligns malicious intention with action and makes it impossible to excuse the king later by claiming his ignorance or innocence. The reader hears the king utter selfish thoughts and passes judgment. After establishing the negative traits that distinguish Agamil's rule, Bonafon contrasts these with the glorious reign of Tanastès. Yet, the golden age is short-lived, and Bonafon ends her novel on an ambivalent note.

After she transforms Agamil into a snake, Ardentine grinds him to a poisonous powder that she forces Tanastès to drink. As a result, Tanastès acquires a sharper resemblance to the real Louis XV. Bonafon assumes the narrative voice to describe the effects of the poison on Tanastès's character: 'Ce caractère ambigu, mêlé de bien et de mal était alors à la mode; ainsi après bien des agitations, il en fut quitte pour se mettre au niveau des hommes ordinaires' (155).[37] The combination of good and bad qualities made Tanastès a credible and complex literary character. Yet, by revealing the king's flaws and inconsistencies, Bonafon dispelled the mystique attached to his person. Although George III of England cultivated this 'ordinariness' to enhance his popularity, French kings who claimed divine sanction for their rule could not pursue this strategy.[38] The readers' sympathy raised expectations about the king's performance that they transferred from the fictional character to the political ruler.

As an author, Bonafon had options for manipulating characters and resolving problems that real life denied to ministers and princes. The police reports confirm that Bonafon's fiction encouraged readers to draw conclusions deemed 'insulting' to the king and his authority.[39] Louis XV was not an imposter waiting to be replaced by a good king hidden in the shadows. In the novel, the doubling of the king's character made it difficult for readers to distinguish between the two versions of Louis XV. Moreover, by the end of the story, Bonafon fuses the good and bad kings in the one body of Tanastès, to account for lingering character flaws. The reliance on fantastic details including metamorphoses, magical potions, and fairies blurred the boundaries between characters and undermined distinctions of birth and rank. Moreover, the king, like everyone else in the story, took shape and direction from the author rather than some higher power. Ultimately, the principle of literary character revealed the subjective nature of all decisions including those of the king

Like Bonafon, the Chevalier de Rességuier based his allegorical novel, *Voyage d'Amatonthe*, on his experience as an insider at Versailles. An officer of the Gardes Françaises, Rességuier took the reader directly into the court of Louis XV through the eyes of a traveler named Timante. The narrator's detachment from court politics enables him to see and describe what the participants themselves fail to grasp. Moreover, this trope reinforces the novel's agenda for reform by alerting the king to abuses and urging him to correct them. Nonetheless, Rességuier's intentions failed to contain the damage to the king's character in a novel that the police described as 'injurieux au Roi, à la Marquise de Pompadour, et aux ministres'.[40]

The *Voyage d'Amatonthe* is a novel in two parts.[41] While part one celebrates the values of hard work and conjugal love, part two dissects the French court and government. In addition to the published version, the police confiscated a manuscript version of volume two that openly denigrated Louis XV and his government. The police feared that the manuscript was circulating at court and wanted to prevent Rességuier from publishing it. Although Rességuier denied the charges, we can assume that the manuscript version had a healthy readership that included the Abbé Raynal, who had commissioned it for the *Mercure de France* before Rességuier was arrested.

The novel opens with a preface outlining the story and the author's intentions to 'peindre le vice et non les vicieux'.[42] Rességuier describes the first part as a banal love story compared to the more philosophical second volume. Close reading, however, reveals an underlying coherence. To begin with, the first part of the story establishes the principle that virtue provides the basis for good government and human happiness. Rességuier pursues this theme through Timante's quest for pleasure and his discovery of love. Upon his arrival in Amatonthe, Timante meets many beautiful women who leave him cold due to their lack of virtue. After marrying Camille, 'une figure douce et aimable, où la vertu, la sagesse, la gaieté se peignent également', Timante departs to seek his fortune at the prince's court.[43] The second part of the novel criticizes royal authority through the theme of a weak prince trapped in a corrupt court. Government serves private ambition not public service. After describing the suffering of a young woman who is abandoned by her lover, Timante uses the episode to condemn the immorality of the court.

In the published version, Rességuier's displays caution in his attack and refuses to name the prince directly. The king fails to lead by virtuous example, and this negligence manifests itself in both the domestic and political spheres. Finding himself alienated by the court's contempt for virtue, Timante decides to flee its dangerous temptations. The novel ends with his return to Camille and his pledge to cultivate their love. The political themes in the manuscript, however, move the king to center stage and spare his character no quarter.[44] Although a less sophisticated writer than Bonafon, Rességuier highlights the influence of the passions in determining human action and links personal debauchery to misrule. Upon his arrival, Timante observes the king for the first time and remarks:

> Le Prince [...] gouverne ses peuples avec douceur, il a
> toutes les qualités que le trône exige. On l'adore dans
> l'Amatonthe. Peut-être serait-il digne des sentiments
> qu'on a pour lui, s'il employoit mieux les avantages dont
> il est pourvû; mais aucun mortel n'est exempt de faib-
> lesse: les passions troublent les cœurs des Rois comme
> ceux des derniers des hommes.[45]

Thus, the narrator lures the reader into a critical position by raising doubts about the prince's inherent superiority. Timante questions the king's judgment in preferring the company of his mistress, a woman of obscure birth, Emise (Madame de Pompadour) to that of his loyal and virtuous wife, the queen. By gaining the reader's confidence in this manner, the narrator establishes the egalitarian principle of character against the hierarchical one of royal authority. While the mortality of the king enables the reader to identify with him, it also undermines his unaccountability.

Compared to Bonafon, Rességuier's characters lack complexity, and his plot is static. Nonetheless, the two novels converge in their portraits of Louis XV as a weak king susceptible to manipulation and caprice. For example, Timante notes that the young prince places his trust in flatterers who distract him with pleasure and blind him to his people's suffering.[46] The narrator establishes a logical connection between royal negligence and military fiasco in the War of the Austrian Succession, describing the latter as a failed venture that drained the country of lives and resources. Rességuier returns to Richelieu's notion of character as a model of behavior only to emphasize how Louis XV has perverted it. The king still leads by example, but his conduct inspires license, abuse, and destruction. Compared to the published novel, the manuscript portrays a well-intentioned king who evokes little respect from other characters or the reader. Unlike Bonafon and Crébillon who attempted to salvage Louis XV and sustain belief in his authority, Rességuier depicted a king so indolent that even the criminals in his kingdom go unpunished.

Although Rességuier initially claimed that he wrote the novel for his own amusement, he later acknowledged his offense in a letter he sent to Louis XV in which he begged for pardon.[47] Like Bonafon, Rességuier assumed responsibility for his text and attributed the creative process to a mixture of youth, imagination, and current affairs. He attempted to excuse his offense by blaming his readers and asserting the innocence of his characters. Thus, the act of writing a novel moved the control of royal character from police officers and ministers to authors and their readers.

Like Bonafon, Crébillon made Louis XV the protagonist of his novel, *Les Amours de Zéokinizul*, and satirized the king's amorous pursuits to raise doubts about his qualifications as a ruler. Although the first edition in 1746 lacked a key, the second edition of 1747 included a printed one at the end of the text. The novel enjoyed immediate success and went through several editions, including an English translation that appeared in 1749. Given Crébillon's track record with the police – imprisoned at Vincennes in 1734 and exiled briefly from Paris in 1742 – his decision to write a political satire of Louis XV appears rash. Although the police identified the novel as dangerous, they never arrested the author, and the book continued to circulate.[48] This leniency is perplexing and suggests that Crébillon succeeded in disguising his criticism to avoid imprisonment. This trick, however, fooled neither the police nor the readers who competed to get their hands on a copy of the novel.

Crébillon sets his allegory in an imaginary African kingdom, the realm of the Kofirans, and traces the early years of the reign of Zéokinizul/Louis XV. The novel blends current affairs with fictional episodes to develop a complex portrait of Louis XV. Crébillon uses the novel to praise Louis XV's virtues, but also reveals his flaws and their consequences. The narrative voice relies on the reader to infer the criticism rather than denounce the king directly. Thus, the novel opens by summarizing the history of the preceding reigns where kings had worked to establish 'le pouvoir arbitraire' and ultimately relinquished power to their ministers. Crébillon captures the desire of the French to love their king while voicing their concerns about his character. Although the king emerges steadfast in battle, he remains restless in love. In fact, Crébillon identifies the king's poor judgment as the cause of the nearly fatal illness he suffered when he joined his troops at Metz in 1744 with the opening of the War of the Austrian Succession. The public rejoiced when the king's confessor banished the unpopular mistress, Madame de Chateauroux, from the king's sickbed and sent for the abandoned queen. Through this description, Crébillon suggests that the king's inability to contain his passions has political consequences, because the health of the realm depended on the body of the king. The author applies the novel's interest in the emotions to dissect the character of the king. He attributes the king's illness to the passions shared by all mortals and effectively removes the royal body from the workings of God or providence. The king's inability to contain his passions enables readers to identify with his reactions. This sympathy, however, comes at the cost of their respect for his character.

The last episode in Crébillon's novel demonstrates the use of free indirect discourse to bring the reader into the king's bedroom and inside his head. The incident warns readers that kings who are blinded by passion will abuse their authority to pursue it. Zéokinizul desires a young beauty named Nasica, who has recently arrived at the court, but Nasica is in love with a young duke or *Bassa*. Zéokinizul decides to send the duke away on a mission to clear the path for seducing Nasica and tells himself:

> L'idée d'un rival chéri ne fut point capable de lui ôter
> l'espérance d'être heureux et comme un Roi fait l'amour
> bien différemment d'un sujet, loin de faire oublier à sa
> maîtresse le jeune Bassa par ses soins et ses tendres
> empressements, il voulut se servir de son autorité pour
> l'éloigner d'elle sur un prétexte honorable.[49]

This extract, where the voice of the narrator blends with that of Zéokinizul, reveals the king intentionally abusing his authority to separate two lovers. This technique makes it impossible for the reader to excuse the king's disregard for his subjects. The king's decision to exploit his status to sate his lust forces readers to question whether his privileges or powers were justified in the first place.

Once banished, the duke tries to write his lover but Zéokinizul intercepts the letters to convince Nasica to forget her lover. In one of these notes, the duke accuses Zéokinizul of separating them and defies his authority: 'en amour une couronne devait être comptée pour rien; [...] c'était le cœur auquel une véritable amant devait s'attacher.'[50] Although Nasica never receives this letter, Crébillon uses the epistolary form to denounce the king and implicate the reader directly in the lovers' plight. Through the resolute duke, Crébillon asserts the claims of the heart against rank, fortune, and even majesty. The principle of love entails a voluntary choice equally available to all characters. This truth, foregrounded in the novel, overpowers the prerogatives of rule.

As Zéokinizul pursues Nasica, he finds himself consistently rebuffed. Yet the dialogic structure of these scenes builds the reader's sympathy for Nasica and distrust of the king. After one of Zéokinizul's declarations of love, Nasica offers a forceful rebuke: 'Ta Hautesse ne peut que m'offrir des vœux coupables, et je périrois plutôt que de les satisfaire.'[51] Even though Nasica believes her lover has deserted her, she refuses to betray him, and her loyalty shames the philandering king. The boldness of her retort must have resonated with readers who could only imagine uttering such words to Louis XV. Even when Zéokinizul abandons all hope of seducing Nasica, he refuses to unite the lovers. After the duke returns to the palace, Zéokinizul imprisons and condemns him to death, reassuring himself that 'sa désobeissance à ses ordres lui fournissait un prétexte plausible de le faire périr, et déjà cette cruelle résolution s'emparait de son cœur'.[52] Crébillon closes on a positive note, however, with a king who recognizes and atones for his errors. Like Bonafon, he emphasizes the king's innate virtue and offers his novel as instruction. One senses that Crébillon wanted Louis XV to encounter himself as Zéokinizul and learn from the experience. Yet, as an author, Crebillon had to attribute motives to his character, and the king's selfish behavior lingered in the reader's mind long after finishing the novel.

Many of the preceding techniques converge in Diderot's early novel, *Les Bijoux indiscrets*.[53] Drawing on the vogue for orientalist tales and libertine literature, Diderot tests fictional techniques to address philosophical problems that drive his subsequent projects. For our purposes, we will focus on Diderot's portrait of Louis XV as the Sultan Mangogul and his mistress Mirzoza, Madame de Pompadour. While Diderot depicted Madame de Pompadour in a flattering light, arguably to secure her favor and protection for the *Encyclopédie*, his treatment of Louis XV exposed the king in an unfavorable, often critical, light.[54] The police identified the danger but did not arrest him until a year later for his *Lettre sur les aveugles*. It is unclear why the *Bijoux* did not trigger a *lettre de cachet*, but the fact that Madame de Pompadour had a copy in her library may explain the crown's leniency.[55] Nonetheless, the police kept their eye on the author and worked to repress the novel that was drawing readers at court and in Paris.

In the opening pages of the novel, Diderot introduces the sultan, Mangogul, by praising his accomplishments in war and government and his promotion of the arts. Diderot's summary of Mangogul's childhood and character identifies the sultan as Louis XV for the contemporary reader. Yet, Diderot cannot resist casting doubt on this portrait with the following remark: 'Le bon sultan que ce fut! Il n'eut jamais de pareil que dans quelque roman français.'[56] With this verbal wink to his reader, Diderot alerts us to his critical agenda and his decision to use his novel to advance it. The reference to fictional kings inscribes *Les Bijoux indiscrets* in two universes, politics and literature, and suggests their interdependence. The reader understands that Mangogul both is and is not Louis XV, a character who represents the real king while embodying Diderot's project for reform if his gamble in writing the novel pays off.

Diderot draws on popular perceptions of Louis XV's weaknesses, the king's melancholy temperament combined with his penchant for pleasure, to structure the novel's central plot. At the start, the reader learns that Mirzoza had secured her status as favorite mistress through her conversational skills, not her prowess in bed. Day after day, Mirzoza regaled the sultan with licentious tales about the sexual escapades of his courtiers. Yet, one day she runs out of stories and advises the king to consult the genie, Cucufa, to find a remedy. Mangogul asks the genie: 'de me procurer quelque plaisir aux dépens des femmes de ma cour [...] Savoir d'elles les aventures qu'elles ont et qu'elles ont eues; et puis c'est tout.'[57] This request reveals the king's willingness to seek diversion at the expense of his subjects' honour and marks him as a despot to eighteenth-century readers.[58] Cucufa gives Mangogul a magic ring that, while rendering the sultan invisible, forces women to recount their sexual escapades whenever he turns it toward them. Speaking through their 'bijoux' not their mouths, the women expose themselves to Mangogul's delectation. Mangogul is delighted with his ring, but Diderot tempers this joy through Cucufa's words of caution: 'Faites un bon usage de votre secret, et songez qu'il est des curiosités mal placés.'[59]

Diderot's adopts a complex narrative strategy in the novel, alternating dialogue and free indirect discourse with the voice of his alleged African author.[60] This fragmented voice shields his criticism by directing irony both at the king and the reader. Mirzoza hints at the destructive potential of the king's reckless pursuit of pleasure – no social bonds will survive his interrogation. Society cannot exist unless desires, including those of an indolent king, are contained. Through Mirzoza's voice, Diderot criticizes a king, Louis XV, who sacrifices the public good for personal pleasure. Thus, the use and abuse of the magical ring provide a metaphor for good and bad government under an absolute monarchy.

Mirzoza implores the sultan to exercise caution with his newfound powers. One hears an echo from *Tanastès* in the sultan's dismissive retort: 'Suis-je donc sultan pour rien?'[61] The exchange between the two protagonists enables Diderot to elicit sympathy and condemnation from the reader for the contrasting viewpoints. The fact that Mangogul not only harbors selfish thoughts but announces them makes a troubling impression. The sultan's lack of remorse forces the reader into the uncomfortable position of witnessing abusive authority.[62] Thus the dialogue between Mangogul and Mirzoza eliminates any possibility for exculpating the king – the reader must judge even as he laughs. Diderot's novel refuses to let the reader shirk his duty to observe, evaluate, and criticize.

Diderot uses different narrative techniques to develop his representation of royal character. Free indirect discourse enables the king to address the reader directly, while dialogue enables other characters to assess his performance. Throughout the novel, Diderot reminds the reader that Mangogul's relentless quest to 'vary his pleasures' drives the plot forward.[63] Yet at key moments, Mangogul displays self-restraint and moral integrity through his reactions. It is difficult to sort through the diverse episodes in the novel and distill a coherent portrait of royal character. This ambiguity arguably reflects Diderot's attitude of cautious optimism toward Louis XV as the king assumed a more active role in the government of his kingdom after the death of his chief minister, Cardinal de Fleury, in

1743.[64] Diderot repeatedly relies on dialogic exchanges between secondary characters to assess Mangogul's reign. Where Bonafon doubled the figure of the king to clarify the positive and negative traits, Diderot uses dialogue to capture divided opinion.

This last point is illustrated in chapter 14, where Diderot contrasts the perspective of a financially ruined senator to that of a retired military officer. After the senator denounces Mangogul's reign in candid and bitter terms: 'Le prince, voyez-vous, gâte bien des choses', the officer rallies to the sultan's defense: 'Tais-toi, malheureux. Respecte les puissances de la terre, et remercie les dieux de t'avoir donné la naissance [...] sous le règne d'un prince dont la prudence éclaire ses ministres [...] qui s'est fait redouter de ses ennemis et chérir de ses peuples.'[65] How did the eighteenth-century reader react to this impassioned exchange? Clearly, given the war and the losses it had entailed, the criticism resonated. Moreover, doubts about Louis XV's competence and integrity persisted amidst the celebrations of his military victories. The praise failed to defuse the precision and impact of the attacks. In this episode, Diderot speaks directly to Louis XV, reminding him that his actions would shape his legacy. The king had a choice and by implication, so did the reader.

Diderot's irony establishes a complicity between the narrator and the reader that promotes the critical epistemology of the novel at the expense of absolute authority. Diderot describes the gatherings of courtiers who meet twice a week in Mirzoza's apartments to listen to stories. In this setting, the king descends from the throne to enjoy the pleasures and freedom of his entourage. Diderot's portrait is sympathetic and emphasizes the egalitarian atmosphere of this salon. Nonetheless, the ease with which the sultan discards the trappings of his regal office highlights the arbitrary nature of his role from the start. Diderot uses the world of fiction to dismantle the fiction of kingship. This last point emerges toward the end of the novel, when Mangogul reappears in Mirzoza's apartment after a prolonged absence and Diderot observes:

> L'auteur africain ne nous apprend ni ce qu'il [Mangogul]
> était devenu, ni ce qui l'avait occupé pendant le chapitre
> précédent: apparemment qu'il est permis aux princes de
> Congo de faire des actions indifférentes, de dire
> quelquefois des misères et de ressembler aux autres
> hommes, dont une grande partie de la vie se consume à
> des riens, ou à des choses qui ne méritent d'être sues.[66]

While the magic ring granted Mangogul extraordinary powers to penetrate the intimate sphere of his subjects, Diderot suggests that Mangogul's essential nature is no different from those over whom he rules. The mundane features of Mangogul's quest for stimulation fail to justify the authority conferred by birth that secures his title. The 'African author' implies that the day may come when kings might not even merit the attention of novelists or their readers.

Conclusions

The preceding discussion shifts our angle for viewing the mechanisms of discourse and power by analysing the role of character in fictional representations of kingship in eighteenth-century France. While we intuitively sense a relationship between criticism and political change in the Age of Enlightenment, our current interpretations assume more than they demonstrate. My goal is not to pile on more evidence of the king's growing unpopularity in the eighteenth century but, rather, to change our idea of how criticism operates to destabilize authority and legitimate resistance. Attending to the discursive form of criticism illuminates its capacity to provoke epistemological rupture within an enclosed cultural system.

This chapter focused on the novel to argue that narrative strategies had subversive implications that extended beyond the stories they recounted. By seizing control of the king's character from the masters of ceremony, authors grounded royal authority in the realm of human action as opposed to metaphysical truth. The king possessed a title that distinguished his social position but not his ontological status: he was subject to the same physiological laws and emotional drives as his subjects. The use of dialogue made the king speak in his own voice, thereby eliminating the traditional escape hatch of blaming evil ministers and conniving mistresses for abuses and errors. The novel drew the worlds of king and reader closer together through narrative techniques that solicited scrutiny, derision, and judgment.

This argument suggests that casting the king as a fictional character ultimately revealed kingship as a fiction. Prior to the eighteenth century, the monarchy had developed an elaborate mythology to justify its authority and instill obedience. Yet the crown never acknowledged its fictional status, because the ceremonies and myths shaped and transcended history. The *romans à clef* that flourished in the 1740s helped dispel the illusions of power. The theory of the divine right of kingship depended on its capacity to suspend belief in the king's mortality. Yet the novel's commitment to verisimilitude and transparency broke this illusion by inscribing Louis XV in the reader's temporal frame. In the novels we have examined, the character of the king referred to a specific king, Louis XV, with his strengths and weaknesses. Despite the geographical displacement and the fantastic elements, these novels eliminated the shields of abstraction and metaphor for the royal character. The reader, by turns, listened to, empathized with, and questioned a character whose claims to superior reason were repeatedly belied by his thoughts and actions.

The decision to cast the king as a character in a novel establishes an analogy between kingship and fiction. Once the king acquires fictional character, he loses control of his political character. The epistemological assumptions that guided fiction challenged those of divine right monarchy. Since its inception in France, the novel aligned itself with experiment, criticism, and moral improvement. Authors accomplished these goals by entertaining readers with sex, adventure, fantasy, and satire. They relied on dialogic techniques that encouraged readers to inhabit characters and situations and apply them to their own concerns. These principles were antithetical to those that guided royal spectacles designed to dazzle the assembled public.

Clearly, novels cannot bear the explanatory weight for the political shifts we associate with the eighteenth century. They provide one example of how form – in this case fiction – affects meaning. By rejecting the abstractions of philosophical treatises for recognizable experiences, novels communicated directly with their readers. Readers were, in turn, empowered to form their own opinions and discuss them with others, a process that sharpened skills of interpretation and distinction. Moreover, while authors could design neat solutions for their flawed characters, their stylistic techniques raised doubts about rule in the minds of their readers. Fiction opened the king's character to a new kind of criticism, one that threatened his ontological status more than identifying specific areas of neglect. The content of these stories illuminates concerns of the period, but, more important, they demystify the royal character.[67] Louis XV became a familiar fictional character at the same time that he withdrew from the public eye, a pattern that reflects his timidity and discomfort in ceremony. Novels filled the gap left by the king's retreat from the public gaze and assumed the role of representing him to his subjects, high and low.

One last point to consider in the passage from political to literary character entails the intimacy and individualization associated with reading in the eighteenth century. We can assume that these novels were read aloud in small groups and by individuals in the comfort of their salons, studies, and reading rooms. In either case, however, the gesture differs from the crowd gathered to watch the king eat dinner or enter a city. These small volumes resembled a miniature portrait that readers could contemplate and appropriate in personal and diverse ways. Readers cultivated self-awareness as they engaged these texts and developed responses to them. The didactic energy of fiction compelled readers to improve themselves and their society by learning from the examples they encountered. In addition, these novels targeted Louis XV himself, explicitly or implicitly, with their tales of error and redemption. Yet, if the king failed to mend his ways, the novels summoned readers to resist abuse and neglect through the supporting characters who exemplified principles of moral courage and enlightened ideology.

Many of these novels remained popular throughout the eighteenth century. They inspired authors writing in the 1770s who incorporated the tropes and techniques of these allegories into scabrous and incendiary histories of Louis XV's reign. The fictions from the earlier part of the century became the history of the pre-revolutionary decades.[68] Where the earlier novels captured an ambivalent political and cultural climate, the later accounts offered a starker tale of abusive authority and moral decay. Literary character replaced mythology for discussing royal authority, and these discussions presented politics as individual struggles for self-fulfillment in the face of social and institutional obstacles. The dialogic structure of the novel and the rise of reading as an introspective activity encouraged readers to respond to what they read, to formulate criteria for judging themselves and others. Moreover, novels contributed to the enlightened idea of the individual in which character was a social artifact not an essential property. Character took shape in response to the pressures of other characters and circumstances. When the king became a fictional character, he acquired emotional depth to make him credible but lost the charisma that had guaranteed his authority. The moral weight of political character drained out of the king's body, fed into the emerging nation, and contributed there to modern ideas of national character.

Popular Monarchy in the Age of Mass
Media

Staging Modern Monarchs. Royalty at the World Exhibitions of 1851 and 1867

Maria Grever

In 1792 Thomas Paine compared the monarchy with something kept behind a curtain, 'about which there is a great deal of bustle and fuss, and a wonderful air of seeming solemnity; but when, by any accident, the curtain happens to be open – and the company see what it is, they burst into laughter'. According to Paine, a passionate republican who was involved in the American Revolution, nothing of this could happen in the representative system of government. Like the nation itself, this kind of government 'presents itself on the open theatre of the world in a fair and manly manner'. Whatever 'its excellences or defects, they would be visible to all,' he argued. 'It exists not by fraud and mystery; it deals not in cant and sophistry; but inspires a language that, passing from heart to heart, is felt and understood.'[1] Paine fiercely rejected the hereditary system of the monarchy, 'a silly and contemptible thing', and its lack of rationality; he accused monarchs and their adherents of deceiving the public by impressing their imaginations with spectacle and pedigree.

Yet this kind of republican discourse evaporated largely after 1815; it resurfaced in France only after the disposal of the Second Empire and was hardly accepted elsewhere. It was precisely the imaginative appeal of the monarchy that compassed a rather secure and prominent position of *constitutional* kings and queens within national life of the nineteenth century. To be able to survive, particularly after 1870, European monarchies had to adapt to parliamentary supremacy and to transform into popular institutions, thus becoming an integral part of the new cult of the nation. During a preceding stage of 'monarchical constitutionalism', crown, cabinet, and parliament had staged a struggle for power behind the scenes or even in the fullness of publicity, because monarchs still stood for legitimate political power. In France (1851) and Prussia (1864-1867), the crown had even managed to focus political power on the sovereign and his ministers.

Even before 1870, however, monarchs aspired to fortify their position by publicly underlining their role as symbols of the vitality and stability of nation, society, and state. The publicness or suggested visibility of monarchs to all citizens of the nation, advanced by modern mass media, proved to be of incalculable value for the creation and continuation of the constitutional monarchy. Media historian John Plunkett points to the most important feature of Queen

Victoria's successful media-making, what he calls 'mediation': an act of linking and connection. In his view the emerging mass print and visual culture in the 1850s shaped the public character of the British monarchy: it provided the queen's subjects with an intimate and personal interaction with the monarchy.[2] Although newspapers were not able to print photographic portraits until the end of the nineteenth century, the new media evoked a modern perspective on the British monarchy. The queen's ubiquitous presence in written reports and printed cartoons in newspapers and magazines bridged different individual experiences in the industrializing mass society and created a sense of belonging to the national community. Images of the whole British royal family were constantly available on a diverse assortment of media, ranging from engravings and magic lantern shows to street ballads and photographs. Moreover, royal visits and tours stimulated the reciprocal interest present between the British monarch and her subjects. In 1843 the *Penny Satirist* simply declared that Victoria was kept by the nation as a spectacle and that it was only right that she should be seen; it was her duty to show herself.[3]

What makes Queen Victoria especially interesting in this respect is that both her self-representation in staged photographs and the descriptions of her regional tours and civic duties in magazines contributed to the image of an ordinary monarch, a middle-class woman with whom people could easily identify.[4] In 1860 the English royal family also permitted publication of *carte-de-visite* portraits of Victoria, Albert, and their children in a simple, domestic setting. Soon, pictures of the royal family and royal events began to circulate. More or less the same phenomenon happened somewhat later in the Netherlands. In the 1890s the Dutch Queen Regent Emma devised a media strategy to make the monarchy more visible. To strengthen the bond with the Dutch, Emma toured with her daughter across all provinces. At one of these occasions in 1892, when they visited Friesland, Wilhelmina showed up in the traditional costume of this northern province, a tribute to 8,000 Friesian girls and women. The visit turned out to be a tremendous success and stimulated national feelings. Yet the real novelty was Emma's commission two years later to photograph the young Wilhelmina dressed in Friesian outfit at the palace Het Loo, and the selling of these images as picture postcards.[5] The successful interaction with the media of both Victoria and Emma represented a recovery and reassertion of the monarchy after an all-time low.[6]

The birth of new media in the burgeoning mass culture of the nineteenth century coincided with a more general political and cultural transition of the monarchic institution. In Western European countries, the concept of a divine and absolute monarchy was eroded by the growing power of cabinet and parliament, to which monarchs responded by exploring the boundaries of what was left of their power.[7] At the same time, leading politicians increasingly valued the monarchy for its ability to forge a national identity and thus to prevent uncontrollable revolutionary events. Particularly the revolutions of 1830 and 1848 in Europe, and the 1857 revolt in India against the British proved a real scare and had an enormous impact on political culture. The staging of *national* monarchs above all conflicting parties proved to be an effective instrument to mitigate class differences. This policy was strengthened by an increasing susceptibility of the masses for the pomp and circumstance of the monarchy. The visibility of the Crown might stimulate the consolidation of the nation and consequently the justification of its imperial expansion. Although both kings and queens objected to being 'mere representation', they knew that within a constitutional monarchy the only solid basis for their position lay in a theatrical support of the nation. Functioning as vehicles of national feelings, monarchs used a symbolic and ritual language either to exalt royal influence or to conceal its weakness. In order to maintain some political power, their first priority was to win the favour of the general public.

In the changing media structures, world exhibitions played a particularly influential role in the framing of royal representation and popular spectatorship. Being part of a broader visual culture, these grand spectacles offered an unprecedented opportunity to promote a populist monarchy and to sustain a royal culture industry on a mass scale, while thousands of visitors had a chance to gaze at 'real' kings and queens. Watching royals became part of a growing entertainment industry. In the words of Vanessa Schwartz: 'Real life was experienced as a show at the same time that shows became increasingly lifelike.'[8]

In this essay I will compare some articulations of the emerging popular monarchy at the world exhibitions of 1851 and 1867: how monarchs exposed themselves and represented their nation with modern means and (re-)invented discourses, and how the masses consumed and (re-)appropriated this royal spectacle. It will become evident that David Cannadine's chronology about the populist invention of the British monarchy between the late 1870s and 1914 does not hold.[9] Yet, my main goal is to show how the impact of world exhibitions furthered the reconfiguration of Western monarchies into popular, national institutions. Evidently these modern sites attracted many royals. They exchanged the latest news on family relations and political developments, explored national repertoires and compared the achievements of the exhibiting countries, while experiencing the possibility to be seen by large crowds from different backgrounds.

World Exhibitions and Visual Culture

The world exhibitions that became *en vogue* in the second half of the nineteenth century primarily celebrated scientific and technological progress by enforcing competition between Western nations. For more than fifty years,

local and national exhibitions in several European countries had been organized to promote industry and agriculture. Just like the national version, the
idea of a world exhibition originated in France. When the French were planning for another national exposition in 1849, the Minister of Agriculture and
Commerce, Louis-Joseph Buffet, proposed that it should be open to foreign
participants. In the end, the French organizers rejected the whole idea out of
fear for revolutions and the sapping of their economic protection policy. When
the British architect Matthew Wyatt and the manufacturer Henry Cole visited
the Paris exposition, they conceived the notion of an international exhibition
of industry. With the support of Prince Albert and other manufacturers, Cole
successfully launched the project in London in 1851.[10]

Other Western countries soon followed and copied this format. Until 1900,
millions of visitors came to the extensive sites of industry and artisanship in
London, Paris, Vienna, Philadelphia, Chicago, Brussels, and other cities, to see
manufactured goods, tools, machinery, arms, inventions, architecture, art,
exotic objects, animals, and people on display. These metropolises managed
extraordinary educational projects out of distant lands and peoples. The essential performative character of world exhibitions, with a duration of six to seven
months, was evident in the tremendous amounts of money and energy invested
in mass festivities and rituals, such as the opening of the exhibition by the
political elite, the reception of foreign royals, the presentation of winning
medals for specific exhibits, and the organization of international conferences.

In contrast to national exhibitions, world exhibitions were organized so as
to match the classification of the exhibited items with explanatory walking
tours, a strategy probably derived from the classical mnemonic techniques.[11] In
this sense, world exhibitions were layered narratives, articulating specific temporal and spatial experiences. The organizers and exhibitors presented their –
sometimes contradictory – visions of society by the construction of rooms,
halls, and pavilions, the selection and ordering of objects, the textual explanation, and the marketing of the exhibition. The whole layout gave meaning to
the objects on display, whereas walking tours and guides helped the visitors to
link the elements and to make the world exhibitions 'readable'. Illustrated
maps guided spectators through the buildings and brought the colonies within
reach; detailed catalogues explained the different objects; engravings and picture postcards of exhibits and specific festivities were sold to the public as a
kind of fair souvenir.

Despite differences in rhetoric and design, all world exhibitions expressed
some important Enlightenment features, such as: the encyclopedic urge to clas-
sify every single object, a desire for a visual overview of the world as a whole,
and an extreme emphasis on progress and the future. The 'super-plot' of every
world exhibition was the advancement of Western civilization: 'the world had
to be seen as being in some kind of advancing flux, with a stable – and

inevitable – future of plenty on the horizon.'[12] Hence, by and by world exhibitions visualized on a gigantic scale the increasingly asymmetrical power relations in society. Interestingly enough, almost from the start, the past played a significant role in the designs of the exhibition plan. Demonstrating the latest inventions and modern lifestyles evoked – whether implicitly or explicitly – a view of what the exhibitors considered old fashioned and traditional. Eventually, world exhibitions overwhelmingly articulated the need to link the past with the present and the future – in the words of Reinhart Koselleck, to bridge the growing gap between 'the space of experience' and 'the horizon of expectations'.[13]

What exactly do we know about the public's perception of the world exhibitions? Historical sources such as official procedures, minutes of committees, correspondence with private exhibitors, and printed exhibition catalogues generally shed more light on the intentions of the organizers. A central committee of the host country always provided for the construction of the industrial palace, the set-up of halls and pavilions, the selection and ordering of objects, and the marketing of the exhibition. The governments of participating countries installed official national committees – if possible, officially headed by a king or royal prince – that arranged the most important and characteristic exhibits of their country. These committees intended to showcase somehow a kind of national identity. To require the cooperation of grand entrepreneurs and to raise the enormous amounts of money needed, government support was absolutely necessary. Last but not least, the involvement of royal houses facilitated fund-raising, because royalty often ascribed a sense of magic and glamour to the ceremonials.

With regard to public perceptions, there are reports about visiting experiences in the newspapers and illustrated journals, letters of ordinary people and observations of famous writers and activists such as Charles Dickens, Karl Marx, Susan B. Anthony, Frederick Douglas, and Louis-Ferdinand Céline. From these sources we know that visitors were young and old, men and women, illiterates and intellectuals, labourers and entrepreneurs, politicians and aristocrats. Encouraged by their employees, large groups of artisans and other employees visited the exhibitions. In this respect, world exhibitions articulated, in Jürgen Habermas's terms, the changing public sphere of the nineteenth century, the space where people with no stake in the outcome of the debate discussed issues of general interest. Since the Enlightenment, this has been the arena in which new forms of citizenship were moulded. At the time of the first world exhibitions, the 1850s and 1860s, the aristocratic elite of Europe stood to lose its self-evident role in governing the nations, while the middle classes and working classes would in principle gain full citizenship rights. Yet, according to Nancy Fraser, the public domain was never a monolithic entity but consisted of various, sometimes overlapping publics and counter-publics.[14]

Precisely the multiform character of the public created new forms of inclusion and exclusion, and new possibilities of opening horizons and transgressing boundaries. World exhibitions served as modern, urban spaces for public consumption and entertainment, combining different visual attractions.

Yet, the sheer number of innovations and the unprecedented crowds of spectators caused many to experience the intended order as total chaos.[15] In the last decades of the nineteenth century, the bourgeois worried increasingly about the dangers of the masses. They feared the commercialization of culture, the degrading level of art and the mixture of different publics on one location.[16] The exhibition grounds could be 'invaded' by all sorts of people. To handle the densely packed crowds, the designers drew up schedules of fixed opening hours and viewing days for certain exhibits or performances. Newspapers and guides allowed visitors to familiarize themselves with the vast exhibition. There were special walking tours for white middle-class women which took them to shops and parks, providing an opportunity for leisurely viewing without male companions. While wandering on the exhibition grounds, they seemed to challenge the male concept of the flâneur. Particularly the 1893 World's Columbian Exposition in Chicago assured them a safe cultural place by masking the social dangers of mixing classes and ethnic groups. Yet, this strolling was, above all, connected to the rituals of urban commodity consumption.[17] Women had become important targets for selling goods, making their husbands spend.

According to Anne McClinctock, visitors shared the experience of the gaze: the privilege of watching, the power and freedom to meander, to choose where to look, to indulge in the pleasure of the gaze and yet remaining anonymous in the crowd.[18] The imaginary bird's-eye view, reproduced in maps and tourist guides, displayed the world exhibition as a distant panorama, offering the illusion of mastery and comprehension.[19] Walking at exhibition grounds also suggested the idea of being at the centre of a world in which one could readily survey its farthest reaches as well as its past and future, while measuring the differences between inferior and superior civilizations. Hence, visitors shuffled side by side through halls and pavilions. Both the design of the rooms and the display of the objects, products and people with information plaques steered the spectators in their interpretation. But they also retained considerable freedom of choice. Visitors could move about as they pleased, skip over exhibits or return for a second look, comparing observations with others. They could weave together all these impressions into their own stories. Thus, while the narratives of the world exhibitions articulated features of new temporal and spatial experiences, they also allowed the public to 'refigure' its plots.

Royal visits undergirded the prestige of world exhibitions with real and imagined spaces, displaying industrial goods and the latest technical inventions with imperial spectators and colonial 'objects'. Kings, queens, princes, and princesses symbolized a romantic or heroic past and offered many people something to cling to in the rapidly changing world of the day. From their point of view, monarchs considered these exhibitions a splendid opportunity to link themselves to modern society and to embody their nation. Watching the set-up of colonies with people on display, they could imagine themselves reigning a large colonial empire. Their presence might suggest that they approved of industrial progress and were still in charge of their country's future. However, because royals were instrumental to the fair's prestige, they ran the risk of becoming a commodity spectacle that could easily demystify their status. In that sense world exhibitions formed perfect tryouts for the popular monarchy: royalties tried to exploit the crowd's gaze effectively while simultaneously protecting their sacral image. But they could not completely control the perception of their image. Apart from political pressures, the expanding media structures with modern print techniques and new possibilities for the public's appropriation were far too complex. This becomes clear if we take a closer look at the world exhibition's festivities in London (1851) and Paris (1867).

Domestic Royalty at the Great Exhibition

In the 1790s the American politician Thomas Paine had announced the advent of meritocracy and the downfall of the monarchy, that irrational and silly institution. Nevertheless, more than seventy years later, the English economist Walter Bagehot considered the monarchy an important 'theatrical show', a disguise for the real workings of government, which were all the more effective for going on in secret. Although his argument actually obfuscated the real power of the Lords, Bagehot did not cling to the *ancien régime* of the absolute monarchy. He deliberately distinguished between the appearance and the reality of power, what he called 'the dignified parts' and the 'efficient parts [...] of the Constitution'.[20] The 'dignified parts' referred to monarchy and the Lords, performers who put on a good show; the 'efficient parts', Commons and the Cabinet, did the real work of governing the country. Each of these parts had its own dignified and efficient aspects; even the monarchy had its efficient side. The dignified parts of the government were a disguise or outward (mis)representation of the efficient parts. Particularly the dignified parts of the monarchy were necessarily 'the theatrical elements – those which appeal to the senses [...]. That which is mystic in its claims [...]; *that which is seen vividly for a moment, and then seen no more*'.[21] The mere idea of coming close to the 'real' monarchy, if only for a few seconds, could throw people into a rapture and stimulated the process of imagining the nation. The crucial component of this magical spell was the mixture of inapproachability and nearness of the royal family.

One of the first orchestrated shows of the popular monarchy occurred on 1 May 1851, when the British Queen Victoria opened the Great Exhibition of the

Works of Industry of All Nations in London's Hyde Park. Some 24,000 guests and authorities squeezed into the Crystal Palace, with thousands of people packed in the streets to catch a glimpse of the Queen and her family. Nine state carriages were driven quickly along the route, while the clocks of all Anglican churches in England announced the opening.[22] At twelve o'clock sharp the Queen, Prince Albert and their two little children entered the Crystal Palace. While everyone rose from the seats and a choir of 600 voices sang *Britannica Rules*, the procession strode to one end of the transept where they reached a platform with a throne under a baldachin.[23] Albert explained the purpose and history of the event and offered the official catalogue to the queen. After a prayer and Handel's *Hallelujah*, Queen Victoria made her inspection tour through the Crystal Palace and finally opened the Exhibition. The choir sent forth *God Save the Queen*, trumpets sounded and cannons boomed. The *Illustrated London News* reported:

> The ceremonial was one [...] without precedent or rival. The homage paid by the Sovereign of the widest empire in the world to the industry and genius of both hemispheres, will not fill a page in history as a mean and unsubstantial pageant. While the race of man exists, this solemn and magnificent occasion will not readily fade away from his memory [...].[24]

Prince Albert, although at first reluctant to become involved, had devoted himself energetically to the Great Exhibition. By the time of its closing in October, more than five million visitors had attended the exhibition. This success brought distinction to England and greatly improved Albert's reputation. When he had married Victoria, there had been significant opposition to the German prince of Saxe-Coburg-Gotha. Being a foreigner and the queen's cousin, his activities often roused much suspicion, particularly amongst the English aristocracy. Moreover, there was no clear public role for Albert. No wonder newspapers ridiculed him for being mere decoration. The Great Exhibition had offered the prince an excellent opportunity to prove his patriotic loyalty and, indirectly, to promote himself. At the same time the exhibition organizers – liberal politicians, manufacturers, architects, civil engineers – used the monarchy to sell the idea of an international exhibition. Consequently, the Crystal Palace became the project that linked the royal family to middle-class values.[25]

According to Tom Nairn, Albert also metamorphosed into the first and most important of all royal impresarios. Together with Victoria he created a new image of the royal family, according with both social and national needs: 'a matriarchally inclined symbol-family bringing home a traditionalist national identity to ever-wider circles of population.'[26] For the opening ceremonial

Fig. 1. Opening of the Great Exhibition (1851-1852), *by Henry Courtney Selous (1803-1890). In the middle: Queen Victoria, Prince Albert and their children. Left and right: dignitaries and guests with the Chinese man He-Sing.*

Albert had deliberately staged a domestic setting. The private family of the queen secluded from public gaze was revealed for all to see in a glass house amidst displays of modern industry, the latest inventions and new sciences. In this way the royal family personified Great Britain's leading position in the modern world.[27] In behaving publicly like members of the middle class, Victoria and Albert set an example for their subjects to consider themselves members of a middle-class nation who could share in its power and prosperity.[28] The combination of domesticity and royal grandeur appealed to the masses; it stimulated a collective sense of belonging to a national unity. At the same time this family image obscured the unequal society of the British empire: the sharply separated social classes, ranks, and ethnic groups with the monarch at the top of this hierarchy, buttressed by tradition and religion. Victoria's performance also demonstrated the constitutive role of gender in the making of national identity: as a woman she symbolized both the biological reproduction of true (white and Protestant) members of the nation and the cultural transmission of English values.[29]

According to historian Jeffrey Auerbach, contemporaries were struck by the social mixing in the Crystal Palace. Indeed, people of every class and rank came to visit the Great Exhibition. Soon after the opening, *Punch* printed a cartoon showing 'Her Majesty, as She Appeared on the FIRST of MAY, Surrounded by "Horrible Conspirators and Assassins"'.[30] Yet the drawing itself shows the royal family quietly walking through the Crystal Palace surrounded by animated well-dressed ladies with gentlemen behind them, apparently from the middle classes, who were settled along the principal avenues and galleries. The masses flocked in after 26 May, when the shilling days started. Only then did social mixing take place among upper, middle, and working classes. Nevertheless, this kind of social encounter was a rare phenomenon. Even more exceptional was the fact that the queen attended the Crystal Palace frequently, before and after the opening, sometimes passing workmen, exhibitors and ordinary visitors.[31] One of the main characteristics of world exhibitions was the creation of a social space where different classes, genders, and ethnic groups could coexist and observe each other. But bringing these groups into closer proximity also enforced hierarchies and differences. Particularly in the last decade of the nineteenth century, the bourgeois increasingly feared the masses and the mixture of different publics on one location. Journalists often reported on densely packed crowds flooding the exhibition grounds.[32] While 'only' six million people came to the Crystal Palace in 1851, the Paris World Exposition of 1900 attracted 50 million visitors.

HER MAJESTY, as She Appeared on the FIRST of MAY, Surrounded by "Horrible Conspirators and Assassins."

Fig. 2. Cartoon 'The Queen and Her subjects', Punch (3 May 1851).

Although the number of foreigners during the Great Exhibition was relatively small, English journalists warned against the dangers of foreign visitors. Xenophobic pamphlets about Turkish, Russian, Prussian, and Jewish travellers stimulated prejudices and evoked curiosity after 'exotic' people. Newspapers and cartoons referred to 'dark looking fellows' and 'black men with fearful eyes and teeth'. One of *Punch*'s drawings shows the Crystal Palace as an exhibit packed with Oriental-looking people, with Western spectators gawking at them.[33] Other caricatures depict black visitors from non-Western countries as primitive beings. Drawings and caricatures like these were the first expressions of a globalizing society, emphasizing a supposed gap between so-called inferior and superior civilizations. Later, at the world exhibitions of 1873 and 1878, indigenous people from the colonies worked as restaurant personnel; since the Amsterdam world exhibition in 1883, they were put on display as objects, often under humiliating circumstances.[34] Yet spectatorship was not a privilege for white, middle-class Westerners. In these public spaces visitors and displayed people interacted, playing with the very boundaries that the world exhibitions helped to set up. Visitors particularly discovered the return gaze and the agency of non-Western performers.[35]

A hilarious incident during the opening of the 1851 Great Exhibition showed something of the confusion of the organizers about how to treat Oriental guests. The foreign officials assembled in the nave included a mysterious Chinese man, clothed in satin, silent but seemingly at ease. The sight of him shaking hands with the Duke of Wellington led observers to believe that he was a Chinese Mandarin. Then suddenly, during the singing of the *Hallelujah Chorus*, he pushed his way through the crowd to the throne, began to bow repeatedly to the queen and tried to kiss Victoria's feet. Since no one knew who he was, but not wanting to offend him, they let him attend the procession that toured the Palace. It turned out that this man, called He-Sing, was no Mandarin but the proprietor of a Chinese junk, moored at a pier in the Thames. There he performed Chinese swordplay with his crew every night.[36] Obviously, He-Sing had played a convincing role in the opening ceremony, demonstrating the vulnerable boundaries between the 'real' and the spectacle of a mass event. This *petite-histoire* also illustrates that class and status could privilege over colour and ethnicity. In his book *Ornamentalism,* Cannadine emphasizes that the British Empire was above all a complex *social* hierarchy: it was not exclusively based on the collective, colour-code ranking of social groups, but depended as much on the more venerable colour-blind ranking of individual social prestige. He points to the new culture of ornamentation in the British Empire, with a pseudo-medieval spectacular of rank and inequality. The British hailed the ruling princes in South Asia as the 'native aristocracy of the country'; their support was vital for the stability of the Indian Empire.[37]

The Great Exhibition also linked progress to consumerism. Exhibitors showed the large public the newest goods and persuaded them to buy products that would bring the industrial world into their homes. The display of historical objects and images from the past made a good contrast with the Exhibition's general message of modernity. As a consequence, the exhibition produced a tension between modernity and tradition. While some groups cherished anti-modern sentiments and feared the loss of tradition, others had optimistic feelings about the industrial mass society. In this ambivalent atmosphere, opponents and adherents of the Great Exhibition used the monarchy – the institution that supposedly symbolized a glorious past – for their own purposes and commercial interests. A contradictory combination of progress and nostalgia was well illustrated in the pictures of a jewel cabinet made for Queen Victoria by Ellington and Company and exhibited at the Crystal Palace. Whereas Albert advocated internationalism, free trade, and progress, the image of the royal couple shows him standing in armour and Victoria sitting in late medieval dress with a child near her lap.[38]

But the cabinet's pictures reveal something else as well. While Victoria embodies domesticity and motherhood without any explicit references to her position as queen regnant, Albert obviously represents an ideal of English masculinity by combining the fighting spirit of the medieval knight with the chivalrous guardianship of the modern gentleman. This image of the royal couple might have expressed the queen's desire to claim for her German-speaking husband an English identity, an ideal woman hardly could achieve. According to Elizabeth Langland, narratives of Englishness at the time of Victoria developed into an increasingly masculine construction.[39] Hence, immediately after the opening, the Queen credited the success of the Crystal Palace both to Albert and to England. In her view he had demonstrated successfully the superiority of the English and what true Englishness meant in the world. Six years later the Queen could endow Albert with the official title of Prince Consort. Although Albert became a leading national figure, he remained a foreigner, certainly in the eyes of the aristocrats. His ties with the middle classes and his involvement in the construction of a domestic image of the Queen and the monarchy defined him as Victorian but alienated him from the discourse of 'true' Englishness.

Keeping up Appearances at the Paris Exposition Universelle

In 1867 the French Emperor Louis-Napoleon Bonaparte was determined to outdo the English in the size and magnificence of the fourth world exhibition. More than 11 million people came to the *Exposition Universelle et Internationale* in Paris.[40] Napoleon III was in urgent need for this megaproject to enhance his political status and to place France in the centre of the civilized world, because European monarchs considered him a parvenue emperor, linked to the French Revolution, who had seized his power by a coup d'état and had established a dictatorial emperorship by the grace of people's favour.[41] He was never fully accepted by the age-old royal houses who used to govern by divine right. Whereas the Great Exhibition had been a compromise between private initiative and state intervention, supported by a cautious Prince Albert, a French Imperial Committee produced the concept for the whole Exposition, and groups of state officials executed the plans. French manufacturers were not in charge; the emperor was, along with his government and some experts, particularly mining engineer Frédéric Le Play.

Le Play had designed a plan that articulated a desire for a harmonic, rational society. His utopian palace, built on the Champs de Mars, consisted of seven concentric oval galleries and resembled the Coliseum in Rome. In the roofed-over galleries, objects were displayed according to specific categories. By touring one gallery, spectators could compare countries in a particular category. The outer ring was reserved for shops, restaurants and cafés from the participating countries. The next and largest ring was full of steel and smoke; there were power looms, spinning machines, typesetting machines, locomotives and cannons. The innermost ring was devoted to the (mainly French) history of labour. Sixteen radial cross-sections offered exhibition space to the various countries, so that a pie-shaped cross-section showed all exhibits from a single

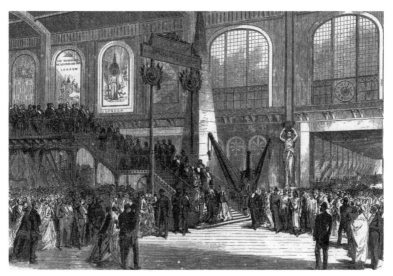

Fig. 3. Grand Album de l'Exposition Universelle 1867.
Opening ceremony of the Paris Exposition Universelle 1867 by Emperor Napoleon III.

country. Just like England's Great Exhibition, the 1867 Exposition focused on the doctrine of progress, but this time the organizers devoted much more attention to the evolutionary process of the innovations.[42] Hence, the importance of historical settings and rituals.

The opening ceremony was planned for April 1. To cover up the still-unfinished Exposition, a kind of Potemkin façade was constructed with textile and paint.[43] It did not disturb the theatrical opening, which deliberately aimed for a close association with the triumphal marches of the Roman emperors. Louis-Napoleon, an admirer of Julius Caesar,[44] toured with the Empress in an open carriage through the streets of Paris to make himself visible for some 100,000 (apparently) exulting people. Thousands of workmen, the majority with their picks and shovels hoisted in the air and the others holding tricolour flags surmounted with gilt eagles, were ranged on each side of the road.[45] When the emperor entered the building via *la Porte d'honneur* (triumphal arch), soldiers and labourers formed a line, while music played. Napoleon surveyed the building, the Exposition sections, the organizing committees and its exhibitors. Members of foreign monarchies, such as the Dutch Crown Prince William of Orange, joined the imperial procession. When the Emperor and Empress quit the palace, they made their way through cheering crowds.

This ritual lacked the sophisticated mix of enchantment and domesticity that had characterized the opening of the Crystal Palace. Being at the centre of the 1851 Great Exhibition, Queen Victoria had self-evidently incarnated the whole English nation. The opening ceremony of the 1867 Exposition mainly intended to reinforce the idea of the paternal care of the French emperor for his people. However, considered from a gender perspective, there was at least one interesting similarity: the (self)representation of Albert and Louis-Napoleon referred to the figure of the active male agent of modernity. Both men played their roles in the making of the nation with other men. But also in this respect, differences dominated the scene. Prince Albert had offered his queen and wife a modern world under a glass house, a world which might gradually downgrade traditional social hierarchy and its titles. Committed to middle-class interests, he strove for free trade and peace among nations.[46] Whereas the British queen had appropriated the attitude of a modern monarch and thus became imitable for the upcoming classes, the French emperor seemed to shore up the *ancien régime*, disguised in a modern shape. The military character of ceremonies and rituals during the 1867 Exposition explicitly emphasized social hierarchy within a corporative state.

The cult of Louis-Napoleon and the Bonaparte family reached its climax at the awarding of prizes on July 1. The glass court of the huge industrial section, the *Palais de l'Industrie*, was transformed into a classical Roman circus with ten award trophies set up in the centre. The building was filled with more than 20,000 selected visitors, including royalty. The Emperor dominated the circus like a *paterfamilias*. Situated on top of the largest platform, he was surrounded by the Empress and their son, by representatives of European courts and oriental royals.[47] The whole stage suggested not only the international acceptance of Napoleon's regime but also the support of his government by the French people. Yet, at that time, despite some liberal reforms and a gradual process of parliamentarization, Louis-Napoleon Bonaparte still ruled a rather authoritarian, centralized, imperial nation-state. The military organization of the exhibition awards clearly demonstrates this. The triumphant prizewinners descended the state staircase, marched like an army through the circus behind a flag of their professional group to honour the emperor and finally took their places near one of the trophies. After several speeches, some members of the group (always

Fig. 4. Grand Album de l'Exposition Universelle 1867.
Official distribution of exhibition awards at the Champs-Élysées Palace, 1 July 1867.

patrons or employers) were allowed to climb the stairs to receive their awards from the emperor. This over-organized ritual ended with a triumphal march of the emperor. Representatives of all national committees were introduced to Napoleon while their national anthem was played.[48]

A remarkable and new feature of the 1867 Exposition was the gathering of so many Western and non-Western monarchies with their dignitaries at one location. About fifty royal visitors attended the opening, such as the Emperors of Russia and Austria, the Dutch Queen Sophie and her two sons, the Belgian King and Queen, the son of Queen Victoria, the King and Queen of Prussia, the Ottoman Sultan Abdülaziz and his nephew, the Viceroy of Egypt, and the Japanese Mim Bou Tayou (brother of the Taîkoun or ruler).[49] Perhaps world exhibitions evoked the international socialist movement, but they certainly echoed 'the international of monarchies' of previous times. In these gatherings, royalty connections, social status and grandeur overruled ethnic and colour differences.[50] The 1867 Exposition also produced a genuine royal culture industry. Week after week there were huge festivities to celebrate the presence of one member of royalty after another: the gala in the Paris Opéra to honour the Russian Tsar; special rituals for the arrival of the Turkish Sultan (his tour through the streets of Paris, the welcome by the Emperor's son and his visit at the palace of L'Elysée); a ball at the town hall to honour all foreign royals; a spe-

REPRÉSENTATION DE GALA A L'OPÉRA, EN L'HONNEUR DE L'EMPEREUR DE RUSSIE

Fig. 5. Grand Album de l'Exposition Universelle 1867.
Gala at the opera in honour of the Russian Tsar Alexander II.

cial military reception for the Austrian Emperor; and the presentation of the winning awards.

Artists, often commissioned by publishing companies, made accurate engravings of these events with a very good likeness of the royals. The *Grand Album de l'Exposition Universelle 1867* consists of 150 impressive wood engravings made by French and foreign artists. Plunkett describes the revival of the wood engraving and the subsequent development of an illustrated press already in the 1840s, thus before the advent of photography. One result in England was an accumulation of realistic and satiric images of Queen Victoria.[51] World exhibitions were an important impetus in this culture industry, because the organizers had to set up the publication of special journals, albums and illustrated maps to attract visitors. Several engravings of world exhibition albums or journals appeared in foreign journals, and consequently reached a large public that in the future could recognize the royals because of the realistic images.[52] At the exhibitions, visitors also could buy picture postcards and photographs.

Apart from political motives, royals were also invited to the world exhibitions for commercial reasons. The organizers addressed the public by official and spectacular announcements of the arrival of kings and queens in the newspapers. In this way they tried to attract more visitors, making royalty a part of the display and an object of entertainment.[53] The mass press played an

S. M. L'EMPEREUR D'AUTRICHE RENDANT AUX DAMES DE LA HALLE LEUR; VISITE

Fig. 6. Grand Album de l'Exposition Universelle 1867.
Arrival of the Austrian Emperor Franz Jozeph.

important role in the interaction between spectacle and spectator.[54] Journalists prepared the visitor's perception by describing the details of the royal visits to world exhibitions: how they were dressed, what kind of jewels, the family relations, and the genealogies of the monarchies they represented. Many were eager to come close to the unapproachable elite, to gaze at emperors, kings, queens, princes, and princesses while they were watching new technologies or experiencing modern inventions such as navigating an air balloon. Royalty attracted ordinary people for obvious reasons of imagination and appropriation. The opportunity to actually see 'real' representatives of distant countries and ancient monarchies, if only for a glimpse, made the world exhibitions increasingly lifelike. Being at the same site where royalty had been enhanced the status of visitors. Absorbed by the royal spectacle, they may have learned about other countries and their place in the world. The sight of magnificently dressed queens chaperoned by sturdy kings in military uniforms also suggested that fairy-like monarchs carefully ruled their countries and protected their people – fantasies which were nostalgic escapes from a disagreeable present.

The official invitation policy of the Imperial Committee had reflected Napoleon's strategy to consolidate his internal position and to strengthen his international alliances – this was certainly the case when the Prussian King came to the Exposition accompanied by Chancellor Bismarck. In March 1867, just before the opening of the Exposition Universelle, Napoleon's reputation had been severely damaged in the crisis about the status of Luxemburg with Germany. The Dutch called for a conference attended by France, Prussia, Austria, the Netherlands, and England in London, 7-11 May, where all parties were reconciled. Probably to make a gesture, the Prussian King came to the Paris Exposition, but his state visit did not really improve the relationship with France. In 1870 the French-German war broke out, and the alliance with the Russian Emperor, gloriously sealed at the 1867 Exposition, turned out to be of no value. The second empire had become history. One could thus conclude in hindsight that the 'dignified parts' of French governmental power – so much appreciated at the Exposition Universelle – could not conceal the failure of the 'efficient parts' anymore.[55]

Performing the Nation

At first sight, the attempt to sanctify the world exhibitions with royalty may have contributed to the demystification of the represented monarchies. Yet these spectacles also offered them the opportunity to come to terms with mass society and to understand their new performing role within national frames. At exhibition sites, royals could experiment with that complex mixture of magic attraction, grandeur and 'ordinariness' of kings and queens. It was also the beginning of a phenomenon to which Anne McClintock refers when she suggests that the singular power of nationalism since the late nineteenth century has been its capacity to organize a sense of popular, collective unity through the management of a mass national *commodity spectacle*.[56]

In Benedict Anderson's well-known account of nation formation, the newspaper was central to the growing awareness of a national identity, which he considers a cultural and imaginative process, not identical to state formation and definitions of citizenship. Print culture gave people new ways to think about themselves and to relate to each other. Anderson's image of middle-class men reading their morning newspaper over breakfast while getting ready to go to work points to the importance of mass media for the dissemination of ideas about a national community. In my view, McClintock rightly criticizes Anderson for neglecting the influence of visual culture. Nationalism 'takes shape through the visible, ritual organization of fetish objects – flags, uniforms, airplane logos, maps, anthems, national flowers, national cuisines, and architectures as well as through the organization of collective fetish spectacle'. Despite the commitment of European nationalism to the idea of the nation-state as the embodiment of rational progress, she argues, 'nationalism has been experienced and transmitted primarily through fetishism – precisely the cultural form that the Enlightenment denigrated as the antithesis of Reason'.[57] The public's fascination for royalty at the world exhibitions in 1851 and 1867 relates to that sentiment. But royalty also manifests itself in different shapes within different environments.

The boastful and military performance of the people's Emperor Louis-Napoleon at the World Exhibition of 1867 revealed the fake and ephemeral character of the Second Empire. The presence of many foreign royals masked its own poor situation. Yet the different role of Victoria at the 1851 Exhibition was not only a matter of character or gender. According to Nairn, England/Britain should be interpreted *really* as a 'disguised Republic', a republic since the Glorious Revolution of 1688 in the sense of a 'Parliamentary Sovereignty', hidden, ornamented and preserved by the Windsor monarchy.[58] The Windsor Crown, he argues, functions as a barrier against the people's sovereignty and republican democracy. In 1792 Thomas Paine could not foresee that the monarchic institution would benefit from the new media to perform spectacles that mobilized masses and consequently shaped the modern English nation-state, even in the twenty-first century. The French Second Empire had been a last gasp of plebiscitary autocracy, an attempt to actually subordinate the modern to the traditional.

In 1878 the Third Republic of France organized another World Exhibition in Paris. At the crowded opening ritual, when President Mac Mahon entered the main building with many royals, people cheered 'Vive la République!'[59] French royalty belonged to the past. It was now represented by the display of ancient jewellery of the French crown, set up in one of the exhibition rooms, left to the public's vivid imagination and referring to a distant past.

The Emperor's New Clothes.
The Reappearance of the Performing
Monarchy in Europe, c. 1870-1914

Jaap van Osta

In recent years the Dutch monarchy has attracted public attention through a series of impressive ceremonies. Both the marriage of Crown Prince Willem-Alexander and the funerals of Prince Claus and Princess Juliana and Prince Bernhard, in 2002 and 2004, respectively, were spectacular events, brilliantly staged and skilfully handled. They demonstrated that in the Netherlands the 'theatre of the state' is being well conducted under Queen Beatrix. However, in the meantime, a quarrel[1] within the Dutch royal family, which revealed by accident the secret powers of the Crown, caused much of the recently gained respect to be lost. The conclusion that can be drawn from these recent events in the Netherlands is that the attraction of the monarchy nowadays is grounded mainly in its ceremonial, not political, aspect. Furthermore, as I can detect no substantial difference on this point between the situation of the Dutch monarchy and other European monarchies, it seems clear that the role of monarchy as an institution in our present postmodern era is basically ceremonial. I will try to demonstrate that the reappearance of the 'ceremonial monarchy', i.e., a monarchy based essentially upon royal performance, is the outcome of the desacralization of the monarchy and the democratization of politics: a long historical development, which goes back to the aftermath of the French revolution.

The Monarchy as a 'Sociodrama'

It has long been assumed that since the nineteenth century the institution of monarchy had been doomed to die. After all, the French Revolution had put an end to the absolute power of the monarch who governed by the grace of God and had deprived the monarchy of its inherent right to exist. What exactly was the position of the monarch in the constitutional era? Halfway through the nineteenth century, when the political role of the Crown was seriously curtailed, at least in Western European nations, it became necessary to devise a new role for the monarchy if it was to have a significant future existence. The monarchy had to be 'reinvented', as it were.

Theoretically, this process of transforming the monarchy was not at all complicated. The French Revolution had put the fate of the monarchy ultimately into the hands of the people. As a 'people's monarchy', the institution had to be popular by definition, and henceforth monarchs who reigned by the grace of their subjects had one single purpose: to find favour with the people. Yet, what did 'popular' mean in the early nineteenth century? There was no easy answer to this question, so it was just as well that the question initially was not expressly put. In the first half of the nineteenth century, the constitutional monarchy was 'popular' because it left room for the ideals and ambitions of the wealthy and educated classes, who more and more came to dominate political life in Western European countries. By the second half of the century, when increasingly larger sections of the population were politically involved by the extension of the franchise, the question of what was meant by 'popular monarchy' could no longer remain unanswered. Slowly, the answer emerged. Independently, political thinkers such as the German Lorenz von Stein and the Italian Angelo Camillo De Meis conceived of a mediating role for the monarchy: the king, by promoting a policy of reform, would collaborate to reduce social tensions and, in doing so, would be instrumental in holding the nation together.[2] It was up to the politicians to make room for the monarchy's new function and to adapt the king to his new role.

The huge popularity the monarchical institution enjoyed around the turn of the century proves that the efforts of politicians to 're-invent' the monarchy had not been without success. By taking advantage of nationalist sentiments, they had launched a popularity campaign for the benefit of the state, with the prominent figure of the monarch at its head. As in early modern times, the monarch's role would be essentially a *performing* one: vested with all the splendour of monarchical ritual, the monarch would be presented as the vivid symbol of continuity and consensus to which the whole nation might defer.[3]

How should we understand this popularity campaign? In theory, it is not at all easy to make propaganda for something not tangible, a symbol, which only lives in the human imagination. Fortunately, the monarchy itself offered the solution, for it is by definition a human institution in that it is carried by a person of flesh and blood. Apart from this one person, there is nothing. But it proved to be enough. In the mid-1860s, the English journalist Walter Bagehot had already intuited that it should not be difficult to elicit emotional and affectionate feelings for crowned heads from the masses, the only condition being for royals to play their parts well. Bagehot wrote that as a 'family on the throne' they ought to behave as common people as much as possible, for this would enable their subjects to identify with them easily, which was what really mattered.[4] 'Lead a private life publicly' is what Bagehot suggested royals should do, and this seems to be exactly the key to the success of present-day monarchs, namely, the idea that royals are at once like us and not like us.[5]

From the 1870s onward, everywhere in Europe new forms of monarchical representation developed. First, monarchs became, more than previously, public figures. As the Crown's popularity depended upon the monarch's visibility, new occasions were created where emperors and kings could be seen. So, following the example of Queen Victoria, who together with the entire royal family had appeared 'in state' at the opening of the Great Exhibition in London in 1851,[6] European royalty gathered in Vienna in 1873 for the opening of the World Exhibition – a colourful assembly of foreign princes, which the young Sigmund Freud, who was there to see the carriage procession drive by, irreverently described as 'made up exclusively of mustachios and medals'.[7] Second, increasing numbers of 'human' events in royal families – such as births, marriages and funerals – were transformed along Bagehotian lines into national events in order to make the identification between the monarch and the people real. As brilliant editions of ordinary events, they caught the attention of the public. In addition, extraordinary events such as coronations and royal jubilees were equally seized upon as opportunities to present the monarch to the people, public appearances being the principal *raison d'être* of the monarchy. These royal celebrations were occasions for national ceremonies, defined by Elizabeth Hammerton and David Cannadine as 'examples of consensual, secular religion'.[8] As demonstrations of national unity they would be highly valued in governmental circles. Sometimes voices to the contrary could be heard,[9] but these failed to put the authorities off, since most such celebrations proved extremely successful. It even happened that they were repeated shortly afterwards, for no apparent reason.[10]

By means of these national celebrations, which were a 'calculated combination of the ritual and the prosaic', as Simon Schama put it,[11] the monarchy entered into the collective consciousness of the nation as a 'human' institute, functioning at the level of *sociodrama*. It was a remarkable approach to royalty, making it more dignified while at the same time more banal, a combination that – as we have seen in previous contributions – worked well also in other historical contexts.

The Reappearance of the 'Performing Monarchy'

It is not difficult to see that the royal ceremonies organized at the turn of the nineteenth century helped the monarchy to survive. They helped to transform the monarchy from an institution of dwindling political power into a tremendously effective centerpiece of national identity.

The first and best example of such ceremonies can be found in British history. In the 1860s, when the general public highly resented Queen Victoria's withdrawal from public life after the death of the Prince Consort in 1861, the visibility of the Crown became a matter of major concern and discussion. Both the royal household and the government feared that the queen's unpopularity might have a destabilizing effect on political life, so they tried to persuade her to resume her royal duties in the way the public required. 'It is impossible to deny that H.M. is drawing too heavily on the credit of her former popularity,' Lord Halifax, the Lord Privy Seal, wrote to Henry Ponsonby, the Queen's private secretary, adding ominously that 'Crowned Heads as well as other people must do much that was not necessary in former days to meet the altered circumstances and altered tone of modern times'. What was meant by 'altered circumstances' and 'altered tone' he specified as follows:

> The mass of the people expect a King or Queen to look
> and play the part. They want to see a Crown and Scep-
> tre and all that sort of thing. They want the gilding for
> the money [...] It is not wise to let them think [...] that
> they could do without a sovereign who lives [in a palace]
> as any private lady might do.'[12]

In 1871 the British government, alarmed by the news of the proclamation of the French Republic following military defeat in the Franco-Prussian war, decided to act. The Prince of Wales, Victoria's eldest son, fell ill and when he, to the general relief of the people, finally recovered, Prime Minister Gladstone devised a plan to capitalize upon the general mood by staging a public ceremony of thanksgiving, a religious service at St Paul's Cathedral preceded by a grand procession through London starting from Buckingham Palace – at which the Queen and the Prince would be seen by the ordinary people for whom there would be no pews in St Paul's.[13] In a discussion with the Queen, who naturally was much against the plan and only accepted it on condition that the *show*, as she sardonically termed the ceremony, would be carried out properly, Gladstone stressed the historic importance of the thanksgiving, calling it a 'great public act' through which the monarchy's new meaning and importance could be demonstrated. 'Royalty,' he said:

> [...] was in one point of view a symbol, and one of great
> consequence: its character and duties had greatly
> changed among us in modern times but perhaps in the
> new forms they were not less important than in the old.'

In Gladstone's view, the purpose of the thanksgiving was to exercise a positive effect on 'the future of the Monarchy & of the country as connected with it', and to that end he wanted all the traditional pomp that could be mustered to be brought into play for a public that had no experience of such a spectacle.[14] The Thanksgiving Ceremony of February 1872, defined by one historian as 'the first truly national festival of modern times',[15] marked a turning point for the monarchy in Britain. What Gladstone had intuited in 1871, later politicians could no longer afford to ignore, namely that a more democratic nation demanded greater state and show, just as Bagehot had predicted.[16]

British and Continental Experiments

Just like the Thanksgiving Ceremony of 1872, both the Golden and Diamond Jubilees of Queen Victoria, in 1887 and 1897, respectively, were equally master-pieces of Britain's 'theatre of state'. Elsewhere a similar development occurred. The reappearance of the 'performing monarchy' in the Netherlands dates from the period of the Regency of Queen Emma (1890-1898), when the Queen, widow of the deceased King William III, together with her daughter, the infant Queen Wilhelmina, travelled the country to pay a number of introductory visits.[17] It was their way of giving the Dutch monarchy a human face, as in the reign of William III it had turned more and more invisible. In Belgium the situation was similar, although modernization had to wait for the death, in 1909, of the controversial King Leopold II. More contemporaneous was the situation in Germany. Since 1888, Germany had been ruled by Emperor Wilhelm II, who himself was convinced that it was essential that a modern monarch be visible. He therefore travelled frequently – so frequently, in fact, that he was nick-named the *Reisekaiser,* or peripatetic emperor.[18]

These European initiatives to modernize the monarchy led roughly to the same situation everywhere: the rise of a popular, national monarchy. Yet there are differences in style. For instance, in Britain the popularization of the monarchy resulted in a ceremonial monarchy, a monarchy of 'invented' traditions as Cannadine put it, clearly different from the informal monarchy that arose in the Netherlands. These distinctions were caused by circumstances that differed between the two countries. A closer look at some of the striking differences between certain European monarchies will clarify how specific national contexts influenced the form and style of the monarchies that developed.

For the British monarchy, the late Victorian revival of state and show is inextricably bound up with the rise of the British Empire, unrivalled in history, which demanded a symbol on which to fix its feelings of national unity and self-conceit. The monarchy was a convenient object, and it was subsequently adorned with all the ceremonial trimmings suitable for a great nation. This occurred in the last decades of Victoria's reign, with a reluctant queen insisting that she did not want to be made a fool.[19] So, as it happened, the ceremonial monarchy, so typical of the present-day British monarchy, actually dates from after her death in 1901[20] and is bound up with her successor Edward VII, who reigned for no more than nine-and-a-quarter years but whose very important contribution was to prepare the British monarchy for the age of entertainment.[21]

Obviously, British efforts to adorn the monarchy did not remain unnoticed. Other nations envied the display of power it heralded, so they sought to upgrade their own monarchies after the British example. In their turn, these monarchy 'decorators' faced problems and obstacles which offer insight into the peculiarities of the country concerned. For instance, in Italy many politicians contemplated following the British example, spurred by the fact that the Italian state, finally unified in 1861, had not made an easy start. Italian nationalist feeling had never run high, and politicians consequently put all their hopes in the monarchy. King Victor Emmanuel II was expected to put lots of work into his job, but unfortunately did not! For instance, he refused to take up residence in Florence when it became the capital of the kingdom in 1864, arguing that this choice was only temporary. So the national state had to do without a national court, and things did not improve when Rome was added to Italy in 1871. Only when the king died in 1878, would politicians take revenge on the king by staging an extravagant funeral, committing his bodily remains – against his last wishes – to Rome's Pantheon. As a matter of fact, they almost literally copied the ceremonial the Belgians had invented for the state funeral of their first king three years earlier.[22]

For all this royal stubbornness, the government had every reason to complain, and it did so in 1881, when Prime Minister Crispi opened his heart in a parliamentary debate and said:

> Whenever the king desires to attend a parliamentary meeting and I notice that the chairman's seat is taken away to be replaced by a wooden throne, I feel humiliation deep within my heart. In London such meetings with the head of state take place in the House of Lords, where a throne (not made of wood, but of bronze and gold) is available, permanently and visibly. It has never occurred to anyone there that it would be there only temporary. For a throne must, like a state, be solid and look solid.[23]

Savoy's *parvenu* monarchy was unable to fulfil its historic role of unifying the Italian people, and in the end Crispi, who had privately turned republican, would search for alternative ways to consolidate the fragile structure of the state. These alternatives, disastrously, led to Africa. The ceremonial upgrading of the Italian monarchy did not come off.

The Dutch monarchy had been rather unceremonious from its origin, reflecting the nation's history – proudly republican – and character – typically bourgeois and non-aristocratic. Late nineteenth-century attempts to enhance its ceremonial character were equally modest.[24] Typically, the most remarkable contribution, linked to *Prinsjesdag* or the State Opening of Parliament, came off 'spontaneously' and was not the work of politicians. The initiative to build the Golden State Coach was taken by the people of Amsterdam, who wanted to give a present to Queen Wilhelmina when she ascended the throne in 1898. They raised money and ordered a golden coach from a local firm, which was presented to the Queen at the time of her inauguration. The Golden State Coach would become the distinguishing mark of the Dutch monarchy, playing, from 1903 onwards, a prominent role in the annual ceremony of *Prinsjesdag,* which came to be staged regularly in the ancient *Ridderzaal* (Hall of Knights) in The Hague, a spectacular scene of recent restoration.

The idea of *Koninginnedag* (Queen's Day), the nation's extremely popular holiday celebrating the monarchy, was not an invention of politicians but emanated from a private citizen, Mr. J.W.R. Gerlach, who was the editor of a local newspaper, the *Utrechts Provinciaal en Stedelijk Dagblad.* Concerned about the growing social and political tensions that threatened the nation in the 1880s, the editors proposed to celebrate the birthday of the then four-year-old Crown Princess Wilhelmina as a day of national reconciliation and rejoicing.[25] The idea, although not completely new as the birthday of the reigning king had traditionally (but irregularly) been an occasion for festivities, gained immediate popularity. In 1885 *Prinsessedag* (Princess's Day) was celebrated for the first time in the city of Utrecht, with various festivities, especially for children, spontaneously organized and sponsored by the local authorities.[26] By 1890, when Princess Wilhelmina became Queen Wilhelmina (and, consequently, *Prinsessedag* became *Koninginnedag*), almost all towns and cities had followed suit.

The Role of the Media

Looking at these modern Dutch traditions, two things come to mind. First, both the Golden State Coach and *Koninginnedag* were spontaneous initiatives, coming from various sections of the population – in the former case the common Amsterdam people and in the latter the middle classes. They originated from below, although the governing classes surely did not underrate their importance. This point is confirmed by recent local studies that date the rise of nationalist and royalist popular feeling in the Netherlands to the 1870s.[27] The popular origin of these monarchical traditions must be underscored, as it seems to have been no different in other countries. In Britain, where the invented tradition argument has created the picture of royal ceremonies being imposed upon the public by cunning politicians, the reality was in fact different. The Thanksgiving Ceremony of 1872 originated from the popular interest in the Prince of Wales's illness, which Gladstone subsequently exploited for his own political ends. Equally, the two Victorian jubilees came off by popular demand. The Liberals, who were in office in 1886, explicitly refused a request for government sponsorship of a celebration until there was a marked expression of popular interest in the event.[28]

An interesting question related to the increased popular interest in the monarchy, and a question that until now has been neglected by the historians, concerns the role played by the media. Many signs indicate that this role was big indeed, especially after the 1880s, when the yellow press began to bring news that was at the same time more nationalized and more 'human'. The celebration of the Diamond Jubilee in 1897, for instance, had much to do with the launch in 1896 of Alfred Harmsworth's *Daily Mail*, Britain's first truly popular newspaper. With its blend of human interest stories and jingoism, the *Mail* had a keen nose for anniversaries, and the paper was the first to notice that the 77-year-old queen was about to become the longest-reigning sovereign in British history – and to suggest that this landmark should not be left unnoticed. To be sure, such newspaper-meddling was no longer new in the 1890s. In fact, the Thanksgiving Ceremony of 1872 had already been what we would now call a media event, both in the way the press took up the story of the prince's illness, thus creating popular interest in the monarchy, and in the way it prepared the public for the ceremony, producing an endless stream of articles on the coming event. As for the Dutch *Koninginnedag*, the crucial role played by the press in its rise has already been pointed out.

Commercialization

The success of the 'performing monarchy' depended not only on the efforts of the media as a go-between but also, equally, on the way in which the monarchy became commercialized. Royal ceremonies led to an outpouring of commemorative pottery, as national and local authorities everywhere began to distribute plates, mugs and other gifts in order to keep the memory of these ceremonies alive. For instance, for the Golden Jubilee of 1887, the British government ordered as many as 45,000 china mugs from the Royal Doulton factories at Burslem, Staffordshire, to be handed out to London schoolchildren in the week of the jubilee.[29] These souvenirs became an essential part of the popularity campaign, being the physical expression of the abstract monarchy. Of course, the commercialization of the monarchy was not entirely new, but new was the extent of it. The huge popularity of the monarchs caused the monarchy to become big business, as manufacturers cashed in on the appeal of royal ceremonial to a mass market which had never existed before.

The booming memorabilia market would lead to some remarkable international intersections. For instance, the enamel beaker commemorating the coronation of Emperor Nicholas II of Russia in 1896, currently known as the 'cup of sorrow', was produced by a Bohemian firm known by the name of its founders, Ignatius and Rudolf Gottlieb. The company, founded around 1880 in the town of Brno, employed around 1,500 workers in the 1890s and specialized in the production of specially designed purpose-made beakers, samples of which went on journey around the world. The story of this Russian beaker, among a number of souvenir gifts distributed among the people at a festival on the Khodynka Field outside Moscow, is well known. The festival turned into a disaster, when the crowd, alarmed by the rumour that insufficient beakers had been ordered, overran the guards and surged towards the pavillions, resulting in more than 2,600 casualties – men, women and children – of which more than half were trampled to death.

Less well known is what happened to the hundreds of beakers that remained undistributed following the stampede. They were stored and probably would have rusted away had a Dutch trader with a typically Dutch business instinct not read about the disaster of the Khodynka Field in the newspapers. He subsequently devised a plan to buy the entire lot for one rouble each and bring them to the Netherlands, in view of the forthcoming inauguration of Queen Wilhelmina in 1898. A coloured cardboard cut-out of the young queen was pasted onto the front to cover the Russian monogram, and the Dutch coat of arms was placed on the Russian double-headed eagle on the reverse (Figures 1 and 2). The beakers, sold exclusively in The Hague for 30 cents each, were not a success (Figure 3). Once used and washed they lost their cardboard accessories, and not a day had passed before newspaper articles appeared calling the beaker a swindle.

As a rule, commercial activity surrounding royal celebrations contributed to their success, but it also provoked criticism. Some people were annoyed by the commercialization of these national ceremonies, fearing that it might undermine their 'holy' character. For instance, the decision taken in 1896 to celebrate Queen Victoria's Diamond Jubilee, barely ten years after her Golden Jubilee, encountered criticism as people suspected it had been dictated by economic considerations only. An all-time low was reached in 1902, when the coronation of Victoria's successor had to be postponed at the last minute because the king fell ill. All coronation mugs had to be withdrawn from the market. Hotels and guesthouses in London were faced with cancelled reservations from one day to the next. It was a tough financial blow, and in the frantic first moments it was even suggested that a substitute should be found to take the king's place. With the substitute well wrapped in the coronation robe, no one would notice the fast-change trick, it was thought.[30] Again, critics argued that the coronation of the king had become, in the mind of too many people, a show instead of a sacrament. But, in truth, ceremonies that celebrated a monarchy which had ceased to be a divine investiture and had became an institute of popular

Fig. 1. Front side of the Russian beaker showing (left) the original mono-grams N (of Nicholas) and A (of Alexandra) in Cyrillic together with the year 1896, and (right) the red cardboard picture of Queen Wilhelmina and the year 1898 pasted onto it. The beaker is made of enamel covering tin, dec-orated in red and blue, with a golden border.

Fig. 2. Back side of the same beaker showing (left) the double-headed eagle emblem (the Russian state coat of arms) and (right) the Dutch royal coat of arms placed over it.

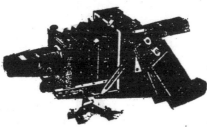
Fig. 3. Newspaper advertisement announcing the exclusive sale of the so-called Russian Coronation beaker, at the price of 30 cents, at a local party goods store in The Hague.

consent had nothing to do with the sacramental. Thomas Richards, commenting on the frenetic mood of the British public at the time of the Golden Jubilee, has made a point when he concluded that 'majesty is made, not born [...] (that is to say) it is manufactured'.[31]

Conclusion

In my survey of the 'performing monarchy', its reappearance and its character, I have stressed the importance of national conditions – sociocultural as well as political – as being responsible for its ultimate shape. However, if the monarch no longer rules but reigns and if the adulation and adoration of the people are basically a matter of identification, the historian will, in the final analysis, of necessity take royal performance into account as well, which means that the historiography of the modern monarchy cannot do without the personalized and biographical approach. Bagehot's famous statement that a monarchy's key asset is its 'human nature' implies that the 'performing monarchy' had to steal the hearts of the people. The 'royal fairy tale', in which monarchs appear to live a normal daily life like you and me, appeals to the popular imagination in a way of which mere politicians can only dream. The more kings and queens appear to be humans of flesh and blood, the more spontaneously they kiss and hug each other, the better the monarchy performs.

So the historian need not shrink from probing into the characters and the personal lives of royals, knowing that in the 'performing monarchy' the estimation of the Crown as an institution is bound up with the personal popularity of the monarch whose job it is to lead a private life publicly.[32] The *magical touch of royalty* is a kind of charismatic radiance between grandeur and banality. Not every king or queen found the balance. A few references must suffice. The success of the 'performing monarchy' in Britain was, to a degree, Queen Victoria's personal success. Contrary to what she might have thought of herself, she was a very great actress who played her public role exactly as she was expected to.[33] In contrast, the growing difficulties that besieged the Russian monarchy after 1900 were clearly caused in part by theatrical incompetence, with an ineffectual Tsar and a dysfunctional Tsarina. In Italy a similar situation developed during the reign of the uninspiring, diminutive King Victor Emmanuel III, resulting in a temporary popularity during the years of fascism of the Duke of Aosta of the rival cadet branch of the House of Savoy.[34]

As we have seen, the long nineteenth century was a period of transition in which absolute monarchies 'by the grace of God' were replaced by constitutional monarchies 'by the grace of popular favour'. The gradual democratization and involvement of 'the people' in politics were coupled by the reshaping of the performing monarchy as an ideal structure of identification and political affection.

Cannadine, Twenty Years on. Monarchy and Political Culture in Nineteenth-Century Britain and the Netherlands

Henk te Velde

David Cannadine's article about the British monarchy and the invention of tradition has been the single most influential article on the history of monarchy since at least the 1960s. His contribution to the volume on invented traditions edited in 1983 by Eric Hobsbawm and Terence Ranger paved the way for a new cultural approach to the history of monarchy.[1] But it also played a part in the redirection of political history that was going on at the time. The present essay will concentrate on the beneficial as well as the detrimental effects Cannadine's article has had in this last respect. Historian Michael Kuhn devoted an important part of his otherwise useful PhD dissertation to refuting Cannadine's thesis of the invention of tradition. According to Kuhn, Cannadine's theory was overly functional, flawed and excessive, teleological, because it allegedly advocated a conspiracy thesis. It even seemed to be Marxist, which today is the most damning condemnation that can be levelled at a historian.[2] Cannadine's work has, nonetheless, been criticized as being too royalist and conservative, and Cannadine himself argues convincingly that he steers a middle course between a neglect of the importance of the monarchy by left-wing historians and an uncritical approach by more conservative ones.[3] In this sense Cannadine's article was one sign that a new common ground was emerging where historians of different persuasions could meet. One of the interesting features of the new cultural political history, it has been argued, is that it has contributed to the partial disappearance of older, politically inspired historiographical controversies about high and low politics and has led to a common interest in the cultural setting of politics.[4] Kuhn's book about the British monarchy at the end of the nineteenth century is an example of this and is itself actually so dependent on Cannadine that it in fact reinforces Cannadine's argument by qualifying or refining it, even if Cannadine himself perhaps would not agree.

Kuhn argued that Cannadine's article sits uneasily between an older social history approach, on the one hand, according to which ritual was just a means used by the elite to hide their real interests, and on the other, an approach which sees ritual as constituting society, which would be the view of cultural anthropologists. He uses this as criticism, but it seems that this precisely captures the reasons why Cannadine was so successful. The success of the article was of course not due only to its own merits but also to its timing. Just as the book about festivals during the French Revolution by Mona Ozouf[5] was one of the first signs of a new cultural approach to the history of the Revolution, so Cannadine's article and the volume on the invention of tradition were a first announcement of a new cultural approach to late nineteenth-century political history in particular. It allowed for social and political historians to meaningfully study the cultural side of monarchy – and the idea of invention of tradition made it possible to do this also for politics in general – without crossing from socio-economic determinism to cultural determinism. It bridged the gap between political and social history, and its ambiguities contributed to its success.

When Cannadine explained his approach in the prologue to his book about the British aristocracy (1990), he said he wanted 'to lay bare the reality behind the myths that [members of the patrician élite] invented or believed about themselves'.[6] This seems to be a case of straightforward debunking, but as Cannadine has demonstrated in a number of studies, he is not the crude debunker Kuhn makes him out to be. He is genuinely interested in the cultural side of monarchy and of power in general in its own right,[7] although at times he is fiercely critical of the role of the monarchy in British society. His ambiguity is even clearer in his article about Victoria as 'the last Hanoverian sovereign' (1989). Cannadine sets out to explain that the purpose of the article is to *criticize* the idea that the Victorian monarchy was a modern invention! He writes that 'there are conventional royal wisdoms and practices which survive across the centuries with amazing tenacity'. This seems to be a complete negation of the idea of the invention of tradition, although a few pages before he had said that the early Victorian monarchy was still in many ways a continuation of the previous period, but that 'by the end of Victoria's reign the British monarchy had indeed been fundamentally transformed'.[8]

If we accept the idea that Cannadine's ambiguities contributed to his success, this is not to say that no criticism of Cannadine is possible; on the contrary. Perhaps the most obvious form of criticism touches upon the idea of the invention of tradition itself. As Kuhn and others have pointed out, what has been termed invention has in fact often been a kind of conscious systematization, reordering and structuring of elements that already existed previously, albeit in a loose way, rather than real invention. Cannadine's work itself suggests that he has been aware of this problem from the beginning, but did not always find a satisfactory solution to it. The expression 'invention of tradition' seems to suggest invention from scratch, which is an idea most historians almost instinctively reject. There is a parallel to the study of nationalism here. After the first wave of studies by scholars such as Ernest Gellner, Benedict Anderson and partly also Hobsbawm himself, who seemed to argue that nationalism was a nineteenth-century construction and invention pure and simple, there was renewed interest in older forms of national consciousness which to a certain extent prefigured the full-blown nationalism of the late nineteenth century.[9] In his recent inaugural lecture Cannadine said: 'most of us who write on modern monarchies know less than we should about their ancient, medieval and early modern predecessors, and so fail to appreciate sufficiently what those traditional functions were, or just how much they have been diminished and adapted in more recent times.'[10] This could be read as a plea for a new but critical interest in long-term developments and continuity.

In many respects Cannadine's use of the idea of the invention of tradition has proved to be inspiring but also controversial, and the popular pastime of historians of always looking for earlier beginnings has, for instance, resulted in a book by Cannadine's partner Linda Colley, who showed that some elements of the popular monarchy were prefigured by developments in the period of the French Revolution.[11] More recently, John Plunkett, partly building on older literature, argued that the huge public interest in the British monarchy was not an invention of the late nineteenth century but already existed in the 1830s, at the beginning of the reign of Queen Victoria, whom he calls the 'first media monarch'. This interest was not stimulated by large carefully organized state festivals like the jubilees at the end of Victoria's reign but, rather, by quasi-spontaneous visits to the people, which were popular precisely because they *refrained* from the military pomp and excessive pageantry of later years. Plunkett draws attention to the nineteenth-century constitutionalist discourse on populism, which has recently received a lot of attention from historians, and says: 'It was through the interlinked discourses around the People and the constitution that Victoria's first tours and visits were endlessly played out.'[12]

Though Plunkett does not use the expression, it could be argued that the monarchy was at this time an 'essentially contested political concept', an institution whose political meaning could be interpreted differently by different parties. Some perhaps would say that at the end of the nineteenth century the monarchy was perceived as being above parties, but that before that period it was still a party in political conflicts. It is true that the political role of the monarchy became less manifest, but this does not mean that the partisan stance of the queen was more obvious at the start of her reign than at the end. There is little doubt that Victoria preferred the Tories to the Liberals at the end of her reign and that she started with a preference for the (conservative-liberal) Whigs. But until the second half of the nineteenth century, the old concept of the good king with bad counsellors on the one hand and the limited suffrage on the other still made it possible to use the monarchy as a popular and in fact 'democratic' counterbalance to the rule of the oligarchic Whig House of Commons: King and People against parliament. Not only radical critics of the existing politics did so, the conservative Disraeli forcefully used the same argument in his early novels, too: 'power had been transferred from the crown to a parliament, the members of which were appointed by an extremely limited and exclusive class, who owned no responsibility to the country, who debated and voted in secret.'[13] The monarchy could be used as a rhetorical argument by very different political groups.

If it is true that the monarchy was part of a discourse on populism at the beginning of Victoria's reign, this suggests that the growth of the popularity of the monarchy from the 1870s was less sudden than Cannadine would have it. But conversely, it also points to the fact that the monarchy was and remained very much part and parcel of political life. Only if a very limited definition of politics is being used could it be argued that monarchy really retreated from politics in the second half of the nineteenth century. The classical view maintains that by the 1870s the monarchy was rapidly changing into an institution outside the political arena, the power of which lay in its symbolic rather than its practical political capital. This view was of course canonized by Walter Bagehot, who differentiated between the 'efficient' parts of the constitution, such as the Cabinet and the House of the Commons, and its 'dignified' parts, such as the House of Lords and in particular the monarchy.[14] It could be argued that Cannadine is to a large extent a follower of Bagehot, and he has concentrated on the symbolic side of the monarchy. As I will argue in the remainder of this essay, there is a clear downside to this approach which separates the monarchy from Cabinet and Commons: the distinction between the dignified and the efficient parts of the constitution easily leads to the conclusion that 'real' politics does not include cultural elements and that the dignified and cultural elements of the constitution are not 'real' politics. This conclusion, however, would make it difficult to understand the meaning of politics in the nineteenth century.

The Cultural Aspect of British Parliament

According to some authors, the Bagehotian distinction tended to obscure the real political power the queen still exercised at certain moments.[15] More important for the purposes of the present essay, however, is the other side of the coin. By concentrating exclusively on the monarchy, Cannadine's new cultural view of politics completely overlooked the symbolic and cultural side of *parliamentary* politics. In a recent article about the famous residence of Parliament, the Palace of Westminster, Cannadine has written about the symbolic side of the Commons, but only about the building itself, and the purpose of the article was to show that the building was devised to honour the monarchy and was hardly the parliament of the people until at least the end of the nineteenth century. It was a sombre, uncomfortable building, closed to the outside world, the domain of a small aristocratic elite.[16] In certain respects this may be true, but, remarkably, there is an obvious parallel between changes in the position of the monarchy and changes in political life in general. Though subsequent research has shown that much of the invention of tradition took place in the 1900s, under Victoria's successor Edward VII, the crucial decades in Cannadine's story are clearly the 1870s and 1880s. These decades witnessed changes not only in royal ritual but also in political life. The 1870s were the years of 'the duel' between the radical liberal William Gladstone and the conservative Benjamin Disraeli, as the historian Ensor already put it in the 1930s. It was a period of unprecedented public interest in politics, stimulated not only by the personalization of politics but also by Gladstone's revolutionary mobilizing of the people in his election campaigns and his use of public meetings. New political organizations emerged, and although British election campaigns had always been popular events, formal politics had probably never been as popular as they were from the 1870s.

This was not only a matter of sober politics. Politicians became the equivalent of today's pop stars. To quote Ensor once again, in the 1870s:

> there were no film stars, no football champions, no
> speed supermen, no male or female aviators, no tennis
> heroes or heroines. [...] The people's daily fluctuations of
> excitement, of expectancy, of hero-worship, which are
> dissipated now over these and many other fields, were
> concentrated then upon the House of Commons. [...]
> Parliamentary speeches were reported prominently and
> at length in all the newspapers; they were read aloud and
> discussed in homes and public-houses. Points scored or
> lost in debate across the floor of the House of Commons
> were not merely noted by the members present, but followed with rapt attention throughout the country.
> Working men canvassed the form and prospects of parliamentary leaders.[17]

This passion for politics clearly had much to do with its spectacular and cultural sides. Gladstone in particular became a popular hero, famous for his speeches in the Commons, for the way in which he addressed public meetings, but also for his favourite pastime, felling trees. Bits of the wood of the trees he felled were cherished as souvenirs or even relics.[18] At the same time, New Journalism began to pay close attention to human interest in politics. Newspapers had always closely followed parliamentary politics, but this had meant mainly verbatim reports of debates. Now sketch writers wrote about the atmosphere of the House of Commons, the prominent political personalities and the comic and exciting scenes in the House. Some had done so since the 1850s, but in the

1880s sketch writing really became popular. Journalists such as T.P. O'Connor (who was also a MP) and Henry Lucy were famous sketch writers. They commented on the theatrical aspects of monarchy *and* parliamentary politics.[19]

Both Gladstone and Disraeli played vital roles in the development of the ritual surrounding the monarchy. They both urged Victoria to appear in public and to assume her duties as a democratic and dignified queen. It is a well-known fact that the Queen had a great liking for the charming Disraeli but an extreme dislike of Gladstone – 'that *half-mad firebrand* who would soon ruin anything, and be a *Dictator*',[20] and who was in her eyes an excited and dangerous populist. 'A salient fact of late nineteenth-century Britain was that the two figures who most symbolized the nation and the age, Queen Victoria and Gladstone, did not get on.'[21] As most (modern) biographies of both Victoria and Gladstone testify, she complained that the slightly pathetic and rather solemn Gladstone used to address her as if he was addressing a public meeting. Victoria's preferences are sometimes explained as either strictly political or purely personal,[22] but something more can be said about them. Perhaps Victoria felt threatened by Gladstone. According to Gladstone himself, her antipathy was to a certain extent inspired by jealousy: 'She can't bear to see the large type which heads the columns of newspapers by "Mr Gladstone's movements", while down below is in small type the Court Circular.'[23] Elizabeth Longford, perhaps Victoria's most prominent biographer, also writes that Victoria was 'profoundly jealous of Gladstone' and adds: 'The "People's William" competed with the "People's Victoria".'[24] Some liberals thought that the Queen disliked Gladstone because the old liberal leader had acquired quasi-royal status himself. A liberal review cited a tour by Gladstone in Edinburgh which followed the same route as the Queen had done previously; the Grand Old Man had even used the same sort of open carriage.[25] Victoria must have seen Gladstone as a competitor. Plunkett shows the popularity of the monarchy among other things by counting the number of commercial portrait photographs that were taken. Gladstone was one of the very few people outside the royal family whose picture was taken almost as often as Victoria's.[26]

Disraeli, in contrast, was not nearly as popular in the country as Gladstone. He was seen as essentially a House of Commons man who revelled in the games politicians liked to play. According to Bagehot, 'the special influence of this great gladiator never passed the walls of the amphitheatre', and an early sketch writer stressed Disraeli's 'elegantly artificial' qualities as a political actor, but only within the walls of the House.[27] He was no competitor of Victoria's. In fact, he hoped that the popularity of the Queen would contribute to the popularity of conservatism. This fit in with conservative conceptions of democratization. Gladstone's popularity rested on the assumption that he was the people's tribune, and his work was directed toward the political mobilization of the responsible common people. The conservatives also favoured democracy, but wanted to link it to nation, empire and monarchy, and did not want to politicize the people as Gladstone tried to do.

By studying the monarchy, Cannadine was able to show the fertility of a cultural view of politics, but by focusing exclusively on the monarchy he contributed to the continuation of a Bagehotian division between the showy dignified parts of politics and its efficient parts where the 'real' political battles were fought. But in practice the two elements of politics were inextricably connected. There could be no democratic politics without a certain amount of 'theatre', in particular in periods such as the late nineteenth century when new classes had to be mobilized. This is particularly clear in Britain. Right down to the present-day, not only public life in general but politics in particular have retained a strong public theatrical aspect. In 1859, when *The Times* was still arguing that Britain did not need a theatrical monarch, the journal wrote about parliament: 'They say that we have lost as a nation our theatrical taste; but the truth is Parliament is our theatre. [...] The Romans had their gladiatorial fights, the Middle Ages had their tournaments, Spain has her bullfights even now', and Britain had her parliamentary combats.[28]

Almost sixty years later, Josiah Wedgwood, who started the history of Parliament, wrote: 'the man who steps into the English Parliament takes his place in a pageant that has ever been filing by since the birth of English history.'[29] This last quotation is taken from an article by David Cannadine, who wrote about royal pageantry, but Wedgwood's remark did not immediately lead to further reflection on his part. Because there was no written constitution in Britain, continuity in the constitution was not self-evident. The appeal to 'age-old' customs was therefore as vital in the case of the House of Commons as it was in the case of the monarchy, and almost as rhetorical. It could be argued that Parliament also went through a process which came close to the invention of tradition. Rules were adapted, the building was changed, and even if we accept Cannadine's argument that Parliament used to be a closed bulwark of aristocracy, it is clear that it ceased to have this quality at the end of the nineteenth century. At this time, sketches in the new mass press familiarized the public with the cultural aspects of Parliament, many new popular histories of Parliament appeared, and Parliament's prestige was at its apex. British Parliament already had the mythical role of protector of the freedom of the people, but probably for the first time many people really became acquainted with 'the inner life of the House of Commons'. This was the title of a new compilation of sketches by William White from the 1850s and 1860s, issued in 1897 and then reaching a new audience.[30]

It is of course no coincidence that Cannadine chose the British monarchy to demonstrate the invention of tradition. No other monarchy was theatrical and at the same time constitutional. But the theatrical aspect was not typical of the British monarchy alone; it also characterized British politics in general. This is not to say that the representational side of British politics were mere shallow theatre but, rather, that politics was a serious business and a real struggle and at the same time a very nice and exciting pastime. If we separate monarchy from the rest of politics, we would probably continue Bagehot's separation of dignified and efficient parts of politics. But if we take the cultural approach to politics seriously, we should also study the cultural elements of what is considered as the heart of the representational system. Even if it could be argued that the administrative side of politics, the Cabinet and the civil service, lacked this exciting cultural quality, it is clear at least that its representational side, including the House of Commons and its members, possessed it.

The Netherlands

In order to show that the interrelationship between changes in the public face of the monarchy and changes in the public side of politics was not unique to Britain, a few remarks about the situation in the Netherlands are useful. There are remarkable parallels between the development of a liberal parliamentary system and of democracy in the two countries. Even the dates of important changes in the constitution almost match, with the high tide of parliamentary politics in the middle of the nineteenth century, the growth of the 'caucus' and organized extra-parliamentarian political parties in the latter part of the nineteenth century and the adoption of general suffrage around the First World War. But there was also a huge contrast between the political cultures. The Dutch Parliament has always been rather quiet, and established politics most of the time was more about administration than about mobilization of the common people. The Parliament in The Hague did not attract a lot of attention, at least not compared with Westminster at the end of the nineteenth century. Or perhaps one should say that the Dutch Parliament only attracted a mass audience when it became the home of the tribunes of the people. And those tribunes were not parliamentary orators such as Gladstone, but religious or socialist party leaders who started as outsiders and wanted to mobilize the people in order to create extra-parliamentary political parties.[31] Neither the state nor Parliament was at the centre of this type of politics, but the social groups of Protestants, Catholics or socialist workers were.

This was matched by the development of the monarchy in the Netherlands. As Jaap van Osta showed in a comparative study of the British and Dutch monarchies, the Dutch monarchy was not nearly as ceremonial and theatrical as the British.[32] But at the end of the nineteenth century, there were important developments in the Netherlands as well. When new mass political parties emerged, the Queen's Birthday was introduced as a national holiday to counterbalance the mobilization of separate socio-political groups by the royalist mobilization of the people as a whole.[33] Just as the political parties first developed in society rather than in The Hague, this holiday was a private and local initiative, with conservative-liberal groups acting as local committees almost in the way local political parties had first acted. Orthodox Protestants who were normally staunch supporters of the royal family of Orange at first did not like these competitors in the struggle for the attention of the common people. There was the same sort of tension between Queen Wilhelmina and the popular and theatrical Protestant party leader and Prime Minister Abraham Kuyper as between Victoria and Gladstone; Wilhelmina also accused Kuyper of acting as a king. In a way they were competitors. Wilhelmina and her mother Emma got on much better with quiet Protestant or conservative-liberal notables who played the same part that Disraeli played in Britain.[34]

Conservative liberals tried to use the monarchy as a means to unite the Dutch people in a period of rapidly changing social and political relations. Orthodox Protestants, Catholics and socialists each constructed their own world and mobilized their part of the common people. This implied a new type of mobilizing politics the old liberals abhorred. They tried to hold on to their idea of politics as a game of notables, but they realized that the populist appeal of the monarchy was a powerful means of attracting support. At the same time they themselves seemed to believe the royal fairytale, as is demonstrated by many comments on the inauguration of Queen Wilhelmina which showed how moved many members of the liberal elite were. As Richard Crossmann already noted, Bagehot's rather cynical distinction between the common people, who did not understand parliamentary politics and needed the fairytale of the dignified monarchy, and the elite, who confined themselves to 'real' efficient politics, was dubious.[35]

Also in the Netherlands, many members of the social and political elite were probably as much affected by the myth as were the 'common' people, and the widespread belief in the political power of the monarchy was more than just naiveté. Parliament in The Hague was not very popular, but the monarchy, or to be more precise the Orange family, was. In the Netherlands the mythical role of protector of the freedom and rights of the people was attributed to the Orange family.[36] Ever since William the Silent in the sixteenth century, the royal family was supposed to protect the common people. In the nineteenth century, this took the form of a belief in the power of the king to do away with evil advisers and oligarchic politics and unite with the People. As in Britain, not only radicals voiced such ideas, but also others – for example Kuyper, the orthodox Protestant – who still tried to use the king in their struggle against a liberal education bill in 1878. Somewhat earlier, Multatuli, the celebrated author who at times was radical but at other times conservative, had urged the king to get rid of the boring and oligarchic parliament. In instances such as these, the monarchy was used in political debate and became a contested concept.

These images of the monarchy were not imaginary and naïve dreams but weapons in a political struggle. They are to be compared to the liberal image of the responsible ministers and the principle that the king can do no wrong. Even if this formula was written in the Dutch constitution of 1848, liberals knew that King William III did not want to comply with it and only grudgingly played his role of constitutional monarch. Still, at his death in 1890, they pictured him as an example of constitutional virtue, because it fit in with their political ideals.[37] In all of these cases, efficient and dignified elements of politics *and* monarchy were linked. At the end of the nineteenth century, however, the political role of the monarchy became less ambiguous. The extension of suffrage made it less convincing to picture the monarchy as a stronghold of the people against an oligarchic parliament, and conservative liberals and socialists paradoxically cooperated in assigning the monarchy the role of symbol of conservatism, very popular but not in socialist districts. In 1898 socialist commentators lamented when they saw the common people drink and celebrate on the occasion of the inauguration of Queen Wilhelmina. In some ways this inauguration can be compared to the coronation of Victoria in 1837 at the same age. In both cases, the image of the girlish, seemingly vulnerable young queen moved both the popular and the elite audience.

The new public role of the monarchy also was supported by the monarchy itself. Wilhelmina's father, the unruly and moody King William III, did not want anything to do with public ceremonies. When he died in 1890 his daughter was only ten years old, and Queen Mother Emma acted as regent until 1898. She realized the importance of public relations and took her daughter on a tour around the country to meet her people in the provinces. This was a classic case of the invention of tradition, in the sense of the adaptation and refinement of older practices on a new scale and with new publicity. When the kingdom of the Netherlands was founded at the beginning of the nineteenth century, in reminiscence of the royal state entries of the early modern period or Late Middle Ages, its constitution suggested that the king would visit all his provinces as a kind of series of inaugurations. In 1840 King William II, who liked the showy aspects of his kingship, used the regulation as a pretext for brilliant visits to the provinces. As there was no real need for separate inaugurations in a unitary state, the regulation was subsequently deleted from the constitution, and King William III stayed at home. Emma and Wilhelmina did not need a constitutional regulation to see the importance of the visits, and even today, as when Crown Prince Willem-Alexander married Máxima in 2002, the first thing they did was visit all the provinces of the kingdom. Whereas King William II visited the provinces because the constitution asked him to, in the case of Emma there was a clear strategy. And this strategy was typical of the political and cultural situation in the Netherlands. There were no grand aristocratic ceremonies in the capital or in The Hague; instead, a popular monarchy developed that suited Dutch bourgeois culture and also suited Dutch political culture, which also did not stress the national centre. So the concerted efforts of Emma and Wilhelmina and of the political movements of their time brought about a change in the position of the monarchy. It is still dubious whether we could call this purely and simply the advent of the popular monarchy and the decrease of its political role. It all depends on what we call popular and what we call political.

Conclusion

Democratic politics are simultaneously a fierce struggle and a form of culture, and this is important, too. The study of nineteenth-century political culture has developed since the 1980s, and popular politics have been studied as well.[38] The curious thing is, though, that not much attention has been paid to the development of parliamentary politics in this respect,[39] and that, further, the connection between popular politics and the monarchy has not often been made. Studies that seem to deal with the relations between the monarchy and the people in fact often concentrate on the image of the Queen in the media or on the 'icon' Victoria as a 'commodity'.[40] In this sense they do not remedy a downside of Cannadine's approach of the invention of tradition: in his treatment of the monarchy, this appears to be a top-down process (the elite, not the people, invent royal traditions[41]). Whoever concentrates on 'advertising and spectacle' could be led to conclude that the monarchy was simply a device to delude the people. That, in fact, the people also used the monarchy for their own purposes – distraction but also politics – is something few authors would really want to deny, but it could be interesting to study the popular appreciations of the monarchy as a debate about an essentially contested institution. If we want to understand nineteenth-century politics and monarchy, it is clear that both the popular interest in the monarchy – which was more than a naïve belief in fairytales – and the cultural side of the efficient parts of the constitution, especially the House of Commons, should be taken seriously. Cannadine is one of those who have shown the way toward a cultural political history. It would be a pity if we were to follow his trail so closely that we would confine this approach to the 'dignified' parts of the constitution. Both the study of the social role of the monarchy and the study of political culture in general would profit from an intimate relationship.

The Impossible Neutrality of the Speech from the Throne. A Ritual between National Unity and Political Dispute. Belgium, 1831-1918

Gita Deneckere

The historical and anthropological study of rituals brings the link between ritual and power to the fore and interprets rituals as a form of strategic social behaviour.[1] Where royal rituals are concerned, the premise is all too often that the political role of the monarchy declined in favour of the ceremonial role during the second half of the nineteenth century. That perception must be ascribed to Walter Bagehot, who distinguished between the 'efficient' and the 'dignified' parts of the constitutional monarchy, with the parliament and the government taking part in real politics on the one hand and the monarchy serving as an ornament on the other.[2] In his contribution to this volume, Henk te Velde argues that there should not be such a sharp contrast between 'politics' and 'culture'. He points out the cultural aspects of politics and the political aspects of culture, and in so doing, he adapts important points[3] of David Cannadine's basic intuition about the 'invention' of royal rituals at the end of the nineteenth century.[4] Moreover, Walter Arnstein has pointed out in a recent article that Cannadine passed over an important ceremony: the queen's opening and closing of the Houses of Parliament. This is an annually recurring ritual, as opposed to the one-off ceremonies that Cannadine studied, such as a coronation or a funeral. In this way Cannadine overlooked a ritual that was at its most popular during the early years of Victoria's reign and one that therefore does not fit in with his portrayal.[5]

Research into the rituals of the Belgian monarchy is still in its infancy.[6] The research presented in this article has been done because the annual ritual of the speech from the throne concerns a ritual that has both a political and cultural element, even more so than royal weddings and funerals, which can be regarded as pure power display. In other words, the speech from the throne bears both 'efficient' as well as 'dignified' aspects of royal power. If it is true that the political influence of the monarchy – in the narrow sense – declined in the nineteenth century, how then did the speech from the throne evolve?

In essence, the purpose of the speech from the throne was a symbolic one in the sense that the pact between the monarch and the nation was renewed and ratified every year. That is the precise reason why the socialists in particular wanted to disrupt the speech from the throne at the end of the nineteenth century: to expose the fact that not everyone was represented in parliament. The disruption of the strongly symbolically sensitive circumstance of the speech from the throne was aimed at bringing their demand for universal suffrage to the very pith of public attention. The speech from the throne also had a 'substantive' aspect, as was the case in Great Britain and the Netherlands, where the sovereigns to this day open parliament annually: it conveyed a political message because the king on that occasion announced the government's policy programme. Hence he was the mouthpiece of national politics.[7] The monarchs in Great Britain and the Netherlands still function as the ventriloquist's doll: although they seemingly speak in their own capacity, they merely read a government declaration, as befits a constitutional monarch. This is consistent with the ministerial responsibility and the adage that 'the king can do no wrong' and extends to the king can *say* no wrong; the ministers are responsible for what he says and must cover the immune king. The mere fact that the king speaks bestows an exceptional splendour on the government's address: the role that the speech from the throne plays is a ceremonial one, whereas the government is responsible for the political message. That, at least, is the constitutional standard, the perfect example that Bagehot also had in mind.[8]

In Belgium, the tradition of the speech from the throne can be traced back to the United Kingdom of the Netherlands. King William I addressed the States General from The Hague in one year and from Brussels in the next.[9] After the separation, the Belgian kingdom took over the ritual, and the sovereign made a speech from the throne to the united legislative authority at the opening of Parliament in November. This was, however, only done until the end of the First World War, and not continually. Leopold I delivered the address almost every year from 1831 to 1863, Leopold II only sporadically from 1866 to 1892, and, finally, Albert I twice: in 1910 and 1918. Although there was never an official end to the ritual, no more speeches from the throne seem to have been held after 1918. The Belgian kings address Parliament only at their inauguration. The speech from the throne has been replaced by the government policy statement, read out by the Prime Minister. Why did the speech from the throne disappear for good after the First World War? In order to answer that question, we will first have to examine the ritual context within which the speech from the throne was made and, subsequently, the political nature of the text itself.

The Ritual Context of the Speech from the Throne

'To be national is the great thing,' Leopold I wrote to Victoria in 1837, at that stage the fresh Queen of England.[10] The political counselling that he regularly gave his beloved cousin confirms the statement made by John Plunkett and others that European monarchs were thoroughly aware of their new role concerning 'the nation' and that they had a strongly 'populist' mentality.[11] A very important task that the 'national' monarch had was to see that he was loved by the people, which could only be achieved if the people could *see* the king and queen, either in person or through publicity about them. In the early nineteenth century, when the media were not yet within national reach and public transport had not yet been developed to such an extent that the common people could go to the capital whenever they wished to see the monarchs in all their glory, it was essential for the monarchs to regularly mingle with their subjects. It is apparent from Leopold's correspondence with Victoria that he was well aware of this, and he advised her to travel her own country regularly. Leopold's 'Joyous Inaugurations' and presence at national festivities and ceremonies served the same purpose. In Belgium, which was founded subsequent to a revolution, the king symbolized the country's unity. He was the nation's pivotal figure during the national festivities, the one who sang the praises of the marriage between order (the monarchy) and liberty (the Belgian revolution and the constitution).[12] The ritual of the speech from the throne was also in complete keeping with the marriage between order and liberty, which was sealed by a pact that the monarch had concluded with the nation when he took the oath in 1831. The ritual of the speech from the throne was initiated specifically for the purpose of annually renewing this pact.[13]

Leopold I's oath-taking was full of symbolical meaning. By swearing allegiance to the Belgian constitution, by solemnly promising to honour the Belgian nation's laws and to protect the national independence and the integrity of the territory, Leopold of Saxon-Coburg-Gotha committed himself to the people who formed the foundation of this new nation. In the *Moniteur Belge* (the Belgian Government Gazette), the official mouthpiece of the government, it was emphasized clearly that the revolution accepted Leopold, that Leopold in turn accepted the revolution, and that he was not allowed to deny any of its principles whatsoever. King and people were one and were not to be pulled asunder.[14] During his inauguration Leopold referred to the pact that had been concluded between monarch and subjects in earlier times. Leopold I, in turn, concluded a pact with the nation, as represented by both houses. In so doing, he made himself part of history and maintained continuity with the past. Despite the ideological pluralism and the principle of liberty, the pact was a symbol of the king's vow to preserve the country's unity. A mere two months after taking the oath, the ritual of the speech from the throne was initiated in order to symbolically renew the pact with the nation when Parliament opened. The king repeated the bond with the nation at the place where the nation originated, and at the beginning of the parliamentary year he invited those who represented the people, for their part, to renew the pact by approving the government's policy programme. The solemn ceremony surrounding the speech from the throne was expanded, put the monarchy in the public eye and gave it a character that was clearly national. The procedure of the ritual was rigid, according to strict rules and at a time and place that were very symbolical.

The speech from the throne was an annually recurring ritual that coincided with the opening of the parliamentary session, which was usually on the third Tuesday in November. The ritual itself was centred in the surroundings of two pivotal buildings: the Royal Palace and the Palace of the Nation (the parliament building), which are separated by the Warande Park and lie opposite one another in the heart of Brussels. The area played a crucial role during the Belgian struggle for independence in 1830. The most important battles were fought during the stormy days in September. This is where the Belgian nation 'originated'. Belgium's revolutionary origin was 'compensated' for by placing monumental statues of the 'good' monarchs of the past in the Palace of the Nation, and the intention was to portray the continuity of a long monarchical tradition.[15]

In the parliamentary building, reminders of the period of the Netherlands were wiped out. At the time of the United Kingdom of the Netherlands, the States General were housed in the Palace of the Nation, where the throne remained. In 1831 Belgium adopted the Paris system, according to which the throne was stored again for another year the day after the royal session.[16] This was an expression of the more intensive contact that the new regime wanted to install in the nation, and a sign that the king was subject to the sovereignty of the people.

The opening ceremony of the legislative houses was laid down by a royal decree that was published in the *Moniteur Belge*.[17] While the king was in the Royal Palace, preparing to leave for the Palace of the Nation, the members of the House of Representatives prepared for his arrival. First the procession of the queen and the other members of the family left for the Palace of the Nation, and a few minutes after that twenty-one cannon shots announced the departure of the royal coach.[18] The Brussels civil guard, together with the garrison troops, formed a guard of honour along the route that the king and his family followed. The officials responsible for keeping law and order did not prevent anyone from being a spectator and hailing the royal family. Nevertheless, Leopold I did not feel completely safe, because people from all classes of society followed his route to the House of Representatives.[19]

During the magnificent journey the king was clearly visible to bystanders because he rode his own horse.[20] When he was in uniform and on horseback, the king was a symbol of the defence of the country as he had received it on 21 July 1831. Those wounded in the stormy September days of 1830 received a place of honour in the event: they received the martyrs' tribute. Up to the 1880s, the presence of the wounded emphasized the importance of the revolution for the national feeling and identity.[21] The royal children also took part in the queen's procession. Beginning in 1847, Leopold, the heir to the throne, was allowed to join the royal procession on horseback, and two years later, his younger brother, Philip, was granted the same honour.[22] The two uniformed princes on horseback, both old enough to take over from their father, were a symbol of the perpetuation of the dynasty and the continued existence of the nation in the future. Leopold II's brother continued to accompany the king, who had no male descendants, in the procession of the speeches from the throne up to and including the last one in 1892.[23]

Apart from slight variations in the leading parts of the ritual, there was a steadfast continuity throughout the years in the way in which the king was literally the link between the symbol of the monarchy – the Royal Palace – and the symbol of democracy – Parliament. What happened after the procession also took place according to a rigid pattern. The target audience for the king's speech naturally consisted of members of parliament, senators and ministers, but the diplomatic corps was invited also.[24] On the occasion of the speech from the throne, there were also ladies who attended and therefore sat in the parliamentary semi-circle behind the gentlemen dignitaries, which was extremely exceptional in a time when politics was still very much a gentleman's business. The public gallery was made up mostly of ladies, probably the parliamentarians' spouses. As a result of the great attendance, not all the spectators always had a place to sit or stand.[25]

Only after the king had greeted those present, and all was quiet in the hall, would he make his speech from the throne.[26] After the speech, he would greet the gathering once again, put his hat back on and hand his speech to the Great Marshall, who would in turn give it to the chairman of the royal gathering.[27] Twenty-one cannon shots would signal the start of his departure.

A separate ritual still unfolded in Parliament and the Senate. Each house formulated a separate answer to the king's address. A 'commission de l'adresse' (address commission) was formed in each house. Such commissions would draw up a text in which a reply by the representatives and senators would be formulated. These drafts were then read out to the plenary meeting and were discussed line by line. Consequently, a delegation was formed to convey the answer to the king during an audience they had with him. Finally, there was the king's confirmation, and he therefore had the final say.[28]

Leopold I was clearly conscious of the ritual and the political importance of his speech from the throne. To constantly repeat a ritual in the same way was an important precondition for its success. The king must have realized this, because when he had an accident in 1844 that made it difficult for him to ride on horseback, he did it anyway because that was the manner in which he made his entrance every year:

Being naturally lazy, I have combined the opening of parliament with the procession of the civil guard for a few years now and it was impossible for me to inspect the cavalry and the infantry by coach, like Louis XVIII, because it seemed a little too lazy to my liking. I therefore decided to go on horseback, although not without serious misgivings.[29]

Although the king did not like the ritual opening of parliament, he duly fulfilled this duty almost every year. In 1846 he let it be known almost a year before the time that he had no inclination to open parliament: 'in autumn there are the preparations for our tiresome opening of the chambers.'[30] In 1853 the ministers feared for their positions if the king did not deliver his traditional speech: 'I had wished to avoid the opening of the chambers it being a delicate moment, but the Cabinet they think it would do them harm.'[31] The ceremony would be cancelled only in the most exceptional circumstances. Even when the king had serious bronchitis in 1861, he still gave his speech from the throne, despite his illness.[32] However, when he really was too ill, he was very frank about it: 'Here we are getting near the opening of our chambers; I have not the most distant chance of being able to open them myself. I cannot say that this will make me particularly unhappy.'[33]

In addition to the ceremonial side of the speech from the throne, the central purpose of which was the reconfirmation of the pact between monarch and nation, the speech had also borne a political significance right from the start: on this occasion the king was the interpreter of government policy. The speeches from the throne were therefore per se political (in a narrow sense), but they were never allowed to take sides. Because the speech was a political action – in keeping with the principle that the king had no constitutional responsibility – it had to be approved by the government. The king under no circumstances was allowed to be partial to a particular party or to express his personal opinion. Theoretically, therefore, the ministers had the final say on the contents of the speech, but in practice the Belgian kings did try to influence the way in which the text came into being.

Being a symbol of national unity, the king read out the government's policy programme, and the first thing he did was request support for it, which automatically presupposed a certain amount of consensus in Parliament.

Leopold I and the Ever-Increasing Party Conflict

In the first years subsequent to independence, Belgium had 'unionist' governments, in which Catholics and liberals joined forces to form a strong, united front against a possible threat from the Netherlands. One could not yet really speak of parties with a party policy, nor of political party governments that were supported by a parliamentary majority. Consequently, the government was not certain of Parliament's voting behaviour, and it needed the king to act as mediator. This position afforded the king some influence in the draft of the speech from the throne. The king could, as chief executive power, weigh more heavily on the government than when parties dictated the government policy. He therefore acted in the eyes of the outside world as the one to bridge the gap. Therefore, it is not surprising that, in the beginning of Leopold I's reign, there is much evidence of his manifest interventions in the preparation of the speech from the throne.[34]

The unionist period came to an end after the peace agreement with the Netherlands was signed in 1839. Internally, the different points of view between the liberals and the Catholics were becoming more clearly defined, and there was increasing room for the development of political parties. When the first liberal government was formed in 1847, the Minister of Home Affairs, Charles Rogier, wanted to have the first liberal victory endorsed by a liberal speech from the throne. He wrote a party-partial text, which evoked the following misgiving in Leopold I: 'The principal thing however was that it made me speak the language of our little radical Club l'Alliance so named.'[35] The king did not intend to defend the 'radical' liberal points of view. This actually could put his position as neutral national symbol into jeopardy: 'I expected that the speech would be very reasonable and particularly as all speeches of that description ought to do mild on all subjects which a party question and on which the crown cannot be expected to express opinions.'[36] He informed Rogier: 'Il est de l'essence d'un discours royal d'éviter d'entrer, pour ainsi dire, au cœur des discussions politiques.'[37] Leopold I wanted to deliver a neutral speech from the throne and definitely did not wish to get involved in political arguments, let alone be a mouthpiece for the liberals. He wrote to his father-in-law, Louis-Philippe, the French king:

> Son but paraissait en grande partie de faire exprimer
> mon amour sans bornes pour nos radicaux. La question
> est fort simple: ce qu'ils ont annoncé dans leur pro-
> gramme doit malheureusement être admis comme possi-
> ble, mais le Roi n'a à exprimer ni plaisir ni déplaisir, cela
> est leur affaire.[38]

The king put the government leader under pressure to remove, rephrase or add a number of undesirable sentences. Eventually, Rogier capitulated and adjusted his text to the king's wishes.[39]

In 1857 unionism was definitely something of the past, and the king inevitably lost some of his power to the government parties. The ministers tried to slip sensitive matters such as Belgium's recognition of Italy in 1861 into the speech from the throne. This was much to Leopold I's dissatisfaction, who was of the opinion that it would be much wiser for the government to remain discreet about it because it was too controversial: 'The speech offers difficulties. Contrary to what is done in England they always want here to put things into the speech that ought not according to good taste to be there.'[40] The king requested to have the recognition of Italy removed, which eventually happened.[41]

On close inspection, Leopold I succeeded in maintaining the speech from the throne as a 'national' address. His suggestions to change the text sometimes would be accepted and at other times he was forced to conform to the wishes of his ministers, but he was able to see to it that his neutral position remained unaffected by the words he uttered.

Leopold II as the Government's Mouthpiece: The Subversion of the Speech from the Throne

Leopold II continued the ritual speech but would, unlike his father, only sporadically appear in front of both houses. Eventually, in 1892, seventeen years before his death, he put a stop to it altogether. During Leopold II's reign, very few documents have been preserved in which the ministers communicated with one another or the king, either through a mediator or directly, about the speech from the throne. Unfortunately, little or almost no information is available on the direct role that Leopold II played in editing the speech. However, many of the reasons for the ritual's abandonment can be deduced from the speeches that he delivered.

Leopold II's first speeches from the throne followed the normal procedure. The king delivered his speech to both houses and with almost no really strong preceding arguments, received an answer. Then in 1870 the king addressed Parliament in an extraordinary session three months earlier than usual. A new government had been elected for just one month. Like the elections, the speech from the throne was dominated by the international tension brought about by the French-German war. Leopold II appealed to the patriotism of his country.

> Au moment où les événements du dehors exaltent dans nos cœurs le sentiment de la patrie commune, il me tardait de voir la Représentation nationale réunie autour de moi [...]. Devant une cause aussi sacrée, tous les cœurs belges s'unissent [...]. Dans l'accomplissement de tels

devoirs, peuple et Roi n'auront jamais qu'une âme et
qu'un cri: Vive la Belgique indépendante! Dieu veille sur
elle et protège ses droits.[42]

This appeal in the speech was answered in unison.[43]

This unanimity did not exist for very long, however. The ideological tension between Catholics and liberals clearly mounted in the 1870s. After the elections in the summer of 1878, the radical anticlerical government of Frère-Orban-Van Humbeeck came into being. The new government decided that the time had come to finally make Belgium a secular state. The anticlerical liberals strove towards a complete division between church and state. According to them, the ultimate means to achieve that goal was to put public education under the auspices of the state, whereas previously, the church and the Catholics had taken advantage of the freedom of education to establish their own schools. The Ministry of Public Education was established for the first time in Belgian history, in 1878. The political parties in the meantime had distinguished themselves clearly, and the government could increasingly rely on the parliamentary majority for support. This happened at the expense of the king, who had less and less grip on the governments. This was why Frère-Orban-Van Humbeeck's strong radical-liberal government could put its anticlerical stamp on the speech from the throne. The king declared: 'L'enseignement donné aux frais de l'Etat doit être placé sous la direction et sous la surveillance exclusives de l'autorité civile.'[44]

It was the first time that the ritual of the speech from the throne had ever been so strongly politically tinted. The king no longer put himself forward as the promoter of unity, who surpassed the party differences of opinion and symbolized national unity. He had evolved from neutral 'reader' to mouthpiece of the political party in power. The speech from the throne lost its impetus as a result of its politicization. What the king had said about education was the trigger for the school battle in which Belgium was caught up from 1878 to 1884.[45] The school battle was started in the debate on the address that Parliament was to deliver to the king. The way in which the Senate dealt with this indicates that the First House at that time was still an aristocratic, moderating and reconciliatory body where no strongly political arguments took place.

Depuis après de très longues années du Sénat, c'est-à-
dire, il est d'usage de présenter une adresse qui pût être
votée unanimement par tous les membres de cette
assemblée. Il est bien entendu, comme l'a dit l'honorable baron d'Anethan, que chacun conserve son opinion.[46]

After the problematic speech from the throne in 1878, in which it was abundantly clear that the king had been brought into the party dispute and the speech had become a source of conflict instead of being an instrument to encourage unity, Leopold II held only three more opening speeches. In 1880 he delivered a second speech from the throne that came from Frère-Orban-Van Humbeeck's radical-liberal government. It once again emphasized that education would be developed along the same lines as those laid down in the 1879 law and as they had been announced in 1878. Despite the Catholics' resistance, it did not cross the government's mind to restrain the law. The king once again was forced to endorse the education policy in his speech from the throne.[47] It was the second time that the king was obliged to choose sides in a strongly polarized atmosphere.

Leopold II's last two throne speeches were written during the time of Auguste Beernaert's Catholic government. In 1886, the speech from the throne clearly bore the signs of the social strife that criss-crossed the battle of the parties in the last decennia of the nineteenth century and dominated the political agenda at certain moments. A dramatic social uprising in the spring of 1886 had caused the traditional parties to wake up with a start, and they finally noticed the social problems at hand. In order to put the people at ease, the king spoke about matters such as improving the labourers' situation and legal protection for the weak, and he also announced social reforms. The Commission d'Enquête du Travail, a parliamentary investigation commission, had prepared the matter:

> Eclairé par ses travaux, mon gouvernement aura à vous
> saisir de projets de réformes importantes. Il convient
> notamment de favoriser la libre formation de groupes
> professionnels, – d'établir entre les chefs d'industrie et
> les ouvriers des liens nouveaux sous la forme des conseils
> d'arbitrage et de conciliation – de réglementer le travail
> des femmes et enfants.[48]

Clearly afraid of a repeated performance of the revolutionary upsurge, the government deemed it essential to seize the symbolic moment of the speech of the throne to show its concern. The symbolic gesture in the speech contributed to making the social question a political theme, which gave upcoming socialism an important stimulus. The *Belgische Werkliedenpartij* [Belgian Labour Party] that had been founded in 1885 turned the social struggle into a struggle for political emancipation: as soon as the labourers were represented, they would be able to achieve a parliamentary majority because they outnumbered other social groups, and they would thus be able to get social reforms passed. Because of the lack of political representation, the struggle for the general right to vote was fought outside Parliament, in the streets. That is how it came about that Leopold II's last speech from the throne in 1892 was disrupted by a socialist action. Five days before the speech was to take place, the parliamentary commission rejected a bill proposed by the radical-liberals that favoured the general right to vote. There was no intention to hold Leopold II personally responsible or to aim a direct attack at him personally. The disruption of the speech was a new form of protest that was bold in character and that had an extraordinary reverberation. From that moment on, Leopold II would never show himself in Parliament again. What is ironic is that it was precisely the ritual of the speech from the throne that had made it possible to hold the protest action: since 1891 it actually had been forbidden to hold any form of protest in the 'neutral zone' around the parliament building and the Royal Palace. But because it was so important to have a large cheering crowd present along the route that the king followed on his way to the Palace of the Nation, it was impossible to forbid gatherings in and around the neutral zone on 8 November 1892. The ritual's success depended on exactly such a gathering. However, the public show was thoroughly disrupted by the socialists from Brussels who answered the cheer of 'Vive le Roi!' (Long live the King!) with 'Vive le Suffrage Universel!' (Long live Universal Suffrage) and who unfolded banners during the king's procession. The spectacle was ambiguous, to say the least:

> Tous les chapeaux levés, mais ornés de carton revendica-
> teur, le vol blanc de milliers de rondelles, les chants et les
> cris pareils à des vivats enthousiastes pouvaient, observés
> de loin, donner l'illusion d'une délirante explosion de
> loyalisme.[49]

Right in front of the parliamentary building, it was horribly unclear for whom the crowd's applause was meant: the king or the socialist leader Jean Volders. When someone threw a handful of slips of paper in the direction of the king, his horse started rearing, and the pomp and circumstance completely disappeared.[50] The speech from the throne itself remained neutral and superficial on the sensitive subject of the reform of suffrage. The latter also would necessitate a revision of the constitution. An extension of the right to vote was foreseen for a later date.

> La constitution belge est aujourd'hui la plus ancienne
> du continent. Elle a valu à notre cher pays une longue
> série d'années de paix et de fécond développement: J'en
> ai plus d'une fois, comme vous, proclamé la sagesse [...]
> nos institutions si libérales peuvent être aujourd'hui
> améliorées et rajeunies [...] le corps électoral d'aujour-

d'hui vient de vous donner mandat de réaliser une large extension du droit de suffrage.[51]

At the end of the debate, the members of Parliament cried 'Vive le Roi!,' except the radical liberals (the socialists, as has already been said, were not yet represented in Parliament) who answered with 'Vive le Suffrage Universel!' That was the sign to drop whole packets of slips of paper printed with 'Vive le Suffrage Universel!' down from the public gallery. With this, the profanation of the ceremony was complete. The disruption of the speech from the throne was no real attack on the monarch, but rather a new and spectacular means of enforcing the demand for suffrage. The ritual was seized and subverted in order to let the socialist debate on democratization of the right to vote reverberate with the strongest possible impact. Leopold II subsequently stayed away from Parliament, and as a result the socialists had to wait until Albert I's inauguration to repeat this spectacular form of collective action.

Albert I and the Speech from the Throne As a Source of Conflict

When Albert I took the oath on 23 December 1909, it too was accompanied by a collective action by the parliamentary left, which included socialists at that time. When the new king – who had stage fright – entered the parliamentary semi-circle, he was greeted from the socialist benches with 'Vive le Suffrage Universel!'.[52] On 8 November 1910, almost one year after he had taken the oath, Albert I again addressed Parliament, which made it look as though he wanted to reinstate the lost tradition of the speech from the throne. It took the Council of Ministers, with the king as chairman, two cabinet meetings to prepare it.[53] Thoroughly against the wishes of the Catholic government, the king did all he could to put his stamp on the speech from the throne. Albert I was in fact an ally of the left opposition parties in their struggle to democratize the right to vote and to make primary education compulsory.[54] During the preliminary sessions of the Council of Ministers, the king strongly insisted that the speech from the throne should contain a passage on election reform. The Catholics, who had been in power since January 1908, had a conservative wing who opposed the democratization of the right to vote, but they did so in a very intractable manner. That is why Albert could not convince the Schollaert government to include this subject in the speech. The most important point on the agenda was public education, traditionally *the* divisive element between left and right in Belgium. The socialists, the radicals and even the progressive Catholic wing strove towards compulsory primary education. King Albert I supported the struggle, which was linked to the democratization of the right to vote and to the implementation of general military service, but he was not able to convince the Catholic ministers in this regard. Moreover, it was insinuated in the paragraph that was included in the part on the improvement of public education that the government would subsidize the free Catholic education.[55]

> C'est au père de famille qu'appartient le droit de veiller à l'éducation et à l'instruction de son enfant, de choisir librement et en pleine indépendance l'école à laquelle il le confiera. Mon gouvernement vous proposera des mesures pour garantir efficacement l'exercice de ce droit imprescriptible.[56]

Albert, just like Leopold II in 1878 and 1880, was forced therefore to represent a point of view that was (party) politically tinted. Moreover, the government's vision went against the grain of the king's strategy of taking to heart the demands that the opposition parties had concerning education and the right to vote. He wanted to rise above the political polarization and strive towards a national consensus, which he regarded as essential in the light of international tension. It is apparent from a note that Albert wrote in 1911[57] that he would have undone the 1910 speech from the throne if it had been possible. The impression had been created that, by uttering the words that the Catholic government had put in his mouth, he fully supported the government's policy and committed himself to realizing the Catholic school reformation against the parliamentary minority.[58] Seeing that Albert I was convinced that it was in the national interest to take the demands of the opposition into account, he had done his best to formulate the speech from the throne in these terms. He failed when it came to two crucial aspects: compulsory primary education and the democratization of the right to vote.

Moreover, despite the good preparation and organization, it was impossible to prevent the socialists from marring Albert's first speech from the throne in 1910.[59] On his way from the Royal Palace to Parliament, the king was treated to a shower of small pieces of paper with socialist demands written on them, in the same way as in 1892. The socialist members of Parliament wore red roses in their buttonholes. On their desks lay piles of little pieces of paper with the words 'Dissolution, Vive le Suffrage Universel!' (Dissolution, Long Live Universal Suffrage!). When the king entered Parliament, the socialists stayed seated while the others stood up and shouted 'Long live the King!' Then the pieces of paper with 'Vive le Suffrage Universel!' were thrown about. After the parliamentary session, the socialists also stayed away from the formal dinner at the palace, where the people's representatives were allowed to have a seat at the table. They emphasized their 'separate' status by holding a meeting in the *Maison du Peuple* in Brussels. Once again, the socialists did not aim their disruption at the king personally: 'Nous n'en voulons pas au roi' (We do not have anything against the king).[60]

Albert I, like Leopold II, clearly did not feel much of an inclination to start the speech from the throne up again after what had happened in 1910, but in 1918 he was spurred on to restore the tradition by the enthusiasm around the end of the First World War. The speech from the throne on 22 November 1918 was consistent with the end of the war and was permeated by the nationalistic feeling of unity and victory that accompanied it. The ritual was not disrupted by socialist slogans, but it deviated from the previous speeches from the throne in that there were a few amendments to the procedure. The parliamentary semi-circle was laden with national signs and symbols. The Belgian flag was resplendent in the royal gallery. The national coat of arms and the Belgian lion adorned the hall together with medallions and King Albert's portrait. Many of those present wore their military uniform as a token of honour to the king, their commander during the war. In contrast to the other years, the ritual did not follow a straight time line. The preparations for the king's arrival were made first, as usual. Then, the chairman of the royal session went forward to announce a *Te Deum*: a solemn ceremony in the cathedral. Subsequently, the Minister of Economic Affairs, Edward Cooreman, took the opportunity to give a nationalistic address in which he sang the praises of the king, the queen, all the heroes and those wounded in the war. His address enhanced the national and royalist feelings of all those present. After Cooreman's speech the meeting was adjourned. The session was continued after the procession. As on previous occasions, the king came in behind the royal family, but he held his speech from the parliamentary chairman's desk, not from his throne. His speech was, not surprisingly, strongly nationalistic in character. It was a token of honour to all who had fought and suffered in the war.[61] Patriotic feelings united all parties for a short while, and the speech from the throne seemed to interpret this perfectly.[62]

However, the royal address of 1918 was to become an important source of conflict during the interwar period, because of the promises that had been formulated in them – concessions, in fact, to the demands of the most important pre-war emancipation movements. On the one hand, the speech from the throne announced and proposed the implementation of universal suffrage (one man, one vote) as a type of compensation and reward for the man in the street's pains during the war. The promise was subsequently honoured rather quickly by reforming the constitution in what was, in fact, an unconstitutional manner. The speech from the throne also announced the dutchifying of the University of Ghent, which was the Flemish movement's most important demand. The promise for pacification was, however, put off to a later date because a part of the Flemish movement had burnt its own political bridges by collaborating with the Germans during the First World War. That was a difficult sticking point in a country where the Flemish-Walloon contrasts were made all the more poignant by the collaboration. The official announcement to dutchify aroused a substantial amount of conflict potential surrounding the king as figurehead. The symbolic gesture of recognition made the Flemish movement's argument more forceful, but at the same time King Albert was a national figure par excellence who incarnated Belgium's unity and who, as such, was the one to whom the anti-Flemish movements appealed. The Flemish movement, even in its recent historiography, refers to Albert's speech from the throne as one of the divisive elements of the Belgian system.[63]

Prime Minister Carton de Wiart insisted that the king should again hold his speech in 1920. In his opinion, all parties would benefit from it: 'Vous insistez dans votre nouvelle lettre sur l'accueil favorable que feraient tous les partis à l'annonce d'un discours du trône.'[64] However, Albert I refused to open the Houses of Parliament according to the usual ritual. He would have to make a pronouncement on the curtailment of the military service, and he did not agree with that government point of view. He refused to act as the government mouthpiece in order to avoid creating the impression that he supported its vision.

> Si je parlais, je serais obligés, étant donné mon serment
> constitutionnelle et mon devoir de chef de l'armée, d'af-
> firmer catégoriquement que nous sommes un des pays
> les plus vulnérables au point de vue militaire et que,
> abaisser la durée du temps de service au dessous d'un
> certain terme c'est tomber dans le système des milices.
> Or l'expérience prouve que ces troupes n'ont jamais tenu
> devant une force régulier et bien entraînée. On croit
> trouver un correctif dans un puissant armement mais
> une troupe sans discipline ni cohésion ne saura pas
> défendre cet armement.[65]

Albert I did not want to defend the government's point of view regarding the country's defence by saying words he did not support.

The Speech from the Throne: Short History of a Political Text

Although the ceremonial aspect of the speech from the throne hardly changed between 1831 and 1918, it appears that its political text evolved in terms of the changing sociopolitical context and the king's position in it. Seeing that the struggle between the parties made the realization of a national consensus increasingly less self-evident – except in time of war or threat of war – the speech from the throne became more and more politicized, and the king's words could no longer surpass or remove the divide in a neutral manner. The speech from the throne's political message would, in the long run, undermine the essential function that the ritual had, namely to promote unity. It appears from the Belgian case that, despite the ministerial responsibility, the monarch did exercise influence on the text of the address, and also tried to put his stamp on it. The balance of power among king, government and parliament and the extent to which the government was assured of the support of the parliamentary majority determined the freedom of movement that the king had when editing the speech from the throne. Leopold I succeeded in keeping the speech from the throne more or less neutral and national. In 1878 the government was supported by the parliamentary majority to such an extent that the king was invoked in the party struggle, whether he liked it or not. Via 'his' words he even gave the initial impetus for the school struggle. The ritual of the speech from the throne could no longer fulfil its purpose of promoting unity because the royal address itself became the cause for political struggle.

The democratization of political life at the end of the nineteenth century did not reinforce the pomp and circumstance of the speech from the throne; on the contrary, it actually diminished it even further. In 1892 and 1910 the speeches were marred by the socialists, who saw it as the ideal opportunity to add force to their demand for universal suffrage. A ritual derives its aura from its continuity. Maybe the little information that is offered us in official documents on the socialist disruptions should be seen as a way of protecting the ritual.

Just because this ritual was undermined by (a part of) 'the commoners' at a time when the political debate was dominated by the democratization of the right to vote, it did not mean that no other ritual outside political life in Belgium was not simultaneously invented or reinforced to popularize once again the royal family – not least with the people who had no right to vote. The 'royal fairy tale' was strongly cultivated, especially in Albert I's reign, and the highest authoritative institution once again was brought down to a worldly level. The king's cult status as the personification of the national ideal became stronger with the democratization of political life. The royal family's popularity depended on its image. The royal family romance vouched for the royal heritage and, in so doing, combined the traditional dynastic legitimacy with the modern element of the family romance. Albert assembled his royal family around his uncle Leopold II's coffin upon the latter's death in 1909. With every public appearance, Albert saw to it that he was accompanied by Queen Elisabeth or one of his children. The newspapers were filled with the King's attention to the Queen, Elisabeth's motherly warmth and the family's harmonious appearance. The royal family became the symbol of happiness, love, fertility, heritage, immortality or the public personification of personal desires. By presenting themselves to the people in the way they did, Albert and Elisabeth made it look as though they were the personification of the ideals of masculinity and femininity. The court seemed to be one big, happy family, with Albert as the good *paterfamilias*. Albert I's roles as head of the state and head of the family actually overlapped.

Yet Albert was unable to propagate this image of the father for the fatherland via the speech from the throne. It was under his reign that an end was put to the ritual, paradoxically enough just at the time when he was more popular than ever, after the First World War: a time when there was more pomp and circumstance to the speech than ever before, resulting in a more lasting impression than had ever been the case in the past.

The fact that the speech from the throne became a source of conflict, and could have political repercussions that were at odds with its function to promote unity, explains why the ritual ceased to exist in Belgium, unlike the situation in the Netherlands and Great Britain. Another factor that contributed to the quiet death that the speech from the throne died in Belgium was the intransigence of the Belgian kings. They were never able to completely reconcile their position with their limited constitutional role and therefore refused to be a mere passive instrument of the government.

Public Transcripts of Royalism.
Pauper Letters to the Belgian Royal
Family (1880-1940)

Maarten Van Ginderachter

In the last few years, the writings of 'ordinary people' have been at the centre of scholarly attention, the most notable example being Thomas Sokoll's edition of 758 Essex pauper letters from the period 1731-1837.[1] This renewed interest in sources from 'ordinary people' is part of a recent reaction against one of the central assumptions of the field of discourse studies, viz., that analysing the *production* of a certain discourse amounts to studying its *consumption* in society. According to Jonathan Rose, one cannot judge the impact of a discourse on 'ordinary people' by merely studying the discourse as such, because this method will produce a series of contradictory interpretations of equal value dependent on the position of the researcher. For instance, American radio publicity from the 1930s was clearly gender-stereotyped. Some scholars have inferred from this that female listeners interiorized conservative sex roles, but others have pointed out that they barely listened to these publicity messages and that they saw them 'as just another sales pitch'. Rose's point is that 'there is as much hard evidence for any of these readings [...], which is to say none at all; and we will get no closer to answering these questions unless we shift our attention from the text to the audience'.[2] One way of doing this is by basing our historical research on sources *from* 'ordinary people' and not merely *about* them. Rose for one has accomplished a *tour de force* with his impressive study, *The Intellectual Life of the British Working Class,* in which he entered 'the minds of ordinary readers in history, to discover what they read and how they read it', using memoirs, diaries, interviews, reader letters to the press and fan mail from 'common readers'.[3]

Likewise, when examining popular attitudes towards the monarchy, historians must not limit themselves to the official royalist discourse in the media. However, when searching for sources that go 'beyond' the official rhetoric, they are likely to be confronted with heuristic problems. Documents in which ordinary citizens themselves talk directly to or about 'their' royal family are not that widespread. For the post-World War II period we can rely on oral sources and testimonies, but when all direct witnesses have died, historians cannot be too choosy: 'Beggars can't be choosers'. And it is 'beggars' this article is about.

Since the establishment of an independent Belgium in 1830, numerous citizens have written to the royal family for a number of reasons: to dedicate a poem to the king; to give the heir apparent a present of their own making; to offer congratulations for the birth of a prince or princess; or to offer condolences in death. The most common reason for writing was to ask the royal family for money or help in kind with a so-called *letter of request* or *demande de secours*. A rough estimate suggests that between 1865 and 1934, spanning Leopold II's and Albert I's reigns, the royal family must have received tens of thousands of citizen letters, most of which were letters of request.[4] Only a few hundred, though, have been preserved (as yet uncatalogued) in the Archives of the Royal Palace in Brussels. These letters are unique sources that have not yet been systematically used in historical research.[5]

Using James C. Scott's concept of the 'public transcript', this essay asks to what extent the 'official' royal imagery resounded at the base of society. Scott argues that the way in which the subordinate publicly address the dominant, i.e., the public transcript of their domination, does not tell the whole story. The lower classes have an 'off-stage' discourse, i.e., the hidden transcript, which challenges the powers that be. Or in Scott's own words, the public transcript is 'the open interaction between subordinates and those who dominate' or 'the *self*-portrait of dominant elites as they would have themselves seen'.[6] The hidden transcript is 'a wide variety of low-profile forms of resistance that dare not speak in their own name'.[7] The letters of request that are the subject of this essay constitute the public transcript of royalism as produced by the subordinate. To what extent does it mirror the public transcript of the dominant? This is one of the questions this essay will address.

'To the King'

Turning to the king when in need is an old tradition dating back to the Ancien Regime.[8] Royal philanthropy too has time-honoured roots, but during the eighteenth century the custom of royal gifts to the poor took on a whole new meaning. The idea of popular Sovereignty – the monarch as representing the nation's will – changed the entire context. According to Prochaska, Ancien Regime monarchs were part of 'a warrior tradition of nobility, characterized by self-glorification and an obsession with wealth and influence'. They gave alms not out of 'social pity' but because they believed it would contribute to their salvation, enhance their reputation, show their wealth, overawe their equals and express their authority. These reasons may have continued to play a role, but in the eighteenth century a new idea became the cornerstone of royal philanthropy, viz., 'that privilege entailed responsibility to the less fortunate'. Political theorists began to present monarchs as servants to their people and to base royal power on a kind of 'velvet' paternalism. Monarchs became the neutral heads of a unified, constitutional nation, and popularity became one of the most important justifications of royal power. Royal philanthropy had a new goal, viz., helping to win over the people.[9]

A nineteenth-century Belgian could turn towards a host of authorities when in need. At the top of the 'request pyramid' stood the king, and under him were the Interior or Justice Minister, the provincial governors, the district commissioners and mayors. When a member of the royal family received a letter of request, the palace administration turned to the local authorities to make sure it was *bona fide*. A file was compiled containing a detailed social profile of the requester (sex, address, age, job, wage, family composition, etc.). Most letter-writers did indeed receive help. In 1908 for instance, Prince Albert denied help to a mere 1.5 per cent of the 1328 people who turned to him that year. The large majority (some 1230) received 5 or 10 francs, the remainder an amount between 15 and 350 francs. The total sum he dispensed on philanthropy in 1908 was 15,994.5 francs[10] – at the time when a Borinage miner earned 1257 francs a year or 4.13 francs a day.

Any member of the royal family could be the addressee of these citizen letters, but obviously the king got the most. However, there are some interesting fluctuations in addressee popularity.[11] When Prince Albert became the first in line to succeed his uncle Leopold II after the death of two closer heirs to the throne in 1891, he became steadily more respected than the King, whose popularity suffered from his autocratic leanings and his adventures in the Congo. Prince Albert consequently got more letters of request than Leopold, especially from the lower classes of society. Female members of the royal family were not particularly 'in demand' with the letter writing public until Prince Albert married Elisabeth in 1900. They were the first royal couple to be perceived by the public as a 'normal' family, with loving parents and adorable children. While in Great Britain, the 'feminization of the British monarchy' became an important element in its popularization from the end of the eighteenth century on,[12] in Belgium this only occurred from the beginning of the twentieth century. Before Elisabeth, the queen was merely seen as an appendage to the king, without many public duties. In 1874, for instance, the wife of a small bartender from Liège wished both the king and the queen 'a long and happy life', but for the king this was to 'reign' and for the queen 'to raise her honourable family'.[13] From Elisabeth on, female royals became much more prominent on the public scene (although in family-related gender roles) and consequently received more letters. As caring for the poor was seen as a female quality, people increasingly turned to the Queen for help, especially after World War I consecrated Elisabeth's image as the queen-nurse who cared for her people.

Most letters of request came from people at the bottom of society, but they were not necessarily written on the writer's own initiative. Doctors, priests, local politicians or public writers often stimulated people to turn to the royal family for help, or they wrote on their behalf. Some mayors of municipalities whose poor relief was underfunded systematically channelled their poor to the royal palace. A number of frauds were also active. In 1895, for instance, Prince Albert's administration discovered an impostor from the town of Mons who wrote requests on demand, in exchange for 10 per cent of the amount rewarded by the Prince.[14] It is unlikely, however, that fraud was a widespread phenomenon, given the meticulous way in which requests were examined by the palace administration, the local authorities and the police.

We should bear in mind when reading these letters that, on the one hand, we cannot interpret them automatically as direct, unfiltered statements of the lower classes. In Scott's terminology, they used 'the ideology of the dominant stratum', 'making appeals that remain within the official discourse of deference'.[15] To put it differently, there is always an influence of the hegemonic public transcript. On the other hand, the fact that some letters were mediated by middle-class supporters of the poor should not lead us to underestimate the initiative of 'commoners' to voice their own complaints. Sometimes workers on strike directly appealed to the king as a neutral arbiter to settle labour disagreements. In Brussels, ordinary people went to the royal palace to ask help in person. Some requesters referred to the tradition that the king *had* to offer help on his birthday, the day of his patron saint or the national holiday, thus turning the public transcript of the 'good king' to their own benefit. When members of the royal family made an official visit to a town, people handed over their letter of request personally. Such official visits usually resulted in a sharp increase of requests from that particular town in the following weeks. All in all, there seemed to be a low threshold to write to the royal family. People did not know to whom they should turn in the labyrinth of official institutions, and consequently turned to the first authority figure that sprang to mind: the king. Letter writers did not have to worry about the exact address either; they could simply write on the envelope 'To the King', and the letter would be duly delivered.

Facts and Figures

Based on a sample of 60 letters – 30 taken from the period 1880-1904 addressed to Leopold II and 30 from the period 1925-1938 addressed to Queen Elisabeth[16] – I estimate that roughly half of all letters of request were undoubtedly written by the requesters themselves. The authorship of roughly one-third is unclear. In only one-sixth of all cases is the profession of the requester and spouse unknown. Of those whose professional background is known, 60 per cent are lower class, as determined from profession, place of residence, wage, education and literacy level. As to the sex of the writers, there is an almost perfect balance. The geographical division shows that a quarter came from Brussels[17], a sixth from Flanders and 60 per cent from Wallonia. Of course, these figures have a limited empirical base. We need a larger sample to assess how representative they are.

The palace administration kept an inventory of all letters received. Unfortunately, there is only one inventory left that is truly useful for our purpose, meaning that it contains all or some of the following information: name of the requester, sex, address, reason for the request, profession, family composition and wage. It is the inventory of Prince Albert when he was heir apparent from 1891 until 1909.[18] In this period he received some 18,000 letters from citizens, of which 10,305 were letters of request (only 30 or a mere 0.3 per cent have been preserved). I have sampled the entire year of 1908, in which Prince Albert and his wife Elisabeth received a record of 1328 letters of request from different persons. I will not go into much detail about these figures, but the most striking statistic is that 66 per cent of all letters came from Wallonia, about 26 per cent from the Brussels area, and only 8 per cent from Flanders. How to explain this underrepresentation of Flanders, which at the time represented 60 per cent of the Belgian population? First we need to know whether this distribution applies to all years, but it looks as if this disproportion is a constant, because right to this day there are significant differences in the language of the letters of request. Between 1990 and 1999, King Albert and Queen Paola received approximately 100,000 letters of request, of which 70 per cent on average were written in French and 30 per cent in Dutch (while the current linguistic division in Belgium is 6 speakers of Dutch to 4 francophones).[19] Factors that may have played a role in the linguistic unbalance of letters to Prince Albert in 1908 include local economic situation, unequal rates of literacy (lower in Flanders), efficiency of local poor relief, survival mechanisms in closer-knit Flemish rural communities that precluded asking for help from an outsider, the francophone image of the monarchy as a mental barrier for writing in Dutch to the King, etc. A second remarkable statistic is that 40 per cent of all letters of request to Prince Albert came from one of the four Walloon *mining and steel* districts with a distinct overrepresentation of industry workers (between 85 per cent and 99 per cent of the requesters from these regions whose profession we know were industry workers).[20] In short, the trend in 1908 was that letters of request were a phenomenon of Walloon industrialized centres, but to fully explain these figures additional research is necessary.

What these figures tell us about the popularity of the monarchy at large is not unambiguously clear. First, only a tiny portion of Belgian society actually applied for royal help, but of all institutions people wrote to when in need, the monarchy was likely to receive the most requests. Second, does applying for a royal gift imply adoration or even acceptance of the institution of the monarchy? On the one hand, Scott claims that the subordinate turn the 'hegemonic ideology to good advantage'.[21] In our case, this might mean that letter writers used the official image of the good and benevolent monarch to improve their chances of receiving help. On the other hand, it might be argued that when poor people in a miserable, dead-end situation obtained a royal gift, it was hard for them not to feel grateful towards the person if not the institution of the monarch. In 1926, e.g., a lower-class widow from Charleroi wrote to Queen Elisabeth, her 'Dear Benefactress', but when her application was successful, she jubilantly called the Queen 'Dear Mother'.[22] Why did she use a more affectionate term the second time around? Most likely because she felt truly grateful. If she was only intent on utilizing the official royalist rhetoric to maximize her chances, there is no reason why she would not have written 'Dear Mother' in the first place, as this was a more direct reference to Elisabeth's public image as a mother to her people.

Public Transcripts of Royalism

Letters of request can be used to examine the extent to which the deliberate construction of royal images by the authorities had an impact on public opinion – or in other words how the public transcript of the subordinate and that of the dominant compare.

The royal palace was well aware of the public-relations value of helping the poor. Traditionally, the king donated money when calamities such as mining disasters and inundations occurred, or he dispensed emergency relief (bread and coal) in Brussels during harsh winters. The newspapers were so well aware of these initiatives that it is highly likely they were 'tipped' by press releases. After Albert's marriage to Elisabeth in 1900, the palace actively sought to construct an image of the couple as loving and caring parents. When Prince Leopold (the future Leopold III) was born in 1901, citizens who sent a letter of congratulation received a postcard of Albert and Elisabeth holding hands by their baby's cradle. The captions read: 'Gathered round the cradle of small Prince Leopold' and 'An intimate scene in Prince Albert's palace'.

Through 'press leaks', the public at large was kept abreast of the Prince's philanthropy. In 1908, for instance, the papers were lyrical about an incognito visit of the Princess to a bedridden working-class mother in Brussels. The Princess went there on foot, accompanied by two staff members, carrying meat, wine, bed linen and napkins for the baby. The woman in question, the papers reported, was overcome by 'so much goodness and simplicity'. The Princess left without 'her visit having been noticed in the neighbourhood'.[23]

The royal administration was more discrete about the letters of request, but it was well aware of the impact that donations had on public opinion. In 1908, for example, Prince Albert's secretary admonished his personnel to ignore requests made by a certain Father L'Heureux because 'he asks for money in the name of different people, but he doesn't let them know whom it comes from'.[24]

Autour du berceau du petit Prince Léopold

Propriété de l'édition V. G. Bruxelles.

Fig. 1. Postcard which was sent to citizens who congratulated Prince Albert and Princess Elisabeth on the birth of their first son Leopold in 1901.

This priest dispensed poor relief from the palace without acknowledging its source. The royal gifts were not supposed to be anonymous; people were expected to know that the monarchy was being kind to them. In short, royal gifts were, to use Walter Bagehot's phrase, one of the 'dignified parts' of the institution, meant to inspire the population's reverence. The requesters, who were citizens in a relatively democratic state, did not seem to mind the paternalist implications of the custom. Indeed, most of them turned towards the monarchy precisely because they believed in the king's paternalist duty, or they at least paid homage to the official transcript of the kind monarch.

If we want to use the letters of request to examine to what extent official royal images were held by the public at large, and more particularly by the letter writers, we have to tread carefully. First, nearly 15 per cent of all letters were written not by the person for whom help was requested but by middle-class people who wanted to help a pauper. This is not an insurmountable obstacle and may, in fact, help us to find similarities and differences between lower- and middle-class views.[25] Nonetheless, it does recommend caution. Second, we cannot read these letters as *the* authentic manifestation of very deep and individual feelings, for they show the influence of certain models prescribing how to address a royal and how to make one's request convincing. As Scott argues, when the subordinate address the dominant, their discourse is often 'habitual and formulaic, implying little in the way of inwardness'.[26] Letter writers often employed 'success-enhancing strategies', for instance supporting values they thought pleasing to the dominant classes. However, the fact that the writers most probably used model letters or phrases inspired by their middle-class supporters does not imply that their writings were inauthentic. Borrowings assuredly took place, and our challenge is to examine if and how the poor adapted models to their specific needs. Third, these letters cannot answer the question 'how far images of monarchs grew out of the psychological needs of their subjects, being projected from below on to the crown, and how far they were deliberate political constructions, emanating from central government'.[27] We can merely say that certain images were present both in the official discourse and at the base of society. With these caveats in mind, then, what do the letters of request tell us about the official and subordinate transcripts of the monarchy?

Lower-class letters were generally much shorter and less elaborate than their higher- and middle-class equivalents. Their misery spoke for itself. 'Commoners' had very modest requests. They only asked for 'relief',[28] 'help',[29] a 'small grant',[30] a 'reward',[31] a certain 'amount' of money,[32] or a 'gift'[33] – without specifying what exactly it was they needed, let alone specifically stating the amount of money they wanted. Some did not even ask anything.[34] Nor did they try to counter the bourgeois prejudice about the lower classes as unworthy of help because of their loose morals and their wastefulness. Either they were unaware that this might influence their chances of receiving help, or they simply could not be bothered because they were at their wits' end. They merely painted their own miserable situation and left it up to the king or queen's discretion to decide what to do. Middle- and higher-class people were more likely to ask for a very specific amount of money ('86 francs to pay my rent'[35]) or a concrete intervention of the royal family[36] ('make my creditors go away',[37] 'let me meet you in person',[38] 'attend my concert,'[39] or 'award a pension to my assistant'[40]).

While lower-class people generally kept to the essentials and did not try to embellish their request ('I am in dire straits and need help'), other letter writers tried to justify their claim by giving their moral or patriotic credentials, such as 'I have been serving my community for over 38 years',[41] 'I have received several distinctions',[42] 'I have written a patriotic hymn',[43] 'My father fought in the Belgian Revolution'[44] or 'I have served in the army'.[45] After World War I, active service[46] or a similar experience (German imprisonment[47], execution of family members,[48] war invalidity[49]) was mentioned in a considerable number of lower-class letters, but interestingly none of these were actually written by lower-class people.

Middle-class writers often stressed their family responsibilities or their family situation. They referred to themselves as heads of family, spouses, mothers or fathers.[50] Four letter writers even called themselves 'orphan', although strictly speaking they were not. They were adults[51] with children,[52] or they had still one parent alive.[53] The title *orphan* was clearly seen as an argumentative advantage. Middle-class people who wrote on behalf of lower-class persons were usually more goal-oriented in obtaining help and, consequently, used a very modest tone of phrasing, although their demands were very clear (unlike lower-class demands).

Letters of request actually written by lower-class people were often completely idiosyncratic in their phrasing, neglecting all rules of polite letter writing and addressing the king as 'Mister' as if actually speaking to him.[54] Or, and this was the case for the large majority, they used the traditional templates but with a twist, as they did not master them completely. Lower-class letter writers turned to oral speech forms and phrases or formulas which they thought were appropriate when addressing a grand figure but which were, in reality, impolite. Hélène Van der Linden, the wife of a miner from Gilly, had some kind of model in mind when she wrote to Queen Elisabeth in 1927, but she gave a personal twist to it: 'Awaiting to receive from your kind heart a good answer in which I have deep faith and honour to be with the most profound respect Your Majesty's very humble and obeying servant.'[55] A man from Fleurus had evidently heard that one had to address one's letter 'to Your Majesty'. Hence, he wrote 'To your Majesty': 'I take the liberty of writing to you for something small, if you understand, To Your Majesty'. He ended: 'Please, To Your Majesty, accept the assurance of my respect.'[56] A Protestant worker from near Liège asked a grant in 1892 to build a temple. The man was polite, used grave-sounding phrases, but he addressed the King as 'Your Majesty Leopold II King of the Belgians and President of the Congo'. One can imagine Leopold's dismay given his allergy for all things republican.[57]

Middle-class letter writers (whether they wrote on behalf of someone else or on their own) seemed to make themselves smaller in the face of royal greatness. Repeatedly within the same letter they referred to themselves and their request as 'humble' and 'small',[58] as opposed to the king and the queen's 'enormous royal power'.[59] It is striking that letter writers who explicitly referred to themselves as 'simple' or 'humble workers' were either labour aristocracy (skilled workers who worked on their own or in the artisan sector) or plain middle class.[60] The stock phrase 'I am but a simple worker' seemed to reflect the middle-class view that the worries of the small are essentially unworthy of royal attention, but that the King and Queen in their infinite goodness deign to look down upon them. The fact that this imagery is missing in the letters of lower-class people can be attributed to their insufficient mastery of writing norms – but perhaps also to a popular notion that the great are morally obliged to help the small. This is corroborated by the fact that lower-class people were not completely overawed by their contact with the royal family. They seemed to be under the impression that it was almost their right to receive help. The most extreme case was a young lower-class man who wrote to the king in 1892 requesting the loan of one of the king's uniforms for a carnival procession. He did not bother to introduce himself, and three weeks after his first letter he sent a reminder.[61] Especially after World War I, it was almost inconceivable to the requesters that Queen Elisabeth, who was perceived as a mother to her people, would not intervene on their behalf.

Before World War I, lower-class letter writers hardly appealed to any of the traditional qualities of the good sovereign (justice, wisdom, power), while in the other letters two royal attributes were singled out for praise, viz., kindness ('bonté'[62]) and generosity ('charité'[63]). The idea of the king as 'father of the nation' was generally absent in requests before World War I. Perhaps the idea of Leopold II as a caring father seemed a bit too far-fetched, given the public indignation over his wild lifestyle. It is no coincidence that Leopold II was the favourite target of many caricaturists, while the press published almost no caricatures of his successor Albert, who was seen as a model family man.[64]

Postwar requests addressed to the queen show that the kind, generous and charitable image of Elisabeth had become so popular after her role in World War I that nearly all letter writers, from whichever social class, were influenced by it. Most people addressed her affectionately as 'My dear queen' or 'My dearest Majesty',[65] while Leopold II was always impersonally addressed as 'Your Majesty'. In other words, while before World War I referring to the kindness and generosity of the royal family was merely a middle-class commonplace that was mentioned because etiquette demanded it, after the boost in prestige that World War I gave Albert and Elisabeth, it became a heartfelt and dearly held conviction of all letter writers. At the least, this discourse had become so all-pervading that it could not be ignored.

In showing themselves very modest, in phrasing their letters *comme il faut* and in belittling themselves in the face of royal power, middle-class requesters explicitly appealed to the official transcript. The lower classes, however made little use of these strategies. They did not always seem to master the official transcript sufficiently to put it to conscious use, which puts a new perspective on Scott's insistence that the subordinate deliberately manipulate the dominant values to their own advantage. The official public transcript might at times have been too hard to read (and use) for the lower classes.

Banal vs. Sacral Monarchy

It has often been argued that the success of the modern monarchy hinges upon its ability to appear at the same time as extraordinary and commonplace: the

Fig. 2. *Photograph of Prince Albert posing amongst the miners in 1908.*

king is at once 'one of us' and 'beyond us'. How is this mixture of banalization and sacralization reflected in the letters of request? Although Leopold II's administration sought to popularize a caring and philanthropic image of the royal family, it did not want to present too common an image of the king: he still remained high above his subjects, and in all his greatness he bestowed his gifts upon them. It is no coincidence that Leopold II's portraits all show a stern man in uniform or official attire, while Albert, for instance, posed in the outfit of a miner amongst the colliers when he visited coal mines.

Leopold II was definitely not 'one of us'. It is revealing that in 1907 the King's personal secretary called the gifts to the requesters 'alms'.[66] This term reflects a kind of pre-democratic vision on the hierarchical relationship between monarchs and their subjects. In practice, however, writing a letter of request might have banalized the monarchy, as ordinary citizens invited a royal figure into their daily life.

Generally, we might say that most letter writers' relationship to Leopold II was rather impersonal, and – if at all explicitly mentioned – based on loyalty, devotion or submission to him, while their relationship to Elisabeth was one of love and affection. Under Leopold, middle-class writers had a hierarchical vision of their relationship with the royal family. They usually 'begged',[67] 'sub-mitted' themselves to the King's 'charity'[68] or asked 'forgiveness' for their 'bold-ness' to disturb the King[69] and a few even used the imagery of throwing them-selves at the King's feet.[70] It is equally striking that letter writers who praised Leopold II's compassion for his people were either labour aristocracy or middle class.[71] Hence we can say that the image of Leopold II as philanthropist did not resonate enough in society to be referred to in lower-class letters of request. This changed after World War I, as a more personal relationship between citizen and royal family seemed to replace the hierarchical pre-war one. People turned not to an institution or an unreachable representative of the high life but to a real-life person in whom they personally confided, who was almost a confessor. A housewife whose family was so derelict that they literally had to live in a pigsty wrote in 1926: 'I would thank the good Lord if I could explain my misery to you in person. Oh, good Majesty.'[72] A lower-class housewife from Brussels asked for relief in 1926 because 'Your Majesty [...] you are the only one I can turn to'.[73] Tellingly, the image of falling down at the King's feet was replaced in one letter by 'I reach out my hand to You, whom they rightly call Belgium's Providence'.[74] While to most letter writers Elisabeth was more human and approachable than Leopold II ever had been, there was in a sense also a resacralization of the Queen's role after World War I. Queen Elisabeth's war prestige gave her saintly properties. She was called 'our holy Queen',[75] mother and comforter of her people in a way that was reminiscent of the Virgin Mary.[76] In Elisabeth's image we see the mixture of the extraordinary and the commonplace that has become so vital in the justification of the monarchy in Europe since the eighteenth century: people turned to her as to a friend, they believed in a personal exclusive relationship with the Queen, but at the same time her almost superhuman moral qualities set her apart from ordinary mortals.

Concluding, Linda Colley's appraisal of the British monarchy also applies to the Belgian case. From this small sample of request letters, it appears that in Belgium the image of the king and queen as 'essentially the same as his [or her] subjects' gradually became popularized after Albert's marriage to Elisabeth in 1900. Citizens were prompted to see their royal family 'as unique and as typical, as ritually splendid and remorselessly prosaic, as glorious and *gemütlich* both'.[77]

Notes

Deneckere and Deploige, Introduction

1 Gabrielle M. Spiegel, *Practicing History. New Directions in Historical Writing after the Linguistic Turn* (New York and London: Routledge, 2005), p. 11.

2 Ibid., p. 22

3 For instance, Peter Gay, 'Do Your Thing', in *Historians and Social Values*, ed. by Joep Leerssen and Ann Rigney (Amsterdam: Amsterdam University Press, 2000), pp. 33-44.

4 Michel Foucault, *Surveiller et punir. Naissance de la prison* (Paris: Gallimard, 1975).

5 Michel de Certeau, *L'invention du quotidien. I: Arts de faire* (1980; Paris: Gallimard, 1990, 2nd rev. ed.), pp. 75-81; Idem, 'Le noir soleil du langage: Michel Foucault' and 'Microtechniques et discours panoptique: un quiproquo', in: Idem, *Histoire et psychanalyse entre science et fiction* (1987; Paris: Gallimard, 2002, 2nd rev. ed.), pp. 152-173 and 174-187.

6 Michael Billig, *Talking of the Royal Family* (London-New York: Routledge, 1998, 2nd rev. ed.).

7 See, e.g., Ernst Kantorowicz, *The King's Two Bodies. A Study in Mediaeval Political Theology* (1957; Princeton: Princeton University Press, 1997); *La royauté sacrée dans le monde chrétien (Colloque de Royaumont, mars 1989)*, L'histoire et ses représentations, 3, ed. by Alain Boureau and Claudio S. Ingerflom (Paris: EHESS, 1992); and the provocative Vernon Bogdanor, *The Monarchy and the Constitution* (Oxford: Oxford University Press, 1995).

8 See, e.g., Lynn Hunt, *The Family Romance of the French Revolution* (Berkeley and Los Angeles: University of California Press, 1992); and Susan Dunn, *The Deaths of Louis XIV. Regicide and the French Political Imagination* (Princeton: Princeton University Press, 1994).

9 See, e.g., Peter Burke. *The Fabrication of Louis XIV* (New Haven and London: Yale University Press, 1992); and Kevin Sharpe, *The Personal Rule of Charles I* (New Haven: Yale University Press, 1995).

10 See, e.g., Arlette Farge, *Dire et mal dire. L'opinion publique au XVIIIe siècle* (Paris: Seuil, 1992); Lisa Jane Graham, *If the King Only Knew. Seditious Speech in the Reign of Louis XV* (Charlottesville: University Press of Virginia, 2000); and John Barrell, *Imagining the King's Death. Figurative Treason, Fantasies of Regicide 1793-1796* (Oxford: Oxford University Press, 2000).

11 See Mikhail Bakhtin, *The Dialogic Imagination. Four Essays by M.M. Bakhtin*, ed. by Michael Holquist (Austin: University of Texas Press, 1982), pp. 270-274. See also Michael Billig, *Arguing and Thinking. A Rhetorical Approach to Social Psychology* (1987; Cambridge: Cambridge University Press and Editions de la Maison des Sciences de l'Homme, 1996, 2nd rev. ed), pp. 17-19.

Boureau, How Christian Was the Sacralization of Monarchy?

Translated from the French by Jill Corner and Donald Pistolesi.

1 See the anonymous version of *Merlin*, ed. by Irène Freire-Nunes and trans. with notes by Anne Berthelot, in *Le Livre du Graal*, ed. by Philippe Walter, Bibliothèque de la Pléiade (Paris: Gallimard, 2001), pp. 755-806.

2   Marc Bloch, *Les rois thaumaturges. Étude sur le caractère surnaturel attribue à la puissance royale, particulierement en France et en Angleterre.* Preface by Jacques Le Goff, Bibliothèque des histoires (Strasbourg, 1924; Paris: Gallimard, 1983); trans. by J. E. Anderson as *The Royal Touch: Sacred Monarchy and Scrofula in England and France* (London: Routledge and Kegan Paul, 1973).

3   James George Frazer, *The Golden Bough: A Study in Magic and Religion: A New Abridgement from the Second and Third Editions*, ed. by Robert Fraser (1900, 1906-1915; Oxford: Oxford University Press, 1994).

4   Ralph Giesey, *The Royal Funeral Ceremony in Renaissance France* (Geneva: Droz, 1960).

5   William F. Church, *Constitutional Thought in Sixteenth-Century France. A Study in the Evolution of Ideas* (Cambridge, Mass.: Harvard University Press, 1941).

6   Sarah Hanley, *The Lit de Justice of the Kings of France: Constitutional Ideology in Legend, Ritual, and Discourse* (Princeton: Princeton University Press, 1983).

7   See Giovanni Levi, 'I pericoli del geertzismo', *Quaderni storici*, 58 (1985): 269-277; and Pierre Bourdieu, *Méditations pascaliennes. Eléments pour une philosophie négative* (Paris: Seuil, 1997), pp. 66-67.

8   Ernst H. Kantorowicz, *The King's Two Bodies: A Study in Mediaeval Political Theology* (1957; Princeton: Princeton University Press, 1997).

9   See Jacques Le Goff, *Saint Louis* (Paris: Gallimard, 1992).

10 See Michel Senellart, *Les Arts de gouverner. Du* regimen *médiéval au concept de gouvernement* (Paris: Seuil, 1995), pp. 103-104.

11 Gérard d'Abbeville, *Quolibet* VIII, 1, ed. by Adriaan Pattin, in *L'Anthropologie de Gérard d'Abbeville. Étude préliminaire et édition critique de plusieurs questions quodlibétiques concernant le sujet, avec l'édition complète du* De cogitationibus, Ancient and Medieval Philosophy, I-14 (Leuven: Leuven University Press, 1993), p. 62: 'Secundum hoc ergo Salomon in sompno non meruit donum sapientie, licet ibi obtinuerit ipsum donum, quia non obtinuit illius donum per meritum contemplationis, sed per gratiam revelationis.'

12 See André Vauchez, '*Beata stirps*: sainteté et lignage en Occident aux XIIIᵉ et XIVᵉ siècles', in *Saints, prophètes et visionnaires. Le pouvoir surnaturel au Moyen Âge* (Paris: Albin Michel, 1999), pp. 67-78.

13 On this topic, see Alain Boureau, *Le simple corps du roi. L'impossible sacralité des souverains français* (Paris: Éditions de Paris, 1988).

14 Gilbert Dagron, *Empereur et prêtre: étude sur le césaropapisme byzantin*, Bibliothèque des histoires (Paris: Gallimard, 1996); trans. by Jean Birrell as *Emperor and Priest: The Imperial Office in Byzantium*, Past & Present Publications (Cambridge: Cambridge University Press, 2003).

15 Angelus Clarenus, *Expositio super regulam Fratrum Minorum*, ed. by Giovanni Boccali, Pubblicazioni della Biblioteca Francescana Chiesa Nuova-Assisi, 7 (Assisi: Edizioni Porziuncola, 1995), p. 438: 'sicut Dominus dicit de David, qui comedit panes propositionis quos manducare non licebat nisi solis sacerdotibus.' Angelus Clarenus refers here to Matthew 12.4.

16 Ibid., p. 668: 'Tu es sacerdos in eternum secundum ordinem Melchisedech.'

17 Pierre Toubert, 'La doctrine gélasienne des deux pouvoirs. Propositions en vue d'une révision', in *Studi in onore di Giosuè Musca* (Bari: Dedalo, 2000), pp. 519-540, reprinted in Idem, *L'Europe dans sa première croissance* (Paris: Fayard, 2004), pp. 385-417.

18 See the doctoral dissertation of Elsa Marmursztejn, 'Un troisième pouvoir? Pouvoir intellectuel et construction des normes à l'université de Paris dans la seconde moitié du XIIIe siècle, d'après les sources quodlibétiques (Thomas d'Aquin, Gérard d'Abbeville, Henri de Gand, Godefroid de Fontaines)' (Diss. Paris: Éditions de l'École des Hautes Études en Sciences Sociales, 1999).

19 See Alain Boureau, '*Vel sedens vel transiens*: la création d'un espace pontifical aux XIᵉ et XIIᵉ siècles', in *Luoghi sacri e spazi della santità*, ed. by Sofia Boesch Gajano and Lucetta Scaraffia (Turin: Rosenberg e Sellier, 1990), pp. 367-379.

20 See Alain Boureau, 'Le principe hiérarchique, obstacle à la sacralité royale en Occident?', in *La Royauté sacrée dans le monde chrétien*, ed. by Alain Boureau and Claudio S. Ingerflom (Paris: Éditions de l'École des Hautes Études en Sciences Sociales, 1992), pp. 29-37.

21 The work of Michael E. Moore shows very well how, from Isidore of Seville up to the 'Peace of God' movement (tenth century), the Frankish Church developed a 'social christology' which broke with what has been coined, since Henri-Xavier Arquillière, as 'political Augustinism': the Christian society, through baptism and conversion, identifies itself with the body of Christ and thus should be directed by kings and priests. See Michael Edward Moore, 'La monarchie carolingienne et les anciens modèles irlandais', *Annales - Histoire, Sciences Sociales*, 51 (1996): 307-324; Idem, 'Carolingian Bishops and Christian Antiquity: Distance from the Past, Canon-Formation, and Imperial Power', in *Learned Antiquity. Scholarship and Society in the Near East, The Greco-Roman World, and the Early Medieval West*, ed. by Alaisdair A. MacDonald, Michael W. Twomey, and Gerrit J. Reinink, Groningen Studies in Cultural Change, 5 (Leuven: Peeters, 2003), pp. 175-184; see also Henri-Xavier Arquilliere, *L'Augustinisme politique. Essai sur la formation des théories politiques au Moyen Âge* (Paris: Vrin, 1934).

22 See Alexandre Faivre, *Ordonner la charité. Pouvoir d'innover et retour à l'ordre chrétien dans l'Eglise ancienne* (Paris: Cerf, 1992).

23 Jean Coste, *Boniface VIII en procès. Articles d'accusation et dépositions de témoins (1303-1311). Édition critique, introduction et notes* (Rome: L'Erma di Bretschneider, 1995).

24 Since the beginning of the Carolingian period, Pope Zachary (741-752) had given his support to Pippin the Younger (d. 768), confirming that he who really had the power and not its shadow should be king.

25 See also the chapter of Jeroen Deploige in this volume.

26 Manegold of Lautenbach, *Liber ad Gebehardum*, ch. 30, ed. by Kuno Francke, Monumenta Germaniae Historica, Libelli de lite, 1 (Hannover: Hahn, 1891), p. 365: 'Quod rex non sit nomen nature, sed vocabulum officii.'

27 Cited by Coste, *Boniface VIII en procès*, p. 76.

28 Despite its importance, I treat this last age rather briefly here. See Alain Boureau, *Satan hérétique. La naissance de la démonologie dans l'Occident médiéval (1280-1330)* (Paris: Odile Jacob, 2004).

29 On the notion of *majestas*, see the important work of Yan Thomas, 'L'institution de la Majesté', *Revue de synthèse*, 112 (1991): 331-386; and Jacques Chiffoleau, 'Sur le crime de majesté médiéval', in *Genèse de l'État moderne en Méditerranée*, Collection de l'École française de Rome, 168 (Rome: École française de Rome, 1993), pp. 183-213.

30 See Walter Ullmann, *The Growth of Papal Government in the Middle Ages* (London: Methuen, 1955).

31 Michael Wilks, *The Problem of Sovereignty in the Later Middle Ages* (Cambridge: Cambridge University Press, 1963).

32 Jacques Krynen, *L'Empire du roi. Idées et croyances politiques en France. XIIIème-XVème siècle* (Paris: Gallimard, 1993).

33 Lawrence Moonan, *Divine Power. The Medieval Power Distinction up to its Adoption by Albert, Bonaventure and Aquinas* (Oxford: Oxford University Press, 1994); William J. Courtenay, *Capacity and Volition. A History of the Distinction of Absolute and Ordained Power* (Bergamo: Pierluigi Lubrina Editore, 1990). See also Eugenio Randi, *Il sovrano e l'orologiaio: Due immagini di Dio nel dibattito sulla 'potentia absoluta' fra XIII e XIV secolo* (Florence: Nuova Italia, 1987); and the anthology of translated texts collected under the direction of Olivier Boulnois, *La Puissance et son ombre. De Pierre Lombard à Luther* (Paris: Aubier, 1994).

34 See Alain Boureau, 'L'immaculée conception de la souveraineté. John Baconthorpe et la théologie politique (1325-1345) (Postille sur *Entre l'Église et l'État*, pp. 189-201)', in *Saint-Denis et la royauté. Études offertes à Bernard Guenée*, ed. by Françoise Autrand, Claude Gauvard, and Jean-Marie Moeglin (Paris: Publications de la Sorbonne, 1999), pp. 733-749.

35 See Carl Schmitt, *Political Theology. Four Chapters on the Concept of Sovereignty*, trans. by George Schwab (1922; Cambridge, Mass.: MIT Press, 1985), pp. 46-47.

Deploige, Political Assassination and Sanctification

I am very grateful to Hideki Aotani (Kobe University) for his stimulating comments and to Albert Demyttenaere (University of Amsterdam) for enriching discussions on the occasion of my lecture on 6 April 2004 in Amsterdam on the topic of this chapter.

1   Galbertus Brugensis, *De multro, traditione et occisione gloriosi Karoli comitis Flandriarum*, ch. 15, ed. by Jeff Rider, Corpus Christianorum. Continuatio Mediaevalis, 131 (Turnhout: Brepols, 1994), p. 37: 'Primae horae quoque obsequium finitum erat et de tertia hora responsum finitum, quando *Pater noster* oratum est, quando comes more suo officiose et aperte legendo orabat. Tunc tandem post tot consilia et juramenta et securitates inter se factas, primum in corde homicidae et traditores pessimi comitem devote orantem et eleemosynas dantem, divinae majestati suppliciter prostratum, gladiis confossum et saepius transverberatum, mortuum dimisere. At sui sanguinis rivulis a peccatis abluto et in operibus bonis vitae cursu terminato, martyrum palma comitem Deus donavit. In supremo ergo articulo vitae et mortis accessu vultum dignissime atque regales ad coelum manus inter tot verbera et ictus gladiatorum, quantum potuit, converterat, sic que suum Domino universorum spiritum tradidit et se ipsum Deo obtulit sacrificium matutinum.' English translation: Galbert of Bruges, *The Murder of Charles the Good, Count of Flanders*, trans. by James Bruce Ross (1959; New York: Harper Torchbooks, 1967), p. 119.

2   On this juridical context, see Raoul C. Van Caenegem, 'Galbert van Brugge en het recht', *Mededelingen van de Koninklijke Academie voor Wetenschappen, Letteren en Schone Kunsten van België. Klasse der Letteren*, 40/1 (1978): 3-35 (here pp. 15-16).

3   See François L. Ganshof, 'Le roi de France en Flandre en 1127 et 1128', *Revue historique de droit français et étranger*, 27 (1949): 204-228.

4   Sandy Burton Hicks, 'The Impact of William Clito upon the Continental Policies of Henry I of England', *Viator. Medieval and Renaissance Studies*, 10 (1979): 1-21.

5   Henri Pirenne, *Histoire du meurtre de Charles le Bon comte de Flandre (1127-1128) par Galbert de Bruges suivie de poésies latines contemporaines. Publiées d'après les Manuscrits avec une introduction et des notes*, Collection de textes pour servir à l'étude et à l'enseignement de l'histoire (Paris: Alphonse Picard, 1891).

6   E.g., Heinrich Sproemberg, 'Das Erwachen des Staatsgefühls in den Niederlanden. Galbert von Brügge', in *L'organisation corporative du Moyen Âge à la fin de l'Ancien Régime*, Études présentées à la Commission Internationale pour l'histoire des assemblées d'états, 3 (Leuven: Bibliothèque de l'Université, 1939), pp. 31-88; Ganshof, 'Le roi de France'.

7   E.g., Van Caenegem, 'Galbert van Brugge en het recht'; Dirk Heirbaut, 'Galbert van Brugge: een bron voor de Vlaamse feodaliteit in de XIIde eeuw', *Tijdschrift voor rechtsgeschiedenis*, 60 (1992): 49-62; and Alan V. Murray, 'The Judicial Inquest into the Death of Count Charles the Good of Flanders (1127): Location and Chronology', *The Legal History Review*, 68 (2000): 47-61.

8   E.g., Jan Dhondt, 'Les "solidarités" médiévales. Une société en transition: la Flandre en 1127-1128', *Annales ESC*, 12 (1957): 529-560.

9   E.g., Jan Dhondt, 'Une mentalité du douzième siècle. Galbert de Bruges', *Revue du Nord*, 39 (1957): 101-109; Albert Demyttenaere, 'Mentaliteit in de twaalfde eeuw en de benauwenis van Galbert van Brugge', in *Middeleeuwse cultuur. Verscheidenheid, spanning en verandering*, Amsterdamse historische reeks. Grote serie, 18, ed. by Marco Mostert, Rudi Künzel, and Albert Demyttenaere (Hilversum: Verloren, 1994), pp. 77-129; and Jeroen Deploige, 'Bertulf of Galbert? Kanttekeningen bij Rudi Künzels middeleeuwse droomduiding', *Tijdschrift voor geschiedenis*, 116 (2003): 59-72.

10 E.g., Jacques Le Goff, 'Le rituel symbolique de la vassalité', in *Pour un autre Moyen Âge. Temps, travail et culture en Occident: 18 essais* (Paris: Gallimard, 1977), pp. 349-420.

11 Heinrich Sproemberg, 'Galbert von Brügge - Die Geschichtsschreibung des flandrischen Bürgertums', in *Mittelalter und demokratische Geschichtsschreibung. Ausgewählte Abhandlungen*, Forschungen zur Mittelalterlichen Geschichte, 18, ed. by Manfred Unger, Lily Sproemberg, and Wolfgang Eggert (Berlin: Akademie-Verlag, 1971), pp. 221-374; Walter Mohr, 'Geschichtstheologische Aspekte im Werk Galberts von Brügge', in *Pascua mediaevalia: Studies voor Prof. Dr. Jozef-Maria De Smet*, Medievalia Lovaniensia, 1/10, ed. by Robrecht Lievens, Eric Van Mingroot, and Werner Verbeke (Leuven: University Press Leuven, 1983), pp. 246-262; and Jeff Rider, *God's Scribe. The Historiographical Art of Galbert of Bruges* (Washington D.C.: The Catholic University of America Press, 2001).

12 Mikhail Bakhtin, 'The Problem of Speech Genres', in *M. M. Bakhtin. Speech Genres and Other Late Essays*, ed. by Caryl Emerson and Michael Holquist (Austin: University of Texas Press, 1986), pp. 60-102.

13 Ibid. p. 65.

14 This flow chart will also serve in my forthcoming study *Strategies and Tactics in Medieval Hagiography. Discourse, Church, and Society in the Southern Low Countries, c. 920-c. 1320* (Turnhout: Brepols).

15 See Pierre Bourdieu, 'Genèse et structure du champ religieux', *Revue française de sociologie*, 12 (1971): 295-334; Idem, *Les règles de l'art. Genèse et structure du champs littéraire* (1992; Paris: Seuil, 1998, 2nd rev. ed.).

16 Hans-Robert Jauss, 'Littérature médiévale et théorie des genres', *Poétique. Revue de théorie et d'analyse littéraires*, 1 (1970): 79-101 (here pp. 85-86). See also Idem, *Pour une esthétique de la réception* (Paris: Gallimard, 1978).

17 Michel de Certeau, *L'invention du quotidien. 1. Arts de faire* (1980; Paris: Gallimard, 1990, 2nd rev. ed.), pp. 57-62.

18 Bakhtin, 'The Problem of Speech Genres', pp. 61-62.

19 The concept of a 'hagiographical discourse' was coined by Michel de Certeau, *L'écriture de l'histoire* (Paris: Gallimard, 1975), pp. 274-288. See also Marc Van Uytfanghe, 'L'hagiographie: un "genre" chrétien ou antique tardif?', *Analecta bollandiana*, 111 (1993): 135-188; Deploige, *Strategies and Tactics in Medieval Hagiography*.

20 See, e.g., Michel Foucault, *L'archéologie du savoir* (Paris: Gallimard, 1969); Idem, *L'ordre du discours* (Paris: Gallimard, 1971); and Idem, *Histoire de la sexualité. 1: La volonté de savoir* (Paris: Gallimard, 1976).

21 For an excellent introduction, see Norman Fairclough, *Critical Discourse Analysis: The Critical Study of Language* (London and New York: Longman, 1995).

22 Raoul C. Van Caenegem, 'Historische inleiding: de Vlaamse crisis van 1127-1128', in *De moord op Karel de Goede door Galbert van Brugge*, ed. by Idem and Albert Demyttenaere (Leuven: Davidsfonds, 1999), p. 19.

23 E.g., Suger de St.-Denis, *Vie de Louis VI le Gros*, ed. and trans. by Henri Waquet, Les classiques de l'histoire de France au Moyen Âge, 11 (Paris: H. Champion, 1929); Herimannus Tornacensis, *Liber de restauratione monasterii Sancti Martini Tornacensis*, ed. by Georg Waitz, Monumenta Germaniae Historica. Scriptores, 14 (Hannover: Hahn, 1883), pp. 274-314; and Anselmus Gemblacensis, *Chronicon Sigeberti continuatum*, ed. by Ludwig Bethmann, Monumenta Germaniae Historica. Scriptores, 6 (Hannover: Hahn, 1844), pp. 375-385.

24 Jozef-Maria De Smet, 'Bij de Latijnsche gedichten over den moord op den glz. Karel den Goede, Graaf van Vlaanderen', in *Miscellanea historica in honorem Alberti de Meyer*, Recueil de travaux d'histoire et de philologie, 3/22 (Leuven: Bibliothèque de l'Université, 1946), pp. 418-443.

25 *Epitaphia*, ed. by Jeff Rider, Corpus Christianorum. Continuatio Mediaevalis, 217 (Turnhout: Brepols, 2006), p. 197: 'Hic pupillorum pater, adiutor viduarum, / salvator patriae, zelator et ecclesiarum. / Pax et vita suis, formido et mors inimicis. / Rebus pace suis undique compositis / [...].'

26 Walterus Tervanensis, *Vita Karoli Comitis Flandriae*, ed. by Rider, Corpus Christianorum. Continuatio Mediaevalis, 217, pp. 3-79. See *The Narrative Sources from the Medieval Low Countries* (Ghent, Leuven, and Groningen: Ovid Database, 1996-2006 - http://www.narrative-sources.be), record G010.

27 Nicolaas Huyghebaert, 'Gautier de Thérouanne, archidiacre de Morinie, hagiographe et cano-niste au XIIe s.', in *Dictionnaire d'histoire et de géographie ecclésiastiques*, 20 (Paris: Letouzay et Ané, 1984), cols. 115-116.

28 Galbertus Brugensis, *De multro*, ed. by Rider. See *The Narrative Sources*, record G001. On Galbert's possible role as a notary in the count's administration, see the discussion between Georges Declercq, 'Galbert van Brugge en de verraderlijke moord op Karel de Goede: beschouwingen over tekst en auteur naar aanleiding van een nieuwe uitgave', *Handelingen der Maatschappij voor geschiedenis en oudheidkunde te Gent*, 49 (1995): 71-117 (here pp. 107-108); and Rider, *God's Scribe*, p. 21.

29 Rider, *God's Scribe*, p. 223.

30 I will rely here upon the research results that will be published in Deploige, *Strategies and Tactics in Medieval Hagiography*. See also Idem, 'Hagiografische strategieën en tactieken tegen de ach-tergrond van kerkelijke en maatschappelijke vernieuwingstendensen. De Zuidelijke Nederlanden, ca. 920-ca 1320' (unpublished doctoral thesis, Ghent University, 2002), vol. 2.

31 *Vita Macarii Antiocheni* and *Vita secunda, miracula et elevatio Macarii Antiocheni*, ed. by Godefridus Henschenius, Acta sanctorum, Apr. I (Antwerp, 1675), pp. 875-877 and 878-892; and *Vita Theoderici abbatis Andaginensis seu sancti Huberti in Arduenna silva*, ed. by Wilhelm Wattenbach, Monumenta Germaniae Historica, Scriptores, 12 (Hannover: Hahn, 1856), pp. 37-57.

32 Drogo Bergensis, *Vita Godeliph*, ed. by Nicolaas N. Huyghebaert, in *Drogo van Sint-Winoksbergen. Vita Godeliph* (Tielt and Bussum: Lannoo, 1982), pp. 34-70. See also Georges Duby, *Le chevalier, la femme et le prêtre. Le mariage dans la France féodale* (Paris: Gallimard, 1981); and Renée I.A. Nip, 'The Canonization of Godelieve of Gistel', *Hagiographica*, 2 (1995): 145-155.

33 Gualbertus Marchianensis, *Translatio sancti Ionati in villa Saliacensi*, partially ed. by Ernst Sackur, *Neues Archiv der Gesellschaft für ältere deutsche Geschichtkunde*, 15 (1890), pp. 448-452.

34 See Steven Vanderputten, 'A Miracle of Jonatus in 1127-1128. The *Translatio Sancti Jonati* (BHL 4449) as Political Enterprise and Failed Hagiographical Project', *Analecta bollandiana* (forth-coming; with a new and complete critical edition of the *Translatio*).

35 [Gualbertus Marchianensis], *Huc ades, Calliope*, ed. by Rider, Corpus Christianorum. Continuatio Mediaevalis, 217, pp. 177-184.

36 David W. Rollason, 'The Cult of Murdered Kings and Princes in Anglo-Saxon England', *Anglo-Saxon England* 11 (1983): 11-22.

37 Drogo Bergensis, *Vita sancti Oswaldi*, ed. by Joannes Pinius, Acta sanctorum, Aug. II (Antwerp, 1735), pp. 94-102. See also Nicolaas Huyghebaert, 'Les deux translations du roi S. Oswald à Bergues-Saint-Winnoc', *Revue Bénédictine*, 86 (1976): 83-93; and Idem, 'De twee sermoenen van Drogo van Sint-Winoksbergen over de koning-martelaar St Oswald', *Ons geestelijk erf*, 56 (1982): 97-108.

38 See Robert Folz, *Les saints rois du Moyen Âge en Occident (du VIe au XIIIe siècles)*, Subsidia hagio-graphica, 68 (Brussels: Société de Bollandistes, 1985); and Patrick Corbet, *Les Saints ottoniens. Sainteté dynastique, sainteté royale et sainteté féminine autour de l'an Mil*, Beihefte der Francia, 15 (Sigmaringen: Thorbecke, 1986).

39 See Gábor Klaniczay, 'From Sacral Kingship to Self-Representation: Hungarian and European Royal Saints', in *The Uses of Supernatural Power. The Transformation of Popular Religion in Medieval and Early-Modern Europe*, ed. by Idem (Cambridge: Cambridge University Press 1990), pp. 79-94; and Idem, *Holy Rulers and Blessed Princesses. Dynastic Cults in Medieval Central Europe* (Cambridge: Cambridge University Press, 2002). Hideki Aotani brought to my attention the importance of Klaniczay's work for this topic. See also Hideki Aotani, ['The Martyrdom of Charles the Good, Count of Flanders: Sovereign and the Idea of Rule in Early Twelfth Century'], *The Shrin or the Journal of History*, 82 (1999): 36-67 (published in Japanese, with an English summary).

40 Klaniczay, *Holy Rulers*, p. 152; and Folz, *Les saints rois*, p. 39.

41 *Passio sancti Canuti regis et martyris*, ed. by Marius C. Gertz, in *Vitae sanctorum Danorum* (Copenhagen, 1908-1912), pp. 67-71. For a survey of the surviving manuscripts, see *BHLms, Bibliotheca Hagiographica Latina manuscripta. Index électronique de la Bibliotheca Hagiographica Latina et des Catalogues de manuscrits hagiographiques latins*, version 1, ed. by Centre de recherches 'Hagiographies' des F.U.N.D.P. à Namur and Socii Bollandiani (Louvain-la-Neuve, 1999 - http://bhlms.fltr.ucl.ac.be/). On the contacts between Flanders and Denmark, see also Michael H. Gelting, 'Un prélat flamand aud Danemark au XIIe siècle. Hélie, évêque de Ribe (1142-1162)', *Handelingen van het Genootschap voor geschiedenis gesticht onder de benaming "Société d'Emulation" te Brugge*, 122 (1985): 159-179.

42 See André Vauchez, 'Lay People's Sanctity in Western Europe: Evolution of a Pattern (Twelfth and Thirteenth Centuries)', in *Images of Sainthood in Medieval Europe*, ed. by Renate Blumenfeld-Kosinski and Timea Szell (Ithaca and London: Cornell University Press, 1991), pp. 21-32.

43 *Vita Alberti Leodiensis*, ed. by Iohannes Heller, Monumenta Germaniae Historica, Scriptores, 25 (Hannover: Hahn, 1880), pp. 137-168. See also Raymonde Foreville, 'Mort et survie de saint Thomas Becket', in *Thomas Becket dans la tradition historique et hagiographique. Essays by Raymonde Foreville*, Collected Studies, 130 (London: Variorum, 1981), pp. 21-38.

44 *Non lingua fari*, ed. by Rider, Corpus Christianorum. Continuatio Mediaevalis, 217, pp. 189-191.

45 David Van Meter, 'Eschatology and the Sanctification of the Prince in Twelfth-Century Flanders: The Case of Walter of Thérouanne's *Vita Karoli comitis Flandriae*', *Sacris erudiri*, 35 (1995): 115-131 (here p. 120).

46 Galbertus Brugensis, *De multro*, ch. 69, p. 122: 'Quoniam Deus iniquitates patrum solet vindictae severitate corrigere in tertiam et quartam generationem.' English translation by Ross, *The Murder*, p. 237.

47 See Dhondt, 'Une mentalité du douzième siècle', pp. 107-108; Demyttenaere, 'Mentaliteit in de twaalfde eeuw', pp. 113-116; and Mohr, 'Geschichtstheologische Aspekte'.

48 Galbertus Brugensis, *De multro*, ch. 68-71, pp. 120-126.

49 Walterus Tervanensis, *Vita Karoli*, ch. 28, p. 52: 'Sed huius, rogo, ut ita dicam, martyrii quae fuit causa nisi iustitia ?'

50 On the theocratic conception of the medieval *patria*, which was still predominant in the eleventh century, see Thomas Eichenberger, *Patria. Studien zur Bedeutung des Wortes im Mittelalter (6.-12. Jahrhundert)*, Nationes, 9 (Sigmaringen: Thorbecke, 1991).

51 See Geoffrey Koziol, *Begging Pardon and Favor. Ritual and Political Order in Early Medieval France* (Ithaca and London: Cornell University Press, 1992), pp. 141-143. See also Henri Platelle, 'La violence et ses remèdes en Flandre au XIe siècle', *Sacris erudiri*, 20 (1971): 101-173; and Geoffrey Koziol, 'Monks, Feuds, and the Making of Peace in Eleventh-Century Flanders', in *The Peace of God. Social Violence and Religious Response in France around the Year 1000*, ed. by Thomas Head and Richard Landes (Ithaca and London: Cornell University Press, 1992), pp. 239-258.

52 See Hartmut Hoffmann, *Gottesfriede und Treuga Dei* (Stuttgart: Hiersemann, 1964), pp. 143-158.

53 Especially in the hagiographical works attributed to Werricus Gandensis, *Vita Bertulfi Rentiacensis*, ed. by Johannes Bollandus, Acta sanctorum, Feb. I (Antwerp, 1658), pp. 677-687; and *Vita secunda Winnoci Bergensis*, ed. by Carolus De Smedt, Acta sanctorum, Nov. III (Brussels, 1910), pp. 267-274. See also Bernd Schneidmüller, *Nomen patriae. Die Entstehung Frankreichs in der politisch-geographischen Terminologie (10.-13. Jahrhundert)*, Nationes, 7 (Sigmaringen: Thorbecke, 1987), pp. 96-98.

54 Petrus Pictor, *De laude Flandrie*, ed. by Lieven Van Acker, Corpus Christianorum. Continuatio Mediaevalis, 25 (Turnhout: Brepols, 1972), pp. 56-58; and *Genealogia regum Francorum comitumque Flandriae*, ed. by Ludwig Bethmann, Monumenta Germaniae Historica. Scriptores, 9 (Hannover: Hahn, 1851), pp. 308-312.

55 E.g., Galbertus Brugensis, *De multro*, ch. 5, p. 15, l. 11 and ch. 47, p. 98, l. 28

56 Ibid., ch. 63, p. 116: '[...] quam egregie pro patre et patria moriendum foret'. English translation by Ross, *The Murder*, p. 224. See also Ernst H. Kantorowicz, '*Pro Patria Mori* in Medieval Political Thought', *American Historical Review*, 56 (1951): 472-492. On Kantorowicz's study, see Eichenberger, *Patria*, pp. 12-15.

57 Walterus Tervanensis, *Vita Karoli*, ch. 36, p. 60, l. 5; and Galbertus Brugensis, *De multro*, prol., p. 5, l. 49 and ch. 88, p. 138, l. 34.

58 Ibid., ch. 70, p. 122: 'Deus [...] pro iustitia patriae occisum transduxit in requiem sanctorum.' English translation by Ross, *The Murder*, p. 237.

59 Galbertus Brugensis, *De multro*, ch. 4-5, pp. 11-15

60 Ibid., prol., p. 3.

61 Ibid., ch. 47, p. 97: 'quem justius decuerat fuisse regem quam pessimorum traditorum comitem'. English translation by Ross, *The Murder*, p. 187.

62 [Norman Anonymous], *De consecratione pontificum et regum*, ed. by Heinz Boehmer, Monumenta Germaniae Historica. Libelli de Lite, 3 (Hannover: Hahn, 1897), pp. 662-679. See also Van Meter, 'Eschatology and the Sanctification', p. 116 and *passim*. On the Norman Anonymous, see also Ernst H. Kantorowicz, *The King's Two Bodies. A Study in Mediaeval Political Theology* (1957; Princeton: Princeton University Press, 1997), pp. 42-61.

63 Kantorowicz, *The King's Two Bodies*, p. 89

64 Walterus Tervanensis, *Vita Karoli*, ch. 27, pp. 51-52.

65 Kantorowicz, *The King's Two Bodies*, pp. 93 ff.

66 Galbertus Brugensis, *De multro*, ch. 6, p. 17, l. 27.

67 Ibid., ch. 47, p. 98: 'Idcirco considerate et caute agere vos volo super electionem meae personae, et praemonitos vos rogo ne me alienum a regno faciatis, qui jure et ex debito propinquitatis, si mihi remandaveritis, comes futurus, justus, pacificus, tractabilis et utilitatis communis atque salutis provisor accurro.' English translation by Ross, *The Murder*, p. 188. It should be noted, however, that the notion *ad communem utilitatem* is also mentioned once by Walter of Thérouanne, but not in a same ideologically charged context: Walterus Tervanensis, *Vita Karoli*, ch. 18, p. 44, l. 10.

68 Galbertus Brugensis, *De multro*, ch. 51, p. 100: 'qui utilitati communiter patriae velit et possit prodesse'. English translation by Ross, *The Murder*, p. 193.

69 Galbertus Brugensis, *De multro*, ch. 55, pp. 103-105.

70 Kantorowicz, *The King's Two Bodies*, p. 384. See also the chapter of Alain Boureau in the present volume.

71 Raoul C. Van Caenegem, 'Galbert of Bruges on Serfdom, Prosecution of Crime, and Constitutionalism (1127-1128)', in *Law, Custom, and the Social Fabric in Medieval Europe*, Studies in Medieval Culture 28, ed. by Bernard S. Bachrach and David Nicholas (Kalamazoo: Medieval Institute Publications, 1990), pp. 89-112 (here p. 103).

72 Ludo J. R. Milis, '*Justus ut palma*. Symbolism as a Political and Ideological Weapon on the Seals of Thierry and Philip of Alsace, Counts of Flanders (1128-1191)', in *Ludo Milis. Religion, Culture, and Mentalities in the Medieval Low Countries. Selected Essays*, ed. by Jeroen Deploige, et al. (Turnhout: Brepols, 2005), pp. 249-267 (here pp. 254-250).

73 Gregorius Turonensis, *Decem libri historiarum*, ed. by Bruno Krusch and Wilhelm Levison, Monumenta Germaniae Historica, Scriptores rerum Merovingicarum, 1/1 (Hannover: Hahn, 1951, 2nd rev. ed.). See, e.g., Barbara Rosenwein, 'Inaccessible Cloisters: Gregory of Tours and Episcopal Exemption', in *The World of Gregory of Tours*, Cultures, Beliefs and Traditions: Medieval and Early Modern People 8, ed. by Kathleen Mitchell and Ian Wood (Leiden: Brill, 2002), pp. 181-197; and Rob Meens, 'De kracht van het altaar. Het recht van asiel in kerken bij Gregorius van Tours', *Utrechtse historische cahiers*, 22 (2001): 97-105.

74 I am making an allusion here to the Bakhtinian-inspired essay of Peter Stalybrass and Allon White, *The Politics & Poetics of Transgression* (London: Methuen, 1986). See also Van Meter, 'Eschatology and the Sanctification', p. 131, who argues against the very ritualistic approach of political assassination advocated by Robert Jacob, 'Le meurtre du seigneur dans la société féodale. La mémoire, le rite, la fonction', *Annales ESC*, 45 (1990): 247-263. On the tension between text and reality in the study of ritual, see also the highly critical essay of Philippe Buc, *The Dangers of Ritual. Between Early Medieval Texts and Social Scientific Theory* (Princeton: Princeton University Press, 2001).

75 Guibert de Nogent, *Autobiographie*, ed. and trans. by Edmond R. Labande, Les classiques de l'histoire de France au Moyen Âge, 34 (Paris: H. Champion, 1981).

76 See, e.g., the fine analysis of Trudy Lemmers, *Guibert van Nogents Monodiae. Een twaalfde-eeuwse visie op kerkelijk leiderschap* (Hilversum: Verloren, 1998).

77 The concept of literary history as a history of provocation was developed in a famous lecture by Hans-Robert Jauss, *Literaturgeschichte als Provokation der Literaturwissenschaft* (Konstanz: Universitätsverlag, 1969).

78 This vision was maintained since the publication of Pirenne, *Histoire du meurtre*. See, e.g., also Stephanie Coué, 'Der Mord an Karl dem Guten (1127) und die Werke Galberts von Brügge und Walters von Thérouanne', in *Pragmatische Schriftlichkeit im Mittelalter. Erscheinungsformen und Entwicklungsstufen*, ed. by Hagen Keller, Klaus Grubmüller, and Nikolaus Staubach (Munich: Fink, 1992), pp. 108-129.

79 Galbertus Brugensis, *De multro*, ch. 35, p. 81: 'Et notandum, quod in tanto tumultu rerum et tot domorum incendiis – quae per ignitas sagittas nocte tectis suburbiorum injecerant ab intus, et latrunculi exterius ut sibi aliquid furarentur – et inter tot noctium pericula et tot dierum certamina, cum locum scribendi ego Galbertus non haberem, summam rerum in tabulis notavi donec aliquando, noctis vel diei expectata pace, ordinarem secundum rerum eventum descriptionem praesentem. Et sic secundum quod videtis et legitis in arto positus fidelibus transcripsi.' English translation: Rider, *God's Scribe*, pp. 29-30.

80 Ibid., pp. 1-10.

81 See also the landmark essay of Gabrielle M. Spiegel, 'History, Historicism and the Social Logic of the Text', *Speculum*, 65 (1990): 59-86 [reprinted in *The Past as Text. The Theory and Practice of Medieval Historiography* (Baltimore and London: Johns Hopkins University Press, 1997), pp. 3-28].

82 See, e.g., Hayden White, 'The Value of Narrativity in the Representation of Reality', in *The Content of the Form: Narrative, Discourse, and Historical Representation*, ed. by Idem (Baltimore and London: Johns Hopkins University Press, 1987), pp. 1-25 (here pp. 6-20).

83 Mikhail Bakhtin, *The Dialogic Imagination. Four Essays by M. M. Bakhtin*, ed. by Michael Holquist (Austin: University of Texas Press, 1982). See also John Shotter, 'Bakhtin and Billig: Monological Versus Dialogical Practices', *The American Behavioral Scientist*, 36 (Sept.-Oct. 1992): 8-21.

84 On the place of traditional hagiography in the history of literature, see Mikhail Bakhtin, 'The *Bildungsroman* and Its Significance in the History of Realism (Toward a Historical Typology of the Novel)', in *Speech Genres*, pp. 10-59.

85 See, e.g., Galbertus Brugensis, *De multro*, ch. 8, 57, 71, pp. 21, 106-109, 125-126. See also the important study by Alan V. Murray, 'Voices of Flanders: Orality and Constructed Orality in the Chronicle of Galbert of Bruges', *Handelingen der Maatschappij voor Geschiedenis en Oudheidkunde te Gent*, 48 (1994): 103-119.

86 Galbertus Brugensis, *De multro* ch. 121, p. 168: 'Queratur ergo, cum per mortem alterius Deus pacem vellet restituere patriae, cur magis dispensavit ut moreretur Willelmus comes, qui justiorem causam regendi terram obtinuit, et quare non citius mortuus fuit Theodericus comes, qui injuste superpositus videbatur, aut qua justitia Deus concessit ei consulatum, qui violenter arripuit dignitatem.' English translation by Ross, *The Murder*, pp. 310-311.

87 Dhondt, 'Une mentalité du douzième siècle', *passim*.

88 On this specific point, I am hence not going as far as Jeff Rider, who argues that even Galbert's second part of his *De multro* constitutes a consciously conceived, journalistically organized history of which the central plot is one of 'comital oppression and civil resistance, a fable of the tyrant and the good citizens', foreshadowing John of Salisbury's *Policraticus* of half a century later. See Rider, *God's Scribe*, p. 149.

89 Galbertus Brugensis, *De multro*, ch. 118, p. 165: 'Injuste quidem agebant cives ut, vivo domino suo, alium superponerent dominum, neutro quippe vel juste depulso vel suscepto.' English translation by Ross, *The Murder*, p. 306.

90 White, 'The Value of Narrativity', p. 20. See also Idem, 'Historical Emplotment and the Problem of Truth in Historical Representation', in *Figural Realism. Studies in the Mimesis Effect*, ed. by Idem (Baltimore and London: Johns Hopkins University Press, 1999), pp. 27-42. For a plot analysis in Galbert's work, see also Rider, *God's Scribe*, pp. 131-147.

91 See also Demyttenaere, 'Mentaliteit in de twaalfde eeuw', pp. 126-127.

92 Galbertus Brugensis, *De multro*, ch. 115, p. 161, l. 12.

93 See Van Caenegem, 'Historische inleiding', p. 40 *vs.* Rider, *God's Scribe*, pp. 162-164. See also Murray, 'Voices of Flanders', p. 118.

94 Van Caenegem, 'Galbert of Bruges on Serfdom', p. 104.

95 Galbertus Brugensis, *De multro*, ch. 106, p. 151: 'sine ratione, sine lege Dei et hominum'. English translation by Ross, *The Murder*, p. 284. See also François L. Ganshof, 'Les origines du concept de souveraineté nationale en Flandre', *Revue d'histoire du droit*, 18 (1950): 135-158 (here pp. 153-155).

96 Manegoldus, *Liber ad Gebehardum*, ed. by Kuno Francke, Monumenta Germaniae Historica. Libelli de Lite, 1 (Hannover: Hahn, 1891), pp. 308-430; Van Caenegem, 'Galbert of Bruges on Serfdom', pp. 105-106; see also Horst Fuhrmann, '"Volkssouveränität" und "Herrschaftsvertrag" bei Manegold von Lautenbach', in *Festschrift für Hermann Krause*, ed. by Sten Gagnér, Hans Schlosser, and Wolfgang Wiegand (Cologne and Vienna: Böhlau, 1975), pp. 21-42; and Rider, *God's Scribe*, pp. 154-155.

97 See also Albert Demyttenaere, 'Galbert of Bruges on Political Meeting Culture: Palavers and Fights in Flanders During the Years 1127 and 1128', in *Political Assemblies in the Earlier Middle Ages*, ed. by Peter S. Barnwell and Marco Mostert (Turnhout: Brepols, 2003), pp. 151-192.

98 Van Caenegem, 'Galbert of Bruges on Serfdom', pp. 91-92.

99 On Galbert and his urban audience, see, e.g., Sproemberg, 'Galbert von Brügge – Die Geschichtsschreibung' and Coué, 'Der Mord an Karl dem Guten'.

100 Stephanie Coué, however, has pointed to an interesting difference between Walter and Galbert's 'pragmatic literacy' and motivations: while Galbert was writing primarily for the urban population of Bruges where the most important events took place, Walter was writing for the inhabitants of the Flemish part of the diocese of Thérouanne, south of Bruges, where Furnes, the home town of the Erembald clan, was one of the most important places. See Coué, 'Der Mord an Karl dem Guten', p. 129.

101 See Jeff Rider, '*Vita Karoli comitis Flandrie*', Corpus christianorum. Continuatio Mediaevalis, 217, pp. 3-9.

102 John Shotter and Michael Billig, 'A Bakhtinian Psychology: From out of the Heads of Individuals and into the Dialogues between Them', in *Bakhtin and the Human Sciences. No Last Words*, ed. by Michael Bell and Michael Gardiner (London: Safe, 1998), pp. 13-29 (here p. 19): 'And it is from out of the sea of a people's lived behavioural ideology – "made up of multifarious speech performances that engulf and wash over all persistent forms and kinds of ideological creativity"—that the materials relevant to the official ideologies of ruling elites are selected, and others excluded.'

Lecuppre-Desjardin, 'Et le prince respondit de par sa bouche.'

I would like to thank Susie Sutch for her generous help.

1 Lewis Carroll, *Alice in Wonderland. Through the Looking-Glass* (1865; Ware: Wordsworth Classics, 1992), p. 159.

2 Quentin Skinner, 'On Performing and Explaining Linguistic Actions', *The Philosophical Quarterly*, 21 (1971): 1-21. See also John Langshaw Austin, *How to Do Things with Words* (Oxford: J.O. Urmson, 1962).

3 Ernst Hartwig Kantorowicz, *The King's Two Bodies, A Study in Mediaeval Political Theology* (Princeton: Princeton University Press, 1957; repr. 1998). Jacques Chiffoleau, 'Dire l'indicible. Remarques sur la catégorie du *nefandum* du XIIe au XVe siècle', *Annales E.S.C.*, 45 (1990): 289-324.

4 See the contribution of Alain Boureau in this volume.

5   Exodus 4.15-16.

6   Jacques Le Goff, 'Saint Louis et la parole royale', in *Le nombre du temps: en hommage à Paul Zumthor,* ed. by Emmanuelle Baumgartner (Paris: H. Champion, 1988), pp. 127-136.

7   Philippe de Commynes, *Mémoires,* ed. by Philippe Contamine (Paris: Imprimerie Nationale, 1994), p. 50: 'Mais le dit Morvillier luy rompoit la parolle, disant ces motz: "Monsieur de Charroloys, je ne suis pas venu pour parler à vous, mais à monsieur votre pere".'

8   Ibid., pp. 50-51: 'Le dit conte supplia par plusieurs foys à son pere qu'il peult responde; lequel luy dist: "J'ay respondu pour toy comme il me semble que pere doit responde pour filz. Toutesfoys, si tu en as si grand envye, pensez y aujourdhuy, et demain dy ce que tu voudras".'

9   Ibid., p. 51: 'Et croy bien que si n'eust esté la crainte de son dit pere, qui là estoit present et auquel il adressoit sa parolle, qu'il eust beaucoup plus asprement parlé.'

10 On Philippe de Commynes's character, see Jean Dufournet, *Sur Philippes de Commynes. Quatre études* (Paris: CDU/SEDES, 1982); Joël Blanchard, *Commynes l'Européen. L'invention du politique* (Geneva: Droz, 1996); and Idem, *Philippe de Commynes* (Paris: Fayard, 2006).

11 Philippe Wielant, *Recueil des Antiquités de Flandre,* ed. by Joseph Jean de Smet, *Recueil des Chroniques de Flandre* (Brussels: C. Mucquardt, 1865), IV, p. 55.

12 On Philip Augustus and Louis IX, see Le Goff, 'Saint Louis'. On Charles V, see Liliane Dulac, 'L'autorité dans les traités en prose de Christine de Pizan', in *Discours d'écrivain, parole de prince,* ed. by Liliane Dulac and Bernard Ribémont, *Medievalia,* 16 (1995): 15-24. On Philip the Fair, see Jean Favier, *Philippe le Bel* (Paris: Fayard, 1978; repr. 1998), pp. 1-5. Bernard Saisset is cited here after Elizabeth M. Hallam, *Capetian France, 987-1328* (London and New York: Longman, 1980), p. 278. For the original text, see Pierre Dupuy, *Histoire du Différend d'entre le pape Boniface VIII et Philippe le Bel, roi de France* (Paris, 1655).

13 See recently Elodie Lecuppre-Desjardin, *La ville des cérémonies. Essai sur la communication politique dans les anciens Pays-Bas bourguignons,* Studies in European Urban History, 4 (Turnhout: Brepols, 2004), pp. 165 sq.

14 Ernest Fraser Jacob, *The Fifteenth Century in The Oxford History of England,* ed. by Sir George Clark (Oxford: Clarendon Press, 1961), p. 546; and *Three Books of Polydore Vergil's English History,* ed. by Sir Henry Ellis (London: The Camden Society, 1844), p. 172.

15 Georges Chastellain claims that the Dauphin Louis talked to the city-dwellers and to the merchants 'très aimiablement', without any distance. Georges Chastellain, *Œuvres,* ed. by Kervyn De Lettenhove, 8 vols (Brussels: Heussner, 1863-1866), III, pp. 305-306.

16 During the assembly of the Estates in Tours, 1464, Louis XI pronounced a speech after the president of Toulouse Parliament, Jean Dauwet, without any eloquence, according to chroniclers. Maybe that is why the king was condemned to silence during the assembly of 1468. In Tours in 1468, the royal majesty was enhanced by the decorum. The king wore a long white damask dress brocaded with gold from Cyprus and sable-lined. He appeared under a blue velvet canopy spangled with fleurs-de-lis. For further details, see Jean Favier, *Louis XI* (Paris: Fayard, 2001), p. 313; and Neithard Bulst, 'Louis XI et les États Généraux de 1468', in *La France de la fin du XVe siècle. Renouveau et apogée. Économie, pouvoirs, arts, culture et conscience nationales,* ed. by Bernard Chevalier and Philippe Contamine (Paris: CNRS, 1985), pp. 91-104.

17 Pierre Bourdieu, *Ce que parler veut dire. L'économie des échanges linguistiques* (Paris: Fayard, 1982), pp. 105-107. According to him: 'En fait, l'usage du langage, c'est-à-dire aussi bien la manière que la matière du discours, dépend de la position sociale du locuteur qui commande l'accès qu'il peut avoir à la langue de l'institution, à la parole orthodoxe, légitime.'

18 Thomas Basin, *Histoire de Louis XI,* ed. and trans. by Charles Samaran, 3 vols (Paris: Les Belles Lettres, 1963-1972), III, p. 309.

19 For some developments about that topic, see Cary J. Nederman, 'The Union of Wisdom and Eloquence Before the Renaissance: The Ciceronian Orator in Medieval Thought', *Journal of Medieval History,* 18 (1992): 75-95.

20 Some details about that educational treaty in Bertrand Schnerb, 'L'éducation d'un jeune noble à la cour de Philippe le Bon d'après les Enseignements paternels de Ghillebert de Lannoy', in *Liber Amicorum Raphaël de Smedt. Miscellanea Neerlandica XXV,* ed. by Jacques Paviot (Leuven: Peeters, 2001), pp. 113-132.

21 *Œuvres de Ghillebert de Lannoy,* ed. by Charles Potvin (Leuven: Imprimerie de P. et J. Lefever, 1878), pp. 448-449.

22 Ibid., p. 451: 'Et pour ceste cause, nature a ordonné en nos bouches la langue estre emprisonnée en trois clostures: c'est assçavoir es lèvres, es dens et au palais; voeullant par ce la modérer en ses offices de parler.'

23 Ibid., p. 453: 'Sy te prie, mon filz, que tu t'accointes et accompaignes de gens bien famez, et s'il advient que aulcunes fois l'en te die aulcuns secrès, soyes diligent que la porte de ta bouche soit seurement fermée, et ne le descoeuvre jamais en lieu dont il en puist estre nouvelle. Porte tousjours bonne bouche et ne blasme nulz ne nulles, car tu ne poeus jamais sçavoir les meschiefs ne les fortunes qui te pèvent advenir.'

24 Thomas Basin, *Histoire de Louis XI,* III, pp. 303-304.

25 Ibid., III, pp. 367: 'Il ne pouvait absolument pas retenir sa langue et comme, ainsi que le dit le sage Salomon, 'le péché marche avec le bavardage', il arrivait fréquemment qu'il s'emportât jusqu'à médire des absents, fussent-ils des princes. [...] C'était le plus souvent des mots orduriers, des indécences et des bouffonneries qui sortaient de sa bouche, rien en tout cas qui sentît la gravité et la sagesse.'

26 Louis XI handled humour and irony easily. And he is said to have called 'Toison d'or', the herald of Burgundy, 'Trahison d'Or'. See Favier, *Louis XI,* p. 58.

27 The intervention of Louis of Gruuthuse on the Vrijdagmarkt saved Charles the Bold from a very perilous situation. The lord of Gruuthuse reminded Charles of the importance of sweet words to calm down the crowd. Georges Chastellain, *Œuvres,* V, pp. 267-268: 'Que maugré en ait celuy et celuy ! Que voulez-vous faire ? Nous voulez-vous faire tuer nous trestous et mourir ici honteusement san desfense par votre chaleur ? Où cuidiez-vous estre? Ne veez-vous que vostre vie et la nostre pend à moins que à un fil de soie ? et venez ici rabourer un tel monde par menaces et par dures paroles, qui ne vous poisent , ne ne prisent, par ainsi faire, ne que le moindre de nous; car sont en fureur, là où il n'y a raison, ne lumière. Par la mort que Dieu porta ! Si vous estes contant de mourir, ce ne suis-je pas, que ce ne soit maugré moi: car vous pouvez bien faire autrement , et les rappaiser par doux et sauver vostre honneur et vostre vie.' For more details about that event, see Lecuppre-Desjardin, *La ville des cérémonies,* pp. 294-302; Peter Arnade, 'Secular Charisma, Sacred Power: Rites of Rebellion in the Ghent Entry of 1467', *Handelingen van de Maatschappij voor Geschiedenis en Oudheidkunde te Gent,* 45 (1991): 69-94.

28 *Three Books of Polydore Vergil,* p. 138.

29 See *Medieval Eloquence. Studies in the Theory and Practice of Medieval Rhetoric,* ed. by James J. Murphy (Berkeley, Los Angeles, and London: University of California Press, 1978); Enrico Artifoni, 'Retorica e organizzazione del linguaggio politico nel Duecento italiano', in *Le forme della propaganda politica nel Due e nel Trecento,* ed. by Paolo Cammarosano (Rome: École Française de Rome, 1994), pp. 157-182; Enrico Artifoni, 'L'éloquence politique dans les cites communales (XIIIe siècle)', in *Cultures italiennes (XIIe-XVe siècle),* ed. by Isabelle Heullant-Donat (Paris: Les éditions du Cerf, 2000), pp. 269-296.

30 'The Union of Wisdom'.

31 Marc Fumaroli, *L'âge de l'éloquence* (Paris: A. Michel, 1980; repr. 1994), p. xv: 'La cité terrestre, dans l'Europe postérieure à l'Empire romain, a besoin d'une discipline régulatrice des discours. Comme le droit romain, avec lequel elle a de nombreuses affinités, la rhétorique est génératrice d'ordre civil. Elle renaît et s'impose dès que la violence et la guerre retombent. L'ordre romain, la loi et l'éloquence, retrouve alors ses droits dans la vita activa de la cité et de l'État. Ces barbares qui, en se convertissant au christianisme s'étaient mis à l'école de Rome, avaient une fois pour toutes montré la voie et donné l'exemple. La rhétorique, épaulant le droit, définit l'autorité de la parole, règle ses convenances et ses conventions, elle crée les conditions d'une communauté politique partageant des habitudes stables, et avec elle, d'une économie symbolique qui transforme ces habitudes en coutumes sans les immobiliser ni les figer. Telle est la nécessité élémentaire de l'art de bien dire qui, même au cours de Moyen Âge chrétien, la fait réapparaître obstinément de renaissance en renaissance.' See also Hanna Holborn Gray, 'Renaissance Humanism: The Pursuit of Eloquence', *Journal of History of Ideas,* 24 (1963): 497-514.

32 Gilles Lecuppre, 'Henri VII et les humanistes italiens: élaboration d'une légitimité princière et émergence d'un foyer culturel', in *Rapporti e Scambi tra umanesimo italiano ed umanesimo europeo,* ed. by Luisa Rotondi Secchi Tarugi (Milan: Nuovi Orizzonti, 2001), pp. 51-64.

33 Richard J. Walsh, 'The Coming of Humanism to the Low Countries: Some Italian Influences at the Court of Charles the Bold', *Humanistica Lovaniensa,* 25 (1976): 146-197; Arie Johan Vanderjagt, 'Classical Learning and the Building of Power at the Fifteenth-Century Burgundian Court', in *Centres of Learning. Learning and Location in Pre-modern Europe and the Near East,* ed. by Jan Willem Drijvers and Alasdair A. Mac Donald (Leiden: Brill, 1995), pp. 267-277.

34 Charles Ross in his biography of Edward IV quoted an extract from the *Excerpta Historica* where Edward and Edmund explained to their father that they diligently worked. Charles D. Ross, *Edward IV* (London: Eyre Methuen, 1974), ch. 1: 'And where ye command us by your said letters to attend especially to our learning in our young age, that should cause us to grow to honour and worship in our old age, please it your Highness to wit that we have attended our learning sith we come higher, and shall hereafter; by the which we trust to God your gracious lordship and good fatherhood shall be pleased.'

35 Ibid., p. 341 (*Rotuli Parliamentorum,* V, pp. 462-463; *Rotuli Parliamentorum,* V, p. 372).

36 Ibid., p. 303 (*Records of the Borough of Nottingham,* II, pp. 384-387).

37 *Le Rosier des Guerres. Enseignements de Louis XI, Roy de France, pour le Dauphin son fils* (Paris: typogr. F. Bernouard, 1925).

38 Ibid., ch. 3.

39 Arie Johan Vanderjagt, 'Classical Learning', pp. 268 *sq.*

40 On the library of Guillaume Hugonet, see Anke and Werner Paravicini, 'L'arsenal intellectuel d'un homme de pouvoir. Les livres de Guillaume Hugonet, chancelier de Bourgogne', in *Penser le pouvoir au Moyen Âge. Études offertes à Françoise Autrand,* ed. by Dominique Boutet and Jacques Verger (Paris: Editions Rue d'Ulm, 2000), pp. 261-325.

41 See some examples in *Actes des États Généraux des anciens Pays-Bas,* ed. by Joseph Cuvelier (Brussels: Palais des Académies, 1948), I (1427-1477).

42 See the contribution by Jeroen Deploige in this volume. See also Albert Demyttenaere, 'Galbert of Bruges on Political Meeting Culture: Palavers and Fights in Flanders During the Years 1127 and 1128', in *Political Assemblies in the Earlier Middle Ages,* ed. by Peter S. Barnwell and Marco Mostert (Turnhout: Brepols, 2003), pp. 151-192.

Lecuppre, Ideal Kingship against Oppressive Monarchy

I would like to thank Susie Sutch for her kind advice.

1 'Book of Howth' in *Calendar of the Carew Manuscripts Preserved in the Archiepiscopal Library at Lambeth,* ed. by J.S. Brewer and W. Bullen (London: HMSO, 1871/Nendeln, 1974),V, p. 188.

2 Michael J. Bennett, *Lambert Simnel and the Battle of Stoke* (Gloucester and New York: St Martin's Press, 1987).

3 Gilles Lecuppre, *L'imposture politique au Moyen Âge. La seconde vie des rois* (Paris: Presses Universitaires de France, 2005).

4 Robert Lee Wolff's article, an in-depth inquiry with a substantial bibliography, remains unrivalled: 'Baldwin of Flanders and Hainaut, First Latin Emperor of Constantinople: His Life, Death, and Resurrection, 1172-1225', *Speculum,* 27 (1952): 281-322.

5 Augustinus Stumpf, '*Historia Flagellantium, praecipue in Thuringia – Documenta II: Prophetica Conradi Smedis vel potius Schmid haeresi Flagellatorum infecti (cum glossis cujusdam catholici synchroni)*', *Neue Mittheilungen aus dem Gebiet historisch-antiquarischer Forschungen,* 2 (1836): esp. p. 20: 'Glossa. Ubi dicit quod ipse Cunradus faber Rex sit Thuringiae et Imperator Fredericus debeat nominari et esse [...].'

6 The examples and analyses provided by André Vauchez's classical study can be used for a fruitful comparison with the late medieval ideals of sainthood, independent of political motives: *La*

sainteté en Occident aux derniers siècles du Moyen Âge (1178-1431), d'après les procès de canonisation et les documents hagiographiques (Rome and Paris: École Française de Rome and De Boccard, 1988, 2nd rev. ed.). English trans. by Jean Birrell: *Sainthood in the Later Middle Ages* (Cambridge: Cambridge University Press, 1997).

7   Philippe Mousket, *Historia regum Francorum,* ed. by Adolfus Tobler, Monumenta Germaniae Historica, Scriptores (=MGH SS), 26 (Hannover: Hahn, 1882), pp. 769-770. Everyone at the time made fun of continental Britons, who were said to believe in King Arthur's return. By re-defining the concept of messianism, Virginie Greene once and for all dismissed the so-called belief as a stereotype, 'Qui croit au retour d'Arthur?', *Cahiers de Civilisation Médiévale*, 45 (2002): 321-340.

8   Wolff, 'Baldwin of Flanders', *passim.*

9   He was eventually given a Nietzschean dimension by Ernst Kantorowicz, *Kaiser Friedrich der Zweite* (Berlin: G. Bondi, 1927). It would be unfair, however, not to remember how thoroughly German scholars had re-created the whole character since the second half of the nineteenth century and now looked at him from the dangerous and anachronistic angle of prophecy. For both sources and more recent views, see Klaus van Eickels and Tania Brüsch, *Friedrich II. Leben und Persönlichkeit in Quellen des Mittelalters* (Düsseldorf and Zürich: Artemis & Winkler, 2000).

10 See, for example, the remarkable study by Rainer C. Schwinges, 'Verfassung und kollektives Verhalten. Zur Mentalität des Erfolges falscher Herrscher im Reich des 13. und 14. Jahrhunderts', in *Mentalitäten im Mittelalter. Methodische und inhaltliche Probleme*, Vorträge und Forschungen, 35, ed. by František Graus (Stuttgart: Jan Thorbecke, 1987), pp. 177-202.

11 *Annales Blandinienses,* ed. by Ludovicus Bethmann, MGH SS, 5 (Hannover: Hahn, 1844), p. 33: 'Quo combusto, alter quidam comparens dixit, se ex combustionibus et cineribus dicti combusti fuisse se post triduum resussitatum. Multas perambulans villas et civitates, tandem Gande in cimiterio sancti Bavonis a balivo Gandensi capitur et vinclis ferreis mancipatur; sed tandem a captione balivi liberatus, apud Traiectum inferius patibulo suspenditur.'

12 Three major articles were devoted to Edward II's afterlife, but they all focused on the debate between 'King and no-King', without giving any convincing explanation as to the motives of the impostor: G.P. Cuttino and Thomas W. Lyman, 'Where is Edward II?', *Speculum*, 53 (1978): 522-544; J.C. Russell and E.W. Russell, 'He said that he was the King's Father', *Res publica litterarum: Studies in the Classical Tradition,* 5 (1982), pp. 197-201; Roy M. Haines, 'Edwardus redivivus. The 'Afterlife' of Edward of Caernarvon', *Transactions of the Bristol and Gloucestershire Society*, 114 (1996): 65-86. I try to demonstrate the real meaning of Edward's travels through the continent in Lecuppre, *L'imposture politique*, pp. 367-369.

13 For pseudo-John the Posthumous, see Gilles Lecuppre, 'Continuité capétienne, monarchie universelle et martyre rédempteur: la royauté fantasmatique du Siennois Giannino Baglione (1316-1362)', *Royautés imaginaires (XIIe-XVIe siècle)*, ed. by Anne-Hélène Allirot, Gilles Lecuppre, and Lydwine Scordia (Turnhout: Brepols, 2005), pp. 103-118.

14 Bennett, *Lambert Simnel*; and Ian Arthurson, *The Perkin Warbeck Conspiracy, 1491-1499* (Stroud: Allan Sutton, 1994).

15 *Annales Henrici septimi,* ed. by James Gairdner, Rolls Series, 10 (London: Longman, 1858), p. 398: 'Quæ quidem omnia et singula cum plerisque aliis in deductione causæ latius exprimendis, si præfatis summis pontificibus expressa fuissent aut minus vere non suggesta, procul dubio nullatenus concessisent aut confirmassent concessa, quinimo dictum dominum illustrissimum Ricardum, Eduardi regis filium, in suum regnum restitui et in illius possessionem intronisari mandassent, nec debitos subditorum procerum et aliorum favores suo domino parenti et cognato exhiberi vetuissent, Joadae magni sacerdotis exemplum sicuti, qui Joas regem cruentis aviae manibus ereptum et clam apud amitam alitum in regnum patris restituit et seditiose feminae crudele propositum justa nece prævenit.'

16 Giannino's quest for the Grail is depicted in a simple way throughout his rearranged vernacular autobiography: *Istoria del re Giannino di Francia,* ed. by Latino Maccari (Siena: typog. C. Nava, 1893). See also Lecuppre, 'Continuité capétienne'.

17 British Library, Birch Collection, 4160. A modernized version of the text can be found in *The Reign of Henry VII from Contemporary Sources,* ed. by Albert F. Pollard (London: Longman, 1913), I, pp. 150-155.

18 *Istoria,* pp. 123-125.

19 For a comment on these frescoes, see Hayden B.J. Maginnis, 'Barna [Berna] da Siena', in *The Dictionary of Art* (New York: Grave, 1996), III, pp. 246-247.

20 *Istoria*, p. 125: 'Et tutte queste cose il detto G. patientemente conporto, e sostenne, e sempre ringratiando Idio, e mai non si turbo, ed era contento nell'animo suo di patire, et d'udire quanta villania di lui dovessero dire, e quanto, e quanto stratio, et tormento, e pena gli volessero fare patire, et di qualunche morte lo volessero far morire; et era contento di tutto cio Dio promettesse, che di lui fusse fatto, quasi come se morisse per la fede nostra, et cosi si reputava, dicendo infra se medescimo, che Idio gli faceva grandissima gratia di darli questa tribulatione, e pena in questo mondo, riputando, che fusse per salute, e per bene dell'anima sua, et per sodisfatione di' peccati suoi comessi per lo tempo passato, et che come per questa ragione sperava che Idio gli faciesse gratia di menarlo in paradiso come si fusse martorio, percio che contra ragione, et per falsa cagione era morta.'

21 It is a pity that Ian Arthurson, *Perkin Warbeck Conspiracy*, pp. 146-147, only briefly alludes to the vituperation.

22 For a general background, see Christine Carpenter, *The Wars of the Roses. Politics and the Constitution in England, c. 1437-1509* (Cambridge: Cambridge University Press, 1997).

23 Stanley intrigued to help Warbeck's cause. In fact, every argument specifically or implicitly refers to the late episodes of the civil war, intending to strike a chord among old Yorkists.

24 King Henry VII had married himself Warbeck's 'sister', Elizabeth of York, and given Edward of Warwick's sister to Richard Pole. Hence Henry had shown himself as the York lineage's restorer by that very marriage.

25 For a history of the principality during the period, see Johannes Schultze, *Die Mark Brandenburg,* II: *Die Mark unter Herrschaft der Wittelsbacher und Luxemburger (1319-1415)* (Berlin: Duncker und Humblot, 1961).

26 *Istoria*, p. 50: 'Ben ne parlo, et rivello tutto il fatto a certi suoi segretarii, et intimi amici, de quali molto si confidava, et cosi si stette fino a tanto che misser Giovanni di Valos, il quale tienne la Corona di Francia, fu sconfitto, e preso, et esso misser Philippo suo figliolo, et molti baroni, et cavalieri con lui. E la sconfitta fecie il prenze di Ghalis figlio del Re Adovardo d'Inghilterra, et fu la sconfitta fatta adi 17 di settembre anno 1356: e la novella venne in Siena adi 9 d'ottobre anno detto. Et essendo il detto frate Bartalomeo in Siena parlando di questa sconfitta con molti Ciptadini nobili, et popolari, et ragionando insieme, come la casa di Francia gia lungissimo tempo sempre andava di male in peggio, che mostrava di dovere venire in ruina, allora il detto frate Bartalomeo ad alta bocie ringrato Idio e disse: 'Ora, si vedra la ragione, e la verita di Giovanni.'

27 *The Reign of Henry VII*, p. 150: 'The which season it happened one Henry son to Edmond Tydder-Earl of Richmond, son to Owen Tydder of low birth in the country of Wales-to come from France and entered into this our realm, and by subtle false means to obtain the crown of the same unto us of right appertaining.'

28 *The Chronicle of Lanercost for the Years A.D. 1315-23*, trans. by Harry Rothwell, in *English Historical Documents*. Vol. III, *1189-1327* (London: Eyre and Spottiswoode, 1975), p. 270; for the Latin original, see: *Chronicon de Lanercost*, ed. by Joseph Stevenson (Edinburgh: for the Maitland and Bannatyne Clubs, 1839). See also *Chronica monasterii de Melsa,* ed. by Edward A. Bond, Rolls Series, 43 (London: Longman, 1867), II, p. 336: 'Dicebat mores regis Edwardi cum moribus patris sui aurigae in pluribus concordare, eo quod opera rusticorum naturaliter dilegebat.' A survey of the case can be found in Wendy R. Childs, ' "Welcome, my Brother", Edward II, John of Powderham and the Chronicles, 1318', in *Church and Chronicle in the Middle Ages. Essays Presented to John Taylor* (London and Rio Grande: Hambledon Press, 1991), pp. 149-163.

29 *Die Chronik des Mathias von Neuenburg,* ed. by Adolf Hofmeister, MGH, Scriptores rerum Germanicarum, Nova Series, 4 (Berlin: Weidmann, 1924), p. 261: 'Gens enim terre sibi luxuriam cum filiabus suis et quod liberi sui non sint legitimi nec digni tanto principatu, impingere dicebatur.'

30 See Lecuppre, *L'imposture politique*, chap. 7.

31 William of Ardres, *Chronica Andrensis*, ed. by Johannes Heller, MGH, SS, 24 (Hannover: Hahn, 1879), p. 765: 'Fames hoc anno quam plures opprimit et affligit'; and Albert of Stade, *Annales*, ed. by Johannes M. Lappenberg, MGH, SS, 16 (Hannover: Hahn, 1859), p. 358: 'A.D. 1225. Fames validissima.'

32 The author of the continuation of Martin of Cologne proved perspicacious: 'Sed civitates regno attinentes omnino fidem adhibere volebant propter nimias exacciones, quibus a rege angeriabantur, quorum frequentibus nunciis Wecslare accessit, ut per eorum auxilium civitates ulteriores attingeret' [ed. by Georg Waitz, MGH SS rerum Germanicarum in usum scholarum, 18 (Hannover: Hahn, 1880), p. 358]. To understand those uprisings, consult Thomas M. Martin, *Die Städtepolitik Rudolfs von Habsburg* (Göttingen: Vandenhoeck und Ruprecht, 1976), esp. pp. 159-69.

33 Ian Arthurson, 'The Rising of 1497. A Revolt of the Peasantry?', in *People, Politics and Community in the Later Middle Ages,* ed. by Joel Rosenthal and Colin Richmond (Gloucester: Allan Sutton, 1987), pp. 1-18. Arthurson does not emphasize a genuine switch from a criticism of the government to a radical criticism of the regime.

34 Wolff, 'Baldwin of Flanders', p. 296; Gilles Lecuppre, 'Jeanne de Flandre, traîtresse et parricide: thèmes radicaux d'une opposition politique', in *Reines et princesses au Moyen Âge. Actes du cinquième colloque international de Montpellier. Université Paul-Valéry (24-27 novembre 1999)* (Montpellier: Université Paul-Valéry, 2001), I, pp. 63-74.

35 See, for example, Peter McNiven, 'Rebellion, Sedition and the Legend of Richard II's Survival in the Reigns of Henry IV and Henry V', *Bulletin of the John Rylands University Library of Manchester,* 76 (1994): 93-117.

36 Arthurson, *The Perkin Warbeck Conspiracy, passim.*

37 Frederic Madden, 'Documents Relating to Perkin Warbeck with Remarks on His History', *Archaeologia,* 27 (1838): 153-210, esp. p. 199: 'Simul eius gratia Serenissimus Rex Romanorum eiusque filius archidux Austrie et Dux Saxonie consanguinei mei carissimi. Necnon Reges Dacie et Scotie, qui ad me oratores amicicie et confederationis gratia miserunt.'

38 Bartholomeus de Neocastro, *Historia sicula,* ed. by Giuseppe Paladino, Rerum Italicum Scriptores, 13/3 (Bologna: N. Zanichelli, 1921-1922), pp. 6-7: 'Durante cujus figura dominii, quidam, fraudulenter procedentes, defunctum imperatorem, qui dormiebat jam annis duodecim, ex ingenio Bartholomaei de Mileto et cujusdam notarii Philippi de Catania, apud montem Aetnae, in persona cujusdam pauperis simularunt, patrem in filium arma hostiliter gerere satagentes.'

39 About Serle: *Eulogium historiarum*, ed. by Frank S. Haydon (London: Longman, 1863), III, p. 402: 'Iste confessus est quod quando Rex Ricardus tradidit se duci Lancastriae in Wallia, ipse furatus fuit signetum Regis Ricardi. Et cum Rex Henricus inquireret de occisoribus ducis Gloucestriae, ipse fugiit in Scociam, et inde misit literas dicto signeto signatas ad amicos regis Ricardi, dicens quod ipse viveret, et sic fuit causa mortis multorum. Dixit etiam quod est unus in Scocia similis regi Ricardo, sed non est ipse Ricardus; tamen adhuc non quievit rumor ille de vita ejus. Semper Scoti illum rumorem auxerunt.'

40 About Stanley: *Chroniques de Jean Molinet (1474-1537),* ed. by George Doutrepont and Omer Jodogne (Brussels: Palais des Académies, 1935), I, p. 420: 'Et, de fait, besoignèrent tellement, estans par deçà, par l'envoy de leurs rescriptions ou aultrement, que les plus grans d'Engleterre adhérèrent à la querelle dudit Richart, promettans favoriser à sa descente en Engleterre; dont pluseurs d'iceulx, pour asseurance, lui envoyèrent leur seellés et, entre les aultres, le grant chambellan du roy Henry ensemble plus de quarante lui promirent assistance et quarante mile florins pour soustenir sa querelle'; *The Anglica Historia of Polydore Vergil,* A.D. 1485-1537, ed. by Denys Hay, The Camden Society, n.s. 74 (London: The Camden Society, 1950), p. 74: 'Quidam hoc illud peccatum fuisse ferunt, quod Guillermus alias interloquendum cum Roberto Clyfford, de illo Petro, qui se filium Edwardi prædicabat, dixisset si certo sciret illum filium esse Edwardi Regis, numquam arma contra ipsum ferret', and 76: 'At Guillermus magis fortasse dati quam accepti beneficii memor non æstimabat æquam suis meritis factam esse a Rege remunerationem.' Besides Arthurson, see also W.A.J. Archbold, 'Sir William Stanley and Perkin Warbeck', *English Historical Review,* 14 (1899): 529-534.

41 For more about imposture as a modality of medieval coup d'état, see Gilles Lecuppre, 'De l'essence du coup d'État à sa nécessité: l'imposture, entre fausse légitimité et complot véritable (XIIIe-XVe s.)', in *Coups d'État à la fin du Moyen Âge? Aux fondements du pouvoir politique en Europe occidentale,* ed. by François Foronda, Jean-Philippe Genet, and José Manuel Nieto Soria (Madrid: Casa de Velázquez, 2005).

42 For an introduction: Yves-Marie Bercé, *Le roi caché. Sauveurs et imposteurs. Mythes politiques populaires dans l'Europe moderne* (Paris: Fayard, 1990).

Pieters and Roose, The Art of Saying 'No'

1 Parenthetical references to Montaigne's *Essais* are to the edition by Villey-Saulnier, 3 vols (Paris: PUF, Quadrige, 1992). The anecdote is also mentioned in the biography of Charles IX by Michel Simonin, who is in doubt about the actual circumstances of the events that Montaigne recounts: was it really in 1562, Simonin wonders, and was it really in Rouen? [Michel Simonin, *Charles IX* (Paris: Fayard, 1995), pp. 105-106]. At the time, the first civil war was raging in France, with the Protestants gaining control of a number of large and important regions. In 1562, the royal troops managed to counter the Protestants in the valley of the Loire and in Normandy: 'Rouen, où Antoin de Bourbon trouve la mort, est assiégée et reprise aux huguenots le 26 octobre' [Janine Gerson, *Guerre civile et compromis 1559-1598* (Paris: Seuil, 1991), p. 155]. On 1 November 1562, Charles IX and his mother Catherine de' Medici attended mass in the cathedral of Rouen [cf. René Herval, *Histoire de Rouen* (Rouen: Maugard, 1949), II, p. 81]. Later, from January up to May 1564, in imitation of Francis I and under the instigation of his mother, Charles went on a tour to meet with all of his subjects in an attempt to reconcile Protestants and Catholics.

2 *Jean de Léry. Histoire d'un voyage en la terre du Brésil (1578),* ed. by Frank Lestringant (Paris: Livre de Poche, 1994); Claude Lévi-Strauss, *Tristes Tropiques* (Paris: Plon, 1955).

3 See Frank Lestringant, *Le Cannibale. Grandeur et décadence* (Paris: Perrin, 1994).

4 Charles was only ten when he became king, after the death of his brother Francis II in 1560. He was declared 'majeur' at the age of 14, in Rouen in 1563. See Simonin, *Charles IX*, p. 104. Michel de l'Hospital, with whom we will deal later, provided the legal arguments for the decision: Michel de l'Hospital, *Discours pour la majorité de Charles IX et trois autres discours* (Paris: Imprimerie Nationale, 1993).

5 Michel Foucault, *Sécurité, territoire, population*, Cours au Collège de France, 1977-1978 (Paris: Gallimard, 2004), p. 92 ('Leçon du 1er février 1978'), p. 92.

6 Ibid., p. 196 ('Leçon du 1er mars 1978').

7 Fausta Garavini, *Monstres et chimères. Montaigne, le texte et le fantasme* (Paris: Champion, 1993), p. 277.

8 'Nous ne sçavons pas distinguer les facultez des hommes. Elles ont des divisions, et bornes, mal aysees à choisir et delicates. De conclurre par la suffisance d'une vie particuliere, quelque suffisance à l'usage public, c'est mal conclud: Tel se conduict bien, qui ne conduict pas bien les autres. et faict des Essais, qui ne sçauroit faire des effects. Tel dresse bien un siege, qui dresseroit mal une bataille: et discourt bien en privé, qui harangueroit mal un peuple ou un Prince.' (III, 9, 992) [We cannot distinguish the faculties of men; they have divisions and boundaries that are delicate and hard to determine. To conclude from the competence of a man's private life some competence for public service is to conclude badly. One man guides himself well who does not guide others well, and produces Essays, who cannot produce results; another directs a siege well who could not direct a battle badly, and talks well in private who could be bad at addressing a crowd for a prince.] (Montaigne, *Essays*, trans. by Donald M. Frame (1958; Stanford: Stanford University Press, 1968), p. 759.

9 It is hardly coincidental that Lipsius was one of the first to publish the works of Seneca, foremost of all regal councillors.

10 The distinction derives from Alain Viala, *De la publication* (Paris: Fayard, 2002). To give another example: *L'Anti-Tribonian* by François Hotman (1567), another *protégé* of Michel de l'Hospital's, circulated for quite a while among jurists, without being actually published. In this text, Hotman gives a survey of all the mistakes that were being made by Tribonius, who compiled the main texts underpinning the Roman legal system. Hotman was convinced that traditional French law (common law) should not be replaced by a new legislation based on Roman jurisdiction.

11 La Boétie was eighteen years old when he wrote his text, so Montaigne claims in the editions of the *Essais* that he supervised (I, 28, 195). In the 'Exemplaire de Bordeaux' that Montaigne used for the next edition of his essays (the one that became the first posthumous one), La Boétie's age is changed to sixteen. La Boétie was born in 1530: if he wrote the text at age eighteen, its immediate cause may well have been the violent repression after the rising against the royal taxations during the summer of 1548. On the text's mysterious origins see Simone Goyard-Fabre's extensive introduction to her edition of the *Discours* (Paris: Flammarion, 1983), pp. 36-59.

12 See Montaigne's description of La Boétie in his dedicatory letter to Michel de l'Hospital.

13 La Boétie, *Discours de la servitude volontaire* (Paris: Vrin, 2002), p.25. Subsequent references to La Boétie's text will be given parenthetically, preceded by the indication *SV*. We made use of the English translation, *The Discourse of Voluntary Servitude* by Harry Kurz (1975).
'I see no good in having several lords;
Let one alone be master, let one alone be king.'
Homer puts these words in the mouth of Ulysses, as he addresses the people. If he had said nothing more than 'I see no good in having several lords,' it would have been well spoken. For the sake of logic he should have maintained that the rule of several could not be good since the power of one man alone, as soon as he acquires the title of master, becomes abusive and unreasonable. Instead he declared what seems preposterous: 'Let one alone be master, let one alone be king.'

14 My question will not be, La Boétie writes, which position the monarchy holds in the hierarchy of different forms of government, in the organization of the 'res publica' as he puts it. But he immediately goes on to wonder whether a monarchy can actually be termed a 'res publica': 'pour ce qu'il est malaisé de croire qu'il y ait rien de public en ce gouvernement, où tout est à un' (*SV*, 26).

15 'For the present I should like merely to understand how it happens that so many men, so many villages, so many cities, so many nations sometimes suffer under a single tyrant who has no other power than the power they give him; who is able to harm them only to the extent to which they have the willingness to bear with him; who could do them absolutely no injury unless they preferred to put up with him rather than contradict him.'

16 Montaigne, *Essays*, p. 159.

17 For an analysis of Gramsci's notion of hegemony in the tradition of theories of state, see Norberto Bobbio's 'Gramsci and the conception of civil society', in *Gramsci and Marxist Theory*, ed. by Chantal Mouffe (London, Boston and Henley: Routledge & Kegan Paul, 1979), pp. 21-47.

18 'Too frequently this same little man is the most cowardly and effeminate in the nation, a stranger to the powder of battle and hesitant on the sands of the tournament.' Even though La Boétie seems to refrain from recognizable references to the historical circumstances in which he wrote his text, this particular detail has led commentators to wonder when exactly La Boétie (re)wrote his text. Most argue for 1548, while others take 1561 as the possible date of a later version. In 1559 Henry II died due to an accident on a tournament, to be succeeded by his sick and weak son, Francis II, who in turn was succeeded by his brother, Charles IX.

19 John W. Allen, *A History of Political Thought in the Sixteenth Century*, rev. ed. (London: Methuen & Co., 1957), p. 275.

20 Allen, *A History of Political Thought in the Sixteenth Century*, pp. 275-276.

21 Foucault, *Sécurité, territoire, population*, p. 92 ('Leçon du 1er février 1978').

22 Allen, *A History of Political Thought in the Sixteenth Century*, p. 293.

23 Ibid., p. 296.

24 The translation is Donald Frame's: Montaigne, *Essays*, p. 115.

25 'Resolve to serve no more, and you are at once freed. I do not ask that you place hands upon the tyrant to topple him over, but simply that you support him no longer; then you will behold him, like a great Colossus whose pedestal has been pulled away, fall of his own weight and break into pieces.'

26 Aristotle, *Ethica Nicomachea*, 1103a, 24ff.

27 Michel Spanneut, *Permanence du stoïcisme* (Paris: Duculot, 1973).

28 'If we led our lives according to the ways intended by nature and the lessons taught by her.'

29 See the chapters on 'La physique comme exercice spirituel ou pessimisme et optimisme chez Marc Aurèle' and 'Une clé des *Pensées* de Marc Aurèle' in Pierre Hadot, *Les exercices spirituels et philosophique antique*, rev. ed. (Paris: Albin Michel, 2002), pp. 145-192.

30 'Therefore it is fruitless to argue whether or not liberty is natural, since none can be held in slavery without being wronged, and in a world governed by a nature, which is reasonable, there is nothing so contrary as an injustice.'

31 'Even the oxen under the weight of the yoke complain, /And the birds in their cage lament.'

32 The example is taken from Xenophon's *Cyropaedia*. In the Renaissance, the book was often singled out as one of the books young princes had to read. La Boétie translated the *Oeconomicus*.

33 Marc Bloch points out that it was forbidden to question these miracles until 1541: *Les rois thaumaturges* (Strasbourg: Istra, 1924), p. 327.

34 Arlette Jouanna, Jacqueline Boucher, *Histoire et dictionnaire des guerres de religion* (Paris: Laffont, Bouquins, 1998), p. 1325.

35 'They have insisted on using religion for their own protection and, where possible, have borrowed a stray bit of divinity to bolster up their evil ways.'

36 'Our own leaders have employed in France certain similar devices, such as toads, fleurs-de-lys, sacred vessels, and standards with flames of gold.'

37 At the end of the fifteenth century it was taken that Clovis's coat of arms bore three toads. After his conversion he had them replaced with three lilies; see Michel Pastoureau, *Traité d'Héraldique* (Paris: Picard, 1993), p. 161.

38 See Étienne Pasquier, *Les Recherches de la France* [1565], II, ch. 17, 'Des Nobles, Gens-d'armes, Roturiers, Vilains, Chevaliers, Armoiries de France & plusieurs autres choses de mesme sujet, concernans la Noblesse de France', in *Œuvres*, I (Amsterdam, 1723), pp. 133-142.

39 'Our kings have always been so generous in times of peace and so valiant in time of war, that from birth they seem not to have been created by nature like many others, but even before birth to have been designated by Almighty God for the government and preservation of this kingdom.'

40 In the chapter on superstition and miracles, Montaigne applauds the use of sceptical phrases: 'Le stile à Rome portoit, que cela mesme, qu'un tesmoin deposoit, pour l'avoir veu de ses yeux, et ce qu'un juge ordonnoit de sa plus certaine science, estoit conceu en cette forme de parler. "Il me semble". On me faict haïr les choses vray-semblables, quand on me les plante pour infaillibles. J'aime ces mots, qui amollissent et moderent la temerité de nos propositions: "A l'avanture", "Aucunement", "Quelque", "On dict", "Je pense", et semblables: Et si j'eusse eu à dresser des enfans, je leur eusse tant mis en la bouche, cette façon de respondre: enquesteuse, non resolutive' (III, 1, 1030). [The style in Rome was that even what a witness deposed to having seen with his eyes, and what a judge decided with his most certain knowledge, was drawn up in this form of speech: 'It seems to me'. It makes me hate probable things when they are planted on me as infallible. I like these words, which soften and moderate the rashness of our propositions: 'perhaps', 'to some extent', 'some', 'they say', 'I think', and the like. And if I had to train children, I would have filled their mouths so much with this way of answering, inquiring, not decisive'] (Montaigne, *Essays*, p. 788).

41 Efraim Podoksik, 'Estienne de La Boëtie and the politics of obedience', *Bibliothèque d'Humanisme et Renaissance*, 1 (2003): 83-95.

42 'Such are his archers, his guards, his halberdiers; not that they themselves do not suffer occasionally at his hands, but this riff-raff, abandoned alike by God and man, can be led to endure evil if permitted to commit it, not against him who exploits them, but against those who like themselves submit, but are helpless.'

43 See Laurent Gerbier, 'Les paradoxes de la nature dans le *Discours de la Servitude Volontaire* de La Boétie', in Étienne de La Boétie, *Discours de la Servitude volontaire* (Paris: Vrin, 2002), pp. 115-30.

44 Guillaume de La Perrière, *Miroir politique contenant diverses manieres de gouverner et policer les Républiques, qui sont & esté par cy devant* [1555] (Paris: Vincent Norment, 1567), 6r°.

45 Baldassare Castiglione, *The Book of the Courtier*, trans. by Sir Thomas Hoby (1561; London: J. M. Dent, n.d.), p. 274.

46 The passage is also quoted by Foucault in *Sécurité, territoire, population*, p. 103 ('Leçon du 1er février 1978').

47 Jean-Pierre Cavaillé, 'Langage, tyrannie et liberté dans *Le Discours de la servitude volontaire* d'Étienne de La Boétie', *Revue des sciences philosophiques et théologiques*, 72/1 (1988): 3-30.

48 The text's subtitle is indicative of its central purpose: 'œuvre non moins utile que necessaire à tous les monarches, roys, princes seigneurs, magistrats, et autres surintendants et gouverneurs de Republicques'.

49 Foucault, *Sécurité, territoire, population*, p. 92 ('Leçon du 1er février 1978').

50 Ibid., p. 95. For a brief synthesis of the text, see Jürgen Pieters, 'Normality, Deviancy and Critique. Toward a "Governmental" Reading of Shakespeare's *Measure for Measure*', in *Charles V in Context: Making of a European Identity*, ed. by Marc Boone and Marysa Demoor (Brussels: VUB Press, 2003), pp. 189-205.

51 Foucault, *Sécurité, territoire, population*, p. 248 ('Leçon du 8 mars 1978').

52 Ibid., p. 99 ('Leçon du 1er février 1978').

53 Ibid., p. 238 ('Leçon du 8 mars 1978').

54 Ibid., p. 242 ('Leçon du 8 mars 1978').

55 La Boétie indicates how the tyrant managed very deftly to make use of this image: 'son humanité même, que l'on prêche tant, fut plus dommageable que la cruauté du plus sauvage tyran qui fût onques; pour ce qu'à la vérité ce fut cette sienne venimeuse douceur qui envers le peuple romain sucra la servitude; mais après sa mort, ce peuple-là, [...] éleva une colonne comme 'au père du peuple' (*SV*, 43). 'It seems to me, there was nothing worthwhile, for his very liberality, which is so highly praised, was more baneful than the cruelest tyrant who ever existed, because it was actually this poisonous amiability of his that sweetened servitude for the Roman people. After his death, that people, [...] raised a column to him as to 'The Father of His People'.

56 'Indeed Momus, god of mockery, was not merely joking when he found this to criticize in the man fashioned by Vulcan, namely, that the maker had not set a little window in his creature's heart to render his thoughts visible.'

57 Foucault, *Sécurité, territoire, population*, pp. 233-240 ('Leçon du 8 mars 1978').

58 Ibid., p. 235.

59 Ibid., p. 235.

60 Gil Delannoi, *Éloge de la Prudence* (Paris: Berg International, 1993).

61 We borrow the concept of 'reinvestment', '*Umbesetzung*', from Hans Blumenberg's *Die Legitimität des Neuzeit* (Frankfurt am Main: Suhrkamp, 1999, 2nd rev. ed.).

62 'To see an endless multitude of people not merely obeying, but driven to servility? Not ruled, but tyrannized over?'

63 'Among free men there is competition as to who will do most, each for the common good, each by himself, all expecting to share in the misfortunes of defeat, or in the benefits of victory.'

64 Foucault, *Sécurité, territoire, population*, p. 201 ('Leçon du 1 mars 1978').

65 'Men are like handsome race horses who first bite the bit and later like it, and rearing under the saddle a while soon learn to enjoy displaying their harness and prance proudly beneath their trappings.'

66 Sébastien Charles, 'La Boétie, le peuple et les "gens de bien"', *Nouvelle Revue du XVI siècle*, 17/2 (1999): 269-286.

67 Nannerl O. Keohane, 'The Radical Humanism of Étienne de La Boétie', *Journal of History of Ideas*, 38 (1977): 121.

68 Michel Foucault, 'Qu'est-ce que la critique [Critique et *Aufklärung*]', *Bulletin de la Société française de Philosophie* (1979): 36ff. See also Pieters, 'Toward a 'Governmental' Reading of Shakepeare's *Measure for Measure*', pp. 189-205.

69 Pierre Mesnard, *L'essor de la Philosophie politique au XVIe siècle* (Paris: Boivin, 1936), pp. 389-406.

70 'Whoever could have observed the early Venetians, a handful of people living so freely that the most wicked among them would not wish to be king over them, so born and trained that they would not vie with one another except as to which one could give the best counsel and nurture their liberty most carefully, so instructed and developed from their cradles that they would not exchange for all the other delights of the world an iota of their freedom.'

Sharpe, Sacralization and Demystification

1 See, for example, Michel Foucault, *The Order of Things: An Archaeology of Human Sciences* (New York: Pantheon Books, 1970) and Clifford Geertz, *The Interpretation of Cultures: Selected Essays* (New York: Basic Books, 1973). See Kevin Sharpe, *Reading Revolutions: The Politics of Reading in Early Modern England* (New Haven: Yale University Press, 2000), pp. 11-12.

2 See Stephen Greenblatt, 'Towards A Poetics of Culture', in *The Aims of Representation: Subject. Text/History,* ed. by Murray Krieger (New York: Columbia University Press, 1987) and H. Aram Veeser (ed.), *The New Historicism Reader* (New York: Routledge, 1994); Idem, *The New Historicism* (New York: Routledge, 1989).

3 For an excellent survey of Renaissance rhetorical practices, see Quentin Skinner, *Reason and Rhetoric in the Philosophy of Hobbes* (Cambridge: Cambridge University Press, 1996), part I.

4 Skinner's important early essays are 'Meaning and Understanding in the History of Ideas', *History and Theory,* 8 (1969): 3-53; 'On Performing and Explaining Linguistic Actions', *Philosophical Quarterly,* 21 (1971): 1-21. Skinner's seminal essays have been republished, with changes, in Quentin Skinner, *Visions of Politics,* 3 vols (Cambridge: Cambridge University Press, 2002). See especially vol. I, *Concerning Method*. See also James H. Tully, *Meaning and Context: Quentin Skinner and His Critics* (Princeton: Princeton University Press, 1988); John G. A. Pocock, 'Verbalising a Political Act: Towards a Politics of Language', *Political Theory,* 1 (1973): 27-45; Idem, *Politics, Language and Time: Essays on Political Thought and History* (London: Methuen, 1972); Idem, *Virtue, Commerce and History. Essays on Political Thought and History, Chiefly in the Eighteenth Century* (Cambridge: Cambridge University Press, 1985); Idem, 'Texts as Events: Reflections on the History of Political Thought', in *Politics of Discourse: Literature and History of Seventeenth Century England,* ed. by Kevin Sharpe and Steven Zwicker (Berkeley: University of California Press, 1987), pp. 21-34. For a review of the linguistic turn, see John E. Toews, 'Intellectual History after the Linguistic Turn: The Autonomy of Meaning and the Irreducibility of Experience', *American Historical Review,* 92 (1987): 879-907.

5 Sharpe, *Reading Revolutions,* 20-21; Idem, *Remapping Early Modern England: The Culture of Seventeenth-Century Politics* (Cambridge: Cambridge University Press, 2000), pp. 16-17.

6 It is significant here that the editors and most of the contributors to Daniel Fischlin and Marc Fortier, *Royal Subjects: Essays on the Writings of James VI and I* (Detroit: Wayne State University Press, 2002) are literary scholars.

7 Leah Marcus, Janel Mueller, and Mary Rose (eds.), *Elizabeth I: Collected Works* (Chicago and London: University of Chicago Press, 2000); James Craigie (ed.), *The Poems of James VI of Scotland,* Scottish Text Society, 2 vols (Edinburgh: William Blackwood and Sons, 1955-1958). In the case of James VI and I, historical editors have omitted biblical exegeses and poems from selections of the king's works. See Charles H. McIlwain (ed.), *The Political Works of James I* (Cambridge, Mass: Harvard University Press, 1918) and Johann Sommerville (ed.), *King James VI and I: Political Writings* (Cambridge: Cambridge University Press, 1994).

8 I am currently writing a study of royal representations from Henry VIII to Queen Anne.

9 Sharpe, *Remapping Early Modern England,* pp. 20-21.

10 See Michael T. Clanchy, *From Memory to Written Record: England 1066-1307* (1979; Oxford: Blackwell, 1993, 2nd rev. ed.).

11 David Katz, 'The Language of Adam in Seventeenth-century England', in *History and Imagination: Essays in Honour of H.R. Trevor Roper,* ed. by Hugh Lloyd Jones, Valerie Pearl, and Blair Worden (London: Duckworth, 1981), pp. 132-145; Kevin Sharpe, 'Reading Revelations: Prophecy, Hermeneutics and Politics in Early Modern Britain', in *Reading, Society and Politics in Early Modern England,* ed. by Kevin Sharpe and Steven Zwicker (Cambridge: Cambridge University Press, 2003), pp. 122-163.

12 David Katz, *God's Last Words: Reading the English Bible from the Reformation to Fundamentalism* (New Haven and London: Yale University Press, 2004).

13 Sharpe, *Reading Revolutions,* pp. 27-31.

14 See J. Christopher Warner, *Henry VIII's Divorce: Literature and the Politics of the Printing Press* (Woodbridge: Boydell & Brewer, 1998); P. Neville, 'Richard Pynson: King's Printer' (Diss., London University, 1990).

15 Robert W. Scribner, *For The Sake of Simple Folk: Popular Propaganda for the German Reformation* (Cambridge: Cambridge University Press, 1981); J. Scarisbrick, *Henry VIII* (1968; Harmondsworth: Penguin, 1971), 153-155.

16 Henry VIII, *Assertio Septem Sacramentorum* (1521), ed. by Francis Macnamara, in *Miscellaneous Writings of Henry the Eighth* (Waltham, Mass.: Golden Cockerel Press, 1924). See Louis O'Donovan (ed.), *The Defense of the Seven Sacraments* (New York: Benziger Brothers, 1908).

17 *The Bible in English* (1539); John N. King, 'Henry VIII as David: The King's Image and Reformation Politics', in *Rethinking the Henrician Era: Essays on Early Tudor Texts and Contexts,* ed. by Peter Herman (Urbana: University of Illinois Press, 1994), pp. 78-92; cf. Greg Walker, *Persuasive Fictions: Faction, Faith and Political Culture in the Reign of Henry VIII* (Aldershot: Ashgate, 1996), pp. 92-95.

18 Henry VIII, *A Glasse of the Truthe* (1532), 'To the Readers', sigs A1^V, A3, B2^V.

19 Henry VIII, *A Necessary Doctrine and Erudition For Any Christian Man* (1543).

20 See Paul L. Hughes and James F. Larkin, *Tudor Royal Proclamations I: The Early Tudors* (New Haven: Yale University Press, 1964), pp. 284-286: 34 & 35 Henry VIII cap. 1.

21 *A Glasse of the Truthe,* sigs. E4^v-E8^v.

22 Warner, *Henry VIII's Divorce,* pp. 113, 118; Seth Lerer, *Courtly Letters in the Age of Henry VIII: Literary Culture and the Arts of Deceit* (Cambridge: Cambridge University Press, 1997), p. 113; Henry Ellis (ed.), *Hall's Chronicle* (London: Printed for J. Johnson etc., 1809), pp. 754, 759, 784; Geoffrey R. Elton, *Policy and Police: The Enforcement of the Reformation in the Age of Thomas Cromwell* (Cambridge: Cambridge University Press, 1972), pp. 11, 24, 58, 137; George W. Bernard, 'The Fall of Anne Boleyn', *English Historical Review,* 106 (1991): 584-610.

23 Larkin and Hughes, *Tudor Royal Proclamations,* pp. 244-245: 26 Henry VIII, cap. 13; Sharon L. Jansen, *Political Protest and Prophecy under Henry VIII* (Woodbridge: Boydell, 1991), p. 60.

24 Roy Strong, *Portraits of Queen Elizabeth I* (Oxford: Clarendon Press, 1963); Idem, *The Cult of Elizabeth: Elizabethan Portraiture and Pageantry* (London: Thames and Hudson, 1977); Idem, *Gloriana: The Portraits of Queen Elizabeth I* (London: Thames and Hudson, 1987); Frances Yates, *Astraea: The Imperial Theme in the Sixteenth Century* (London: Routledge, 1975); Helen Hacket, *Virgin Mother, Maiden Queen: Elizabeth I and the Cult of the Virgin Mary* (Basingstoke: Palgrave Macmillan, 1995).

25 See Marcus, *Elizabeth I: Collected Works.* There is no complete edition of Elizabeth's translations. See *Queen Elizabeth's Englishings,* ed. by Caroline Pemberton, Early English Text Society, Original Series 113 (London, 1899; repr. New York: Millwood, 1981).

26 See the frontispiece to John Day, *A Book of Christian Prayers* (1578).

27 *Precationes Privatae Regiae* (1563).

28 Marcus, *Elizabeth I: Collected Works,* pp. 136, 139; Kevin Sharpe, 'The King's Writ: Royal Authors and Royal Authority in Early Modern England', in *Culture and Politics in Early Stuart England,* ed. by Kevin Sharpe and Peter Lake (Basingstoke: Palgrave Macmillan, 1994), pp. 119-120.

29 Julia M. Walker, *Dissing Elizabeth: Negative Representations of Gloriana* (Durham: Duke University Press, 1998).

30 Walker, *Dissing Elizabeth*; and Carole Levin, *The Heart and Stomach of a King: Elizabeth I and the Politics of Sex and Power* (Philadelphia: Penn Press, 1994), ch. 4.

31 Hannah Betts, '"The Image of This Queene So Quaynt": The Pornographic Blazon 1588-1603', in *Dissing Elizabeth,* ed. by Walker, pp. 153-184.

32 See Philippa Berry, *Of Chastity and Power: Elizabethan Literature and the Unmarried Queen* (London and New York: Routledge, 1989); and Levin, *Heart and Stomach.*

33 Levin, *Heart and Stomach,* ch. 7; Anne Barton, 'Harking back to Elizabeth: Ben Jonson and Caroline Nostalgia', *English Literary History,* 48 (1981): 701-731. For a broad survey of the image and appropriation of Elizabeth in history, see Julia M. Walker, *The Elizabeth Icon: 1603 to 2003* (Basingstoke: Palgrave Macmillan, 2003).

34 Figures from the English Short Title Catalogue (ESTC) of the British Library; see Joad Raymond, *Pamphlets and Pamphleteering in Early Modern England* (Cambridge: Cambridge University Press, 2003), pp. 163-165 and fig.1

35 Hughes and Larkin, *Tudor Royal Proclamations,* p. 517.

36 Ibid., p. 522.

37 Raymond, *Pamphlets,* ch. 4

38 Raymond, *Pamphlets,* ch. 2.

39 Elizabeth's famous Golden Speech of 1601 was one of the first parliamentary speeches to be published. See also *A Letter Wherein Part of the Entertainment Unto the Queen's Majesty at Kenilworth Castle* […] *is Signified* (1575); *The Joyful Receiving of The Queen's Most Excellent Majesty Into Her Highness's City of Norwich* (1578); Thomas Churchyard, *A Discourse of the Queen's Majesty's Entertainment in Suffolk and Norfolk* (1578); *The Queen's Majesty's Entertainment at Woodstock* (1585); *The Speeches and Honourable Entertainment Given to the Queen's Majesty in Progress at Cowdray in Sussex* (1591); *The Honourable Entertainment Given to the Queen's Majesty in Progress at Elvetham in Hampshire* (1591).

40 Jürgen Habermas, *The Structural Transformation of the Public Sphere. An Inquiry into a Category of Bourgois Society* (trans. from 1962 German original by Thomas Burger, Cambridge, Mass.: MIT Press, 1989). See also Craig Calhoun, *Habermas and the Public Sphere* (Cambridge, Mass.: MIT Press, 1992).

41 Alexandra Halasz, *The Marketplace of Print: Pamphlets and the Public Sphere in Early Modern England* (Cambridge: Cambridge University Press, 1997); Dagmar Freist, *Governed by Opinion: Politics, Religion and the Dynamics of Communication in Stuart London, 1637-1645* (London: Tauris, 1997). See the forthcoming volume of essays on the public sphere in early modern England by Peter Lake and Steven Pincus (Manchester). I am grateful to the editors for an opportunity to see essays in advance of publication and for stimulating discussion of this subject.

42 David Zaret, *Origins of Democratic Culture: Printing, Petitions and the Public Sphere in Early Modern England* (Princeton: Princeton University Press, 2000); Joad Raymond, 'The Newspaper, Public Opinion and the Public Sphere in the Seventeenth Century', in *News, Newspapers and Society in Early Modern Britain,* ed. by Joad Raymond (London and Portland: Frank Cass, 1999), pp. 109-140; Lake and Pincus, *Public Sphere.*

43 *A Letter Wherein Part of the Entertainment Unto the Queen's Majesty at Kenilworth Castle,* pp. 34-36.

44 *News From The North* (1579). Piers doubts whether magistrates who often bought their posts were chosen by God (sigs. Di-ii).

45 J. Young, *Sermon Preached before the Queenes Maiesty, the Second of March, An. 1576* (1576), sig. Ci.

46 Ibid., sigs. Ci^v, Ciii^v-Cviii, and passim.

47 Franciscus Patricius, *A Moral Methode of Civil Policie* (1576), p. 63.

48 The popular understanding of 'counsel' and its relation to popular politics needs full explication.

49 See, for example, John Brewer and Roy Porter (eds), *Consumption and the World of Goods* (New York: Routledge, 1993); Ann Birmingham and John Brewer (eds), *The Consumption of Culture, 1600-1800: Image, Object, Text* (New York: Routledge, 1995).

50 Douglas Bruster, *Drama and The Market in The Age of Shakespeare* (Cambridge: Cambridge University Press, 1992).

51 See the medals in Edward Hawkins, *Medallic Illustrations of the History of Great Britain and Ireland to the Death of George II* (London: Trustees of the British Museum, 1885; repr. 1969); and Strong, *Portraits of Queen Elizabeth,* p. 134.

52 Ibid., p. 10; Roy Strong, *Artists of the Tudor Court: The Portrait Miniature Rediscovered, 1520-1620* (London: Victoria and Albert Museum, 1983), p. 12; Idem, *The English Renaissance Miniature* (London: Thames and Hudson, 1983), pp. 118-119.

53 Strong, *Portraits of Queen Elizabeth,* 111; and Arthur Hind, *Engraving in England in the 16th and 17th Centuries. Vol. 1: The Tudor Period* (Cambridge: Cambridge University Press, 1952), p. 182.

54 See T.T., *A Book Containing The True Portraiture of The Countenances and Attires of The Kings of England From William the Conqueror Unto Our Sovereign Lady Queen Elizabeth* (1597).

55 See above note 39. Elizabeth was the subject of voluminous verse panegyrics. See, for example, *Puttenham's Partheniades* (1579); *Verses of Praise and Joy Written Upon Her Majesty's Preservation* (1586); Thomas Churchyard, *A Handful of Gladsome Verses* (1592); H.C., *Diana the Praises of His Mistres in Certaine Sweete Sonnets* (1592).

56 Penry Williams, *The Tudor Regime* (Oxford: Clarendon Press, 1979), ch. 11; John Guy, 'The Rhetoric of Counsel in Early Modern England', in *Tudor Political Culture,* ed. by Dale Hoak (Cambridge: Cambridge University Press, 1995), pp. 292-310.

57 George W. Bernard, *War, Taxation and Rebellion in Early Tudor England: Henry VIII, Wolsey and The Amicable Grant of 1525* (Brighton: Harvester Press, 1986).

58 Paul Fideler and Thomas Mayer, *Political Thought and the Tudor Commonwealth: Deep Structure, Discourse and Disguise* (London and New York: Routledge, 1992); Patrick Collinson, 'The Monarchical Republic of Queen Elizabeth I', *Bulletin of the John Rylands Library of Manchester,* 69 (1987): 394-424; Greg Walker, *Writing under Tyranny: English Literature and the Henrician Reformation* (Oxford: Oxford University Press, 2005).

59 R. Malcolm Smuts, 'Court-Centred Politics and The Uses of Roman Historians, c.1590-1630', in *Culture and Politics,* ed. by Sharpe and Lake, pp. 21-44; Idem, *Culture and Power in England, 1585-1685* (Basingstoke: Palgrave Macmillan, 1999), pp. 38-40.

60 Mark Curtis, *Oxford and Cambridge in Transition, 1558-1642* (Oxford: Clarendon Press, 1959), pp. 119, 137; Felix Raab, *The English Face of Machiavelli* (London: Routledge, 1964).

61 See Kevin Sharpe, 'A Commonwealth of Meanings: Languages, Analogues, Ideas and Politics', in *Politics and Ideas in Early Stuart England,* ed. by Kevin Sharpe (London, 1989), pp. 25-27.

62 Ian Dunlop, *Palaces and Progresses of Elizabeth I* (New York: Taplinger Publishing, 1962), p. 56.

63 Sharpe, *Remapping Early Modern England,* pp. 435-436.

64 Marcus, *Elizabeth I: Collected Works,* p. 189.

65 See Jonathan Dollimore, *Radical Tragedy: Religion, Ideology and Power in Renaissance England* (Chicago: University of Chicago Press, 1984); Jean Howard, *The Stage and Social Struggle in Early Modern England* (London and New York: Routledge, 1994), ch. 6; David Kastan, 'Proud Majesty Made a Subject: Shakespeare and the Spectacle of Rule', *Shakespeare Quarterly,* 37 (1986): 459-475.

66 Peter Ure (ed.), *King Richard II,* The Arden Shakespeare (London: Methuen, 1956), p. lix.

67 Hacket, *Virgin Mother,* p. 178; Elizabeth W. Pomeroy, *Reading the Portraits of Queen Elizabeth* (Hamden, CT: Archon Books, 1989), p. 62; Strong, *Portraits of Elizabeth,* pp. 94-95.

68 Robert Ashton (ed.), *James I by His Contemporaries. An Account of His Career and Character as Seen by Some of His Contemporaries* (London: Hutchinson, 1969); Jenny Wormald, 'King James VI and I: Two Kings or One', *History* 68 (1983): 187-209.

69 On Charles I's sacralization of the royal body, see Kevin Sharpe, 'The Image of Virtue: The Court and Household of Charles I', in *The English Court from the Wars of the Roses to the Civil War,* ed. by David Starkey (London and New York: Longman, 1987), pp. 226-260; Idem, *The Personal Rule of Charles I* (New Haven: Yale University Press, 1992), pp. 188-192, 212-219.

70 See Timothy Raylor, *Cavaliers, Clubs and Literary Culture: Sir John Mennes, James Smith and the Order of the Fancy* (Newark, DE: University of Delaware Press, 1994).

71 For an excellent study, see Alastair Bellany, *The Politics of Court Scandal in Early Modern England: News Culture and the Overbury Affair, 1603-1660* (Cambridge: Cambridge University Press, 2002).

72 John Nalson, *An Impartiall Collection of The Great Affairs of State* (1682), vol. II, p. 809. See Harold Weber, *Paper Bullets: Print and Kingship under Charles II* (Lexington: University Press of Kentucky, 1996), especially ch. 4.

73 *Eikon Basilike*, ed. by Philip Knachel (Ithaca: Cornell University Press, 1966); Francis Madan, *A New Bibliography of the Eikon Basilike of King Charles the First,* Oxford Bibliographical Society, 3 (Oxford: Oxford University Press, 1950).

74 See Jane Roberts, *The King's Head: Charles I, King and Martyr* (London: The Royal Collection, 1999).

75 Kevin Sharpe, 'An Image Doting Rabble?: The Failure of Republican Culture in Seventeenth-Century England', in *Refiguring Revolutions: Aesthetics and Politics from the English Revolution to the Romantic Revolution,* ed. by Kevin Sharpe and Steven Zwicker (Los Angeles and London: University of California Press, 1998), pp. 25-56.

76 Eleanor Curran, 'A Very Peculiar Royalist: Hobbes in the Context of his Political Contemporaries', *British Journal for the History of Philosophy,* 10 (2002): 167-208; Jon Parkin, 'Taming the Leviathan: Reading Hobbes in Seventeenth-century Europe', *International Archives of the History of Ideas,* 186 (2003): 31-52. See also the collection of *Early Responses to Hobbes,* ed. by G.A.J. Rogers, 6 vols (London: Routledge and Thoemmes Press, 1996).

77 T. Reeve, *England's Beauty* (1661), p. 34.

78 Benjamin Calamy, *A Sermon Preached Before the Lord Mayor, Aldermen, and Citizens of London at Bow-Church on the 29th of May 1682* (1682), p. 18.

79 Paul Lathom, *The Power of Kings from God: A Sermon Preached in the Cathedral Church of Sarum the XXIX day of June, 1683* (1683), p. 16.

80 Steven Pincus, '"Coffee Politicians Does Create": Coffee-houses and Restoration Political Culture', *Journal of Modern History,* 67 (1995): 807-834; Weber, *Paper Bullets.*

81 Edmund Hickeringill, *The History of Whiggism* (1682), p. 6.

82 Ronald Hutton, *Charles II* (Oxford: Clarendon Press, 1989), pp. 134, 403.

83 Ibid., pp. 359, 421.

84 Ibid., p. 234.

85 See Kevin Sharpe, '"Thy Longing Country's Darling and Desire": Aesthetics, Sex and Politics in the England of Charles II', in *Portraits, Politics, and Women at the Restoration Court,* ed. by Catharine MacLeod and Julia Marciari Alexander (New Haven: Yale University Press for the Yale Center for British Art and Paul Mellon Centre for Studies in British Art, forthcoming).

86 Ibid., passim.

87 See, for example, *A Collection of 86 Loyal Poems* (1683); N. Thompson, *A Choice Collection of 120 Loyal Songs, All of Them Written Since the Two Late Plots* (1684); *A Choice Collection of 180 Loyal Songs All of Them Written Since the Two Late Plots* (1685).

88 Jonathan C.D. Clark, *English Society, 1688-1832: Ideology, Social Structure and Political Practice during the Ancien Regime* (Cambridge: Cambridge University Press, 1985).

89 Edward Gregg, *Queen Anne* (1980; New Haven, Yale University Press, 2001), pp. 147-148; Toni Bowers, 'Queen Anne Makes Provision', in *Refiguring Revolutions,* ed. by Sharpe and Zwicker, p. 67.

90 Ibid.; see Simon Schama, 'The Domestication of Majesty: Royal Family Portraiture, 1500-1800', in *Art and History: Images and Their Meaning,* ed. by Robert Rotberg and Theodore Rabb (Cambridge: Cambridge University Press, 1988), pp. 155-183.

91 See Peter Gay, *Freud for Historians* (New York: Oxford University Press, 1985); Bruce Mazlish, *The Leader, the Led and the Psyche* (Hanover: Wesleyan University Press, 1990). For excellent examples, see Lynn Hunt, *The Family Romance of the French Revolution* (Berkeley: University of California Press, 1992), especially chs. 1 and 2; and Jay Fleigelman, *Prodigals and Pilgrims: The American Revolution against Patriarchal Authority, 1750-1800* (Cambridge: Cambridge University Press, 1982).

Jacobs, King for a Day

1 Sandra Billington, *Mock Kings in Medieval Society and Renaissance Drama* (Oxford: Clarendon Press, 1991), p. 3.

2 Arnold van Gennep, *Les Rites de passage* (1929; Paris: Mouton, 1969); Victor Turner, 'Liminality and the Performative Genres', in *Rite, Drama, Festival, Spectacle. Rehearsals Toward a Theory of Cultural Performance*, ed. John MacAloon (Philadelphia: Institute for the Study of Human Issues, 1984), pp. 19-41.

3 Victor Turner, *The Ritual Process: Structure and Anti-Structure* (Chicago: Aldine Publishing Company, 1969); and Idem, *Dramas, Fields, and Metaphors: Symbolic Action in Human Society* (Ithaca, N.Y.: Cornell University Press, 1974).

4 One of the most famous examples is Natalie Zemon Davis, 'The Reasons of Misrule: Youth Groups and Charivari in Sixteenth-Century France', *Past and Present*, 50 (1971): 41-75.

5 Tacitus, *The Annals*, XIII.15, 2-3, ed. and. trans. by John Jackson, The Loeb Classical Library. Tacitus, 4 (London and Cambridge: Heinemann and Harvard University Press, 1962), p. 24: 'Festis Saturno diebus inter alia aequalium ludicra regnum lusu sortientium evenerat ea sors Neroni. Igitur ceteris diversa nec ruborem adlatura: ubi Britannico iussit exsurgeret progressusque in medium cantum aliquem inciperet, inrisum ex eo sperans pueri sobrios quoque convictus, nedum temulentos ignorantis, ille constanter exorsus est carmen, quo evolutum eum sede patria rebusque summis significabatur. Unde orta miseratio, manifestior quia dissimulationem nox et lascivia exemerat. Nero intellecta invidia odium intendit.' For the English translation, see Shadi Bartsch, *Actors in the Audience. Theatricality and Doublespeak from Nero to Hadrian* (Harvard: Harvard University Press, 1998), p. 14.

6 Bartsch, *Actors in the Audience*, pp. 23-24; James Scott, *Dominance and the Arts of Resistance. Hidden Transcripts* (London: Yale University Press, 1990).

7 The importance of mobilizing other 'worlds' in 'situations' is elaborated in Luc Boltanski and Laurent Thévenot, *De la Justification. Les économies de la grandeur* (Paris: Gallimard, 1991); see Marc Jacobs, 'Actornetwerk. Geschiedenis, sociale wetenschappen. De nieuwe Annales en het werk van Boltanski en Thévenot: een (re)view-artikel', *Tijdschrift voor sociale geschiedenis*, 22 (1996): 260-289.

8 Anne-Marie Le Bourg-Oulé, *Roi d'un jour. Les métamorphoses d'un rêve dans le théâtre européen* (Paris: Albin Michel, 1996), pp. 87-101.

9 See Ronald Hutton, *The Stations of the Sun. A History of the Ritual Year in Britain* (Oxford: Oxford University Press 1996), pp. 1-3.

10 Ibid., *passim*; and Richard Trexler, *The Journey of the Magi. Meanings in History of a Christian Story* (Princeton: Princeton University Press, 1997). One interesting detail I wish to pick out is that the first carved or drawn early Christian representations shows the magi wearing Phrygian red bonnets. See Trexler, *The Journey of the Magi*, pp. 31-32 and Figure 1.

11 Ibid., pp. 78-87.

12 Ibid., pp. 92 and 87.

13 Hutton, *The Stations*, pp. 99-104; Anke Van Wagenberg-Ter Hoeven, *Het Driekoningenfeest. De uitbeelding van een populair thema in de beeldende kunst van de zeventiende eeuw* (Amsterdam: Meertens Instituut, 1997), pp. 16-19.

14 Billington, *Mock Kings*, p. 93.

15 Gilles Li Muisis, *Tractatus tertius*, ed. by Joseph Jean De Smet, in *Recueil des chroniques de Flandre* (Brussels: Commission Royale d'Histoire, 1841), II, pp. 170-171: 'Anno MCCLXXXII, secundum consuetudinem ab antiquo approbatam, cives et filii civium divitum concorditer unam rotundam tabulam concordarunt, et regem elegerunt, et fuit rex electus Johannes, dictus Li Dans.' See Van Wagenberg-Ter Hoeven, *Het Driekoningenfeest*, p. 24, note 51.

16 It evolved to objects in porcelain, in the nineteenth century, or plastics, in the twentieth, and subsequently became a collector's item. See *La phabophilie. Site spécialisé consacré aux fèves anciennes et publicitaires* http://www.fabophilie.com/ [accessed December 2005].

17 Billington, *Mock Kings, passim*.

18 Herman Pleij, *De sneeuwpoppen van 1511. Stadscultuur in de late middeleeuwen* (Amsterdam: Meulenhoff, 1988), pp. 45-54, 73-74.

19 See Trexler, *The Journey of the Magi*, pp. 124-157, esp. 136.

20 The oldest king's letters in the Netherlands are dated from 1577, in Bruges. See, on Bruges, with many examples: Willy L. Braekman, 'Driekoningenavond: koningsbrieven, liederen en gedichten', *Volkskunde*, 98 (1997): 1-40, esp. pp. 18-19; and Van Wagenberg-Ter Hoeven, *Het Driekoningenfeest*, p. 30 and *passim*.

21 Van Wagenberg-Ter Hoeven, *Het Driekoningenfeest*, p. 30.

22 Alfons Thijs, 'Private en openbare feesten: communicatie, educatie en omgaan met macht (Vlaanderen en Brabant, 16de-midden 19de eeuw)', *Volkskunde*, 101 (2000): 81-146, especially 89-90, where sales figures of 6000 copies are mentioned for the Ghent printer Bernard Poelman in 1786, 1787 and 1788.

23 Van Wagenberg-Ter Hoeven, *Het Driekoningenfeest*, p. 35.

24 Le Bourg-Oulé, *Roi d'un jour*, pp. 143-170, 197-200, and 212.

25 Brennan C. Pursell, *The Winter King: Frederick V of the Palatine and the Coming of the Thirty Years' War* (Burlington: Ashgate, 2003).

26 See Elmers A. Beller, *Caricatures of the Winter King of Bohemia* (Oxford: Oxford University Press, 1928).

27 See, along with the study of Maurits Sabbe, *Brabant in 't verweer. Bijdrage tot de studie der Zuid-Nederlandsche strijdliteratuur in de eerste helft der 17e eeuw* (Antwerp: Resseler, 1933); Frances Yates, *The Rosicrucian Enlightenment* (London and New York: Routledge, 1972), p. 22.

28 Braekman, 'Driekoningenavond', pp. 20-23: Abraham Verhoeven also had at least three types of kings' letters in his printing shop. See also Kristin van Damme and Jeroen Deploige, '"Slecht nieuws, geen nieuws." Abraham Verhoeven (1575-1652) en de Nieuwe Tijdinghen: periodieke pers en propaganda in de Zuidelijke Nederlanden tijdens de vroege zeventiende eeuw', *Bijdragen en Mededelingen betreffende de Geschiedenis der Nederlanden*, 113 (1998): 1-22.

29 Sabbe, *Brabant*, pp. 69-70 and the full text on pp. 413-420, for example on p. 419: 'Ministres & senieurs/de He[i]delberg & ailleurs,/N'est il pas chez vous caché?/Ne l'avez pas logé,/Pour chanter comme on souloit/au jour des Roys, le Roy boit.'

30 See the whole text in Sabbe, *Brabant*, pp. 424-426.

31 See the interesting example in Ibid., pp. 98-99.

32 Ibid., pp. 101-108, in particular p. 107.

33 Yates, *The Rosicrucian Enlightenment*, p. 76 (see also pp. 22 and 73-81).

34 Trexler, *The Journey of the Magi*, p. 163.

35 Braekman, 'Driekoningenavond', pp. 20-23, with many references to and reproductions of the kings' letters about Emperor Leopold I (1658-1705).

36 Willem Langeveld, *Politiek per prent. Een inleiding tot de politieke beeldcommunicatie* (Baarn: Ambo, 1989), pp. 47 and 121.

37 Van Wagenberg-Ter Hoeven, *Het Driekoningenfeest*, pp. 201-209.

38 Trexler, *The Journey of the Magi*, p. 179.

39 For example in Sint-Sebastiaan in Haacht, Willy Braekman, *Hier heb ik weer wat nieuws in d'hand. Marktliederen, Rolzangers en Volkse Poëzie van Weleer* (Gent: Stichting Mens en Kultuur, 1990), pp. 468-470.

40 Robert Muchembled, *La violence au village (XVe-XVIIe siècle)* (Turnhout: Brepols, 1989), pp. 356-357.

41 Karen Van Honacker, *Lokaal verzet en oproer in de 17de en 18de eeuw. Collectieve acties tegen het centraal gezag in Brussel, Antwerpen en Leuven* (Kortrijk-Heule: UGA, 1994), pp. 126-128.

42 Trexler, *The Journey of the Magi*, p. 158.

43 See *Œuvres complètes de Voltaire, Tome septième* (Paris: Librairie Hachette, 1876), p. 334 (L'épiphanie de 1741).

44 Paul Downes, *Democracy, Revolution and Monarchism in Early American Literature* (Cambridge: Cambridge University Press, 2002), p. 42.

45 Braekman, 'Driekoningenavond', pp. 24-26.

46 Nicholas Davis, '"His Majesty shall have tribute of me": The King Game in England', in

Between Folk and Liturgy, ed. by Alan Fletcher and Wim Hüsken (Amsterdam and Atlanta: Rodopi, 1997), pp. 97-108. In the early seventeenth century, Captain Robert Dover dressed in cast-off clothes of James I to preside over games in the Cotswolds. This illustrates not an intention to mock the absent (real) king but more the connection between the claim for authority in play and the (example of) royal power.

47 Julio Caro Baroja, *Le Carnaval* (Paris: Gallimard, 1979), pp. 326-327. For examples in France and Italy, see Trexler, *The Journey of the Magi*, pp. 168-169.

48 Hutton, *The Stations of the Sun*, pp. 15-16.

49 Ibid., pp. 102-104.

50 Ibid., p. 106.

51 Billington, *Mock Kings*, p. 95; and John Guy, *Queen of Scots: The True Life of Mary Stuart* (New York: Houghton Mifflin Books, 2004), p. 147.

52 Hutton, *The Stations of the Sun*, pp. 106-107. But see Billington, *Mock Kings*, p. 95, with the story that George Buchanan was appalled by the freedom with the signature of James VI in the 1580s: 'As a lesson, he presented him with a paper which formally transferred regal authority to Buchanan for fifteen days. James signed without reading it, and was treated to Buchanan's imitation of himself.'

53 Ronald Hutton, *The Rise and Fall of Merry England. The Ritual Year 1400-1700* (Oxford: Oxford University Press, 2005), p. 60.

54 Hutton, *The Stations of the Sun,* p. 109.

55 Ibid., p. 110.

56 Van Wagenberg-Ter Hoeven, *Het Driekoningenfeest*, p. 54.

57 Ibid, p. 62.

58 See also Jean-Baptiste Bullet, 'Du festin du Roi-Boit', in *Collection des meilleurs dissertations, notices et traités particuliers relatifs à l'histoire de France, tome dixième,* ed. by C. Leber (Paris: G.-A. Dent, 1838), pp. 36-53 (anastatic reprint on http://gallica.bnf.fr).

59 Baroja, *Carnaval,* p. 329, note 12.

60 In his famous report about monuments and vandalism in 1794, Abbé Grégoire mentions how he witnessed that in Blois a statue of Louis XII was smashed and thrown in the Loire, to the repeated cries '*Le roi boit!*'. Grégoire subsequently pleaded for saving heritage but removing the active royalist signs: the heritage paradigm was born. Henri Grégoire, *Rapport sur les inscriptions des monumens publics: séance du 22 nivôse, l'an II de la République* (Paris: Imprimerie national, 1794), p. 14 (anastatic reprint on http://gallica.bnf.fr); Alyssa Goldstein Sepinvall, *Abbé Grégoire and the French Revolution* (Berkeley: University of California Press, 2005), p. 135.

61 François-Alphonse Aulard, *Mémoires de Chaumette sur la Révolution du 10 août 1792 avec une introduction et des notes* (Paris: Société de l'histoire de la Révolution française, 1893), pp. 15-16 (anastatic reprint on http://gallica.bnf.fr). English translation: 'They gave a big stroke of an axe on another door. Louis XVI himself commanded to open it and started to sway his hat through the air while crying with all his forces: "Long lives the nation" [...] In a twinkling of the eye, the hall was filled with men armed with lances, scythes, sticks enhanced with knives, saws, guns, forks, etc. They put the tables of the Declaration of Human Rights in front of the King. He became baffled and tried to move again in order to recover. Then, there was but a cry: "Approve," they said, "approve the decrees which must save France, reinstall the patriotic ministers, banish your priests, and choose between Coblenz and Paris". The king extended his hand first to one and then to another, continuously shaking his hat. Finally, having discovered a red bonnet in the hands of a citizen, he covered his head with it, and then started to drink a whole bottle "to the health of the sans-culottes", who cried in turn "the king drinks!" He promised everything that the citizens asked. Then, they emptied the apartments bit by bit. [...] Finally, at ten o'clock in the evening, everything was evacuated, and Paris found itself in the greatest calm.'

62 In Bordeaux in 1792 a counsellor tried to suppress the pastrymakers' custom of baking and selling 'gateaux des rois' on Epiphany as this was not compatible with the republican spirit. The city canalized this by introducing new names: 'cakes of liberty' and 'la fête des Sans-culottes'; see Trexler, *The Journey of the Magi*, p. 185.

63 'Corps administratifs, Commune de Paris, séance du 17 Nivôse, l'an 2 de la République', *Gazette des tribunaux et mémorial des corps administratifs et municipaux* (1794): 245-247.

64 The custom was reintroduced two decades later at a royal French court. Significant was Epiphany 1820 in the Tuileries with the members of the royal family. The fact that the Duc d'Orleans was the Bean King that year was later interpreted as an omen for his rise to power in 1830 as the Bourgeois King. See Jean-Baptiste Nervo et al., *Les finances françaises sous la Restauration, 1814-1830* (Paris: Michel-Lévy frères, 1865-1868), I, p. 408 (anastatic reprint on http://gallica.bnf.fr).

Graham, Fiction, Kingship, and the Politics of Character

This article contains research generously supported by the American Council of Learned Societies, the National Humanities Center, and Haverford College. I would also like to thank the editors of this volume for their many and incisive comments.

1 Important studies of the relationship between literature and politics in seventeenth-century France include Joan DeJean, *Tender Geographies: Women and the Origins of the Novel in France* (New York: Columbia University Press, 1991); Christian Jouhaud, *Les Pouvoirs de la littérature: Histoire d'un paradoxe* (Paris: Gallimard, 2000); Hélène Merlin, *Public et littérature en France au XVIIe siècle* (Paris: Belles Lettres, 1994); and Alain Viala, *Naissance de l'écrivain. Sociologie de la littérature à l'âge classique* (Paris: Editions de Minuit, 1985). Gregory Brown evaluates the role of censorship and the social identity of authors in the eighteenth century; see his 'Reconsidering the Censorship of Writers in Eighteenth-Century France: Civility, State Power, and the Public Theater in the Enlightenment', *Journal of Modern History* 75 (2003): 235-268. The theoretical inspiration for much of this early modern work is Bourdieu's account of the emergence of an autonomous literary field in France in the second half of the nineteenth century. See Pierre Bourdieu, *Les règles de l'art: genèse et structure du champ littéraire* (Paris: Editions du Seuil, 1992).

2 On sixteenth-century resistance literature, see *Constitutionalism and Resistance in the Sixteenth Century: Three Treatises*, trans. and ed. by Julian H. Franklin (New York: Pegasus, 1969). On the pamphlet wars during the Fronde, see Christian Jouhaud, *Mazarinades: La Fronde des mots* (Paris: Aubier, 1985); and Jeffrey Merrick, 'The Cardinal and the Queen: Sexual and Political Disorders in the Mazarinades', *French Historical Studies* 18 (1994): 667-699.

3 For an overview of the 'mirror of princes' genre in the Renaissance, see Quentin Skinner, *The Foundations of Early Modern Political Thought*, vol. 1: *The Renaissance* (Cambridge: Cambridge University Press, 1978), pp. 116-128 and 213-243. Renaissance scholars were inspired by their medieval predecessors, such as Sedulius Scottus, *On Christian Rulers and The Poems* (Binghamton: State University of New York Press, 1983). For two French examples, see Régine Lambrech, 'Charlemagne and his Influence on Late Medieval French Kings' *Journal of Medieval History* 14:4 (1988): 283-291; and Lydwine Scordia, 'Le roi, l'or et le sang des pauvres dans *Le livre de l'information des princes*, miroir anonyme dédié à Louis X', *Revue historique* 306:3 (2004): 507-532.

4 For a discussion of La Bruyère's project, see the preface by Louis Van Delft to his edition of *Les Caractères* (Paris: Imprimerie Nationale, 1998), pp. 7-44. Amélie Oksenberg Rorty analyses the evolution of the genre in 'Characters, Persons, Selves, and Individuals', in *Theory of the Novel: A Historical Approach*, ed. by Michael McKeon (Baltimore and London: The Johns Hopkins University Press, 2000), pp. 537-553.

5 Extensive work exists on this topic; see Jean Marie Apostolidès, *Le roi-machine: spectacle et politique au temps de Louis XIV* (Paris: Les Editions de Minuit, 1981); Peter Burke, *The Fabrication of Louis XIV* (New Haven: Yale University Press, 1992); Louis Marin, *Le portrait du roi* (Paris: Editions de Minuit, 1981); and Orest Ranum, *Artisans of Glory: Writers and Historical Thought in Seventeenth-Century France* (Chapel Hill: University of North Carolina Press, 1980). For opposition to the monarchy, see Arlette Farge, *Dire et mal dire. L'opinion publique au XVIIIe siècle* (Paris: Seuil, 1992); and Jeffrey Sawyer, *Printed Poison: Pamphlet Propaganda, Faction Politics, and the Public Sphere in Seventeenth-Century France* (Berkeley: University of California Press, 1990).

6   Sylvana Tomaselli, 'The Death and Rebirth of Character in the Eighteenth Century', in *Rewriting the Self: Histories from the Renaissance to the Present*, ed. by Roy Porter (New York: Routledge, 1997), pp. 84-96. Joan DeJean discusses the breakdown of the self in *Ancients against Moderns: Culture Wars and the Making of a Fin de Siècle* (Chicago and London: University of Chicago Press, 1997), pp. 78-122.

7   Françoise Weil, *L'interdiction du roman et la librairie, 1728-1750* (Paris: Aux Amateurs de Livre, 1986), pp. 137 and 151.

8   Marquis d'Argens, Letter XXXV from *The Jewish Spy* (1744), in *The Augustan Reprint Society*, vol. 32: *Prefaces to Fiction* (Los Angeles: William Andrews Clark Memorial Library, 1952).

9   For a discussion of how royal ceremonies presented the king to the court and the public, see Apostolidès, *Le roi-machine*, pp. 93-113; Arlette Farge, *La vie fragile. Violence, pouvoir et solidarités à Paris au XVIIIe siècle* (Paris: Hachette, 1986), pp. 201-258; and Michèle Fogel, *Les cérémonies de l'information* (Paris: Fayard, 1989).

10 I am drawing on Bakhtin's theory of the novel and the role of parody; see Mikhail Bakhtin, *The Dialogic Imagination*, ed. by Michael Holquist, trans. by Caryl Emerson and Michael Holquist (Austin: University of Texas Press, 1981), p. 23.

11 Bakhtin, *The Dialogic Imagination*, p. 338. Vivian Gruder frames her analysis of pre-revolutionary pamphlet literature and the image of Marie Antoinette in similar terms, although she extends her criticism of recent historiography of the queen in different directions. See Vivian R. Gruder, 'The Question of Marie Antoinette: The Queen and Public Opinion before the Revolution', *French History* 16:3 (2002): 269-298.

12 Michel de Certeau, 'Reading as Poaching', in *The Practice of Everyday Life*, trans. by Steven Rendell (Berkeley: University of California Press, 1984), I, p. 167.

13 Certeau, 'Reading as Poaching', p. 170. Carlo Ginzburg develops the notion of 'a reading filter' in his analysis of the sixteenth-century miller, Menocchio; see *The Cheese and the Worms*, trans. by John and Anne Tedeschi (Baltimore: Johns Hopkins University Press, 1980).

14 Robert Darnton, *The Forbidden Best-Sellers of Pre-Revolutionary France* (New York: Norton, 1995), p. 189. Darnton has recently turned his attention to 'mixed media' in the eighteenth century, including gossip and song, to extend this argument; see 'The News In Paris: An Early Information Society', in *George Washington's False Teeth: An Unconventional Guide to the Eighteenth Century* (New York: Norton, 2003), pp. 25-75; esp. 35-39.

15 *Testament Politique de Richelieu*, ed. by Françoise Hildesheimer (Paris: Société de l'Histoire de France, 1995), p. 287. 'A good reputation is especially necessary to a prince for if we hold him in high regard he can accomplish more with his name alone than a less well esteemed ruler can with great armies at his command. It is imperative that he guard it above life itself, and it is better to risk fortune and grandeur than to allow the slightest blemish to fall upon it [...]', in *The Political Testament of Cardinal Richelieu*, trans. by Henry Betram Hill (Madison: University of Wisconsin Press, 1961), p. 119.

16 See the chapter entitled, 'How a Ruler Should Act in Order to Gain Reputation', in Machiavelli, *The Prince*, ed. by Quentin Skinner and Russell Price (Cambridge: Cambridge University Press, 1988), pp. 76-80.

17 See Richelieu's assessment of Louix XIII's character in Part I, ch. 6: *Qui représente au Roy ce qu'on estime qu'il doit considérer à l'esgard de sa personne* in *Testament Politique*, pp. 192-196.

18 *Testament politique*, p. 242. In English: 'the living law speaking and ruling with more efficacy than all those edicts which might be promulgated to make people seek the good ends desired' (*The Political Testament*, p. 68).

19 *Testament Politique*, p. 196. In English: 'The blows from a sword are easily healed. But it is not the same with blows of the tongue especially if they be from the tongue of a king' (*Political Testament*, p. 41).

20 *Testament Politique*, pp. 197-198. In English: 'Good sense requires that they also close their ears to slander and false information, pursuing and even banishing the authors as most dangerous plagues, often capable of poisoning the hearts of princes, as well as the minds of those who approach them' (*Political Testament*, p. 43).

21 For a discussion of the Academie's place in absolutist culture, see Apostolidès, *Le roi-machine*,

pp. 31-37. Also see Hélène Merlin-Kajman, *L'Excentricité académique: Littérature, institution, société* (Paris: Les Belles Lettres, 2001); and Orest Ranum, *Paris in the Age of Absolutism* (University Park: Penn State University Press, 2002, 2nd rev. ed.).

22 On *lèse-majesté*, see William F. Church, *Richelieu and Reason of State* (Princeton: Princeton University Press, 1972); Lisa Jane Graham, *If the King Only Knew: Seditious Speech in the Reign of Louis XV* (Charlottesville: University of Virginia Press, 2000), pp. 206-208; Orest Ranum, 'Lèse-Majesté Divine: Transgressing Boundaries in Thought and Action in Mid-Seventeenth-Century France', *Proceedings of the Ninth Annual Meeting of the Western Society for French History*, 9 (1982): 68-80; and Alfred Soman, 'Press, Pulpit, and Censorship in France before Richelieu', *Proceedings of the American Philosophical Society*, 120: 6 (1976): 439-463.

23 Montesquieu, *Lettres Persanes*, ed. by Jacques Roger (Paris: Garnier, 1964), p. 173. For an English translation, see *The Persian Letters*, trans. by George R. Healy (Indianapolis and Cambridge: Hackett, 1999), Letter CVII, 179: 'It is said that the character of Western kings can never be known until they have passed the two great tests: selection of their mistress and their confessor. We will soon see both work to capture the mind of this one, and the struggles will be great. For under a young prince these two powers are always rivals, though they become reconciled and allies under an old man.'

24 Bibliothèque de l'Arsenal (hereafter BA), Archives de la Bastille (hereafter AB) 10167, fol. 99v. Unless otherwise indicated, English translations of the original French text are my own: 'The public is talking about a small booklet that is circulating, produced in response to the distractions that the king seeks in his private apartments, people claim that the author is especially impudent because he depicts the king and his favorites in an unflattering light, that he can have no other purpose than to render His Majesty despicable not only before his subjects but also in the eyes of all foreigners into whose hands this booklet happens to fall.'

25 For a discussion of the debates surrounding the novel, see Joan DeJean, *Tender Geographies: Women and the Origins of the Novel in France* (New York: Columbia University Press, 1991); and Georges May, *Le Dilemme du roman au XVIIIeme siècle* (New Haven: Yale University Press, 1963).

26 Claude Crébillon, *Les Égarements du cœur et de l'esprit*, in *Œuvres complètes*, ed. by Jean Sgard (Paris: Garnier, 2000), II, p. 69. For an English translation, see *The Wayward Head and Heart* in *The Libertine Reader: Eroticism and Enlightenment in Eighteenth-Century France*, ed. by Michel Feher (New York: Zone Books, 1997), p. 768: 'Events artfully invented would be naturally expressed. There would be no more sinning against propriety and reason. Sentiment would not be exaggerated; man would at last see himself as he is. He would be dazzled less, but instructed more.'

27 DeJean, *Ancients against Moderns*, pp. 78-123.

28 Darnton, *George Washington's False Teeth*, p. 49.

29 In addition to the four novels I discuss in this article, I have identified other titles that discuss the king and current affairs in this allegorical genre. These include Godard d'Aucour, *Bien-Aimé* (1744); Antoine Pecquet, *Mémoires secrets pour servir à l'histoire de Perse* (1745); Louis de Boissy, *Les filles femmes* (1751); and Marie-Antoinette Fagnan, *Kanor* (1750).

30 For a discussion of censorship and the attack on the novel in the early eighteenth century, see Georges May, *Le Dilemme du roman au XVIIIe siècle*; Georges Minois, *Censure et culture sous l'Ancien Régime* (Paris: Fayard, 1995), pp. 181-230; Daniel Roche, 'La police du livre', in *Histoire de l'édition française*, ed. by Roger Chartier and Henri-Jean Martin (Paris: Fayard, 1984), II, pp. 88-110; and Françoise Weil, *L'Interdiction du roman et la librairie, 1728-1750* (Paris: Aux Amateurs de Livres, 1986).

31 See the reports from Bonnin and La Marche to Marville from 1746 to 1749 in AB 10300. They alerted him to *Les Bijoux indiscrets*. The same dossier contains reports on *Tanastès* and *Zéokinizul*.

32 See Marie Bonafon's prefatory remarks to part two of *Tanastès* where she writes: 'Je dois avertir aussi que l'imprimeur a mis des notes mal-à-propos, telle que l'indication qu'il veut donner de plusieurs personnages, qui est absolument fausse'; and Crébillon, *Les égarements du cœur et de l'esprit*, p. 66.

33 For information on Marie Bonafon and the *Tanastès* affair, see AB 11582. I discuss this case at length in my book, *If the King Only Knew*, pp. 56-95.

34 AB 11733, f. 96. Letter from Rességuier dated 25 January 1751. 'I adored the king, I admired his virtues, and yet I dared to direct my satirical scribbling at him.'

35 Both the Bibliothèque Nationale de France and Bibliothèque de l'Arsenal have copies of *Tanastès*. Bonafon's name does not appear on the title page; see *Tanastès. Conte allégorique* (1745).

36 *Tanastès*, p. 44. 'a king is not made to be victim of the laws he imposes on others'.

37 *Tanastès*, p. 155. 'This ambiguous character, combining the good and the bad was fashionable at the time; thus after considerable agitations, he got off with putting himself on the level of ordinary men.'

38 For a discussion of George III, see John Barrell, 'Sad Stories: Louis XVI, George III, and the Language of Sentiment', in *Refiguring Revolutions: Aesthetics and Politics from the English Revolution to the Romantic Revolution*, ed. by Kevin Sharpe and Steven N. Zwicker (Berkeley: University of California Press, 1998), pp. 75-98.

39 AB 11582, fol. 20.

40 AB 11733, fol. 2: '... insulting to the King, the Marquise de Pompadour, and the ministers.'

41 There are copies of Rességuier's novel at the Bibliothèque Nationale de France and the Bibliothèque de l'Arsenal. I have used the copy at the Arsenal. Rességuier's name does not appear on the title page. See *Voyage d'Amatonthe* (1750).

42 See Rességuier's *avertissement* to the *Voyage d'Amatonthe*: 'to depict vice and not the vicious.'

43 *Voyage d'Amatonthe*, p. 8. 'a sweet and loveable figure, in whom virtue, wisdom, cheerfulness were equally displayed.'

44 For the manuscript version, I have consulted the copy of Rességuier's novel at the Bibliothèque de l'Arsenal (BA MS 6104), as well as the papers seized during his arrest and placed in his dossier; see AB 11733.

45 MS 6104, fol. 1. 'The Prince [...] governs his peoples gently, he has all of the qualities that the throne requires. They adore him in Amatonthe. Perhaps he will be worthy of these sentiments, if he applies the talents with which he is endowed to better ends; but no mortal is exempt from weakness: the passions trouble the hearts of kings like those of the lowest of men.'

46 BA, MS 6104, fol. 10.

47 AB 11733, 52.

48 For information on Crébillon's arrest in 1734, see AB 11509, fols. 227-232. For a discussion of the novel's publishing history, see the introduction by Simon F. Davies in Claude Crébillon, *Œuvres complètes*, ed. by Jean Sgard (Paris: Garnier, 1999), I, 449-450.

49 Claude Crébillon, *Les Amours de Zéokinizul*, in *Œuvres complètes*, I, p. 508. 'The idea of a cherished rival failed to rid him of the hope of being happy and since a king makes love thoroughly differently than a subject, far from making his mistress forget the young duke with his concern and tender attentions, he wanted to use his authority to send the duke away from her on an honorable pretext.'

50 *Les Amours de Zéokinizul*, p. 509. 'in matters of love a crown should have no weight [...] a true mistress should attach herself by the heart.'

51 *Les Amours de Zéokinizul*, p. 511. 'Your Majesty can only offer me guilty wishes, and I would perish rather than satisfy them.'

52 *Les Amours de Zéokinizul*, p. 512. 'his disobedience to his orders provided a plausible pretext for killing him, and already this cruel resolution was taking hold of his heart.'

53 I refer to the following edition of the novel: Denis Diderot, *Les Bijoux indiscrets*, ed. by Jacques Rustin (Paris: Gallimard, 1981). Rustin uses the 1798 edition published by Naigeon, which includes three additional chapters (16, 18 and 19) that Diderot added after the 1748 edition. I have omitted these chapters from my analysis because readers would not have seen them in 1748. I have used this edition because it is readily available and is considered the standard text. The 1748 edition forms the basis of the Hermann edition; see Diderot, *Œuvres complètes*, ed. by Jean Macary, Aram Vartanian and Jean-Louis Leutrat (Paris: Hermann, 1978), vol. 3.

54 For a political analysis of the novel, see Aram Vartanian, 'The Politics of the *Bijoux Indiscrets*', in *Enlightenment Studies in Honour of Lester G. Crocker*, ed. by Alfred J. Bingham and Virgil W. Topazio (Oxford: The Voltaire Foundation, 1979), pp. 349-376.

55 The inventory of her library suggests that Pompadour enjoyed novels and made a point of collecting them, see *Catalogue des Livres de la Bibliothèque de feue Madame la Marquise de Pompadour*, ed. by Jean-Thomas Hérissant Des Carrières (Paris, 1765).

56 Diderot, *Les Bijoux indiscrets*, p. 43. For an English translation, see *The Indiscreet Jewels* in *The Libertine Reader: Eroticism and Enlightenment in Eighteenth-Century France*, ed. by Michel Feher (New York: Zone Books, 1997), pp. 333-542. 'What a good Sultan was he! His equal was nowhere to be found, except in certain French novels', p. 350.

57 Diderot, *Les Bijoux indiscrets*, p. 47. In English: 'To procure some pleasure at the expense of the ladies of my court... For them to tell me of their amorous adventures past and present, no more', p. 353.

58 On the links between forced confessions and despotism in the novel, see Anthony Wall, 'Le bavardage du corps ou *Les Bijoux indiscrets* de Denis Diderot', in *Neophilologus*, 78 (1994): 351-60.

59 Diderot, *Les Bijoux indiscrets*, p. 48. In English: 'Put your secret to good use, and remember that curiosity can be misdirected', p. 354.

60 Diderot's narrative technique has received considerable scholarly attention, but for the purposes of this article, I have found the following useful: Irwin L. Greenberg, 'Narrative Technique and Literary Intent in Diderot's *Les Bijoux indiscrets* and *Jacques le fataliste*', *Studies on Voltaire and the Eighteenth Century* (Oxford: The Voltaire Foundation, 1971), LXXIX, pp. 93-101; Thomas M. Kavanagh, 'Language as Deception: Diderot's *Les Bijoux indiscrets*', *Diderot Studies XXIII*, ed. by Otis Fellow and Diana Guiragossian Carr (Geneva: Droz, 1988), pp. 101-113; and the postface by Jacques Proust to his edition of *Les Bijoux indiscrets* (Paris: Librairie Generale Française, 1972), pp. 341-362.

61 Diderot, *Les Bijoux indiscrets*, p. 55. In English: 'Am I Sultan for nothing?', p. 359.

62 Odile Richard analyses the place of the reader in Diderot's text and the tensions between curiosity and voyeurism; see her '*Les Bijoux indiscrets*: Variation secrète sur un thème libertin', *Recherches sur Diderot et L'Encyclopédie*, 24 (1998): 27-36. Proust also addresses the relationship between knowledge and power in Mangogul's quest; see his postface to *Les Bijoux indiscrets*, pp. 360-362.

63 Diderot, *Les Bijoux indiscrets*, p. 240.

64 I am following Vartanian's analysis; see *The politics of Les Bijoux indiscrets*, p. 358.

65 Diderot, *Les Bijoux indiscrets*, pp. 82-83. In English: 'The Prince, you see, is spoiling things' (378) and 'Quiet, wretch. Show some respect for the powers on earth, and thank the gods for having given you birth [...] under the reign of a prince whose prudence enlightens his ministers, [...] who is feared by his enemies and beloved of his people [...].', p. 379.

66 Diderot, *Les Bijoux indiscrets*, p. 293. In English: 'The African author does not tell us what he had been doing, or how he had spent his time during the preceding chapter. Apparently the princes of the Congo are allowed to do insignificant things, to say silly things, and to resemble other men, who spend a great deal part of life involved in nothing, or at things that are not worth knowing.', p. 524.

67 One could compare the case of fiction to that of Shakespearean theatre, especially *Richard II* and *Henry V*. See Stephen Greenblatt, 'Invisible Bullets: Renaissance Authority and its Subversion, *Henry IV* and *Henry V*', in *Shakespearean Negotiations: The Circulation of Social Energy in Renaissance England* (Berkeley: University of California Press, 1988), pp. 18-47; and Ernst Kantorowicz, *The King's Two Bodies: A Study in Medieval Political Theology* (Princeton: Princeton University Press, 1957), pp. 24-41. For analysis of the impact of print on perceptions of the king in eighteenth-century France, see Roger Chartier, *Les Origines culturelles de la Révolution Française* (Paris: Seuil, 1990), pp. 138-166; Farge, *Dire et mal dire*; and Graham, *If the King Only Knew*. Lynn Hunt focuses on the novel in the pre-revolutionary period; see her *The Family Romance of the French Revolution* (Berkeley: University of California Press, 1992), pp. 17-52.

68 Darnton traces this connection; see his 'The News in Paris: An Early Information Society', in *George Washington's False Teeth*, pp. 49-50.

I would like to thank Siep Stuurman and Coen Tamse for their valuable and inspiring comments.

1   Thomas Paine, *Rights of man* (1791-1792; Harmondsworth: Penguin Books, 1984), part II, ch. 3 'Of the old and new systems of government', p. 182.

2   John Plunkett, *Queen Victoria. First Media Monarch* (Oxford: Oxford University Press, 2003), pp. 7-8.

3   Plunkett, *Queen Victoria*, p. 36.

4   Alison Booth, 'Illustrious Company: Victoria among Other Women in Anglo-American Role Model Anthologies', in *Remaking Queen Victoria,* ed. by Margaret Homans and Adrienne Munich (Cambridge: Cambridge University Press, 1997), pp. 59-78.

5   Maria Grever, 'Matriarch of the Nation. Queen Wilhelmina's Cause', in *Royal Family. Monarchy and Metaphor in European Culture*, ed. by Jo Tollebeek and Tom Verschaffel (Amsterdam: Amsterdam University Press, 2007).

6   Maria Grever, 'Colonial Queens: Imperialism, Gender and the Body Politic During the Reign of Victoria and Wilhelmina', *Dutch Crossing. A Journal of Low Countries Studies* 26:1 (Summer 2002): 99-114 (here p. 100).

7   Eric J. Hobsbawm, *Nations and Nationalism Since 1780. Programme, Myth and Reality* (Cambridge: Cambridge University Press, 1990), p. 84; Hagen Schulze, *States, Nations and Nationalism. From the Middle Ages to the Present* (Oxford: Blackwell Publishers, 1996), pp. 202-203; David Cannadine, 'From Reverence to Rigour. Writing the History of the Modern British Monarchy', *Times Literary Supplement* (23 January 2004), pp. 11-13.

8   Vanessa R. Schwartz, 'Cinematic Spectatorship Before the Apparatus: The Public Taste for Reality in Fin-de-Siecle Paris', in *Cinema and the Invention of Modern Life,* ed. by Leo Charney and Vanessa R. Schwartz (Berkeley: University of California Press, 1995), pp. 297-319, 297.

9   David Cannadine, 'The Context, Performance, and Meaning of Ritual: The British Monarchy and the "Invention of Tradition", c. 1820-1977', in *The Invention of Tradition,* ed. by Eric Hobsbawm and Terence Ranger (Cambridge: Cambridge University Press, 1983), pp. 120-121.

10 Paul Greenhalgh, *Ephemeral Vistas: The* Expositions Universelles, *Great Exhibitions and World's Fairs 1851-1939* (Manchester: Manchester University Press, 1988), pp. 3-26; and Jeffrey A. Auerbach, *The Great Exhibition of 1851. A Nation on Display* (New Haven and London: Yale University Press, 1999), pp. 22-31.

11 Pieter van Wesemael, *Architectuur van instructie en vermaak. Een maatschappijhistorische analyse van de wereldtentoonstelling als didactisch verschijnsel (1798-1851-1970)* (Delft: Technische Universiteit Delft, 1997), pp. 112-113.

12 Greenhalgh, *Ephemeral Vistas*, p. 23.

13 Reinhart Koselleck, *Vergangene Zukunft. Zur Semantik geschichtlicher Zeiten* (Frankfurt am Main: Suhrkamp, 2000), pp. 349-375. For an interpretation of world exhibitions from this theoretical perspective, see Maria Grever, 'Tijd en ruimte onder één dak. De wereldtentoonstelling als verbeelde vooruitgang', in *De ongrijpbare tijd. Temporaliteit en de constructie van het verleden,* ed. by Maria Grever and Harry Jansen (Hilversum: Verloren, 2001), pp. 113-130.

14 Maria Grever and Berteke Waaldijk, *Transforming the Public Sphere. The Dutch National Exhibition of Women's Labor in 1898* (Durham and London: Duke University Press, 2004), pp. 14-15; and Nancy Fraser, 'Rethinking the Public Sphere: A Contribution to the Critique of Actually Existing Democracy', *Social Text* 25/26 (March 1990): 560-581.

15 Auerbach, *The Great Exhibition*, pp. 151-158.

16 Christoph Prochasson, *Paris 1900. Essai d'histoire culturelle* (Paris: Calmann-Lévy, 1999), pp. 140-151.

17 Laura Rabinovitz, *For the Love of Pleasure. Women, Movies, and Culture in Turn-of-the Century Chicago* (New Brunswick: Rutgers University Press, 1998), pp. 178-181.

18 Anne McClintock, *Imperial Leather. Race, Gender and Sexuality in the Colonial Contest* (New York and London: Routledge, 1995), p. 37; and Grever and Waaldijk, *Transforming the Public Sphere*, ch. 4.

19 Robert W. Rydell, *All the World's a Fair: Visions of Empire at American International Expositions, 1876-1916* (Chicago: Chicago University Press, 1984), p. 41; and James Gilbert, *Perfect Cities. Chicago's Utopias of 1893* (Chicago: Chicago University Press, 1991), pp. 65-68.

20 For Walter Bagehot, monarchic theatre was mere theatre, separated from governmental power: *The English Constitution* (London: Henry S. King & Co., 1872), p. 61 (originally published as a series of magazine articles for the *Fortnightly Reviews* in 1866). See Margaret Homans, *Royal Representations, Queen Victoria and British Culture, 1837-1876* (Chicago and London: The University of Chicago Press, 1998), pp. 106-107.

21 Bagehot, *The English Constitution*, p. 64. Italics are mine.

22 'The Queen's Journal, May 1' printed source in Charles H. Gibbs-Smith, *The Great Exhibition of 1851* (London: Her Majesty's Stationery Office, 1951), p. 16.

23 An extensive description of the opening in *Le Palais Crystal. Journal illustré de l'exposition de 1851 et des progrès de l'industrie universelle* (2 May 1851).

24 Quote in Van Wesemael, *Architectuur van instructie en vermaak*, p. 618.

25 Auerbach, *The Great Exhibition of 1851*, p. 61.

26 Tom Nairn, *The Enchanted Glass. Britain and its Monarchy* (London: Hutchinson, 1988), p. 195.

27 Adrienne Munich, *Queen Victoria's Secrets* (New York: Columbia University Press, 1996), pp. 10-11.

28 Margaret Homans, *Royal Representations, Queen Victoria and British Culture, 1837-1876* (Chicago and London: The University of Chicago Press, 1998), pp. 5-6.

29 For this topic, see also Grever, 'Colonial Queens', pp. 103-105.

30 Auerbach, *The Great Exhibition*, p. 152.

31 Auerbach, *The Great Exhibition*, pp. 151-155.

32 *De wereldtentoonstelling van 1878 te Parijs* no. 4, 11 May 1878, p. 74.

33 Auerbach, *The Great Exhibition*, pp. 174-75, 180-185.

34 Grever and Waaldijk, *Transforming the Public Sphere*, ch. 5.

35 Rabinovitz, *For the Love of Pleasure*, pp. 65-66.

36 Description of this incident in *Le Palais de Cristal. Journal illustré de l'exposition de 1851 et des progrès de l'industrie universelle* (Wednesday 7 May 1851). See also Auerbach, *The Great Exhibition*, pp. 178-79.

37 David Cannadine, *Ornamentalism. How the British Saw Their Empire* (London: Penguin Books, 2001), pp. 8-9, 46.

38 Auerbach, *The Great Exhibition*, p. 172.

39 Elizabeth Langland, 'Nation and Nationality: Queen Victoria in the Developing Narrative of Englishness', in *Remaking Queen Victoria*, ed. by Homans and Munich, pp. 13-32, 14.

40 Three previous world fairs had been organized in London 1851, Paris 1855 and London 1862. Brigitte Schroeder-Gudegus and Anne Rasmussen, *Les fastes du progrès. Le guide des Expositions Universelles 1851-1992* (Paris: Flammarion, 1992), p. 76.

41 Adrianus P.J. van Osta, *De Europese monarchie in de negentiende eeuw. Het Britse en Duitse model* (Ph.D. diss., Utrecht University, 1982), pp. 23 and 87.

42 Patricia Mainardi, *Arts and Politics of the Second Empire: The Universal Exhibitions of 1855 and 1867* (New Haven: Yale University Press, 1987).

43 Van Wesemael, *Architectuur van instructie en vermaak*, p. 238.

44 Helped by his Minister of Education Victor Duruy, Napoleon III wrote two volumes on the history of Caesar. See Roger Williams, *The World of Napoleon III 1851-1870* (New York: Collier Books, 1962), pp. 185-87; Eugen Weber, *My France. Politics, Culture and Myth* (Cambridge, Mass., and London: The Belknap Press of Harvard University Press, 1991) p. 31 and p. 37. On the glorification of the military system during the reign of Louis-Napoleon, see Sudhir Hazareesingh, *The Saint-Napoleon. Celebrations of Sovereignty in Nineteenth-Century France* (Cambridge, Mass., and London: Harvard University Press, 2004).

45 Van Wesemael, *Architectuur van instructie en vermaak*, p. 636.

46 Nairn, *The Enchanted Glass*, pp. 41 and 101-102.

47 *Grand Album de l'Exposition Universelle 1867* (Paris: Michel Lévy Frères, 1868), pp. vii-viii, and 100-101, a large engraving of the exposition awards.

48 Van Wesemael, *Architectuur van instructie en vermaak*, pp. 260-62.

49 *Grand Album de l'Exposition Universelle 1867*, engravings of royals on pp. 9, 17, 23, 25, 107, 109 and 111.

50 Martin Malia, *Russia under Western Eyes. From the Bronze Horseman to the Lenin Mausoleum* (Cambridge Mass.: The Belknap Press of Harvard University Press, 1999), p. 9. Quoted in Cannadine, *Ornamentalism*, pp. 8-9, 124.

51 Plunkett, *Queen Victoria*, p. 5.

52 For instance, several engravings that had been published in the *Grand Album de L'Exposition Universelle 1867* popped up in the Dutch journal *De Katholieke Illustratie* of 1867-68. About the influence of engraving techniques, see Marga Altena, *Visuele strategieën. Foto's en films van fabrieksarbeidsters* 1890-1919 (Hilversum: Verloren, 2003), pp. 15 and 47.

53 See also, for observations on royalty, Émile Zola, *Nana*, ed. by Colette Becker (1888; Paris: Dunod, 1994), ch. 3-4.

54 Schwartz, 'Cinematic Spectatorship Before the Apparatus', pp. 297-319.

55 As will be demonstrated by Henk te Velde in the present volume, too easily applying Baghot's ideal of a radical distinction between the dignified and the efficient parts of power, between 'cultural ornaments' and 'real politics', may obscure more than elucidate our understanding of the meaning of politics in the nineteenth century.

56 McClintock, *Imperial Leather*, pp. 368 and 374.

57 McClintock, *Imperial Leather*, pp. 374-75.

58 Nairn, *The Enchanted Glass*, p. 155.

59 *De wereldtentoonstelling van 1878 te Parijs* (11-5-1878) p. 75.

Van Osta, The Emperor's New Clothes

The translation of this article has been made possible in part thanks to a financial contribution from the Vertaalfonds KNAW/Stichting Reprorecht.

1   This family quarrel, the so-called 'Margarita affair', burst out in February 2003 when Princess Margarita de Bourbon de Parme, one of the queen's nieces, and her husband Edwin de Roy van Zuydewijn publicized the feud they had with the royal family. One of their accusations held that Beatrix had gathered information about the princess's future husband all by herself and had spread this information to a third party. In the ensuing parliamentary debate, this appeared to have happened by order of the Queen's cabinet and without the knowledge of the responsible minister. Subsequently, Parliament stipulated in a motion that from now on the Queen's cabinet was to come under full ministerial responsibility.

2   Lorenz von Stein (1815-90) expounded his theory of royalty as a unifying symbol of permanence and national community in his *Geschichte der sozialen Bewegung in Frankreich von 1789 bis auf unsere Tage* (Leipzig, 1850; repr. Munich: Drei Masken Verlag, 1959), esp. III, pp. 14-15 and 36-41. A. C. De Meis (1817-1891)'s passionate appeal to his king to make an indispensable contribution to the process of nation building initially appeared in 1868 in the *Rivista Bolognese,* now in *Il Sovrano. Saggio di filosofia politica con riferenza all'Italia,* ed. by Benedetto Croce (Bari: Laterza, 1927).

3   For a concise summary of this general development, see Jaap van Osta, *Het theater van de Staat. Oranje, Windsor en de moderne monarchie* (Amsterdam: Wereldbibliotheek, 1998), pp. 11-13. For further elaboration of this development in 'guide country' Great Britain, see notably: William M. Kuhn, *Democratic Royalism: The Transformation of the British Monarchy,* 1861-1914 (Basingstoke and New York: Macmillan and St Martin's Press, 1996).

4   *The Collected Works of Walter Bagehot,* ed. by Norman St John-Stevas (London: The Economist, 1965-1986), V: *The English Constitution,* pp. 85-86 and 259. Most characteristically, in *The English Constitution* Bagehot defines the Crown alternately as 'pageant' (p. 90), 'procession' (p. 249) and 'theatrical show' (p. 248).

5   Cf. Judith Williamson, *Consuming passions. The Dynamics of Popular Culture* (London: Marion Boyars Publishers, 1987), p. 75. For an interesting approach of the present-day monarchy, see for instance: Michael Billig, *Talking of the Royal Family* (London and New York: Routledge, 1992).

6   With regard to the trendsetting role of the British monarchy, in 1852 the entire royal family had again appeared at the elaborate funeral procession for the Duke of Wellington. Eight years later, as the Canadian dominions invited the queen to open the new railway bridge, named after her, over the St Lawrence River at Montreal, and to lay the foundation stone of the Parliament Building at Ottawa – an invitation that ran up against Victoria's strong refusal to venture any further from her realm than her husband's beloved Coburg – at the Prince Consort's suggestion the Prince of Wales was sent instead, mindful of the fact that, for the performing roles of the monarchy in the modern era, there was a *family* on the throne to fulfil them. See Stanley Weintraub, *Edward the Caresser. The Playboy Prince Who Became Edward VII* (New York and London: Free Press, 2001), p. 47.

7   Cited in Ronald W. Clark, *Freud, the Man and the Cause* (New York: Random House, 1980), p. 33.

8   Elizabeth Hammerton and David Cannadine, 'Conflict and Consensus on a Ceremonial Occasion: The Diamond Jubilee in Cambridge in 1897', *The Historical Journal,* 24 (1981): 101-146, esp. 113. This is an elaboration of the 'invention of tradition' theory of Cannadine, exposed in his 'The Context, Performance and Meaning of Ritual: The British Monarchy and the "Invention of Tradition", c. 1820-1977', in *The Invention of Tradition,* ed. by Eric Hobsbawm and Terence Ranger (Cambridge: Cambridge University Press, 1983), pp. 101-164.

9   One point of criticism was their frequency. By way of illustration, on the occasion of the centenary of the birth of Emperor Wilhelm I in 1897, Duke George II of Saksen-Meiningen got up to speak in the Bundesrat and said: 'Lately we have been overrun with celebrations, and if the authorities continue to request people to work up enthusiasm for the same matters time and time again, eagerness will gradually decrease.' Helmut Reichold, *Bismarcks Zaunkönige. Duodez im* 20. *Jahrhundert* (Paderborn: Schöningh, 1977), p. 77. Indeed, the German Empire frequently organized national ceremonies to intensify national feelings for the German State, which were not really widespread, as the unification, in 1871, had only been of late. During these celebrations it was always the Prussian King, symbolising the unity of the German Empire, who was in the centre of attention, to the great annoyance of most German sovereigns, who had witnessed their own state being absorbed into the German Empire.

10   A clear example of this is Queen Victoria's Diamond Jubilee in 1897, which was celebrated ten years after her Golden Jubilee in 1887. It was without precedent, and the organization committee only wanted to stress that the queen was the longest-reigning sovereign in British history. Jeffrey L. Lant, *Insubstantial Pageant. Ceremony & Confusion at Queen Victoria's Court* (London: Hamish Hamilton, 1979), p. 215.

11   Simon Schama, 'The Domestication of Majesty: Royal Family Portraiture, 1500-1850', *Journal of Interdisciplinary History,* 17 (1986): 155-183, esp. 155.

12   Arthur Ponsonby, *Henry Ponsonby: Queen Victoria's Private Secretary. His Life and Letters* (London: Macmillan, 1942), p. 72.

13   See Kuhn, *Democratic Royalism,* chapter 2, for an exhaustive account of the thanksgiving ceremony of 1872.

14   *The Gladstone Diaries. With Cabinet Minutes and Prime-Ministerial Correspondence,* ed. by H. C. G. Matthew, 10 vols (Oxford: Oxford University Press, 1968-1994), VIII, pp. 81-82.

15   Freda Harcourt, 'Gladstone, Monarchism and the 'New' Imperialism, 1868-1874', *The Journal of Imperial and Commonwealth History,* 14 (1985): 20-51, esp. 31.

16   This is particularly apt to the jubilees of 1887 and 1897, celebrating the fiftieth and sixtieth anniversaries of Queen Victoria's ascension to the British throne. These were both large-scale ceremonies, whose origins lay not in political manoeuvre but in popular demand. Cf. W. M. Kuhn, 'Queen Victoria's Jubilees and the Invention of Tradition', *Victorian Poetry,* 25 (1987): 108.

17 See M. F. van Kesteren-Halbertsma, 'Bezoeken in het land', in *Wij zijn er nog. Het regentschap van Koningin Emma, 1890-1898. Catalogus bij de gelijknamige Tentoonstelling* (Rijksmuseum Paleis Het Loo, 1989), pp. 54-62; Cees Fasseur, *Wilhelmina. De jonge koningin* (Amsterdam: Balans, 1998), pp. 107-110.

18 Lamar Cecil, *Wilhelm II. Emperor and Exile, 1900-1941* (Chapel Hill and London: University of North Carolina Press, 1996), pp. 25-26; Giles Mac Donogh, *The Last Kaiser. William the Impetuous* (London: Weidenfeld & Nicolson, 2000), p. 39.

19 Of Queen Victoria's reluctance to make public appearances, her correspondence with her ministers offers adequate understanding. *Letters of Queen Victoria. Second Series, 1862-1885,* ed. by George Earle Buckle (London: John Murray, 1926), I, pp. 296 (1866), 391 and 443 (1867), and III, pp. 66-67. Her ministers' critics are wide; see, for instance: *Disraeli, Derby and the Conservative Party. The Political Journals of Lord Stanley, 1849-1869,* ed. by J. R. Vincent (Hassocks: Harvester Press, 1978), p. 214; Michael Pinto-Duschinsky, *The Political Thought of Lord Salisbury, 1854-68* (London: Constable, 1967), p. 182; and *My Dear Duchess. Social and Political Letters to the Duchess of Manchester, 1858-69,* ed. by A. L. Kennedy (London: John Murray, 1956) (Lord Clarendon). See also Christopher Hibbert, *Queen Victoria. A Personal History* (London and New York: HarperCollins, 2000), pp. 307-313.

20 Her magnificent funeral constituted the first of a series of spectacular royal pageants. Its organization is the subject of Jerrold M. Packard's *Farewell in Splendor. The Passing of Queen Victoria and Her Age* (New York: Dutton, 1995).

21 For the pomp and circumstance of the British monarchy in the Edwardian period, see the testimonies of Viscount Esher, the highly influential Court official, and Sir Frederick Ponsonby and Frederick Gorst, in *Journals and Letters of Reginald, Viscount Esher,* ed. by Maurice V. Brett, 4 vols (London: Ivor Nicholson & Watson, 1934-1938), Frederick Ponsonby, *Recollections of Three Reigns* (London: Eyre & Spottiswoode, 1951), and Frederick John Gorst and Beth Andrews, *Of Carriages and Kings* (New York: Crowell, 1956).

22 See Umberto Levra, *Fare gli italiani. Memoria e celebrazione del Risorgimento* (Turin: Comitato di Torino dell'Istituto per la storia del Risorgimento italiano, 1992), pp. 18-40.

23 Cit. Bruno Tobia, *Una patria per gli italiani. Spazi, itinerari, monumenti nell'Italia unita, 1870-1900* (Bari: Laterza, 1991), p. 26. In the same parliamentary debate he stressed that 'in the eyes of the people, the stability of the institutions becomes apparent from the stability of its monuments'. Ibid., p. 208 (note II, 52).

24 Niek van Sas, '*Fin-de-siècle* als nieuw begin. Nationalisme in Nederland rond 1900', *Bijdragen en Mededelingen betreffende de Geschiedenis der Nederlanden,* 106 (1991): 595-609, esp. 602. For an example of the *unceremonial* Dutch way of handling ceremonies, see André I. Wierdsma, 'Religie en politieke rituelen en symbolen in Nederland na 1813', *Bijdragen en Mededelingen betreffende de Geschiedenis der Nederlanden,* 102 (1978): 177-194, esp. 184 and 187.

25 Henk te Velde, *Gemeenschapszin en plichtsbesef. Liberalisme en Nationalisme in Nederland, 1870-1918* (The Hague: SDU 1992), pp. 123-137, and Fasseur, *Wilhelmina,* pp. 71-72.

26 See Van Osta, *Het theater van de Staat,* pp. 130-146.

27 For instance J. van Miert, 'Nationalisme in de lokale politieke cultuur, Tiel 1850-1900', *De Negentiende Eeuw,* 16 (1992): 59-85, and Jan van Miert, *Wars van clubgeest en partijzucht. Liberalen, natie en verzuiling, Tiel en Winschoten 1850-1920* (Amsterdam: Amsterdam University Press, 1994), pp. 91-97.

28 Kuhn, 'Queen Victoria's Jubilees and the Invention of Tradition', p. 108.

29 For the impact of royal memorabilia at the time of the Golden Jubilee, see Thomas Richards, 'The image of Victoria in the year of Jubilee', *Victorian Studies,* 31 (1987): 7-32.

30 Giles St Aubyn, *Edward VII. Prince and King* (New York: Atheneum, 1979), p. 371.

31 Richards, 'The Image of Victoria', 7-32, esp. 19. For the interdependence of the monarchy and advertising, see also his *The Commody Culture of Victorian England: Advertising and Spectacle, 1851-1914* (Stanford: Stanford University Press, 1990).

32 Recent developments in the Dutch media seem to confirm this. Royalty reporting, previously held in low esteem and considered as belonging to the domain of the tabloids, has witnessed a remarkable upgrading in the past few years. For instance, following the BBC's example, the

NOS, the Dutch national broadcasting corporation, has employed its own royalty correspondent since 1999. In addition, considering 'the social significance of the royal family', according to its editor-in-chief, *de Volkskrant,* one of the leading quality newspapers, some time ago engaged two special journalists to cover royal family news [Pieter Broertjes, editor-in-chief, to the author (7/10/2003)]. One of them, Jan Hoedeman, is president of the 'Vereniging van Verslaggevers Koninklijk Huis' (VVKH), an umbrella organization of journalists dedicating themselves to 'serious' reporting on the Royal House against gossip journalism.

33   In her remarkable obituary, written anonymously some weeks after Victoria's death, Mary Ponsonby, widow of Sir Henry Ponsonby, testified that the Queen had the instinct of an actor. She knew how to move like an actor and 'she was never flurried by a space in front of her'. 'The Character of Queen Victoria', in *The Quarterly Review,* cited in William M. Kuhn, *Henry & Mary Ponsonby. Life at the Court of Queen Victoria* (London: Duckworth, 2002), p. 248.

34   For an example of a study on the impact of the personal factor on the stability of the monarchy, see Jaap van Osta, 'Potere reale e potere apparente della Corona. La monarchia italiana e la monarchia olandese a confronto', *Mededelingen van het Nederlands Instituut te Rome/Papers of the Netherlands Institute in Rome. Historical Studies,* 57 (1998): 255-288, in which the Italian and Dutch monarchies are contrasted.

Te Velde, Cannadine, Twenty Years on

1   David Cannadine, 'The Context, Performance and Meaning of Ritual: The British Monarchy and the "Invention of Tradition", c. 1820-1977', in *The Invention of Tradition,* ed. by Eric Hobsbawm and Terence Ranger (Cambridge: Cambridge University Press, 1984), pp. 101-164.

2   William H. Kuhn, *Democratic Royalism. The Transformation of the British Monarchy, 1861-1914* (Basingstoke: Macmillan, 1996), Introduction and *passim.*

3   David Cannadine, 'From Biography to History: Writing the Modern British Monarchy', *Historical Research* 77 (2004): 289-312.

4   Susan Pedersen, 'What is Political History Now?', in *What is History Now?,* ed. by David Cannadine (Houndmills: Palgrave, 2002), p. 42.

5   Mona Ozouf, *La Fête Révolutionnaire, 1789-1799,* La Bibliothèque des Histoires (Paris: Gallimard, 1976); translated into English as Idem, *Festivals and the French Revolution* (Cambridge Mass./London: Harvard University Press, 1988).

6   David Cannadine, *The Decline and Fall of the British Aristocracy* (New Haven/London: Yale University Press, 1990), p. 4.

7   See, e.g., David Cannadine, 'Introduction: Divine Rites of Kings', in *Rituals of Royalty. Power and Ceremonial in Traditional Societies,* Past and Present Publications, ed. by David Cannadine and Simon Price (Cambridge: Cambridge Univesrity Press, 1987), pp. 1-19.

8   David Cannadine, 'The Last Hanoverian Sovereign? The Victorian Monarchy in Historical Perspective, 1688-1988', in *The First Modern Society. Essays in English History in Honour of Lawrence Stone,* ed. by A. L. Beier, David Cannadine, and James M. Rosenheim (Cambridge: Cambridge University Press, 1989), pp. 129, 155, 165.

9   Benedict Anderson, *Imagined Communities. Reflections on the Origin and Spread of Nationalism* (Norfolk: Thetford Press, 1983); Ernest Gellner, *Nations and Nationalism* (Oxford: Blackwell, 1983); Eric Hobsbawm, *Nations and Nationalism since 1780. Programme, Myth, Reality* (Cambridge: Cambridge University Press, 1990); for the second wave one could refer to Anthony D. Smith's work.

10   Cannadine, 'From Biography to History', p. 293.

11   Linda Colley, *Britons. Forging the Nation 1707-1837* (New Haven: Yale University Press, 1992).

12   John Plunkett, *Queen Victoria. First Media Monarch* (Oxford: Oxford University Press, 2003), p. 16.

13   Benjamin Disraeli, *Sybil or the Two Nations* (1845; Harmondsworth: Penguin Books, 1985), p. 38; Plunkett, *Victoria,* pp. 113-118 and *passim.*

14 Walter Bagehot, *The English Constitution* (1867, 1872; Brighton and Portland: Sussex Academic Press, 1997).

15 Frank Hardie, *The Political Influence of Queen Victoria, 1861-1901* (London: Oxford University Press, 1935).

16 David Cannadine, 'Parliament: the Palace of Westminster as the Palace of Varieties' (2000), in Idem, *In Churchill's Shadow. Confronting the Past in Modern Britain* (London: Allen Lane, 2002).

17 Robert C. K. Ensor, *England 1870-1914*, Oxford History of England, 14 (1936; Oxford: Oxford University Press, 1949), pp. 1-2; cf. H. C. G. Matthew, 'Rhetoric and Politics in Britain, 1860-1950', in *Politics and Social Change in Modern Britain*, ed. by Philip J. Waller (Brighton, Sussex, and New York: Harvester Press, 1987), pp. 34-58.

18 See, e.g., the recent biographies below by Colin Matthew, Roy Jenkins and Richard Shannon.

19 I used this material in my Groningen inaugural lecture: Henk te Velde, *Het theater van de politiek. Rede, uitgesproken bij de aanvaarding van het ambt van hoogleraar* (Amsterdam: Wereldbibliotheek, 2003); Plunkett, *Victoria*, p. 205, that the earlier royal reporting already prefigured the later New Journalism.

20 Richard Shannon, *Gladstone. Heroic Minister 1865-1898* (London: Allen Lane, 1999), p. 245.

21 Roy Jenkins, *Gladstone* (London: Macmillan, 1995), p. 332.

22 Cf. Elizabeth Longford, *Victoria R.I.* (London: Weidenfeld & Nicholson, 1964), p. 528: 'Biographers of both Gladstone and Queen Victoria have always found it necessary to decide whether the dislike was political or temperamental.' Or both, but at different stages: 'The Queen's dislike of Gladstone began in political disagreement and became personal.' Philip Magnus, *Gladstone. A Biography* (London: John Murray, 1954), p. 119.

23 The diary of Edward Walter Hamilton, quoted by Jenkins, *Gladstone*, p. 470; Giles St Aubyn, *Queen Victoria. A Portrait* (London: Sinclair-Stevenson 1991; New York: Atheneum, 1992), pp. 445-446.

24 Longford, *Victoria*, p. 528.

25 Richard Williams, *The Contentious Crown. Public Discussion of the British Monarchy in the Reign of Queen Victoria* (Aldershot: Ashgate, 1997), p. 142.

26 Plunkett, *Victoria*, pp. 157, 159-160.

27 Walter Bagehot, *Biographical Studies* (1881; London: Longmans, 1889), p. 368; Edward Michael Whitty, *St Stephen's in the Fifties. The Session 1852-53* (1854; London, 1906), p. 259.

28 *The Times,* 4 February 1859; cf. *The Times,* 11 December 1859, which argues against a theatrical monarchy.

29 Wedgwood in 1917, quoted by David Cannadine, 'Piety: Josiah Wedgwood and the History of Parliament' (1999), in Idem, *Churchill's Shadow*, p. 141.

30 William White, *The Inner Life of the House of Commons*, 2 vols (London: T. Fisher Unwin, 1897).

31 I compared Gladstone to such Dutch charismatic party leaders as the orthodox Protestant Abraham Kuyper and partly also socialist leaders like Pieter Jelles Troelstra and Ferdinand Domela Nieuwenhuis in Henk te Velde, *Stijlen van leiderschap. Persoon en politiek van Thorbecke tot Den Uyl* (Amsterdam: Wereldbibliotheek, 2002).

32 Jaap van Osta, *Het theater van de staat. Oranje, Windsor en de moderne monarchie* (Amsterdam: Wereldbibliotheek, 1998).

33 Henk te Velde, *Gemeenschapszin en plichtsbesef. Liberalisme en nationalisme in Nederland, 1870-1918* (Den Haag: SDU, 1992), ch. 5.

34 Cees Fasseur, *Wilhelmina: de jonge koningin* (Amsterdam: Balans, 1998); Henk te Velde, 'Het "roer van staat" in "zwakke vrouwenhanden". Emma en het imago van Oranje', in *Koningin Emma. Opstellen over haar regentschap*, ed. by Coen Tamse (Baarn: Ambo, 1990), p. 188.

35 Richard H. S. Crossmann, 'Introduction', in Walter Bagehot, *The English Constitution* (London: Watts, 1964), p. 33.

36 For this paragraph see Piet de Rooy, 'De staat verdrukt, de wet is logen', in *De Eeuw van de Grondwet. Grondwet en politiek in Nederland, 1798-1917*, ed. by Niek van Sas and Henk te Velde (Deventer: Kluwer, 1998), pp. 266-294; Wessel Krul, 'Multatuli en Busken Huet als critici van de democratie. Rondom de politieke crisis van 1867', in *Politieke stijl. Over presentatie en optre-*

den in de politiek, ed. by Dick Pels and Henk te Velde (Amsterdam: Het Spinhuis, 2000), pp. 129-150; Henk te Velde, 'Geheimzinnig schijnende diepte. De volkskoning en de omstreden band tussen vorst en volk in de 19ᵉ eeuw', Groniek, 150 (2000): 7-24.

37 Te Velde, Gemeenschapszin, p. 138.

38 A short discussion of British studies in Pedersen, 'Political History'.

39 But see, e.g., Joseph S. Meisel, Public Speech and the Culture of Public Life in the Age of Gladstone (New York: Columbia University Press, 2001).

40 E.g., Plunkett, Victoria; Thomas Richards, 'The Image of Victoria in the Year of Jubilee', Victorian Studies, 31 (1987): 7-32; Virginia McKendry, 'The Illustrated London News and the Invention of Tradition', Victorian Periodicals Review 27/1 (Spring 1994): 1-24.

41 However, Hobsbawm shows in Invention of Tradition, ed. by Ranger and Hobsbawn, that this is not generally the case in processes of invention of tradition.

Deneckere, The Impossible Neutrality of the Speech from the Throne

1 David I. Kertzer, Ritual, Politics and Power (New Haven: Yale University Press, 1989); and Catherine Bell, Ritual Theory, Ritual Practice (Oxford and New York: Oxford University Press, 1992).

2 Walter Bagehot, The English Constitution (1867, 1872; Brighton and Portland: Sussex Academic Press, 1997).

3 Henk te Velde, 'Cannadine, Twenty Years on. Monarchy and Political Culture in Nineteenth-Century Britain and the Netherlands' (in this volume). See also William H. Kuhn, Democratic Royalism. The Transformation of the British Monarchy, 1861-1914 (London: Macmillan, 1996).

4 David Cannadine, 'The Context, Performance and Meaning of Ritual: The British Monarchy and the "Invention of Tradition," c. 1820-1977', in The Invention of Tradition, ed. by Eric Hobsbawm and Terence Ranger (Cambridge: Cambridge University Press, 1983), pp. 101-164.

5 Walter L. Arnstein, 'Queen Victoria Opens Parliament: The Disinvention of Tradition', in Historical Research, 63 (1990): 178-194.

6 Mise-en-scène. Keizer Karel en de verbeelding van de negentiende eeuw, ed. by Robert Hoozee, Jo Tollebeek, and Tom Verschaffel (Antwerp: Mercatorfonds, 1999); Margot de Smaele, 'Hier zijn wij! Een sociaal-politieke benadering van de nationale viering van het zilveren ambtsjubileum van Leopold I (1856)', De Negentiende Eeuw 26 (2002): 17-48.

7 Jean Stengers, L'action du Roi en Belgique (Brussels: Racine, 1996), pp. 167-177; Emmanuel Gerard, 'Kamer versus regering? Vertrouwensstemmingen, begrotingsdebatten en interpellaties', in Geschiedenis van de Belgische Kamer van Volksvertegenwoordigers 1830-2002, ed. by Emmanuel Gerard, et al. (Brussels: Kamer van Volksvertegenwoordigers, 2003), pp. 251-289.

8 See, inter alia, for the distinction between standard and reality concerning Walter Bagehot's influential ideas: Irène Diependaal, 'Bagehot revisited. De sluipgang van drie koninklijke 'recht-en' in het Nederlandse parlementaire bestel', Jaarboek Parlementaire Geschiedenis (2005): 89-101.

9 Thijs Van Leeuwen, et al., Pracht en Praal op Prinsjesdag (Zaltbommel: Europese Bibliotheek, 1998), p.20.

10 Letters of Queen Victoria, 1837-1861, ed. by A. C. Benson and Lord Esher (London: J. Murray, 1907), pp. 78-79.

11 John Plunkett, Queen Victoria. First Media Monarch (Oxford: Oxford University Press, 2003).

12 Jeroen Janssens, De Belgische natie viert. De Belgische nationale feesten 1830-1914 (Leuven: Universitaire Pers, 2001), pp. vii-xi, 243-248.

13 Gustaaf Janssens, 'Het pact tussen vorst en natie', in Mise-en-scène, ed. by Hoozee, Tollebeek, and Verschaffel, pp. 160-162.

14 Moniteur Belge (MB), 23 July 1831, n.38; see also Janssens, 'Het pact tussen vorst en natie', p. 161.

15 See Marnix Beyen and Rik Röttger, 'Het streven naar waardigheid. Zelfbeelden en gedragsco-des van volksvertegenwoordigers', in *Geschiedenis van de Belgische Kamer van Volksvertegen-woordigers*, ed. by Emmanuel Gerard, et al., pp. 342-343.

16 W. Van den Steene, *Het Paleis der natie* (Brussels: Belgische Overheid, 1981), pp. 187-188.

17 Archives Royal Palace (ARP), Fonds Leopold II, no. 636, protocol booklet 1870.

18 ARP, Fonds Leopold II, no. 636, protocol booklet, s.d.

19 ARP, correspondence between King Leopold I and Queen Victoria, Leopold I to Victoria, 11/11/1842, (II/2).

20 ARP, Fonds Leopold II, no. 636, protocol booklet, s.d.; MB day of the speech from the throne.

21 MB 1880, 10/11/1880, no. 315.

22 ARP, Correspondence between King Leopold I and Queen Victoria, IV/I, 11/11/1847; AP, 1849, 13/11/1849.

23 *Annales Parlementaires* (AP) 1866, 13/11/1863; AP 1886; AP 1892.

24 MB, 1836, no. 315, 9/11/1836.

25 MB 1833, 1834, 1842, 1843.

26 AP and MB, ARP protocol booklet.

27 MB and AP

28 Beyen and Röttger, 'Het streven naar waardigheid', p. 345.

29 Leopold I's letter to Emmanuel van Mensdorff-Pouilly, 23 October 1844 (originally in French), in Jean Puraye and Hans-Otto Lang, *Lettres de Léopold I à sa sœur la princesse Sophie, à son beau-frère Emmanuel, comte de Mensdorff-Pouilly, à son neveu Alphonse, comte de Mensdorff-Pouilly. 1804-1864* (Liège: Vaillant-Carmanne, 1973), p. 337.

30 ARP, correspondence between King Leopold I and Queen Victoria, III/3, 21/2/1846.

31 ARP, correspondence between King Leopold I and Queen Victoria, VI/2, 13/10/1853.

32 ARP, correspondence between King Leopold I and Queen Victoria, IX/1, 7/11/1861.

33 ARP, correspondence between King Leopold I and Queen Victoria, VIII/2, 28/10/1859.

34 Stengers, *L'action du Roi en Belgique*, pp. 168-171 gives the most striking examples.

35 ARP, correspondence between King Leopold I and Queen Victoria, IV/1, letter from Leopold to Victoria, 11/11/1847.

36 ARP, correspondence between King Leopold I and Queen Victoria, IV/1, letter from Leopold to Victoria, 7/11/1847.

37 General Archives (GA) Brussels, Archive Charles Rogier no. 105, letter from Van Praet to Charles Rogier, 7/11/1847: 'It is essential that a speech from the throne avoids entering the cen-tre of the political discussion, so to speak.'

38 Cited in Stengers, *L'action du Roi en Belgique*, pp. 170-171: 'His [Rogier's] aim seemed to be, in broad outlines, for me to express my endless love for our liberals. The matter is extremely sim-ple: what they have announced in their programme must unfortunately be made possible, but the king can express neither pleasure nor displeasure, that is their task.'

39 Ernest Discailles, *Charles Rogier (1800-1885) d'après des documents inédits. Tome troisième (1839-1852)* (Brussels: J. Lebègue et Compagnie, 1894), pp. 208-209; see also Stengers, *L'action du Roi en Belgique*, pp. 169-170.

40 ARP, Correspondence between King Leopold I and Queen Victoria, IX/1, letter from Leopold to Victoria, 7/11/1861.

41 Stengers, *L'action du Roi en Belgique*, p. 170.

42 AP, 8/8/1870, opening of the special legislative session of 1870: 'When all the outside events evoke a common feeling of love for the fatherland in us, I long to see the national house reuni-ted around me [...]. The Belgian hearts unite in the face of such a sacred cause [...]. When ful-filling such tasks, the people and the King will have only one soul and one voice: Long live inde-pendent Belgium! May God watch over it and protect its rights.'

43 *L'Indépendance belge*, 11/8, address to the Senate; *L'Indépendance belge*, 15/8, address to the House of Representatives.

44 AP, 12/11/1878, opening of the legislative session, royal session of 12 November 1878: 'By creating a special ministry of public education, my Government has clearly announced the resolve to carefully watch over this noble and grand interest. Teaching paid for by the State must be pla-ced under the exclusive leadership and watchful eye of the civil authorities.'

45 Gita Deneckere, *Geuzengeweld. Antiklerikaal straatrumoer in de politieke geschiedenis van België, 1831-1914* (Brussels: VUB Press, 1998), pp. 99-144.

46 AP, Senate, Dewandre, 15/11/1878: 'For many years the Senate has been in the habit of delivering an address that was voted unanimously by the members of this assembly. As the honourable d'Anethan has said, it is well understood that everyone has kept his opinion to himself.'

47 AP, 9/11/1880.

48 AP, 9/11/1886: 'Inspired by their work, my government will take on important reform projects. It is only right to allow professional groups to join forces freely – in order to establish new bonds between industrial bosses and labourers in the form of arbitration and conciliation councils – to regulate work for women and children.'

49 Fritz Fischer, *Ecrit sur le sable. Cinquante ans de journalisme* (Brussels: s.n., 1947), p. 5: 'All the hats were lifted, but adorned with cardboards of protest, there were millions of round pieces of white paper, the songs and cries sounded like enthusiastic cheers, and when seen from a distance, it gave the illusion that it was a delirious explosion of loyalism.'

50 Deneckere, *Geuzengeweld*, p. 281.

51 AP 1892, royal session of 8 November 1892, p. 77: 'The Belgian constitution is the oldest on the continent today. It has long granted our dear country years of peace and prolific development: I have proclaimed its wisdom on more than one occasion [...] our institutions that are so liberal can be improved and renewed today. [...] Today's electoral body has just given you the mandate to realize a great extension of the right to suffrage.'

52 Marie-Rose Thielemans and Emile Vandewoude, *Le Roi Albert au travers de ses lettres inédites 1882-1916* (Brussels: Office Internationale de Librairie, 1982), pp. 57, 348.

53 The reports of the Council of Ministers dated 21/10/1910 and 28/10/1910 have not been traced.

54 Deneckere, *Geuzengeweld*, p. 339.

55 Thielemans and Vandewoude, *Le Roi Albert*, pp. 63-64.

56 AP, 1910-1911, royal session of 8 November 1910: 'It is the father of the family who has the right to watch over the education and instruction of his child, to make a free and independent choice as to the school to which he wishes to entrust his child. My government will propose measures to effectively guarantee the exercise of this inalienable right.'

57 Jacques Pirenne, 'Un mémoire du Roi Albert sur la chute du cabinet Schollaert (8 juin)', *Mededelingenblad van de Klasse der Letteren en der Morele en Staatkundige Wetenschappen. Koninklijke Academie van België*, 5th series, 57:10-11 (1971): 439.

58 Stengers, *L'action du Roi en Belgique*, p. 172.

59 Deneckere, *Geuzengeweld*, pp. 338-339.

60 AP 1910-1911, 8/11/1910.

61 AP 1918-1919, 22/11/1918.

62 AP 1918-1919.

63 Lode Wils, *Frans Van Cauwelaert afgewezen door Koning Albert I. Een tijdbom onder België* (Antwerp: Hadewijch, 2003).

64 GA Brussels, Carton de Wiart archive, letter from King Albert I to Minister Carton de Wiart, 20/11/1920: 'In your new letter you insist that all parties would welcome the announcement of the speech from the throne.'

65 GA Brussels, Carton de Wiart archive, letter from King Albert I to Minister Carton de Wiart, 20/11/1920: 'If I spoke, I would be obliged under the constitutional oath that I took and my duty as head of the army, to categorically confirm that we are the most vulnerable country from a military point of view and that, to reduce the military service to under a certain term is to stoop to the level of a militia system. Experience proves that these troops have never served under a normal and well-trained force. They think that they will find a corrective in powerful arms but an army without discipline or unity of purpose can never hope to defend such arms.'

1   Thomas Sokoll, *Essex Pauper Letters. 1731-1837* (Oxford: Oxford University Press, 2001). See also the special issue on petitions of the *International Review of Social History*, 46 (December 2001); and the special issue on 'Pratiques d'écriture' of the *Annales. Histoire, sciences sociales*, 56, 4-5 (July-October 2001).

2   Jonathan Rose, *The Intellectual Life of the British Working Class* (2001; New Haven and London: Yale University Press, 2002), pp. 5-6. Compare Geoff Eley and Keith Nield, 'Farewell to the working class?', *International Labor and Working-Class History*, 57 (2000): 1-30 (esp. 14); Heinz-Gerhard Haupt, Michael G. Muller, and Stuart Woolf, 'Introduction', in *Regional and National Identities in Europe in the XIXth and XXth Centuries*, ed. by Idem (The Hague: Kluwer Law International, 1998), pp. 1-21 (esp. 4); Martyn Lyons, 'La culture littéraire des travailleurs. Autobiographies ouvrières dans l'Europe du XIXè siècle', *Annales. Histoire, sciences sociales*, 56 (2001): 927-46; Sokoll, *Essex Pauper Letters*, pp. 5-6.

3   Rose, *The Intellectual Life*, p. 1.

4   Estimate based on surviving inventories of letters received: *Indicateur particulier* 1863-1898 [Brussels, Royal Palace Archives (subsequently abbreviated to BRPA), Reading room]; *Demandes de secours, gratifications, souscriptions (correspondance entrée)* 1902-1923 *(registre G102)* (BRPA, Cabinet Albert I. 10); *Indicateur générale* 1923-1978 (BRPA, Reading room); *Indicateurs 227-228 Service de la Reine* 1921-1939 (BRPA, Secrétariat Reine Elisabeth. 227-228); *Registres des lettres entrées (demandes d'emplois, de secours, de distinctions honorifiques, [...])* 1894-1909 (BRPA, Commandements Prince Albert, 1-10ter, 11). For Leopold I's reign from 1831 until 1865 virtually no material has survived, we cannot even guess how many letters he originally received. The custom is still very much alive: King Albert II and Queen Paola still receive some 10,000 requests each year (Annual reports of the social secretariat of the Queen, 1995-1999. Documents provided by the Keeper of the Archives of the Royal Palace).

5   In Belgium, the traditional literature on the monarchy has not dealt with royal philanthropy or with the letters of request, and there is little relevant international research.

6   James C. Scott, *Domination and the Arts of Resistance. Hidden Transcripts* (New Haven and London: Yale University Press, 1990), p. 18.

7   Scott, *Domination and the Arts of Resistance*, p. 19.

8   E.g., Natalie Zemon Davis, *Fiction in the Archives. Pardon Tales and Their Tellers in Sixteenth Century France* (Cambridge: Polity Press, 1987); and Arlette Farge and Michel Foucault, *Le désordre des familles: lettres de cachet des Archives de la Bastille au XVIIIe siècle* (Paris: Gallimard, 1982).

9   Frank Prochaska, *Royal Bounty. The Making of a Welfare Monarchy* (New Haven and London: Yale University Press, 1995), p. 8.

10   BRPA, Commandements Prince Albert, 12.

11   These overall impressions are based on the surviving inventories of letters received, see note 4.

12   Linda Colley, *Britons. Forging the Nation 1707-1837* (New Haven: Yale University Press, 1992), p. 272.

13   'Pour élever votre honorable famille' Marie-Louise Faust to the royal couple, 6 Feb. 1880 [in French] (G62/13). All translations by the author.

14   BRPA, Commandements Prince Albert. Registres A. Affaires avec suite. no. 1, 7 Dec. 1895.

15   Scott, *Domination and the Arts of Resistance*, 95.

16   Letters to Leopold II: BRPA, Cabinet Leopold II, Commandements du Roi, G61/32; G62/13; G70/42; G73/33; G73/40; G74/16; G74/20; G81/05; G82/16; G82/33; G86/15; G87/07; G88/02; G91/03; G91/14; G93/38; G94/10; G94/18; G94/43; G98/58; G99/07; G99/55; G100/47; G102/121; G102/164; G102/248; G102/249; G102/254; G102/36; G102/58. Letters to Elisabeth: BRPA, Secrétariat Reine Elisabeth,. Secours I 47; I 61; I 69; I 70; I 87; I 90; I 92; I 105; I 146; I 156; I 169; I 183; I 207; I 211; I 212; I 219; I 220; I 224; I 231; I 234; I 246; I 297; I 330; I 336; I 343; I 346; I 350; I 352; I 356; I 394. All subsequent references are abbreviated to G (letters to Leopold II) and I (letters to Elisabeth). I have chosen this particular sample because these (uncatalogued) series were the most readily available.

17 Around World War I the urban area of Brussels consisted of the following *communes*: Anderlecht, Elsene/Ixelles, Etterbeek, Koekelberg, Laken, Schaarbeek, Sint-Gillis, Sint-Jans-Molenbeek, Sint-Joost-ten-Node, Sint-Lambrechts-Woluwe, Sint-Pieters-Jette, Ukkel and Vorst.

18 *Registres des lettres entrées (demandes d'emplois, de secours, de distinctions honorifiques,....)* 1894-1909 (BRPA, Commandements Prince Albert, 1-10ter, 11).

19 Annual reports of the social secretariat of the Queen, 1995-1999. Documents provided by the Keeper of the Archives of the Royal Palace.

20 For more detailed figures, see Maarten Van Ginderachter, 'Vaderland in de Belgische Werkliedenpartij (1885-1914). Sociaal-democratie en nationale identiteit from below' (unpublished doctoral thesis, Ghent University, 2004), pp. 763-770.

21 Scott, *Domination and the Arts of Resistance,* p. 94.

22 'Cher bienfaitrisse' Mélanie Wéry [a widowed housewife from Charleroi] to Queen Elisabeth, 3 Nov. 1926 [in French] (I 105); 'Cher Mère' Idem 31 Jan. 1927 (I 105).

23 'Tant de bonté et de simplicité', 'sans que sa visite eût été remarquée dans le quartier'. *Le Peuple,* 11 Feb. 1908, p. 1.

24 'Ne plus rien donner à l'abbé L'Heureux; il sollicite des dons pour différentes personnes, mais il ne leur fait pas connaître les noms des donateurs.' BRPA, Commandements Prince Albert, Index 10bis no. 14416, entrance 1 April 1908.

25 I will quote only letters whose authorship is unquestionable (being undoubtedly written by the requester him/herself or on his/her behalf).

26 Scott, *Domination and the Arts of Resistance,* p. 93.

27 Helen Hackett, 'Dreams or Designs, Cults or Constructions? The Study of Images of Monarchs', *Historical Journal,* 44:3 (Sept. 2001): 811-823 (esp. 822).

28 Hélène Amélie Van Der Linden [the wife of a miner from Gilly (Wallonia)] to the Queen [in French], 27 Jan. 1927 (I 156); Marie Beaujean [the wife of a miner from Meux (Wallonia)] to the Queen [in French], 16 April 1927 (I 231); Pétronille Van Poppel [the wife of a wickerworker from Sint Gillis (Brussels)] to the Queen [in French], 10 Dec. 1926 (I 220).

29 Berthe-Marie Blondeau [a married wandering seller of shoes from Sint Gillis (Brussels)] to the Queen [in French], 1 Oct. 1926 (I 90); Henriette Lebon [a married woman from Arquennes (Wallonia)] to the Queen [in French], 12 May 1926 (I 246).

30 Gérard Blistain [a Protestant worker from Jemeppe sur Meuse (Wallonia)] to the King [in French], 11 Oct. 1892 (G88/02).

31 Marie-Louise Faust [the wife of a small bartender from Liège] to the royal couple, 6 Feb. 1880 [in French] (G62/13); Thomas Monami [a married arms worker from Herstal (Liège)] to the King [in French], 29 March 1885 (G73/33).

32 Elie Albert [a Belgian sailor staying in Dunkerque] to the King [in French], 16 April 1885 (G73/40).

33 Charles Tordeur, Louis Boudin and Henri Nitelet [resp. a blacksmith and two industrial day labourers from Pont-à-Celles (Wallonia)] to the King [in French], 3 Dec. 1891 (G86/15).

34 Achille Paturiaux [a married machinist with the State Rail from Quaregnon (Wallonia)] to the King [in French], 1 Nov. 1895 (G94/10); Marie Anciaux [the wife of a wandering musician from Rochefort (Wallonia)] to the Queen [in French], 29 Jan. 1927 (I 211).

35 Marie Mathieu [an unmarried woman from Ghent (Flanders)] to the King [in French], 9 May 1903 (G102/164).

36 Narcisse Tordeur [a widowed bank clerk from Elsene (Brussels)] to the Queen [in French], Dec. 1925 (I 394).

37 M. Maryssael [the wife of a former alderman of the city council from Ostend (Flanders)] to the King [in French], 5 July 1895 (G93/38); Florentin Gilon [an unmarried blacksmith with his own shop from Awirs (Wallonia)] to the King [in French], 16 June 1899 (G98/58).

38 Bertrand Numa [a clerk with the State Rail from Brussels] to the King's secretary [in French], 3 Nov. 1889 (G82/33).

39 Marcel Grégoire [a music teacher from Tongeren (Flanders)] to the King [in French], 3 Dec. 1888 (G81/05).

40 F. J. De Beck [a priest from Nederename (Flanders)] to the King [in French], 14 March 1881 (G70/42).

41 Ibid.

42 François-Guillaume Yanne [a married former mechanic in the Congo from Seraing sur Meuse (Wallonia)] to the King [in French, letter written by a middle-class supporter on his behalf], 14 April 1904 (G102/254).

43 Marcel Grégoire [a music teacher from Tongeren (Flanders)] to the King [in French], 3 Dec. 1888 (G81/05).

44 Justinien Van Drooghenbroeck [an independent gilder from Brussels] to the King [in French], 9 Jan. 1903 (G102/121).

45 Florentin Gilon [a married painter who studied at the Académie des Beaux Arts de Liège from Chênée (Wallonia)] to the King [in French], 16 June 1899 (G98/58); Joseph Gérard [a married mechanics worker from Mons (Wallonia)] to the King [in French, letter written by a middle-class supporter on his behalf], 27 July 1899 (G99/07).

46 Narcisse Tordeur [a widowed bank clerk from Elsene (Brussels)] to the Queen [in French], Dec. 1925 (I 394); Mathieu Lejeune [a married supply clerk from Schaarbeek (Brussels)] to the Queen [in French], Jan. 1927 (I 352).

47 Alexandre Wiliski [a married miner from Naninne (Wallonia)] to the Queen [in French, letter written by a middle-class supporter on his behalf], March 1928 (I 69).

48 Marcelle Flamand [an unmarried apprentice-milliner from Châtelet (Wallonia)] to the Queen [in French, letter written by a middle-class supporter on her behalf], 17 June 1926 (I 146).

49 Marcelle Francois [the wife of a slate worker from Namur (Wallonia)] to the Queen [in French, letter written by a middle-class supporter on her behalf], 15 Jan. 1927 (I 336); Hubert Glineur [a married manual labourer from Vorst (Brussels)] to the Queen [in French, letter written by a middle-class supporter on his behalf], 15 Jan. 1927 (I 346).

50 Ursule Cabut [the wife of a lumberjack from Rochefort (Wallonia)] to the Queen [in French, letter written by a middle-class supporter on her behalf], 29 July 1938 (I 234); Philomène Brigode [the wife of a miner from Jumet (Wallonia)] to the King [in French, letter written by a middle-class supporter on her behalf], 22 Aug 1885 (G74/16); Elisabeth Rivez [a widow from Brussels, working as a rag-and-bone woman] to the King [in French, letter written by a middle-class supporter on her behalf], 28 June 1902 (G102/58); Marcel Grégoire [a music teacher from Tongeren (Flanders)] to the King [in French], 3 Dec. 1888 (G81/05); M. Maryssael [the wife of a former alderman of the city council from Ostend (Flanders)] to the King [in French], 5 July 1895 (G93/38); Mrs. Servais Crochet [the wife of a mechanic in the Congo from Glain (Wallonia)] to the King [in French], 2 July 1900 (G99/55); François-Guillaume Yanne [a married former mechanic in the Congo from Seraing sur Meuse (Wallonia)] to the King [in French, letter written by a middle-class supporter on his behalf], 14 April 1904 (G102/254); Alexandre Wiliski [a married miner from Naninne (Wallonia)] to the Queen [in French, letter written by a middle-class supporter on his behalf], March 1928 (I 69); Louis Delplanque [a married miner from Cuesmes (Wallonia)] to the Queen [in French, letter written by a middle-class supporter on his behalf], 15 Dec. 1926 (I 169); Marcelle Francois [the wife of a slate worker from Namur (Wallonia)] to the Queen [in French, letter written by a middle-class supporter on her behalf], 15 Jan. 1927 (I 336); Hubert Glineur [a married manual labourer from Vorst (Brussels)] to the Queen [in French, letter written by a middle-class supporter on his behalf], 15 Jan. 1927 (I 346); Juliette Conchariere [the wife of a miner from Châtelet (Wallonia)] to the Queen [in French, letter written by a middle-class supporter on her behalf], 24 Jan. 1927 (I 343).

51 Marie Mathieu [an unmarried woman from Ghent (Flanders)] to the King [in French], 9 May 1903 (G102/164).

52 Mrs. Servais Crochet [the wife of a mechanic in the Congo from Glain (Wallonia)] to the King [in French], 2 July 1900 (G99/55).

53 Marcelle Flamand [an unmarried apprentice-milliner from Châtelet (Wallonia)] to the Queen [in French, letter written by a middle-class supporter on her behalf], 17 June 1926 (I 146); Augustine Crockart [the widow of a supply clerk from Brussels] to the King [in French], 18 April 1902 (G102/36).

54 'Monsieur' Elie Albert [a Belgian sailor staying in Dunkerque] to the King [in French], 16 April 1885 (G73/40).

55 'Dans lattente [*sic*] de recevoir de votre bon cœur un bonne [*sic*] rèponse dont jai [*sic*] le ferme foi et l'honneur dêtre [*sic*] avec le plus profond espoir de Sa Majesté la très humble et obéissante Servante.' Hélène Amélie Van Der Linden [the wife of a miner from Gilly (Wallonia)] to the Queen [in French], 27 Jan. 1927 (I 156).

56 'Je prends la respectueuse liberté de vous écrire pour une petite chose, si vous comprenez, à Sa Majesté'; 'Veuillez à Sa Majesté recevoir l'assurance de ma parfaite considération votre humble et dévoué serviteur'; Edouard Tamenne [from Fleurus] to the King [in French], 22 Feb. 1892 (G87/07).

57 'A sa Majesté Léopold II Roi des Belges et président du Congo'; Gérard Blistain [a Protestant worker from Jemeppe sur Meuse (Wallonia)] to the King [in French], 11 Oct. 1892 (G88/02).

58 Elisabeth Rivez [a widow from Brussels, working as a rag-and-bone woman] to the King [in French, letter written by a middle-class supporter on her behalf], 28 June 1902 (G102/58); F.J. De Beck [a priest from Nederename (Flanders)] to the King [in French], 14 March 1881 (G70/42); Mrs. Servais Crochet [the wife of a mechanic in the Congo from Glain (Wallonia)] to the King [in French], 2 July 1900 (G99/55); Augustine Crockart [the widow of a supply clerk from Brussels] to the King [in French], 18 April 1902 (G102/36); Bertrand Numa [a clerk with the State Rail from Brussels] to the King's secretary [in French], 3 Nov. 1889 (G82/33).

59 'Votre grande puissance royal' Florentin Gilon [an unmarried blacksmith with his own shop from Awirs (Wallonia)] to the King [in French], 16 June 1899 (G98/58); 'votre haute attention' Victor Fosty and Constant Gofette [two married slate workers from Oignies (Wallonia)] to the King [in French, letter written by a middle-class supporter on their behalf], 31 Jan. 1894 (G91/14); 'votre généreuse condescendance' Bertrand Numa [a clerk with the State Rail from Brussels] to the King's secretary [in French], 3 Nov. 1889 (G82/33).

60 Victor Fosty and Constant Gofette [two married slate workers from Oignies (Wallonia)] to the King [in French, letter written by a middle-class supporter on their behalf], 31 Jan. 1894 (G91/14); Laure Keymeulen [an unmarried milliner from Brussels] to the King [in French], 9 April 1904 (G102/249); Alexandre Wiliski [a married miner from Naninne (Wallonia)] to the Queen [in French, letter written by a middle-class supporter on his behalf], March 1928 (I 69); Louis Delplanque [a married miner from Cuesmes (Wallonia)] to the Queen [in French, letter written by a middle-class supporter on his behalf], 15 Dec. 1926 (I 169).

61 Edouard Tamenne [from Fleurus] to the King [in French], 22 Feb. 1892 (G87/07).

62 Joseph Gérard [a married mechanics worker from Mons (Wallonia)] to the King [in French, letter written by a middle-class supporter on his behalf], 27 July 1899 (G99/07); Florentin Gilon [an unmarried blacksmith with his own shop from Awirs (Wallonia)] to the King [in French], 16 June 1899 (G98/58); Mrs. Servais Crochet [the wife of a mechanic in the Congo from Glain (Wallonia)] to the King [in French], 2 July 1900 (G99/55); Augustine Crockart [the widow of a supply clerk from Brussels] to the King [in French], 18 April 1902 (G102/36).

63 F. J. De Beck [a priest from Nederename (Flanders)] to the King [in French], 14 March 1881 (G70/42); M. Maryssael [the wife of a former alderman of the city council from Ostend (Flanders)] to the King [in French], 5 July 1895 (G93/38); François-Guillaume Yanne [a married former mechanic in the Congo from Seraing sur Meuse (Wallonia)] to the King [in French, letter written by a middle-class supporter on his behalf], 14 April 1904 (G102/254)

64 Laurence Van Ypersele, 'L'image du roi dans la caricature politique en Belgique de 1884 à 1914', *Revue belge d'histoire contemporaine*, 26 (1996): 133-164 (esp. 146-147).

65 'Oh! bonne Majesté', Yvonne Vander Elst [a married woman from Meslin-l'Evêque (Wallonia)] to the Queen [in French], 15 Aug 1926 (I 61); 'ma souveraine bien-aimée', Louis Delplanque [a married miner from Cuesmes (Wallonia)] to the Queen [in French, letter written by a middle-class supporter on his behalf], 15 Dec. 1926 (I 169); 'notre aimable Souveraine', Mathieu Santre [a married agricultural labourer from Vielsalm (Wallonia)] to the Queen [in French, letter written by a middle-class supporter on his behalf], Dec. 1926 (I 219); 'Bien chère Majesté', Marie Beaujean [the wife of a miner from Meux (Wallonia)] to the Queen [in French], 16 April 1927 (I 231); 'Chère Souveraine', 'Chère Majesté', Mathieu Lejeune [a married supply clerk from Schaarbeek (Brussels)] to the Queen [in French], Jan. 1927 (I 352).

66 'Aumônes', Edmond de Carton de Wiart to E. Delvoie, 31 Oct. 1907 (G102/713).

67 F. J. De Beck [a priest from Nederename (Flanders)] to the King [in French], 14 March 1881 (G70/42); Philomène Brigode [the wife of a miner from Jumet (Wallonia)] to the King [in French, letter written by a middle-class supporter on her behalf], 22 Aug 1885 (G74/16); Florentin Gilon [an unmarried blacksmith with his own shop from Awirs (Wallonia)] to the King [in French], 16 June 1899 (G98/58); Marie Mathieu [an unmarried woman from Ghent (Flanders)] to the King [in French], 9 May 1903 (G102/164).

68 Charles Tordeur, Louis Boudin, and Henri Nitelet [resp. a blacksmith and two industrial day labourers from Pont-à-Celles (Wallonia)] to the King [in French], 3 Dec. 1891 (G86/15).

69 M. Maryssael [the wife of a former alderman of the city council from Ostend (Flanders)] to the King [in French], 5 July 1895 (G93/38); Marcel Grégoire [a music teacher from Tongeren (Flanders)] to the King [in French], 3 Dec. 1888 (G81/05).

70 'C'est à vos genoux Sire que je viens vous suplier', 'je me prosterne à vos pieds', Elisabeth Rivez [a widow from Brussels, working as a rag-and-bone woman] to the King [in French, letter written by a middle-class supporter on her behalf], 28 June 1902 (G102/58); 'je vous en prie à genoux car je ne sais pas ce qui me reste à faire', Marie Mathieu [an unmarried woman from Ghent (Flanders)] to the King [in French], 9 May 1903 (G102/164).

71 M. Maryssael [the wife of a former alderman of the city council from Ostend (Flanders)] to the King [in French], 5 July 1895 (G93/38); Florentin Gilon [an unmarried blacksmith with his own shop from Awirs (Wallonia)] to the King [in French], 16 June 1899 (G98/58); Bertrand Numa [a clerk with the State Rail from Brussels] to the King's secretary [in French], 3 Nov. 1889 (G82/33); Victor Fosty and Constant Gofette [two married slate workers from Oignies (Wallonia)] to the King [in French, letter written by a middle-class supporter on their behalf], 31 Jan. 1894 (G91/14); Augustine Crockart [the widow of a supply clerk from Brussels] to the King [in French], 18 April 1902 (G102/36).

72 'Combien je remercierais le bon Dieu si je pouvais vous dire toute ma misère et ma peine à vous même. Oh! bonne Majesté', Yvonne Vander Elst [a married woman from Meslin-l'Evêque (Wallonia)] to the Queen [in French], 15 Aug. 1926 (I 61)

73 'Surtout Sa Majestez excusez moi que je vous et [sic, ai] fait cette demande mais je ne recois [sic] pas du bureau secour [sic] et ses [sic] a vous seul que je puis faire cette demande s.v.p', Pétronille Van Poppel [the wife of a wickerworker from Sint Gillis (Brussels)] to the Queen [in French], 10 Dec. 1926 (I 220).

74 'C'est une orpheline tres souffrante et malheure [sic] qui ose venir Vous tendre la main, à Vous que l'on surnomme avec raison: la Providence de la Belgique', Marcelle Flamand [an unmarried apprentice-milliner from Châtelet (Wallonia)] to the Queen [in French, letter written by a middle-class supporter on her behalf], 17 June 1926 (I 146).

75 'Notre Sainte Reine', 'Notre Auguste et vénérée souveraine. Sa bonté, sa bienveillance, sa sainte charité sont souvent présents à ma mémoire', Delphine Pir [an unmarried governess from Brussels] to the Queen [in French], 21 Jan. 1935 (I 297).

76 'Je sé [sic] que S M la Reine Elisabéth éter trer [sic] charitable pour son pleuble [sic]', Marie Anciaux [the wife of a wandering musician from Rochefort (Wallonia)] to the Queen [in French], 29 Jan. 1927 (I 211); 'Soyiez [sic] notre protectrice', Mathieu Santre [a married agricultural labourer from Vielsalm (Wallonia)] to the Queen [in French, letter written by a middle-class supporter on his behalf], Dec. 1926 (I 219); 'je sai [sic] que sa Majesté a un si bon Cœur pour les Malheureux', Marie Beaujean [the wife of a miner from Meux (Wallonia)] to the Queen [in French], 16 April 1927 (I 231); 'Connaissant votre bon cœur de Mère pour la Belgique', Hélène Amélie Van Der Linden [the wife of a miner from Gilly (Wallonia)] to the Queen [in French], 27 Jan. 1927 (I 156); 'Cher Mère', Mélanie Wéry [a widowed housewife from Charleroi] to Queen Elisabeth, 31 Jan. 1927 [in French] (I 105); 'Dans ma tristesse et mon désespoir, ne sachant à qui recourir, j'ai pensé à ma Reine, la Mère des pauvres et des malheureux', Juliette Conchariere [the wife of a miner from Châtelet (Wallonia)] to the Queen [in French, letter written by a middle-class supporter on his behalf], 24 Jan. 1927 (I 343); 'Notre reine si bonne, si compatissante aux maux de ses sujets', Marie-Louise Merckaert [an unmarried private teacher from Sint Joost ten Node (Brussels)] to the Queen [in French], Dec. 1926 (I 224); 'votre

bonté légendaire envers les malheureux', Henri Nison [a divorced knife grinder from Flémalle-Haute (Wallonia)] to the Queen [in French, letter written by a middle-class supporter on his behalf], 29 Dec. 1926 (I 207); 'Connaissant les bontés de Sa Majesté pour les malheureux et Son grand désir de leur venir en aide quand Elle le peut', Narcisse Tordeur [a widowed bank clerk from Elsene (Brussels)] to the Queen [in French], Dec. 1925 (I 394); 'Notre Chère et bien aimée Souveraine que nous aimons et respectons toujours car comme dit le Proverbe qui donne au pauvres prette [*sic*] à Dieux. Votre nom si remarquable parmi toute la Belgique entière qui vous appelle leur bonne mère', Elisabeth Nicolas [an unmarried level crossing guard with the State Rail from Chênée (Wallonia)] to the Queen [in French], 9 Sept 1926 (I 92).

77 Colley, *Britons. Forging the Nation*, p. 232.

Notes on Contributors

Alain Boureau, Directeur d'Études at the École des Hautes Etudes en Sciences Sociales, Paris; author of, among others, *Satan hérétique. Histoire de la démonologie (1280-1330)* (Paris: Odile Jacob, 2005); *La Loi du royaume. Les Moines, le droit et la construction de la nation anglaise (XIe-XIIIe siècles)* (Paris: Les Belles Lettres, 2001); *Le droit de cuissage: la fabrication d'un mythe, XIIIe-XXe siècle* (Paris: Albin Michel, 1995); *Histoires d'un historien, Kantorowicz* (Paris: Gallimard, 1990); and *Le Simple corps du roi: l'impossible sacralité des souverains français, XVe-XVIIIe siècle* (Paris: Les Editions de Paris, 1988); co-editor (with Claudio S. Ingerflom) of *La royauté sacrée dans le monde chrétien* (Paris: EHESS, 1992).

Gita Deneckere, Associate Professor of Modern History, Ghent University; author of, among others, *Les Turbulences de la Belle Époque (1878-1905)* (Brussels: Complexe, 2005); *Het katoenoproer van Gent in 1839. Collectieve actie en sociale geschiedenis* (Nijmegen: SUN, 1999); *Geuzengeweld. Antiklerikaal straatrumoer in de politieke geschiedenis van België, 1831-1914* (Brussels: VUB Press, 1998); and *Sire, het volk mort. Sociaal protest in België, 1831-1918* (Antwerp: Hadewijch, 1997).

Jeroen Deploige, Associate Professor of Medieval Cultural History at Ghent University; author of *Strategies and Tactics in Medieval Hagiography. Discourse, Church, and Society in the Southern Low Countries, c. 920-c. 1320* (Turnhout: Brepols, forthcoming); and *In nomine femineo indocta. Kennisprofiel en ideologie van Hildegard van Bingen (1098-1179)* (Hilversum: Verloren, 1998); co-editor (with Ludo Milis, et al.) of *The Narrative Sources from the Medieval Low Countries* (Ghent, Leuven, and Groningen: Ovid Database, 1996-2004 – http://www.narrative-sources.be).

Lisa Jane Graham, Associate Professor at the History Department of Haverford College (PA); author of *If the King Only Knew: Seditious Speech in the Reign of Louis XV* (Charlottesville: University of Virginia Press, 2000); co-editor (with Christine Adams and Jack R. Censer) of *Visions and Revisions of Eighteenth-Century France* (University Park, PA: Penn State University Press, 1997).

MARIA GREVER, Professor of Theory of History and Historiography, Erasmus University Rotterdam; author of, among others, *Strijd tegen de stilte. Johanna Naber (1859-1941) en de vrouwenstem in geschiedenis* (Hilversum: Verloren, 1994); co-author (with Berteke Waaldijk) of *Transforming the Public Sphere. The Dutch National Exhibition of Women's Labor in 1898* (Durham: Duke University Press, 2004); co-editor (with Harry Jansen) of *De ongrijpbare tijd. Temporaliteit en de constructie van het verleden* (Hilversum: Verloren, 2001).

MARC JACOBS, Director of the Flemish Centre for the Study of Popular Culture and Associate Professor of History and Heritage Studies at the Catholic University of Brussels; co-editor (with Peter Scholliers) of *Eating out in Europe. Picnics, Gourmet Dining and Snacks Since the Late Eighteenth Century* (Oxford: Berg, 2003).

GILLES LECUPPRE, Assistant Professor of Medieval History, University of Paris X-Nanterre; author of *L'imposture politique au Moyen Âge. La seconde vie des rois* (Paris: Presses Universitaires de France, 2005); co-editor (with Anne-Hélène Allirot and Lydwine Scordia) of *Royautés imaginaires (XIIe-XVIe siècle)* (Turnhout: Brepols, 2005).

ELODIE LECUPPRE-DESJARDIN, Assistant Professor of Medieval History, University of Lille III; author of *La ville des cérémonies. Espace public et communication politique dans anciens Pays-Bas Bourguignons* (Turnhout: Brepols, 2004); co-editor (with Anne-Laure Van Bruaene) of *Emotions in the Heart of the City: 14th-16th Century* (Turnhout: Brepols, 2005).

JÜRGEN PIETERS, Associate Professor at the Department of Dutch Literature, Ghent University; author of, among others, *Speaking with the Dead. Explorations in Literature and History* (Edinburgh: Edinburgh University Press, 2005); and *Moments of Negotiation: The New Historicism of Stephen Greenblatt* (Amsterdam: Amsterdam University Press, 2001); editor of *Critical Self-Fashioning: Stephen Greenblatt and the New Historicism* (Frankfurt am Main: Peter Lang, 1999).

ALEXANDER ROOSE, Assistant Professor at the Department of French Literature, Ghent University; co-editor (with Benjamin Biebuyck, et al.) of *Negen muzen, tien geboden: historische en methodologische gevalstudies over de interactie tussen literatuur en ethiek* (Ghent: Academia Press, 2005).

KEVIN SHARPE
Leverhulme Research Professor and Professor of Renaissance Studies at Queen Mary, University of London; author of, among others, *Reading Revolutions:*

The Politics of Reading in Early Modern England (New Haven: Yale University Press, 2000); *Remapping Early Modern England: Studies in Political Culture* (Cambridge: Cambridge University Press, 2000); and *The Personal Rule of Charles I* (New Haven: Yale University Press, 1995); co-editor (with Steven N. Zwicker) of *Reading, Society, and Politics in Early Modern England* (Cambridge: Cambridge University Press, 2003); *Refiguring Revolutions: Aesthetics and Politics from the English Revolution to the Romantic Revolution* (Berkeley: University of California Press, 1998); and *Politics of Discourse: The Literature and History of Seventeenth-Century England* (Berkeley: University of California Press, 1987); co-editor (with Peter Lake) of *Culture and Politics in Early Stuart England* (Basingstoke: Palgrave Macmillan, 1994).

HENK TE VELDE, Professor of Dutch History, University of Leiden; author of *Stijlen van leiderschap: persoon en politiek van Thorbecke tot Den Uyl* (Amsterdam: Wereldbibliotheek, 2002); and *Gemeenschapszin en plichtsbesef: liberalisme en nationalisme in Nederland, 1870-1918* (The Hague: SDU, 1992); editor of, among others, *Political Transfer* [*European Review of History*, 12:2 (2005) - special issue]; co-editor (with Frank R. Ankersmit) of *Trust: Cement of Democracy* (Leuven: Peeters, 2004).

MAARTEN VAN GINDERACHTER, Postdoctoral fellow of the Research Foundation – Flanders at the Department of Modern History of Ghent University; author of *Het rode vaderland. De vergeten geschiedenis van de communautaire spanningen in het Belgische socialisme voor WOI* (Tielt and Ghent: Lannoo and Amsab, 2005); and *Le chant du coq. Nation et nationalisme en Wallonie depuis 1880* (Ghent: Academia Press, 2005).

JAAP VAN OSTA, Lecturer at the Department of Italian Language and Culture, Utrecht University; author of *Het theater van de staat: Oranje, Windsor en de moderne monarchie* (Amsterdam: Wereldbibliotheek, 1998); *Drie vorstinnen. Brieven van Emma, Wilhelmina en Juliana* (Amsterdam: Arbeiderspers, 1995); and *Geschiedenis van het moderne Italië: tussen liberalisme en fascisme* (The Hague: Nijgh & van Ditmar, 1989).

List of Illustrations

Cover

Jacob Jordaens, *Le roi boit. Repas de famille le jour de la Fête des Rois* [The King Drinks. Family Meal on the Feast of Epiphany] (c. 1638-1640), Musée du Louvre, Paris, France (© Photo RMN – © Jean-Gilles Berizzi).

Chapter 6 – Kevin Sharpe

p. 109, fig. 1. Souvenir plate in honour of Queen Elizabeth (1600), Museum of London, England (© Museum of London).

Chapter 7 – Marc Jacobs

p. 121, fig. 1. Mosaic of the *Adoration of the Magi* (561), Sant'Apollinare Nuovo, Ravenna, Italy.

p. 124, fig. 2. Vasco Fernandes (?), *The Adoration of the Magi* (c. 1504), Museu Grão Vasco, Viseu, Portugal (© Instituto Português de Museus).

p. 125, fig. 3. *Characters on a Kings' Letter*, by a collaborator of Maerten van Cleve (1575), collection J. Borms, Scheveningen, Netherlands [from Anke Van Wagenberg-Ter Hoeven, *Het Driekoningenfeest. De uitbeelding van een populair thema in de beeldende kunst van de zeventiende eeuw* (Amsterdam: Meertens Instituut, 1997), p. 34].

p. 129, fig. 4. Romeyn de Hooghe, *L'Epiphane du Nouveau Antichrist* (1689) [from John Landwehr, *Romeyn de Hooghe the Etcher. Contemporary Portrayal of Europe 1662-1717* (Leiden: A.W. Slijthoff, 1973), p. 217].

p. 130, fig. 5. Louis Raemaekers, *The Three Kings from the East* (1914) [from Harry Perry Robinson and Edward Garnett, *The Great War: A Neutral's Indictment. One Hundred Cartoons by Louis Raemaekers* (London: The Fine Art Society, 1916), plate 1].

Chapter 9 – Maria Grever

p. 169, fig. 1. Henry Courtney Selous, *Opening of the Great Exhibition* (1851-1852), Victoria and Albert Museum, London, England (© V&A Images).

p. 170, fig. 2. Cartoon 'The Queen and Her Subjects', *Punch*, 3 May 1851.

p. 173, fig. 3. *Opening Ceremony of the Paris Exposition Universelle 1867 by Emperor Napoleon III* [from *Grand Album de l'Exposition Universelle 1867* (Paris: Michel Lévy Frères, 1868), p. 9].

p. 175, fig. 4. *Official Distribution of Exhibition Awards at the Palace Champs-Élysées, July 1, 1867* [from *Grand Album de l'Exposition Universelle 1867*, p. 100-101].

p. 176, fig. 5. *Gala at the opera in honour of the Russian Tsar Alexander II* [from *Grand Album de l'Exposition Universelle 1867*, p. 17].

p. 177, fig. 6. *Arrival of the Austrian Emperor Franz Jozeph* [from *Grand Album de l'Exposition Universelle 1867*, p.107].

Chapter 10 – Jaap van Osta

p. 190, fig. 1. Front side of Russian beaker (1896), DenRon Collections, Amsterdam, Netherlands (reproduced by permission).

p. 190, fig. 2. Back side of Russian beaker (1896), DenRon Collections, Amsterdam, Netherlands (reproduced by permission).

p. 191, fig. 3. Newspaper advertisement (1898).

Chapter 13 – Maarten Van Ginderachter

p. 229, fig. 1. Postcard of the birth of Leopold III of Belgium (1901), Royal Palace Archives (Cabinet Leopold II, Commandements du Roi, G 84/20), Brussels, Belgium.

p. 233, fig. 2. Photograph of Prince Albert posing amongst miners (1908), *Welt und Haus*, 8 January 1908, p. 11-13.

Index

Canute IV (King of Denmark, 1080-1086) 36, 43
Carroll, Lewis 55
Carton de Wiart, Henri 219
Cassianus Bassus (Constantin Cesar) 91
Castiglione, Baldassare 91
Catherine de' Medici (Queen Consort of France) 85, 251n
Caturce, Jean de 131
Céline, Louis-Ferdinand 165
Certain, Simon 107
Certeau, Michel de 9-10, 17, 38-39, 141, 239n
Charlemagne (King of the Franks, 768-814; Emperor of the Romans, 800-814) 122
Charles I the Bold (Duke of Burgundy, 1467-1477) 14, 56-58, 61-64, 246n
Charles I (King of England, King of Scots, King of Ireland, 1625-1649) 111-113, 135, 258n
Charles II (King of England, King of Scots, King of Ireland, 1660-1685) 16, 100, 114-115
Charles V the Wise (King of France, 1364-1380) 122, 245n
Charles IX (King of France, 1560-1574) 79, 85, 89, 251n, 252n
Charles I the Good (Count of Flanders, 1119-1127) 13, 35-37, 39-48, 50, 52-54, 64
Charles IV (Holy Roman Emperor, 1355-1378) 122
Charles V (Holy Roman Emperor, 1530-1556) 58, 122
Chastellain, Georges 245n-246n
Chateauroux, Madame de 151
Chaumette, Pierre Gaspard 137
Chiffoleau, Jacques 55
Choisnet, Pierre 63
Christ 13, 27, 29-31, 47, 65, 71, 101, 113, 117, 120-123, 128, 130, 131-133, 237n
Christopher (Saint) 65
Church, William F. 26
Cicero, Marcus Tullius 62-63
Claudius (Roman Emperor, 41-54 BCE) 119
Claus von Amsberg (Prince of the Netherlands) 181
Clifford, Robert 250n
Clovis (King of the Franks, 481-511) 89, 253n
Cole, Henry 164
Colley, Linda 195, 234
Collinson, Patrick 110
Columella 91
Columbus, Christopher 124
Commynes, Philippe de 56-57, 59, 64, 245n
Cooreman, Edward 218
Coué, Stephanie 244n
Count of St Pol 132
Courtenay, William 33
Crébillon fils, Claude Prosper Jolyot de 145-146, 150-153, 266n
Crispi, Francesco 186
Crossmann, Richard 201
Cucufa (Denis Diderot, Les Bijoux indiscrets) 154
Cyrus the Great (Emperor of Persia, 559-529 BCE) 88

Dagron, Gilbert 29
Darcy of Platen, Lord 65
Darnton, Robert 141-142, 146, 264n, 267n

Dauwet, Jean 245n
David (King of Israel) 28-30, 236n
De Coster, Anthoen 131
De Hooghe, Romeyn 128, 129
DeJean, Joan 145, 264n
Della Fonte, Bartolomeo 62
De Meis, Angelo Camillo 182, 270n
Deneckere, Gita 19
Deploige, Jeroen 13
Devereux, Robert (Earl of Essex) 105
Dhondt, Jan 51
Dickens, Charles 165
Diderot, Denis 155, 266n-267n
Disraeli, Benjamin 19, 195, 197-198, 201
Douglas, Frederick 165
Dover, Captian Robert 262n
Downes, Paul 132
Dudley, John (Duke of Northumberland) 134
Dudley, Robert (Earl of Leicester) 105, 107
Durkheim, Émile 26
Duruy, Victor 269n

Edmund (Earl of Rutland) 247n
Edward the Confessor (Saint; Anglo-Saxon King of England, 1042-1066) 43
Edward I (King of England, 1272-1307) 73
Edward II (King of England, 1307-1327) 69, 73-74, 133, 248n-249n
Edward III (King of England, 1327-1377) 73, 133, 249n
Edward IV (King of England, 1461-1483) 14, 56, 58, 61-62, 64, 70, 247n-248n, 250n
Edward VI Tudor (King of England and of Ireland, 1547-1553) 104, 106, 134
Edward VII (King of the United Kingdom, 1901-1910) 185, 197, 272n
Eichenberger, Thomas 241n
Elisabeth (Princess of Bavaria, Queen Consort of the Belgians) 21, 220-221, 225-228, 229, 231-234
Elizabeth I (Queen of England and of Ireland, 1558-1603) 15-16, 100-101, 104-113, 115, 134, 256n-258n
Elizabeth of York (Queen Consort of England) 249n
Elizabeth Stuart (Princess of Scotland, Queen Consort of Bohemia) 127
Emise (Chevalier de Rességuier, Voyage d'Amatonthe). See Pompadour, Madame de.
Emma (Queen Regent of the Netherlands) 162, 185, 201-203
Ensor, Robert C.K. 197
Erembalds (Flemish clan) 36, 40, 45, 51, 244n
Essex, Earl of. See Devereux, Robert.
Eu, Earl of 56

Fagnan, Marie-Antoinette 265n
Fairclough, Norman 39
Fava, Guido 62
Ferdinand II (Holy Roman Emperor, 1620-1637) 127-128
Ferdinand-Philippe, Prince (Duke of Orléans) 263n
Ferrers, George 134
Ficino, Marsilio 62